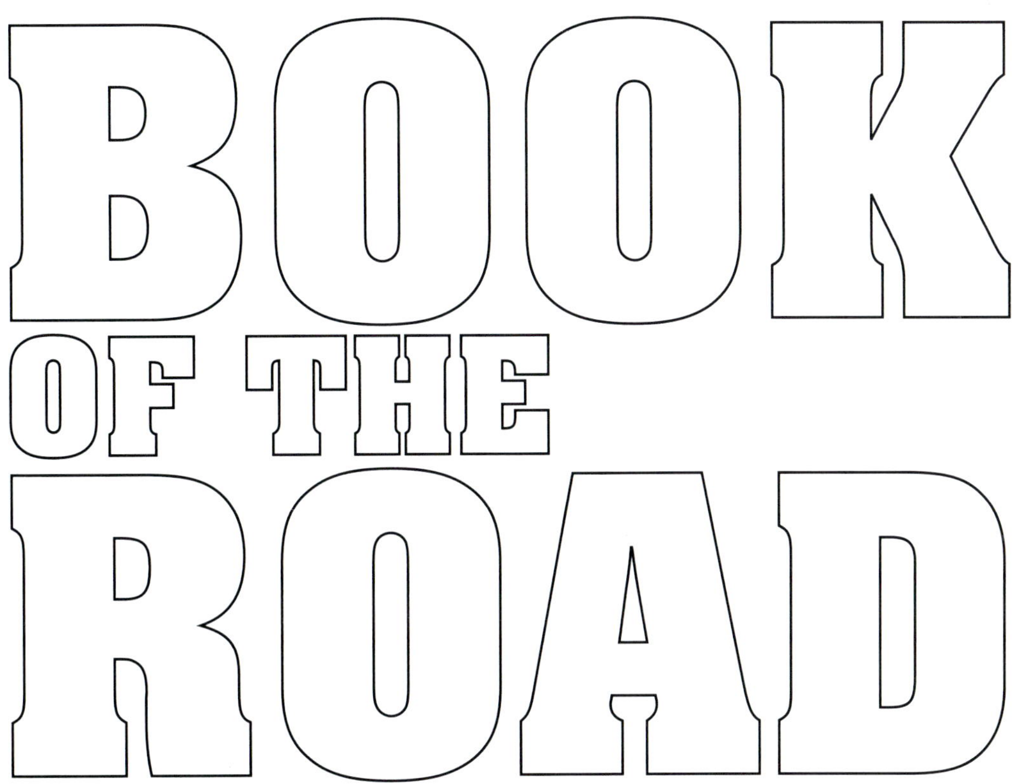

YOUR SOUTH AFRICAN
MOTORING BIBLE

This edition published in 2012 by MapStudio™ South Africa

ISBN 978-1-77026-384-0

Production Manager John Loubser

Cartographic Manager Christine Flemington

Project Cartographers Rudi de Lange, Malcolm Palmer, Ryan Africa & Braam Smit

Assistant Cartographers Liezel Bohdanowicz & Daniella Levin

CD-Rom & Digital Compilation Anthony Davids

Researchers Anthony Davids, Derek Schröeder-Nel & Denielle Lategan

Production Fiona Moosa

Marketing Manager Sandy Christie (sandyc@mapstudio.co.za)

Feedback research@mapstudio.co.za

MapStudio

Wembley Square, 6 Solan Street, Gardens, Cape Town

PO Box 1144, Cape Town, 8000

Tel: 0860 10 50 50

www.mapstudio.co.za

Printed & Bound by CTP Printers, Cape Town

MAIN CONTENT OVERVIEW

Book of the Road

LEGEND TO MAPS

Main map section legend, for pages 18 - 93

Tarred Untarred

Under Construction

- Freeway / national road
- Main road
- Secondary road
- Route numbers (N1, R21, R110, B1, P1, N110)
- Distance in kilometres (15)
- Distance in kilometres on freeways / national roads (15)
- Railway
- International / provincial boundary
- National park and game reserve
- Delta
- Built up area

- Capital or city
- Major town
- Secondary town
- Satellite town
- Other town
- Settlement
- Station
- Water feature
- Pan
- Marsh

- Major airport
- Airfield
- Ferry / pontoon
- Lighthouse
- Major spot height
- Mountain pass
- Border control
- Information
- Toll route
- Toll plaza
- Petrol station
- Accommodation

- Place of interest & historical site
- Provincial heritage site
- Shipwreck
- Battleground
- Waterfall
- Wine estate & wine sales
- Nature reserve & bird sanctuary
- Park entrance
- Water hole
- Hiking trail
- 4x4 trail
- Diving site & whale watching
- Caravan park & camp site

Elevation

3400 - 3482m
3300 - 3400m
3200 - 3300m
3100 - 3200m
3000 - 3100m
2900 - 3000m
2800 - 2900m
2700 - 2800m
2600 - 2700m
2500 - 2600m
2400 - 2500m
2300 - 2400m
2200 - 2300m
2100 - 2200m
2000 - 2100m
1900 - 2000m
1800 - 1900m
1700 - 1800m
1600 - 1700m
1500 - 1600m
1400 - 1500m
1300 - 1400m
1200 - 1300m
1100 - 1200m
1000 - 1100m
900 - 1000m
800 - 900m
700 - 800m
600 - 700m
500 - 600m
400 - 500m
300 - 400m
200 - 300m
100 - 200m
0 - 100m

Scale 1 : 750 000

0 10 20 40 60 80 Km

Street map section legend, for pages 94 - 157

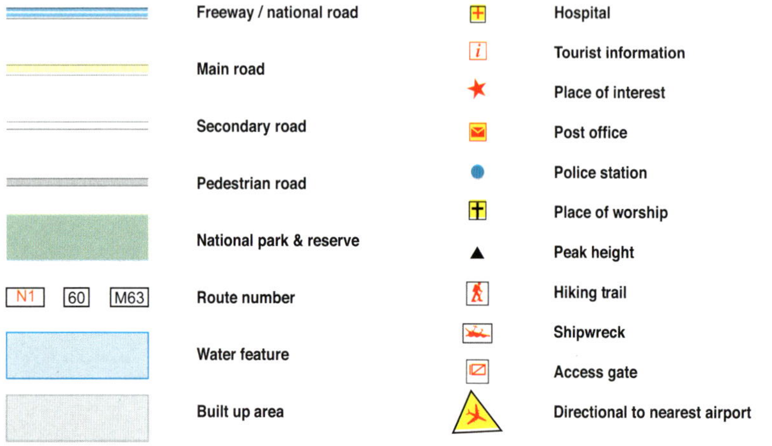

See also map overview pages 14 - 15 >>

Main cities are full-page maps and are indicated in grey (below ▼)

Other street maps are shown in order of appearance & alphabetically (below ▼)

NOTE: some names were changed during production. These are marked with an ✶ and do not follow alphabetical order

STREET MAP CONTENTS

See also map overview pages 14 - 15 >>

STREET MAP CONTENTS

See also map overview pages 14 - 15 >>

TOURIST REGIONS & SITES

Popular tourist regions & sites appearing in main maps

UNESCO World Heritage Sites are shown with (WHS)

Towns with historic interest shown with ✶

Main map page reference for historic towns are shown in brackets

TOURIST REGIONS & SITES

Popular tourist regions & sites appearing in main maps

OVERVIEW MAP OF SOUTH AFRICA

With GPS waypoints for major junctions

See also detailed GPS waypoint maps on page 168 >>

GPS Waypoints for Major Junctions

J1	33°53'06.89"S	18°31'52.92"E	J32	25°27'03.12"S	30°42'35.02"E
J2	34°13'38.67"S	19°25'44.69"E	J33	23°04'41.75"S	29°54'31.18"E
J3	34°05'16.94"S	20°05'26.17"E	J34	23°16'03.03"S	28°26'12.96"E
J4	34°05'37.02"S	21°15'04.27"E	J35	24°17'13.52"S	28°58'54.82"E
J5	33°59'07.37"S	22°30'32.68"E	J36	24°55'08.66"S	28°22'22.19"E
J6	33°49'09.52"S	22°21'16.45"E	J37	25°38'45.65"S	28°16'29.69"E
J7	33°01'31.16"S	18°06'24.59"E	J38	25°40'54.54"S	28°16'45.79"E
J8	32°21'50.38"S	18°56'21.46"E	J39	26°02'34.05"S	28°06'08.13"E
J9	32°10'23.26"S	18°52'03.59"E	J40	26°15'49.06"S	27°57'24.24"E
J10	33°13'28.34"S	20°34'54.32"E	J41	25°43'46.12"S	27°39'57.36"E
J11	32°22'35.01"S	22°31'37.07"E	J42	25°32'42.08"S	26°04'44.54"E
J12	31°53'04.81"S	23°05'00.19"E	J43	26°20'29.92"S	26°18'18.33"E
J13	32°15'00.39"S	24°32'07.63"E	J44	25°51'48.64"S	25°38'46.56"E
J14	31°29'49.21"S	25°00'19.78"E	J45	26°57'31.42"S	24°43'56.14"E
J15	33°36'43.84"S	25°54'49.89"E	J46	27°39'24.78"S	27°14'59.54"E
J16	32°57'49.68"S	27°55'11.63"E	J47	28°29'56.73"S	26°59'52.09"E
J17	32°00'23.03"S	27°00'15.07"E	J48	27°19'24.26"S	28°46'36.22"E
J18	30°41'36.58"S	26°42'31.92"E	J49	28°17'16.19"S	29°08'01.49"E
J19	31°35'18.03"S	28°47'24.22"E	J50	29°17'51.19"S	27°27'08.88"E
J20	30°45'10.01"S	30°25'58.31"E	J51	29°12'05.37"S	26°11'27.63"E
J21	29°50'26.62"S	30°57'26.06"E	J52	28°44'56.14"S	24°45'56.08"E
J22	29°48'21.86"S	30°58'42.11"E	J53	28°06'46.15"S	24°51'12.63"E
J23	29°13'26.69"S	30°00'17.67"E	J54	27°53'55.73"S	22°57'45.61"E
J24	28°35'15.69"S	29°36'32.13"E	J55	28°27'36.77"S	21°14'26.97"E
J25	28°00'44.37"S	32°14'18.03"E	J56	29°07'30.62"S	19°23'55.76"E
J26	27°02'27.02"S	30°48'48.83"E	J57	29°39'41.58"S	17°53'33.64"E
J27	26°08'55.77"S	30°46'15.05"E	J58	29°41'23.27"S	22°44'26.84"E
J28	26°31'17.01"S	29°59'07.76"E	J59	30°34'44.76"S	23°30'37.07"E
J29	26°27'11.36"S	29°27'57.69"E	J60	31°04'32.28"S	24°25'55.92"E
J30	25°53'35.96"S	29°15'42.85"E	J61	30°43'59.36"S	25°05'05.63"E
J31	25°49'46.36"S	29°31'43.29"E			

KEYPLAN MAP OF MAIN MAP PAGES

See also main map pages 18 - 93 >>

KEYPLAN MAP OF MAIN MAP PAGES

See also main map pages 18 - 93 >>

KEYPLAN MAP OF STREET MAP PAGES

See also street map pages 94 - 157 >>

North West
Vryburg (154)
Kuruman (127)
Sishen (145)
Upington (151)
KIMBERLEY (125)
Griquatown (121)
Alexander Bay (106)
Port Nolloth (139)
Springbok (146)
Prieska (140)
Northern Cape
Carnarvon (112)
Williston (156)
Victoria West (152)
Atlantic Ocean
Vredendal (154)
Vanrhynsdorp (152)
Calvinia (112)
Lambert's Bay (128)
Clanwilliam (114)
Beaufort West (108)
Graaff-Reinet (119)
Citrusdal (114)
Vredenburg (153)
Saldanha Bay (143)
Langebaan (129)
Western Cape
Tulbagh (149)
Ceres (113)
Darling (115)
Malmesbury (130)
Ladismith (128)
Calitzdorp (111)
Oudtshoorn (135)
Uniondale (150)
Paarl (135)
Wellington (155)
Worcester (157)
Bellville (108)
Robben Island (141)
CAPE TOWN (94)
Victoria & Alfred Waterfront (152)
Cape Town Peninsula (95)
Camps Bay (112)
Hout Bay (123)
Muizenberg (133)
Simon's Town (144)
Strand (148)
Robertson (142)
Franschhoek (118)
Montagu (132)
Ashton (107)
McGregor (131)
Barrydale (108)
Stellenbosch (147)
Somerset West (146)
Grabouw (119)
Greyton (120)
Swellendam (148)
Heidelberg (122)
Caledon (111)
Riversdale (141)
Hartenbos (121)
George (118)
Mossel Bay (133)
Sedgefield (144)
Wilderness (155)
Knysna (126)
Plettenberg Bay (137)
Humansdorp (124)
St Francis Bay (147)
Stilbaai (Still Bay) (148)
Witsand (156)
Kleinmond (125)
Hermanus (123)
Gansbaai (118)
Bredasdorp (110)

See also street map pages 94 - 157 >>

REGULATORY SIGNS

Control signs

Yield

One-way roadway

No entry

Command signs

Minimum Speed

Keep left

Proceed right only

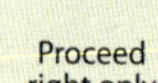

Turn right

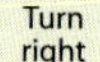

Pay toll

Goods vehicle only

Prohibition signs

Speed limit

Height limit

Left turn ahead prohibited

Right turn prohibited

U turn prohibited

Overtaking prohibited

Stopping prohibited

Parking prohibited

Goods vehicle prohibited

Reservation signs

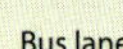
Bus lane

Limited parking

Comprehensive signs

Dual carriageway freeway

Single carriageway freeway

Derestriction signs

Dual carriageway freeway

Exclusive secondary signs

Maximum stay. Applies only during times on days specified

WARNING SIGNS

Road layout signs

Crossroad

End of dual road (to right)

Side road junction from right

Staggered junction

Y-junction

Sharp junction (to left)

T-junction

Direction of movement signs

Traffic circle

Sharp curve (to left)

Hairpin bend (to right)

Concealed driveway (right)

Combined curves (first to right)

Two-way traffic

Two-way traffic crossroad

Symbolic signs

Traffic signals

Traffic control "stop" ahead

Traffic control "yield" ahead

Pedestrian crossing

Wild animals

Motor gate (to left)

Tunnel

Road narrows from one side only (right)

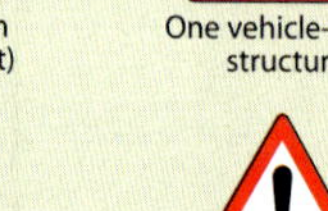
One vehicle-width structure

Drift

Gravel road begins

Speed humps

Slippery road

Falling rocks (from right)

General warning (any type of danger ahead)

Emergency flashing light

Railway crossing

Steep downhill ahead

Hazard marker signs

Danger plate (pass to left)

Danger plate (pass to right)

Double railway crossing

Sharp curve chevron (left)

Sharp curve chevron (left)

T-Junction chevron

GUIDANCE SIGNS

Route marker signs

Direction signs

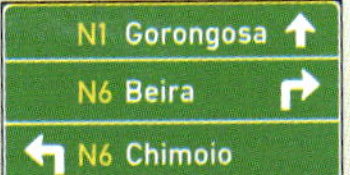

Advance direction sign

Confirmation signs

Location signs

Street Names

Provincial Borders

Freeway Name

Direction sign symbols

Airport

Mine

Alternative route

Toll route

Supplementary plate signs

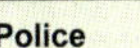
Police

Tow-away zone

Tourism signs

Race course

Golf course

Scenic route

View point

Waterfall

Hiking trail

National Park

General tourist attraction

Museum

Theatre

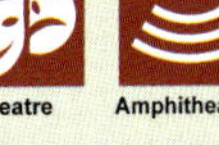

Amphitheatre

Parking area

Tourist information

Accommodation facility

Bed and breakfast

Rooms (bed only)

Caravan site

Camp site

Roadside stall/ Curio shop

Shop

Crocodile farm

Bird park/ sanctuary

Ostrich farm

Ostrich farm

Snake park

Botanical gardens

Wine cellar

Historic Mine

Boat launch

Police

Hospital (with name)

SOS call station

Telephone

Filling station and workshop

Filling station

Workshop

Tow-in service

Truck service

INFORMATION SIGNS

300m

Cul-de-sac

Right of way

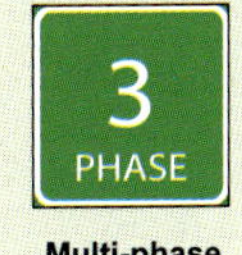

Multi-phase robots

Information centre

Diagrammatic signs

Restriction/prohibition applicable in right lane

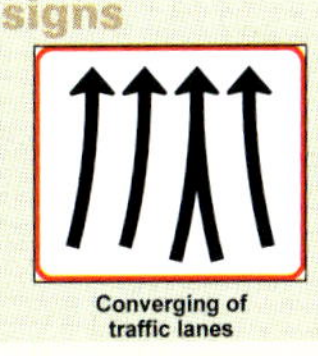
Converging of traffic lanes

ROAD SURFACE MARKINGS

Regulatory

Mandatory direction arrows

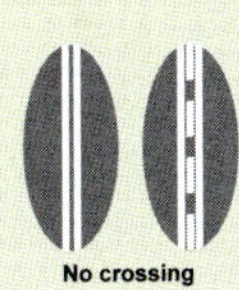
No crossing

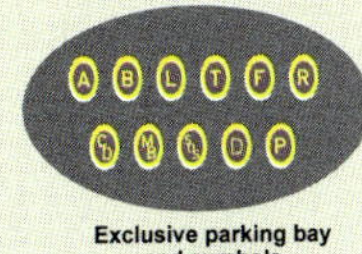

Exclusive parking bay and symbols

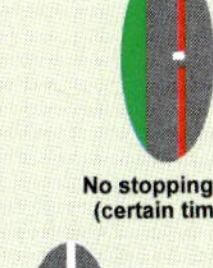
No stopping line (certain times)

No Parking

Yield line

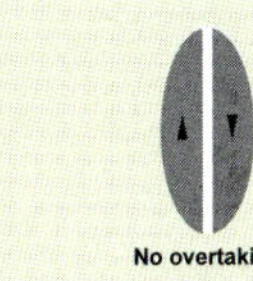
No overtaking

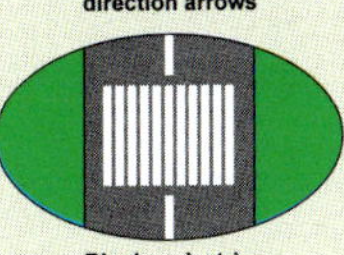
Block pedestrian crossing

Warning

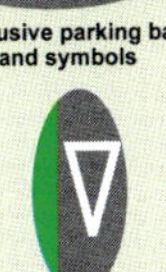
Railway crossing ahead

Yield sign ahead

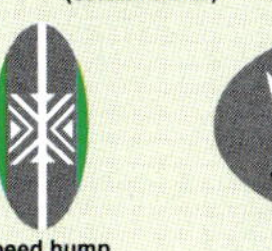
Speed hump

No overtaking or no crossing ahead

Guidance

Airport

12

13

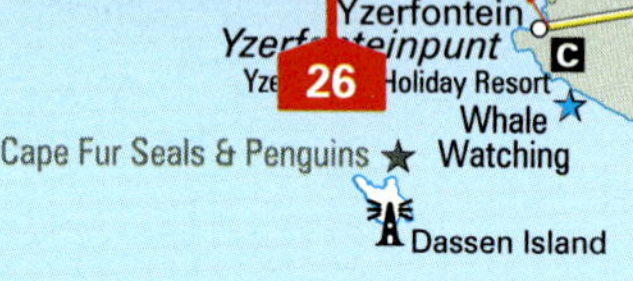

Atlantic Ocean

AW

AX

AY

1 Rietvlei Bird Sanctuary (AW 13)
2 World of Birds (AW 13)
3 Mariner's Wharf (AX 13)
4 Van Riebeeck's Hedge (AW 13)
5 Historic Mile (AX 13)
6 Chapmans Peak Drive (AX 13)
7 Kirstenbosch Botanical Gardens (AW 13)
8 Table Mountain NP (AX 13)
9 Castle of Good Hope (AW 13)
10 V & A Waterfront (AW 13)
11 Noon Gun (AW 13)
12 Dueyang Family (AW 13)
13 Winton 1934 (AW 13)
14 Athens 1865 (AW 13)
15 Thermopylae 1899 (AW 13)
16 Seafarer 1966 (AW13)
17 Het Huis te Kraaiestein 1698 (AW 13)
18 Antipolis 1977 (AW 13)
19 Romelia 1977 (AW 13)
20 Maori 1909 (AX 13)
21 Boss 400 (AX 13)
22 Astor (AX 13)
23 Katzmaru 1970 (AX 13)
24 Kakapo 1900 (AX 13)
25 Clan Munroe 1905 (AX 13)
26 Thomas T Tucker 1942 (AX 13)
27 Nolloth 1965 (AX 13)
28 Phyllisia 1968 (AX 13)
29 Shir-Yib 1970 (AX 13)
30 Tania 1972 (AX 13)
31 Phoenix 1829 (AX 13)
32 Parama 1862 (AX 13)
33 Clan Stuart 1914, Katwyk Aan Rhyn 1786, Die Gebroeders 1792, Bato 1806 (AX 13)
34 Onze Molen Homestead (AW 13)
35 Durbanville Hills (AW 13)
36 Boulders Beach (AX 13)
37 Diving Site (AW 13)
38 Diving Site (AW 13)
39 Oudekraal (AW 13)

Yzerfontein
Yzerfonteinpunt
Whale Watching
Cape Fur Seals & Penguins
Dassen Island
Darling
Ormonde
Flower Reserves
Oudepost Wild Flower Reserve
Waylands Wild Flower Reserve
Mission Station
Water Mill 1840
Mamre
Mission Station 1808
Ganzekraal Resort
Bokbaai
Atlantis
Bokpunt
Koeberg Nuclear Power Station
Ou Skip
Melkbosstrand
Philadelphia
NG Church
Havana Hills
Blouberg Hill
Battle of Blouberg 1806
Bloubergstrand
Robben Island
Rietvlei Nature Area
Durbanville
Diemersdal
Meerendal
Table Bay
Milnerton
Altygedacht
Tygerberg
Parow
Bellville
Canal Walk
Grand West
Cape Town International
CAPE TOWN
Table Mountain
Rhodes Memorial
Mostert's Mill
Hout Bay
Llandudno
Groot Constantia 1685
Constantia Winelands
Constantia Uitsig
Wolfgat NR
Strandfontein Pavilion & Tidal Pool
Noordhoek
Muizenberg
Kommetjie
Rhodes' Cottage
Slangkop
Fish Hoek
False Bay
Just Nuisance Statue
Scarborough
Penguin Colony
Simon's Town
Camel Rock
Table Mountain National Park
Old Cannon
Da Gama Monument 1497
Dias Monument
Lighthouse
Cape of Good Hope
Diving Site
Dias Beach
Cape Point
Kanonkop
Cloof
Abbotsdale
Sonnekus
Kalbaskraal

1 Victorian, Edwardian & Georgian Buildings (AW 14)
2 Bokomo Mill (AW 14)
3 Taal Monument (AW 14)
4 Butterfly World (AW 14)
5 'Hugo se Huis' Monument (AW 14)
6 Bandits Grave (AW 14)
7 Le Grand Chasseur (AW 15)
8 Robertson (AW 15)
9 Car Museum (AW 14)
10 Libertas Amphitheatre (AW 14)
11 Jan Joubertsgat Bridge (1823) (AW 14)
12 Harold Porter Botanical Garden (AX 14)
13 Bobbejaans (AW 14)
14 Wolwekloof (AW 14)
15 Krom River (AW 14)
16 Hawekwas Conservation Area (AW 14)
Atlantic Ocean
Walker Bay
Malmesbury
Wellington
Worcester
Paarl
Stellenbosch
Somerset West
Strand
Gordons Bay
Robertson
McGregor
Villiersdorp
Caledon
Hermanus
Stanford
Gansbaai
Grabouw
Elgin
Botrivier
Franschhoek
Riviersonderend
Greyton
Genadendal
Napier
Elim
Kleinmond
Betty's Bay
Pringle Bay
Rooiels
Pearly Beach
Die Dam
Quoin Point
Cape Agulhas
HUGUENOT TOLL TUNNEL
Hottentots-Holland NR
Kogelberg NR
Riviersonderend NR
Salmons Dam NR
Walker Bay NR
Agulhas NP
Fernkloof NR
Grootbos PR
Boontjieskraal NR
Theewaters NR
Haweqwa NR
Limietberg NR
Waterval NR
Ben Etive NR
Fonteintjiesberg NR
Bokkeriviere NR
Vrolijkheid NR
Dassiehoek NR
Karoo Desert National Botanical Garden
Hex River Pass
De Doorns
Sir Lowry's Pass
Franschhoek Pass
Shaws Pass
Houwhoek Pass
Du Toitskloof
HMS Birkenhead 1852
Birkenhead 1852
Shark Cage Diving
Whale Watching
Diving Site
AW
AX
AY

16
28
17
AW
AX
AY
19
Touws River
Karoo Lodge
Hugo
Avondrust
Bokwaterkloof
Elandskloof
Matjiesgoedkop
1257m
Tapfontein
Anysberg Nature Reserve
Anysberg Nature Reserve
Prinsrivier Dam
Prins
Touws
Anysberg
Kareevlakte
Buffelspoort
Rouxpos
Vleilar
Nougaspoort
Gecko Rock Eco-Trail
Leeuwenboschfontein 4x4
Hoek van die Berg
R318
Brak
Pieterfontein Dam
Tractor Trips
Burgers Pass
Spioenkop
Circular Route
Drie Berge
Hot Mineral Springs
Triangular Trail
Pat Busch PR
Montagu
Montagu
Langkloof
Historic Fort
Klaas
Bloupunt
Tafelkop
Roodezandt
Voogdsrivier
Kogmanskloof Pass
Montagu Mtn Reserve
Major's Hill
Ashton
Springfield
Cheese Factory
Clairvaux
Van Loveren
Wolvendrift & Goedverwacht
Nordale
Vrolijkheid NR
Cheese Factory
Rooikat
Van Zylshof
Bonnievale
Bonnievale
McGregor
Langverwacht & Janéza
Weltevrede
Merwespont
Nooitgedacht
Rietrivier
Proteavallei
Proteavallei
Marloth NR
Forest Station
Goedgeloof Hut
Boskloof Hut
Wolfkloof Hut
Church Square
Rheenendal Mill
Drostdy
Scenic Drive
Swellendam
Jubilee
Kam'Bati 4x4
Buffelsjagrivier
Buffelsjagrivier Dam
Soothey's Arms
Oupas 1734
Suurbraak
Bontebok National Park
Lang Elsie's Kraal
Low Bridge, Drift
Boesmans
Stormsvlei
Riviersonderend
Photo Museum
Riviersonderend
Boerboonfontein
Mont Eco Nature Reserve
Bellair Dam
Poortjieskloof Dam
Sanbona Nature Reserve
Groot
Klipbok Trail
Joubert Tradauw
Tradou
Die Lange Huis B&B
The Berrydale Hotel
Tradouw Guesthouse
Jacaranda Lodge
Barrydale
Barrydale
Tradouws Pass
R324
Boosmansbos Wilderness Area
Forest Station
Grysbok & Bushbuck Trail
Grootvaderbosch Nature Reserve
Warmwaterberg Nature Reserve
Warmwaterberg Spa
Ronnie's Sex Shop
Radioactive Springs
Touwsberg Private Nature Reserve
Plathuis
Doring
Wapadskloof
Brandrivier
Brand
Heidelberg Wildflower Garden
Heidelberg Hotel
Stone Post Office
Heidelberg
Korinte-vet Dam
Renier
Askraal
Duiwenhoks
Slang
R322
Western Cape
Vermaaklikheid
Dipka
Napkei
R319
Kwassiebos
Protem
Klipdale
Kykoedie
R317
Sour
Hansiesrivier Gold Mine
Malgas Hotel
N.G. Church 1856
Malgas
4by4
Ostrich Trail
Westfield
Breë
De Hoop
Potberg Trail
Barry Church
Kapstylhuise 1887
Puntjie
Historic Homesteads
Wydgeleë
Potberg Enviromental Education Centre
Cape Vulture Colony
Whale Trail
Port Beaufort
Witsand
Witsand
Kadie 1865
Merasheen 1947
Whale Watching
Infanta
Whale Watching
Cape Infanta
St Sebastian
Whale Watching
Bucha Bushcamp
Tierhoek
Picnic Spot
Koppie-Alleen Hut
Vaalkrans Hut
De Hoop Nature Reserve
Hamerkop Hut
Hiking & MTB Trails
Bird Watching
De Hoop
Whale Watching
Vlei Trails
Koppie Alleen
Whale Trail
Die Mond
De Hoopvlei
Potberg
Kars
R316
Elandshuis
NG Church
Napier
Ox Wagon Monument
Giant Milkwood Tree
Church Hall and Manse
Bredasdorp
Shipwreck Museum
Bontebok Fence Monument
Geelkop NR
Kosiers Kraal Game Farm
Heuningberg NR
Historic Watermill
Mission Station
Die Herberg Resort
R319
Kassiesbaai Fishing Village
Skipskop
Hooppunt
Clan McGregor 1902
Waenhuiskrans
Fisherman's Cottages
Waenhuiskrans NR
Waenhuiskrans & Arniston
Waenhuiskrans Cave
Forest Station
De Mond
De Mond NR
Maggie 1843
Arniston 1815
Diving Site
Soetendalsvlei
Voëlvlei
Tsaba-Tsaba NR
Bird Watching
Bird Watching
Fisherman's Cottages
Hotagterklip
Agulhas NP
Struis Bay
Diving Site
L'Agulhas Caravan Park
Whale Watching
Struisbaai
Oriental Pioneer 1974
L'Agulhas
Lighthouse Museum
Lighthouse 1848
Cape Agulhas
1 Hodges Bridge (AW 16)
2 Soekershof Maze (AW 16)
3 Thatch Roof Church (AY 16)
4 Harbour Lights (AY 16)
5 Struisbaai Caravan Park (AY 16)
6 Cogman's Kloof (AW 16)
7 Berg-en-dal (AW 16)
8 Breederivier Lodge (AX 17)
9 Sterna Trail (AY 16)
Indian Ocean

Bosluiskloof
Die Hel
18
Seweweekspoort
Gamkaskloof
29
Voortrekker Memorial
Scenic Drive
Swartberg Trail
Bothashoek
19
Cango Caves
Koos Raubenheimer Dam
Rus-en-Vrede Waterfall
Matjiesrivier
Doringkloof
Grootkraal
Towersig
CJ Langenhoven's Birthplace
Bojaankop Trail
Matjiesvlei
Groenfontein
The Retreat Guesthouse
Kruisrivier Guesthouse
Kruisrivier
Schoemanspoort
De Oude Meul Country Lodge
Angora Rabbit Farm
Herrieskloof 1929
De Rust
Ladismith
Zoar
Amalienstein Mission Station
Huisrivier Pass
Museum & Succulent Garden
Fish Eagle Resort
Coetzeespoort
Schoemanshoek
Cango Ostrich Farm
Buffelsdrift Game Lodge
Mons Ruber
Ladismith Klein Karoo NR
Boplaas
Calitzdorp
Historic Churches
Spekboom Cottages
Anna Sophia
Eerste Pastorie
Remhoogte
Oudtshoorn Ostrich Farm
Cheetah & Crocodile Wildlife Park
Cango Wildlife Ranch
Greylands Ostrich Farm
Kerkrand
Badshoogte
Oudtshoorn
Bongolethu
Dysselsdorp
Kammanassie
Kammanassie Dam
Suspension Bridge
Safari Ostrich Farm
Oudtshoorn Experimental Farm
Chandelier Game Lodge
Rooiberg Pass
Calitzdorp Spa (Hot Springs)
The Stables
Tierkloof
Highgate Ostrich Farm
Minwater
Brakpoort
Gamkaberg NR
Oukraal
Doring
Blossoms
Van Wyksdorp
Groot
Mavuradonha
Derde
AW
Eseljag
R328
Voortrekker Gedenkplaat
Attakwaskloof Monument 1689
Outeniqua NR
Swartberg State Forest
Old Tollhouse
Pass to Pass Trail
Herold
Montagu & Old Smithy
Doring River
Outeniqua Pass
Old Smithy
Topping
Cradocks
Outeniqua
Kamma
Bonniedale Holiday Farm
Attaquaskloof
Jonkersberg State Forest
Forest Office
Old Tollhouse
R327
Waboomsberg
Langberg
Cloetes Pass
Robinson Pass
Ruiterbosch
Blanco
Red Berry Farm
George
Corbelled Houses
Eight Bells
Bado Kidogo Bird Farm
Garden Route Mall
Toll House
Die Poort
Ruitersbos Forest Walk
George Airport
Pacaltsdorp
Garcia Pass
Weyers
Herbertsdale
Brandwag
Wolwedans
Pine Creek
R102
Herolds Bay
Thembalethu
Vals
St Barnabas Anglican Church
Nyaru Game Lodge
Botlierskop Game Farm
Groot Brakrivier
Beach Walks
Stone Church
Zeekoegat 1785
Du Plessis Pass
Hartebeeskuil Dam
Klein Brakrivier
Riversdale
Mossel Bay
Julius Gordon Africana Centre
ATKV Holiday Resort
Dibiki Resort
Hartenbos
Rosebud 1888
Werner Frehse NR
Dekriet
Albertinia Hotel
Gourits
Gourits River Bridge
Bartlesfontein
Stink
PetroSA
Kwa-Nonqaba
Fonteine
Albertinia
Aloe Vera Factory
Bungee Jumping
Danabaai
Garden Route Casino
Post Office Tree
Cape St Blaize Cave
Whale Watching
Droëvlakte
R305
Vleesbaai
Riethuiskraal
Johnson's Post
Lappiesbaai Resort
Ellensrust
Cape Vacca (Kanonpunt)
Gouritzmond
Still Bay
Palinggat Homestead
Geelkrans & Pauline Bohnen Nature Reserve
Rein's NR
Bird Hide
Ancient Fish Traps (Visvywers)
Haliartus 1932
Jongensfontein
Groot Jongensfontein
Still Bay
Cape Barracouta
AX
22
1 CP Nel Museum, Fosters Manor & Gottland House (AW 19)
2 The Cave (AX 19)
3 Herolds Bay (AX 19)
4 Fancourt Golf Course (AW 19)
5 Bartolomeu Dias Museum Complex (AX 19)
Indian Ocean

AY

AW
AX
AY
20
30
21

Indian Ocean

AY

23 AX

Indian Ocean

AY

Graham Hotel
Eagle's Nest B&B
Fairbairn Nature Reserve
1820 Settlers Monument
45
26
33
27
Fallodon
Thomas Baines NR
Bloukrans Pass
22
Canoeing
Settler's Dam
Langholm
12
Salem
12
Waters Meeting II Nature Reserve
Nolukhanyo
Restored Settler Houses
Bathurst
The Pig 'n Whistle Hotel
Waters Meeting 1 NR
Bibury Fossil Exposure
63
Mpekweni Holiday Resort
Fish River Sun Hotel
Fort D'Acre
Great Fish Point
Settlers Church
Seafield
Green Fountain Caravan Resort
Horshoe Bend
Southwell
Kowie Hiking Trail
Intaka Lodge
R343
Kariega Game Reserve
Port Alfred
Medolino Holiday Resort
Willows
22
Quinn Sculpture Garden
Alexandria
Rosedale
25
26
Leopard's Kloof
Nongqawuse's Grave
Forest Station
Emlanjeni Private Game Reserve
Kasouga Beach
Kasouga
Kariega
Kenton-on-Sea
Boesmansriviermond
Dias Cross Memorial 1488
Intsomi Lodge
Boschhoek
Boknes
Cannon Rocks Holiday Resort
Cannon Rocks Holiday Resort
Ntdaros 1930
Cape Padrone
1 Nautilus
Milkwood Manor
Lazy Daze
Amanzi (AW 26)
2 Halyards Hotel
Ferryman's
My Pond
Portofino (AW 27)
Indian Ocean
AW
AX
AY

12
37
13
AT
AU
AV
18
1 !Khwa ttu Guesthouse (AV 13)
2 Pelican Beach Resort
Stywelyne Campsite (AU 13)
3 Tienie Versveld Flower Reserve & Wetland (AV 13)
4 Rondeberg Private Nature Reserve
Jakkalsfontein Private Nature Reserve (AV 13)
5 Harold Versveld Flower Reserve (AV 13)
6 Salt Factory
Carinus Bridge (AU 13)
7 Lamberts Bay Hotel (AT 13)
8 Lambertsbaai Campsite (AT 13)
9 River Lodge Guesthouse
Vredendal Hotel
Voorsorg Guesthouse
Tharrakamma Guesthouse (AT 13)
10 Whale Watching (AU 13)
11 Whale Watching (AU 13)
12 Bird Hide (AT 13)
Atlantic Ocean
Bushman Paintings
Lutzville
Vleermuisklip 1661
Saldanha/Sishen Railway Bridge
Lossand
Olifants
Vredendal
Stoumann's
Estuary Boat Trips
Papendorp
Strandfontein
Horseshoe Strandfontein
Strandfontein Beach
Grave of Richard Freyer's Wife
Bamboesbaai
Diving Site
Doringbaai
Spruitdrif
Bergkraal
Klawer
Rock Art Tours
Stellar
Kleipan
Rooiduinpunt
Heerenlogement Cave
Heerenlogement
Diving Site
Diamond Diving Boats
Panorama Park
Bird "Island"
Lambert's Bay
Panorama Park Trail
The Dunes Trail
Annual Crayfish Festival
Whale Watching
Desert Hiking Trail
Jakkals
Graafwater Hotel
Whale Bone House
Wolfhuis
Leipoldtville
Kreefbaai
Wadrif Salt Pan
Eland
Elands Bay Hotel
Elandsbaai NR
Crayfish Industry
Large Wild Olive Grove
Elandsbaai
Diving Site
Baboon Point
Verlorevlei
Sandberg
Redelinghuys
Jakkalskloof
Castle Trail
Historic Ammunition Store, Ruins & San Art
Noordkuil
Rocherpan Nature Reserve
Bird Hide
Papkuil
Dwarskersbos
Stompneuspunt
St Helena Bay
Dwarskersbos Resort
Cape St Martin
Vasco da Gama Nautical Museum
Sea Trader 1971
Da Gama Monument
Stompneus Bay
Midwest
St Helena Bay
Laaiplek
Historic Fisherman's Cottage
Saint Helena Hotel
Paternoster Fish Market
Riviera Hotel
Velddrif
Paternoster Hotel
Tietiesbaai
Paternoster
Port Owen
Bird Watching
Salt Works
Cape Columbine
Prosesfontein Monument
Vredenburg
Langrietvlei Wetlands
Die Witsand
Spanjaard
Bergrivier
Kersefontein
Jacobsbaai
Fossil Park
Langebaanweg
Saldanha Holiday Resort
Tabakbaai Resort
Blue Bay Lodge
Saldanha
SAS Saldanha Military Base
Penguins
Club Mykonos
Air Force Base
North Head
Mussel Rafts
Diving Site
Saldanha Bay
Langebaan
Open-Air Restaurant
South Head
Postberg Nature Reserve (Seasonal only)
West Coast National Park
Kraalbaai
Plankiesbaai Picnic Area
Tzaarsbank Picnic Area
Bird Hide
Churchhaven
VOC Beacon
Geelbek Environmental Centre
Bird Hide
Geelbek Trails
!Khwa ttu Main Gate
16 Mile Beach
Blombosch Trail
Lime Furnaces
Whale Watching
Yzerfontein
Yzerfonteinpunt
Yzerfontein Holiday Resort
Whale Watching
!Khwa ttu Bush Camp
Ormonde
Flower Reserves
Cape Fur Seals & Penguins
Dassen Island
North Terminal De la Caille's Arc of Meridian
McClear Base
Aurora
Salt Works
Sauer
Bushman Art
Groot-berg
Historic Fountain
Koringberg
Fossil Site
Hopefield Lodge
Hopefield
Historic Cape Dutch Homesteads
Moorreesburg
Wheat Museum
Ganskraal
Kiekoesvlei
Rust
Hildebrand (1902)
Museum
Art & Craft Route
Darling
Oudepost Wild Flower Reserve
Kanonkop
Waylands Wild Flower Reserve
Darling
Mission Station
Water Mill 1840
Cloof
Abbotsdale
Boesmans
R362
R363
R364
R365
R399
R27
R45
R311
R307
R315

14
38
15
Rock Pigeon Route
Bo-Kloof
Oorlogskloof NR
Maskamsig
Vanrhijn & Latsky Radio Museum
Vanrhynsdorp
Cactus Nursery
Anglo-Boer War Fort
Urionskraal
Keiskie se Poort
Bloukrans Pass
Brak
Koebee
Bloukrans
Botterkloof
Doringbos
R364
Northern Cape
Rock Paintings
AT
Bulshoek Barrage
Rondeberg Resort
Wolfdrift
Lorraine
Travellers Rest
Bushman's Kloof Lodge
Pakhuis Pass
Bushmans Kloof
De Pakhuys Guest Farm
Uitspankraal
Die Bos
Doring
Biedou
Biedouwvallei
Biedouw Valley
Steenrug
Olifants
Klein Kliphuis
Guided Rooibosch Tours
Dr CL Leipoldt's Grave
Clanwilliam
Clanwilliam Dam
Old Gaol (Jail) Museum
Boschkloof
Krakadouw
Heuningvlei Forest Station
Clanwilliam Dam
Karukareb Safari Tents
Historic Village
Rietvlei
Wuppertal
'Veldskoen' Shoe Factory
Tra-tra
Varschfontein Cottage
Elandsberg
Tankwa-Karoo National Park
Die Kleine Schuur
Rondegat
Elandskloof
Jamaka
Eselbank Waterfalls
Cederberg Wilderness Area
Algeria
Uitkyk
Tweefontein
R355
Tankwa
Tankwa Guesthouse
Onder-Wadrif
La Rhyn
Gekko
Cederberg Cottage
Wolfberg Arch
Driehoek
Wolfberg Cracks
Cederberg Chalets
Matjiesrivier NR
Paleisheuwel
Suikerbossie
Sewefontein
Sanddrif Resort
Cederberg
Dwarsrivier
Cederberg
Maltese Cross
Sneeuberg
Scenic Paleisheuwel Drive
Robyn
Krom
Nieuwoudt Farmhouses & Waterwheel
Die Mond
AU
28
Kromrivier
Cederberg Oasis
Citrusdal Caravan Park
Johan van Zyl
Citrusdal
Het Kruis
Citrus Creek
Citrusdal
Brandkraal
Piekenierskloof
Die Berghut
Middelberg Pass
Graskop
Mount Ceder
Joubert's Werf
Martien's Werf
Piekenierskloof Mountain Lodge
Blinkwater
Droërýskloof
The Baths
The Baths
Kunje
Berg en Dal
Eendekuil
McGregor's Cottage
Treetops
Kardouw
Silverspruit
Hexberg NR
Blinkberg Pass
Bobbejaankrans
Bergstroom
The Baths
Restcamp
Gansfontein
R365
N7
Pools
R303
Versveld Pass
Bergstroom
Piketberg
Beaverlac Nature Reserve
Wittewater
Winkelshoek
Beaverlac
De Hoek
Org de Rac
Waterval Trail
Nieuwedrift
Cheese Factory
Groot Winterhoek Forest Station
Porterville
Groot Kliphuis
Club Elani Resort
Porterville Historic Mill
Klein Kliphuis
Op die Berg
Tulbagh (Porterville)
Hut 1
Hut 2
Perdevlei
Oppiberg Guesthouse
De Tronk
1 Clanwilliam Hotel
Elephant River Guesthouse
Clanwilliam Lodge (AT 14)
2 Bergriver Historical Cemetery (AV 14)
3 Peace of Heaven Campsite
Waterval Campsite
Laatson Campsite (AV 14)
4 Montpellier (AV 14)
5 Lemberg (AV 14)
6 Kloofzicht (AV 14)
7 Paddagang (AV 14)
8 Witzenberg Country Estate (AV 14)
9 Waverley Hills Hiking Trail (AV 14)
10 Wild Olive Farm (AV 14)
11 Ceres Inn Guesthouse
Belmont Hotel (AV 15)
12 Dennebos Campsite
Die Eiland Campsite (AV 14)
13 Morgansvlei (AV 14)
Western Cape
Halfmanshof
Vier En Twintig
Grootwinterhoek Wilderness Area
Lochlynne Dam
Kruis
Swartkop se Dam
AV
Isle of Sky
Twee Jonge Gezellen
Monbijou Historical Buildings
Saronsburg
Rijks
Gydo Pass
Hottentotskloof
Die Venster
Touwsrivier Reserve
Sand
Vleitjies
R311
Klein-berg
Tulbagh
Prince Alfred Hamlet
Theronsberg Pass
R46
Ongegund (Birthplace of Gen. JC Swuts)
Gouda
Drostdy
Witzenberg Game Park
Matroosberg
Smalblaar
Touws
Loganda Karoo Lodge
Nuwekloof Pass
Waterval
Pine Forest Holiday Resort
Swaarmoed Pass
Historic Buildings & Museum
Riebeek-Wes
Sonkwasdrift
Forest Station
Voëlvlei Dam
Ceres
Nduli
Lakenvallei Dam
Bokkeriviere NR
Verkeerdevlei Dam
Aquila Game Farm
Pulpit Rock
Allesverloren
Wild Flowers
Titus
Hugo
Riebeek-Kasteel
Waverly Hills
Wolseley
Old Toll House
Hex River Pass
Matroosberg
Cartwright's Museum and Biggest Oak Tree in RSA
Riebeek
Pieter Cruythoff 1662
Wolseley Hotel
Blockhouse
Tunnel
Paardenberg NR
Michell's Pass
Ben Etive NR
Pine Forest Holiday Resort
Swartland
Hermon
Malmesbury
Waterval NR
Romansrivier
19
De Doorns
The Observatory
Bailey's Peak
Lategangskop
Bergsig
Soetendal

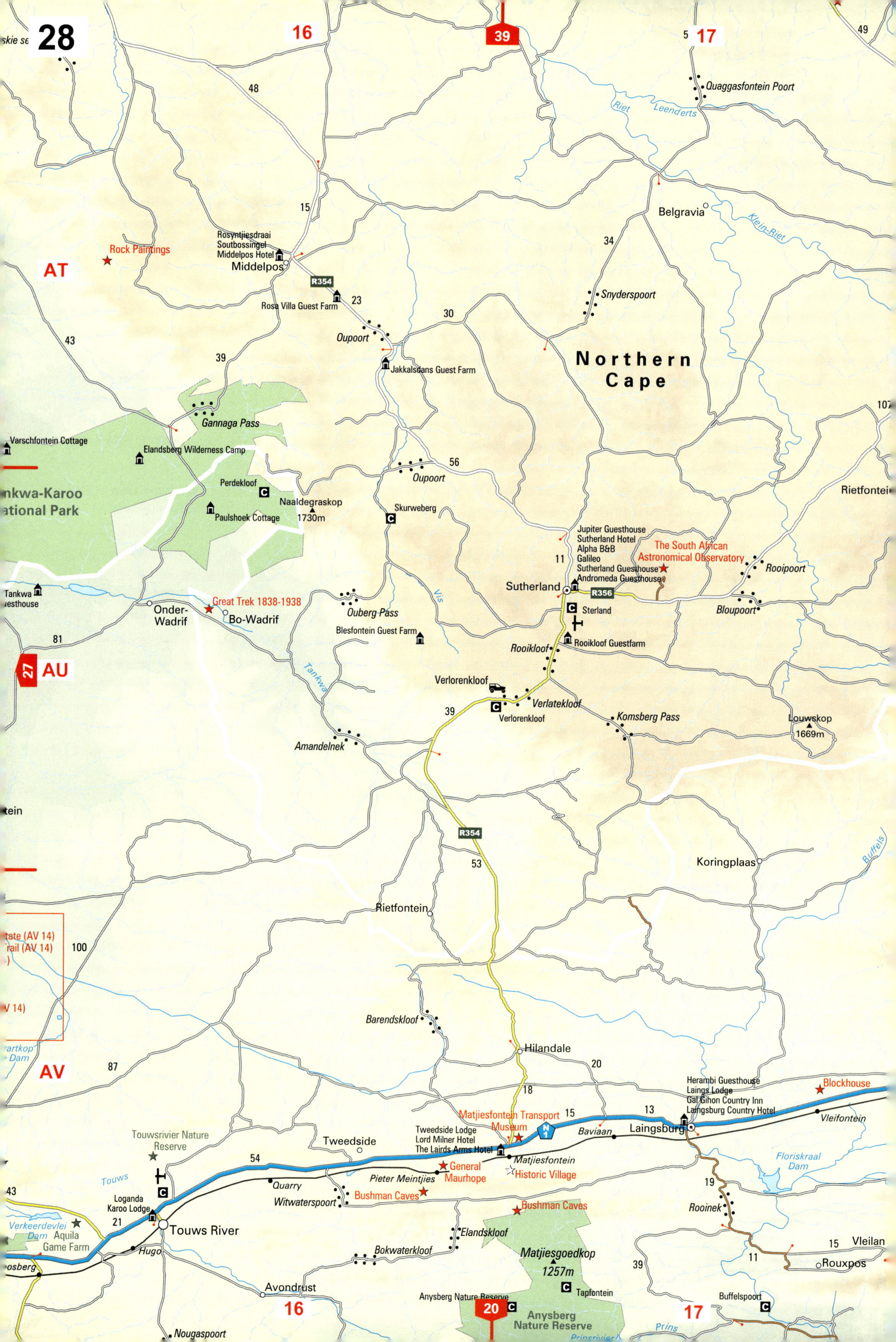

16
39
17
Quaggasfontein Poort
Belgravia
Rock Paintings
AT
Rosyntjiesdraai
Soutbossingel
Middelpos Hotel
Middelpos
R354
Rosa Villa Guest Farm
Oupoort
Snydersspoort
Northern Cape
Jakkalsdans Guest Farm
Gannaga Pass
Varschfontein Cottage
Elandsberg Wilderness Camp
Perdekloof
Naaldegraskop
1730m
Paulshoek Cottage
Oupoort
Skurweberg
Jupiter Guesthouse
Sutherland Hotel
Alpha B&B
Galileo
Sutherland Guesthouse
Andromeda Guesthouse
The South African Astronomical Observatory
Rooipoort
Sutherland
R356
Sterland
Bloupoort
Great Trek 1838-1938
Onder-Wadrif
Bo-Wadrif
Ouberg Pass
Blesfontein Guest Farm
Rooikloof
Rooikloof Guestfarm
AU
Verlorenkloof
Verlatekloof
Verlorenkloof
Komsberg Pass
Louwskop
1669m
Amandelnek
R354
Koringplaas
Rietfontein
Barendskloof
Hilandale
AV
Heerambi Guesthouse
Laings Lodge
Gal Gihon Country Inn
Laingsburg Country Hotel
Blockhouse
Matjiesfontein Transport Museum
Laingsburg
Vleifontein
Tweedside Lodge
Lord Milner Hotel
The Lairds Arms Hotel
Baviaan
Touwsrivier Nature Reserve
Tweedside
Matjiesfontein
Historic Village
Floriskraal Dam
General Maurhope
Pieter Meintjies
Quarry
Witwaterspoort
Bushman Caves
Loganda Karoo Lodge
Rooinek
Bushman Caves
Verkeerdevlei Dam
Aquila Game Farm
Touws River
Elandskloof
Vleilan
Hugo
Bokwaterkloof
Matjiesgoedkop
1257m
Rouxpos
Avondrust
Tapfontein
Anysberg Nature Reserve
Buffelspoort
16
20
Anysberg Nature Reserve
17
Nougaspoort

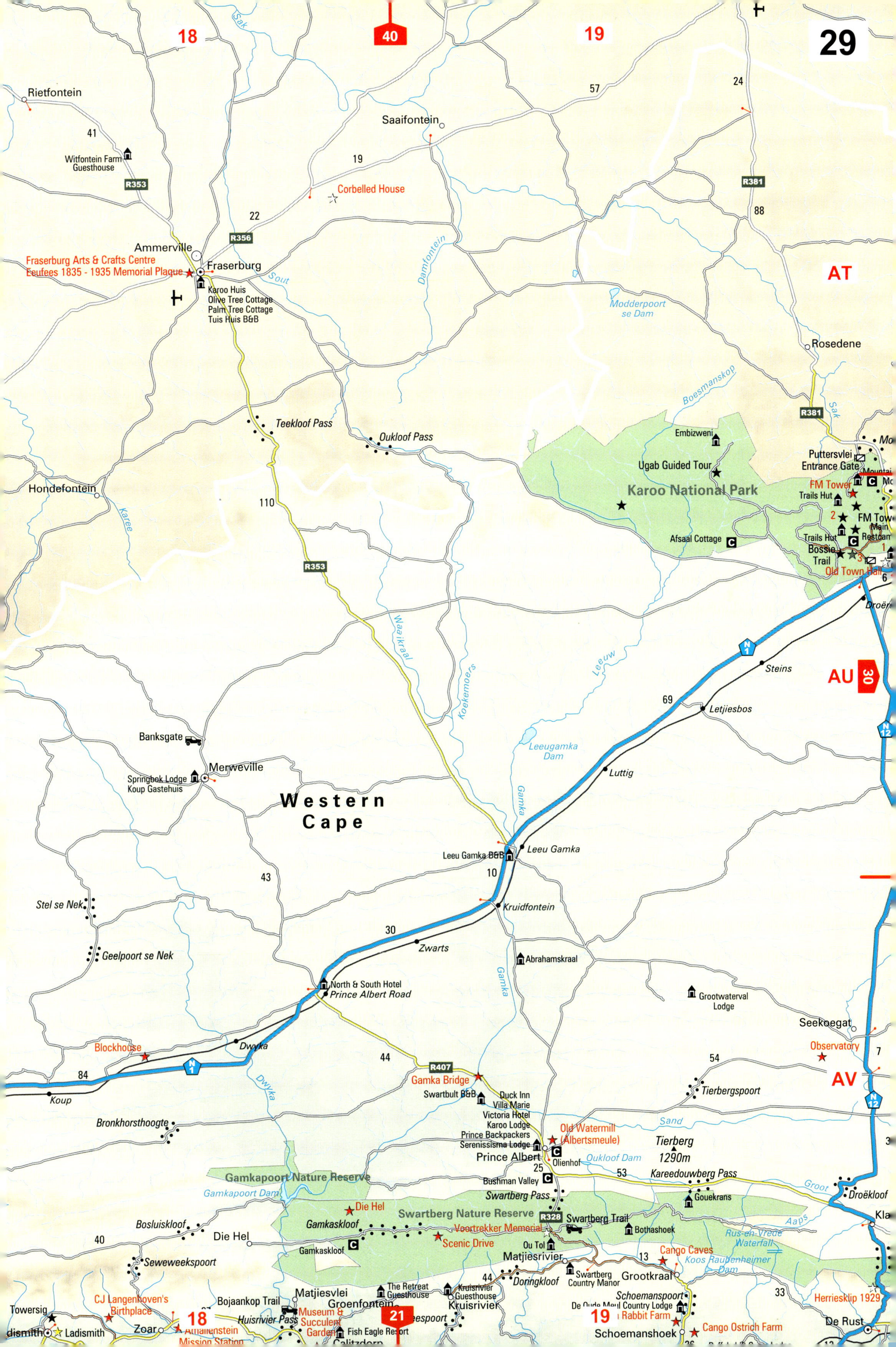
18
40
19
Rietfontein
41
Witfontein Farm Guesthouse
R353
Saaifontein
57
24
19
Corbelled House
R381
88
22
R356
Ammerville
Fraserburg Arts & Crafts Centre
Eeufees 1835 - 1935 Memorial Plaque
Fraserburg
Sout
Damfontein
AT
Karoo Huis
Olive Tree Cottage
Palm Tree Cottage
Tuis Huis B&B
Modderpoort se Dam
Rosedene
Boesmanskop
Sak
R381
Teekloof Pass
Oukloof Pass
Embizweni
Puttersvlei Entrance Gate
Ugab Guided Tour
FM Tower
Karoo National Park
Trails Hut
Hondefontein
Karee
110
Afsaal Cottage
Bossie Trail
Old Town Hall
R353
Waaikraal
N1
Steins
AU
30
Leeuw
69
Letjiesbos
Koekemoers
Banksgate
N12
Leeugamka Dam
Merweville
Springbok Lodge
Koup Gastehuis
Luttig
Western Cape
Gamka
Leeu Gamka B&B
Leeu Gamka
10
43
Kruidfontein
Stel se Nek
30
Zwarts
Geelpoort se Nek
Abrahamskraal
Gamka
North & South Hotel
Prince Albert Road
Grootwaterval Lodge
Seekoegat
Blockhouse
Dwyka
Observatory
44
54
7
84
N1
R407
Gamka Bridge
AV
Koup
Swartbult B&B
Duck Inn
Villa Marie
Victoria Hotel
Karoo Lodge
Prince Backpackers
Serenissima Lodge
Dwyka
Tierbergspoort
N12
Bronkhorsthoogte
Old Watermill (Albertsmeule)
Sand
Tierberg 1290m
Prince Albert
Olienhof
Oukloof Dam
25
53
Kareedouwberg Pass
Gamkapoort Nature Reserve
Bushman Valley
Gamkapoort Dam
Swartberg Pass
Gouekrans
Groot
Droëkloof
Die Hel
Swartberg Nature Reserve
R328
Swartberg Trail
Aaps
Bosluiskloof
Gamkaskloof
Voortrekker Memorial
Bothashoek
Rus-en-Vrede Waterfall
40
Die Hel
Scenic Drive
Gamkaskloof
Ou Tol
Matjiesrivier
Cango Caves
13
Seweweekspoort
Koos Raubenheimer Dam
44
Doringkloof
Swartberg Country Manor
Grootkraal
The Retreat Guesthouse
Kruisrivier Guesthouse
Kruisrivier
Schoemanspoort
33
CJ Langenhoven's Birthplace
Bojaankop Trail
Matjiesvlei
Groenfontein
Herrieklip 1929
Towersig
De Oude Meul Country Lodge
Museum & Succulent Garden
Huisrivier Pass
21
Rabbit Farm
18
19
Cango Ostrich Farm
De Rust
Ladismith
Zoar
Amalienstein Mission Station
Fish Eagle Resort
Calitzdorp
Schoemanshoek

Northern Cape
Western Cape
Beaufort West
1 Formula 1 Hotel - Beaufort West
Springbok Lodge
Tree Top Guesthouse
Grandmas B&B
Viltra Inn (AU 20)
2 Fonteinjieskloof Trail (AU 20)
3 Bird Hide (AU 20)
Hutchinson
Verster
Houdenbeck B&B
Biesiespoort
Skietkuil B&B
Karoo Guesthouse
Joalani
Wagenaarskraal
Hillcrest
Travalia Lodge
Three Sisters
3 Sisters Guest Farm
Kromrivier
Rosedene
De Jagers Pass
Restvale
Nelspoort
The Vale
Molteno Pass
Puttersvlei Entrance Gate
Mountain View Hut
Mountain View Camp Site
FM Tower
Trails Hut
Roseberg Pass
Ko-Ka Tsara Bush Camp
Waterval Camp Site
Main Restcamp
Lemoenfontein Game Lodge
Bossie Trail
Old Town Trail
Beaufort West Dam
N.G. Church
Pap Dam
Droërivier
Renosterkop
Lemoen
Buffels
Kariega
Olive Grove Guest Farm
Letjiesbos
Blydskap Farm
Wiegnaarspoort
Amos
Rietbron
Seekoegat
Observatory
Beervlei Dam
Volstruisleegte
Kommandokraal
Perdepoort
Trompetterspoort
1364m
Soetendalspoort Trail
Droëkloof
Klaarstroom
Groot
Aaps
Rus-en-Vrede Waterfall
Meiringspoort
Herriesklip 1929
De Rust
Willowmore
Die Royal Hotel
The Willow Historical Guestho
Vondeling
Buyspoort
Ghwarriepoort
Olifants
Rooiloop
Barandas
20
21
22
29
41
AT
AU
AV
N1
N9
N12
R61
R63
R306
R329
R381

22
42
23
Lessingshoogte
Kranskop
2052m
Snyderskraal
Weltevreden
Guest Farm
Owl House Museum
Nieu-Bethesda
Aasvoëlkrans Guesthouse
De Toren
Guest Cottage
Brandkraal
Murraysburg
Huis Spitskop B&B
Five Roses Guesthouse
Mulberry Cottage
Rooipoort
Lootsberg
Pass
Rooinek
Bethesdaweg
AT
Wapadsberg
Pass
Koloniesplaas
Naudeberg Pass
Elandskloof
Great Fish
Clifton Guesthouse
Oudeberg Pass
Bird Hide
Magnificent-View
Cottage
Vanryneveldspas Dam
uMasizakhe
Camdeboo National Park - Main Entrance
Graaff-Reinet
Andries Pretorius Monument
Driekoppe Trail
Valley of Desolation
Old Mission Church
Eerstefontein Day Trail
Old
Magazine
Camdeboo
National Park
Munnikspoort
Adendorp
Petersburg
1 Urquhart Caravan Park
Impangele Guesthouse
The Lazy Zebra B&B
Avondrust Guesthouse
Drostdy Hotel - Ferreira House
Red Geranium B&B
Trackers Inn Guesthouse
Aloe Lodge Self Catering (AU 23)
Barakke
Behulpsaam
Uitkyk
Pagel House B&B
Villeria Guesthouse
Aberdeen Hunters Lodge
Kamdebdo
Aberdeen
Thembalesizwe
De Hoop
Dam
Charlwood
Eastern
Cape
Kendrew
AU
32
Sundays
R338
Marais
Aberdeen Road
Kaapse Poortjie
R337
Oatlands
Soutpansnek
Jansenville
The Cottage
Oak Villa
Sondags
Klipplaat
Charles
Hotel
Heuningklip
Swanepoelspoort
Miller
Humefield
Mount Steward
Waterford
AV
Greystone
Naroegaspoort
1230m
Glenmore Farm
(4x4 Trail)
Timbila
Game Reserve
Bhejane
Game Reserve
Knoetze
Toorfonteinpoort
Kamferspoort
Baroe
Narrasnek
Addo Elephant
Park - West
Waaipoort
Salt Pan's Nek
Noorspoort
Guesthouse
Seekoeinek
Wolwefontein
R329
Haaspoort
Noorspoort
Blaauwbosch
Private Game
Reserve
Kleinpoort
Steytlerville
Karoo Theatrical Hotel
Steytlerville Villa
Groot
Baviaanskloof
Adolphuspoort

32
KwaNonzame
24
43
25
Klein Brak
Tafelberg
Groot-Brak
R391
R390
Hofmeyr
Teviot
Die Pondokkie
Karoobos Guesthouse
Vlekpoort
Dwarsvlei
Kelly-Patterson Dam
Witkransnek
N9
N10
35
56
R401
Conway
Grassridge Dam
13
55
Rooinek
34
Groot-Brak
Grassridge Dam Monument
25
R401
Lootsberg Pass
62
63
Great Trek 1838
Groot Brak
Visrivier
R390
AT
Wapadsberg Pass
Koloniesplaas
30
Spitskopvlei
18
R61
Agter Sneeuberg
14
Post Chalmers
Baroda
1 Oude Pastorie
The Irelander
Dirosie
Sir John Cradock
Shalom (AT 25)
Elands
Groot-Vis
Commando Drift NR
Kommandodrif Dam
59
28
Elandskloof
Great Fish
Mountain Zebra National Park
Ubejane Trail
Egg Rock
Mountain Zebra National Park - Main Gate
Cradock Spa
Cradock
Rooiplaat
Old Parsonage
Lingelihle
Tarka
Kranskop
Doornhoek Heritage Site
Doornhoek Guest House
Rest Camp
Halesowen
Lake Arthur
Tarka
Petersburg
R390
Olive Schreiner's Tomb
Swaershoek Pass
35
Barakke
39
Mortimer
45
Coetzerskloof
55
R390
Drennan
Bezuidenhout Grave
Cameron' Glen
N10
R337
37
Glenrock
14
Swaershoek
Witmos
Daggaboersnek
Glen Lynden Church 1828
31
AU
52
R63
18
Daggaboersnek
Baviaans
Pearston
Eastern Cape
Bosberg Nature Reserve
Wienandsnek
Blyderivier Dam
8
13
58
Bruintjieshoogte
Die Kaia
Blue Crane
Glen Avon Farm
Somerset Lodge
Eastpoort
Bedford
Somerset East
48
The Angler & Antelope Luxury Guesthouse
KwaNojoli
12
24
31
Cookhouse
Great Trek 1838
25
R337
Slagtersnek Monument 1816
Golden Valley
Long Hope
Vogel
Witdrift
Middleton
Sondags
26
Sheldon
60
63
R75
Waterford
15
Little Fish
Great Fish
Darlington Dam
Volkers
R400
70
R335
AV
8
Klipfontein
Wapadskloof
Greystone
R400
27
18
Darlington Lake Lodge
23
Canteen Poort
Addo Elephant National Park - West Entrance
Bedrogfontein
Swartwaterspoort Pass
Riebeeck-East
9
13
19
Salt Pan's Nek
41
Ann's Villa
12
Wit
Sundays
Wolwefontein
Addo Elephant National Park
Kabouga Guesthouse
17
Suurberg Pass
Aliceda
Langrugskloof
Narina
Kleinpoort
Mvubu
32
Valleyview
Olifantskop
Grasvlakte Safari Lodge
Kabouga Section - East Gate
Slagboom
Suurberg
35
Bushman Sands
Zuurberg Mountain Inn
Bellevue
Glenconnor
Kirkwood
Bontrug
Kronenhoff Guesthouse
Kirkwood Hotel
Sunday's River Citrus Co.
28
River Bend Lodge
11
17
25
16
Thorndale Safari
Woodall
Addo Eco Trail
Karrega
R336
The Lookout
Narina
Paterson
Shamwari Game Reserve
18
24
24
R342 Entrance
Coerney
9
10
25
R342
Longlee Manor
Breeding Research
32
The Elephant House
15
11
Kadauw Climb Out Point
Adolphuspoort
Sunland
Woodbury Lodge

Touch the Sky Trail
26
The Stagger Inn
R397
Penhoek Pass
44
Andriesberg
2106m
Grootvlei
Tsawulayo
27
Hoggs Kloof
Garryowen
Askeaton
Zitapileni
R392
Qoqodala
Lady Frere
R359
Bongolo Nek
Driver's Drift
Xonxa Dam
Lubisi Dam
Southeyville
1 Lindenhof Guesthouse
Reflection
Ikamva Lodge
Likhaya Guesthouse
Brown Hotel
Panorama Guesthouse
Amatola Mountain View
Grosvenor Lodge Hotel
Hemingways (AV 27)
Bailey
Bowker's Park
McDonald's Farm
Sunken Garden
Bonkolo Dam
Longview Lodge
Twin Oaks B&B
Queenstown
Ezibeleni
Linga Longa B&B
Mzwaphi Guest Farm
Graceland Lodge
Mlungisi
Fincham's Nek
AT
Qamata
Bholotwa
St Marks
Cofimvaba
Swart-kei
Dutch Reformed Parsonage
Skaapkraalpoort
World War I Monument
1922 Bulhoek Rebellion
MCA Shepstone 1861
Blanco Holiday Farm
Indwe Lodge
Lily Fountain Lodge
Knowsley Country Cottage
Headquarters Thibet Park
Tarka Post
Fundani Trail Camp
Volstruisnek
Bushman Art
Otterford Lodge
Phumlani Trail Camp
Tsolwana Game Reserve
Bushman Art
Whittlesea
Sada
Klipplaat
Tylden
Waqu
R351
R351
Spring Valley
De Beers Pass
Besterskop
1995m
Kenwyn B&B
The Gig B&B
Cathcart
Thorn
Thomas
Sole
Waterdown Dam
R345
1820 Settlers Milestone
Thomas River
Devil's Bellows
R344
Mankazana
Nico Malan Pass
Old Thomas River
Forest Station
Forest Station
Katberg Pass
Katberg Forest Station
Readsdale
Post Retief Barracks 1836
Gedenksteen van Post Retief se Moorhuis
Forest Station
Balfour
Oakdene
Big Thomas
Little Thomas
AU
34
Stutterheim
Fort Fordyce Boshoek Outspan
Blue Rock
Intloni Lodge
Mpofu Hut
Liddleton
Mpunzi Lodge
Mpofu Lodge
Mpofu Game Reserve
Fort Armstrong
Seymour
Elands
Michel's Pass
Katrivier Dam
Cata Forest Station
The Rev George Barre 1857
Fortified Ranch
Hogsback
Hogsback Pass
Hogsback Inn
Arminel Mountain Lodge
Maylodge Cottages
Blue Moon
Valley View
Dontsa Pass
Gubu Dam
Kubusi
Cowie
Kaalhoek
Waterkloof
Lourie Rest House
Voortrekkergedenksaal 1828-1874
Forest Station
Harris Hut
Blinkwater
Oorlog Gedenkteken 1850
Evergreen
Castle Eyre 1852
Keiskammahoek
Sandiles Grave 1878
Rabula Road 1880
Red Hill Pass
R346
Adelaide
Midgley's Hotel
Fort Fordyce NR
Water Hill 1860
Martello Tower
Fort Hare
Gaika's Grave 1829
Rooikrans Dam
R352
Fort Beaufort
Bofolo
TRN Town Lodge
The Oak
Alice
Stewart Memorial
Fort Hare
Ncera
Braunschweig
Bailie's Grave
Mgqakwebe
Middledrift
PM Motel
Amatola View Guesthouse
BHISHO
King William's Town
Breidbach
Zwelitsha
Koonap
R344
Pewuleni
Debe
Mdizeni
Ngqokweni
Main Entrance - Northern Gate
Nottingham Lodge
Fort Willshire
Forest Station
Laing Dam
Forest Station
Bothas
Mvubu
Mbabala Lodge
Naudeshoek
Qibira
Zalara
Doubledrift Game Reserve
Andries Vosloo Kudu Nature Reserve
Doubledrift Game Reserve - Southern Gate Entrance
Keiskamma
Sittingbourne
R350
Great Fish
Carlisle Bridge
Fort Brown
Bucklands
Double Drift
Breakfast Vlei
Milkwood Tree 1835
Fort Brown
Kamadolo Gate Entrance
AV
Helspoort Pass
Committees
R345
R72
Valley of Ancient Voices
Katberg Pass
Peddie
Watch Tower 1841
Brakkloof
Pluto's Vale
Wooldridge
Bell
R345
New Year's
Fort Selwyn
Makanas Kop
Hamburg
GRAHAMSTOWN
Grahamstown Municipal
Clock Tower
National English Literary Museum
Fraser's Camp Adventures
Mgwalana
Birha
Gqutywa
Wesley
Graham Hotel
Eagle's Nest B&B
Fairbairn Nature Reserve
1820 Settlers Monument
Mtati
Fallodon
Lalibela Game Reserve
Thomas Baines NR
Bloukrans Pass
Kap
Settler's Dam
Canoeing
Langholm
Bisbury Fossil Exposure
Mpekweni Holiday Resort
Dwala
Tree Tops
Salem
Waters Meeting Nature Reserve
25
Nolukhanyo
Restored Settler Houses
Bathurst
27
Fish River Sun Hotel
Fort D'Acre
Boesmans
N2
N6
R63
R67
R61

Garryowen
Cala
Indwepoort
Askeaton
Lufuta
Frere
Kwaaimans Pass
Forest Station
Ncorha Dam
Lubisi Dam
Southeyville
Tsojana Dam
AT
Qamata
Cofimvaba
Qombolo
St Marks
Garner's Drift
Hange
Tsomo
Nobokhwe
Satansnek
Ngcobo
All Saints Nek
Police Camp
Tsazo
Tylnapoort Pass
Langdon
Coghlan
Clarkebury
Whit
Ntibane
Bityi
Mbashe
Mbashe Bridge
Munyu
Mputi
Thusong Guesthouse
Dutywa
Ntisana
Ebende
Taleni
Willowvale
Ciko
Nyokana
Eastern Cape
Xolobe
Catholic Cross
Nqamakhwe
Sole
Bholo
Thomas River
Mgwali
Butterworth
Palm Springs
Bibby's B&B
KwaNofodosi
Toleni
Great Kei River Bridge
Kei Cuttings
Cats Pass
Manu
Mazeppa Bay Hotel
Mazeppa Bay
Centani
Cebe Nature Reserve
Bowker Bay
Wavecrest Hotel
Wavecrest
Seagulls Beach Hotel
Trennery's Hotel
Qholora Mouth
Kei Mouth Ferry
Kei Mouth
Morgan Bay
Morgans Bay
Double Mouth
Double Mouth NR
Haga-Haga
Cape Henderson Nature Reserve
Lalapanzi Self Catering Cottages
Jesse Lodge
Game Reserve
The Cock Inn Guesthouse
Rocky Ridge Private Reserve
Morgan Bay Hotel
Mpethu
Quko
Stutterheim
Dohne
Fortified Ranger's Cottage 1878
Wriggleswade Dam
Kubusi
Battle of Draaibosch 1877
Komga
Red Valley
The Nortons Granta
Grays
Sandiles Grave 1878
Amabele
Country
Waterfalls Hiking Trail
Kei Road
Macleantown
Tainton
Cintsa East
Cintsa Beach
Cintsa West
East London Coast NR
Kwelera NR
Gonubie
Beacon Bay
Bonza Bay
Nahoon Beach
Nahoon Beach
Historic Buildings
Nahoon Dam
PM Motel
Amatola View Guesthouse
BHISHO
King William's Town
Berlin
Breidbach
Zwelitsha
Mdantsane
Potsdam
Laing Dam
Eocene Fossil Site
Bridle Drift Dam
Buffalo River
Umtiza NR
EAST LONDON
Fort Glamorgan
Heritage Site
Dawn
East London
Lagoon Valley Resort
Umtiza NR
Kidd's Beach NR
Sea View
Breeze Inn
Kidd's Beach
Kidd's Beach Caravan & Camp
Chalumna
Kayser's NR
Kayser's Beach
AV
AU
Bell
Hamburg
Hamburg Beach
Wesley
Holiday Resort
Indian Ocean
1 Kei Mouth Caravan Park (AU 29)
2 The Thatches Holiday Accommodation
The White House Lodge
Kei Sands Accommodation (AU 29)
3 The Manderson Hotel
The Putter's Green
The Shire Eco Lodge
The Bagatelle (AU 28)
28
29
33
45

Matanzima
Misty Mount
Libode
Mlengana Pass
46
Gemvale
31
MTHATHA
Buntingville
Rock of Execution
Ntshilini
Eden Self Catering Cottages
The Creek Self Catering
Dick King 1842
Port St Johns
Silaka NR
Tombo
Lloyds
Tribal Office
Old Bunting
Ngqeleni
Sebeni Forest Station
Forest Station
Hiking Trail
Umngazi River Bungalows
Boulder Bay
Viedgesville
Nothintsila
Forest Station
Mpande Bay
Mqanduli
Hluleka NR
Hluleka
Hluleka National Park Gate
Forres Bank 1958
Dick King 1842
Forest Station
Forest Station
Old Morley
Jojweni
Tshani
Coffee Bay
Coffee Bay
Forest Station
Raptors View
Black Rock
Hole in the Wall
Indian Ocean
Mbolompo Point
Forest Station
Alderley
Forest Station
Bull's Inn
Rothmere
Hobeni
The Haven Hotel
The Haven
Dwesa Nature Reserve
Hiking Trail
O'Bell 1914
Forest Station
Dwesa Chalets & Campsite
Nqabarha
AT
AU
AV
1 Nenga River Lodge
4 Winds Guest Lodge
Sea Shells Guesthouse
Geckos Guesthouse
The Coffee Shack Backpackers
The Coffee Shack Backpackers - Campsite
The Coffee Bay Hotel & Conference Centre
Ocean View Hotel in Coffee Bay (AT 30)
2 Karibu Guesthouse
The Mangrove Resort
The Lodge
The Lily Lodge
Bulolo Holiday Camp (AT 31)
3 Port Saint Johns Hotel
The Jungle Monkey Backpackers
The Island Backpackers Lodge
Ferry Point Camping
Gecko Moon Guesthouse
Karibu Guesthouse
Umzimvubu Retreat (AT 31)
4 Gigi's Self Catering
Hole in the Wall Hotel
Bayview Lodge (AT 30)
5 Anchorage Hotel
The African Pot Mdumbi Backpacker
Mdumbi Backpackers (AT 30)

10 48 11

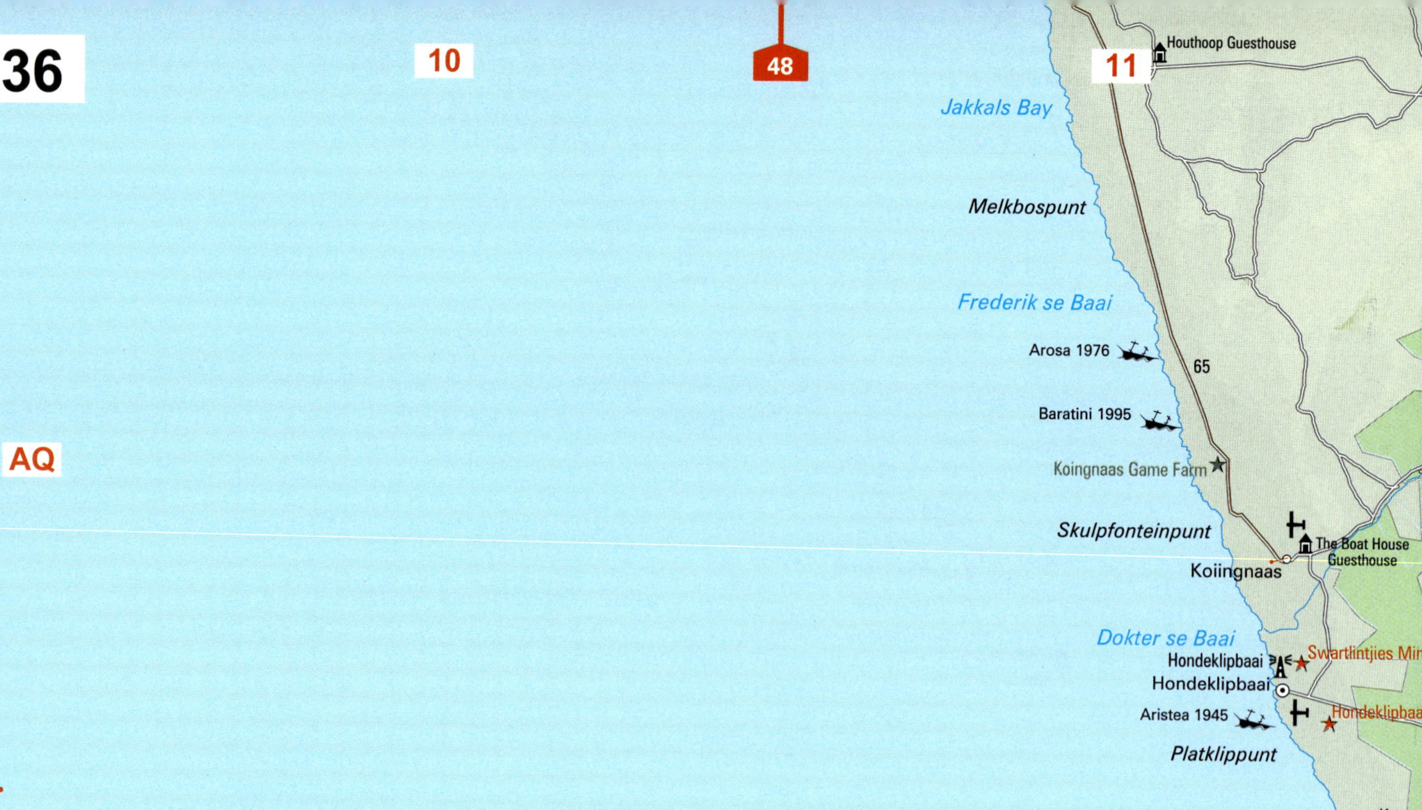

AQ

AR

Atlantic Ocean

AS

10 11

Northern Cape
Western Cape
Namaqua National Park
Atlantic Ocean
Kommaggas
Matjiesklooof
Mesklip
Burke's Pass
Wildeperdehoek Pass
Messelpad Pass
Buffels
Rietfontein
Brak
Gamoep
R355
Kamassies
Rooifontein
Swartlintjies
Skilpad Section
Farm Stall
Skilpad Wildflower Gardens
Soebatsfontein
Start of Korhaan Walking Trail
Cosy Mountain
Pedroskloof Guestfarm
Bailey's Pass
Bowerskop
Kamieskroon Hotel
Kamiesberg Pass
Kamieskroon
Kamieskroon Caravan Park
Grootvlei Pass
Barter's Grave 1902
Methodist Church 1855
Leliefontein
Platbakkies
Stofvlei
Spoegrivier
Karkams
Wallekraal
Spoeg
Studer's Pass
Witwater
Hartbees
Groen
Aalwynsfontein
Langkloof
Bitter
Garies
The Letterklip 1902
Sophia Guesthouse
Garies Guesthouse
Garies Hotel
Kliprand
Breekskip Camp
Skietloodbaai
Grootberg 1021m
Ottaspoort
Nariep
Galjoen Bay
Rooiwalspoort
Swart Doring
Groenriviersmond
Noupoort
Namaqua 1876
Island Point
Kotzesrus
Rietpoort
Roman Catholic Mission Church
Meulsteenberg 434m
'Boerewinkel' General Store
Bitterfontein
1 Dawn Ridge
Mara's Guesthouse
Dunroven (AS 13)
Langklip
Paddagat
Komkans
Klein-Goerap
Oppiekoffie
Nuwerus
Victorian Architecture
Merhof's Castle
Sout
Hoek Bay
Malkop Bay
Blinkwater Bay
Geustyn se Gat
Waterklip
R363
Ratelgat Griqua Heritage Site & Rock Art
Landplaas
Kliphoek
Skaapvlei
Koekenaap
Bushman Paintings
Lutzville
Melkboomsdrift Lodge
Vleermuisklip 1661
Olifants
Vars
R362
Saldanha/Sishen Railway Bridge
Lossand
Vredendal
Stoumann's
Estuary Boat Trips
Anglo-Boer War
Vanrhyn
Maskam
Cactus
AQ
AR
AS
W
N7
R27
12
13
49
26
38
59
68
46
34
50
35
22
15
61
17
55
66
23
31
25
27

14
50
15
1 Vanrhynsdorp Resort
Van Rhyn Guesthouse
Namaqua Country Lodge (AS 14)
2 Rooidakhuis Guesthouse
Van Zijl Guesthouse
Nieuwoudtville Hotel
Nieuwoudtville Caravan Park
Olive Caravan Park (AS 14)
3 Die Blou Naartjie Guesthouse
Die Dorphuis Self Catering
Rolbos Guesthouse
Hantam Hotel
Die Tuishuis (AS 15)
Granaatboskolk
AQ
Konnes se Pan
Dwaggas Soutpan
R358
Stofvlei
Northern Cape
Kromkop
Kliprand
Grootberg
37 AR
Western Cape
R355
Windmill Museum
Loeriesfontein
Noute Guesthouse
Loeriesfontein Hotel
Boesmanland
R357
Meulsteenberg 434m
Doring
Rietfontein
Driekop Dam
Brandkop
Klein Doring
Kleinfontein
AS
Nieuwoudtville Falls
Die Blomhuis
Historic Sandstone Buildings
Wildflower Reserve
Nieuwoudtville
Vanrhyns Pass
Vlakhoeksberg 1530m
Akkerendam NR
Karee Dam
Calvinia
Klipwerf Campsite
Calvinia Campsite
Grootdrif
Leopard Trap
Rietvlei
Brakwater
Pramkoppie
Swartkliphuis
Olienhoutbos
Suikerbosfontein
Bo- Kloof
Kameel se gat
Oorlogskloof NR
Oorlogskloof
Rock Pigeon Route
Vars
Maskamsig
Vanrhijn & Latsky Radio Museum
Vanrhynsdorp
Cactus Nursery
Anglo-Boer War Fort
Urionskraal
Keiskie se Poort
Bloukrans Pass
Brak
27
15

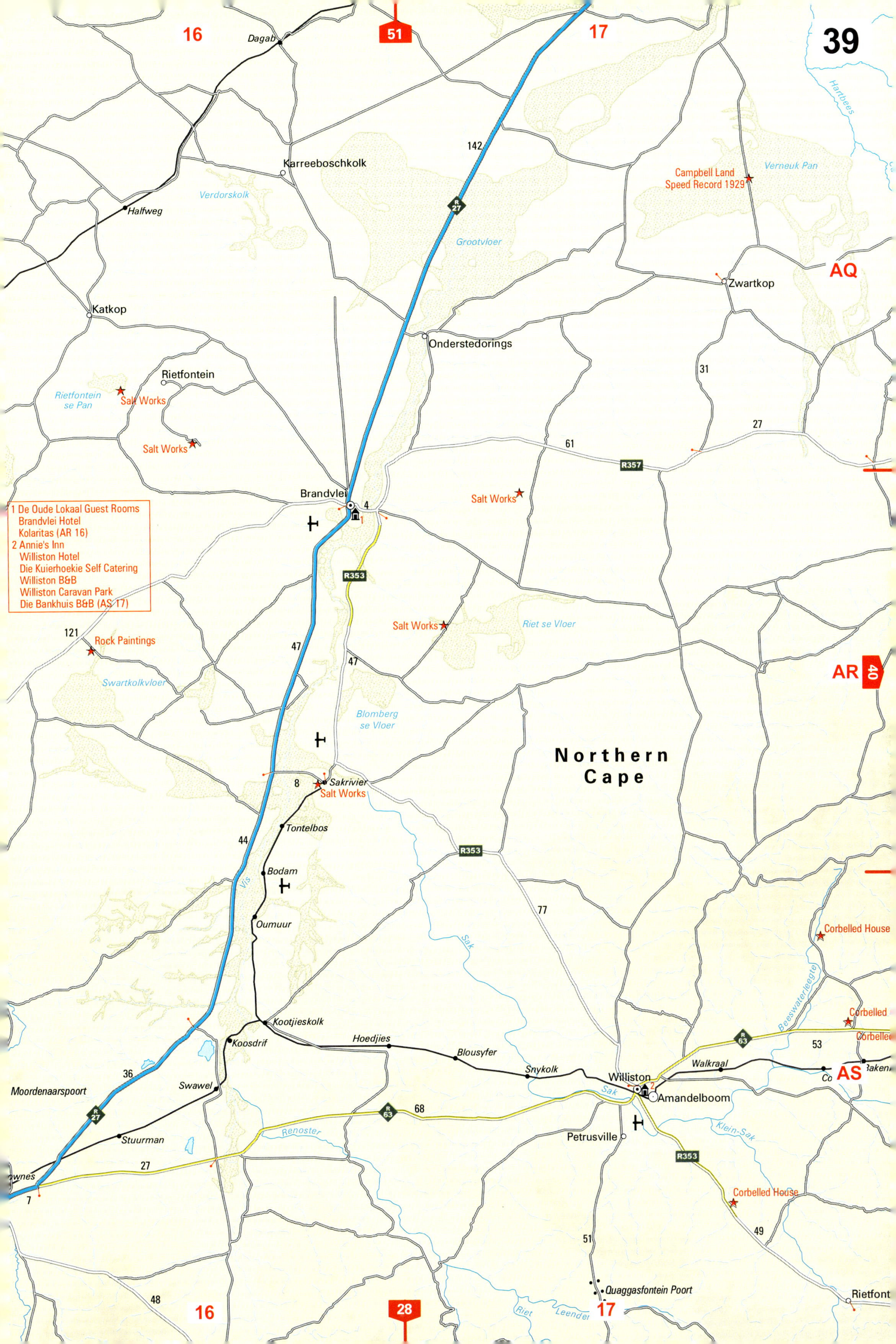

16
Dagab
51
17
142
Karreeboschkolk
Halfweg
Verdorskolk
Grootvloer
Campbell Land
Speed Record 1929
Verneuk Pan
Hartbees
AQ
Zwartkop
Katkop
Onderstedorings
Rietfontein
Rietfontein
se Pan
Salt Works
Salt Works
31
27
61
R357
Brandvlei
4
Salt Works
1 De Oude Lokaal Guest Rooms
Brandvlei Hotel
Kolaritas (AR 16)
2 Annie's Inn
Williston Hotel
Die Kuierhoekie Self Catering
Williston B&B
Williston Caravan Park
Die Bankhuis B&B (AS 17)
R353
Salt Works
Riet se Vloer
121
Rock Paintings
47
47
Swartkolkvloer
AR
40
Blomberg
se Vloer
Northern
Cape
8
Sakrivier
Salt Works
Tontelbos
44
R353
Bodam
Vis
Oumuur
77
Sak
Corbelled House
Beeswaterleegte
Kootjieskolk
Corbelled
Corbelled
Koosdrif
Hoedjies
Blousyfer
53
Snykolk
Walkraal
Williston
AS
36
Swawel
Moordenaarspoort
Amandelboom
68
Sak
Renoster
Petrusville
Klein-Sak
Stuurman
R353
27
7
Corbelled House
49
51
Quaggasfontein Poort
48
16
28
Riet
Leendert
17
Rietfont

18
52
19
Diemansputs
Lekkerleleegte
Hartbees
Verneuk Pan
Land
rd 1929
Copperton
143
R361
Carnarvonleegte
AQ
Zwartkop
74
Carnarvonleegte
7
27
57
Van Wyksvlei Hotel
Van Wyksvlei
Van Wyksvlei Dam
Salt Works
Boesak
Mekataanspoort
R361
57
Kalksloot
71
Louisvale
39
AR
R386
Renosterpoort
R384
46
Carnavon Hotel
Ons Huisie B&B
Out of Africa Guesthouse
Voortrekker Park Campsite
Tip Top Guesthouse
Palace Guesthouse
Kareebospoort
Bonteheuwel
Carnarvon Experimental Farm
Carnarvon
12
12
Blounek
9
Peerboom
Louwspla
R 63
64
Heuwels
Klipkolk
Luttigshoop
Droëputs
Corbelled House
Corbelled House
Goraas
Kareebergleegte
Gansvlei
63
Corbelled House
Beeswaterleegte
Corbelled House
Advance
R 63
53
Sterling
AS
Bakenklip
Cocopan
103
R 63
Gansvlei
4 Seasons Guesthouse
Peppertree Cottages
Blue House
Rus 'n Bietjie
12
R308
Brak
Loxton
Corbelled House
49
Sak
Rietfontein
18
29
57
19
24
Saaifontein
41

Prieskapoort
Grovè
20
Karabee
Keikamaspoort
53
21
Redlands
Grootdoring
Salt Works
Salt Works
Strydenburg
Aloe Garden
Upstairs Guesthouse
Excelsior Hotel
Klein Begin
Brak
AQ
Omdraaisvlei
Sodium
Salt Works
Ongers
Salt Works
Minnieskloof
Houtwater Dam
Voëlgeraas
Broken Dam
Giesenkraal
Bushman Paintings
Hunters Home Hotel
Die Katte
Vosburg
Vosburg Caravan Park
Britstown
Mirage Guesthouse
Transkaroo Country Lodge
Britstown
Sweetfontein
Northern Cape
Volstruispoort
Salt Works
Smartt Syndicate Dam
AR
42
Groen
Beyersburg
Sandkop
Waaipunt
Eselskloof
Deelfontein
Pampoenpoort
Marthasput
Sterkaar
Kweekwa
Ongers
Merriman
De Klerk
Wildebeeste
Welvanpas
AS
Brakpoort
Van Amstel
Soutpoort Dam
Victoria West
Ossewatrek 1838
Victoria West Dam
Victoria West Caravan Park
Rest-a-While Guesthouse
Die Pophuis Hoekie
Kingwills
Hickmans Country Lodge
Die Peperboom
Meltonwold
Aspeling Dam
Meltonwold Guestfarm
Meltonwold Guestfarm
Barnard
Hutchinson
Hutchinson
Verster
20
Northern Cape
30
Houdenbeck B&B
21
R357
R386
R403
R384
R384
R403
R398
R63
N10
N12
N1

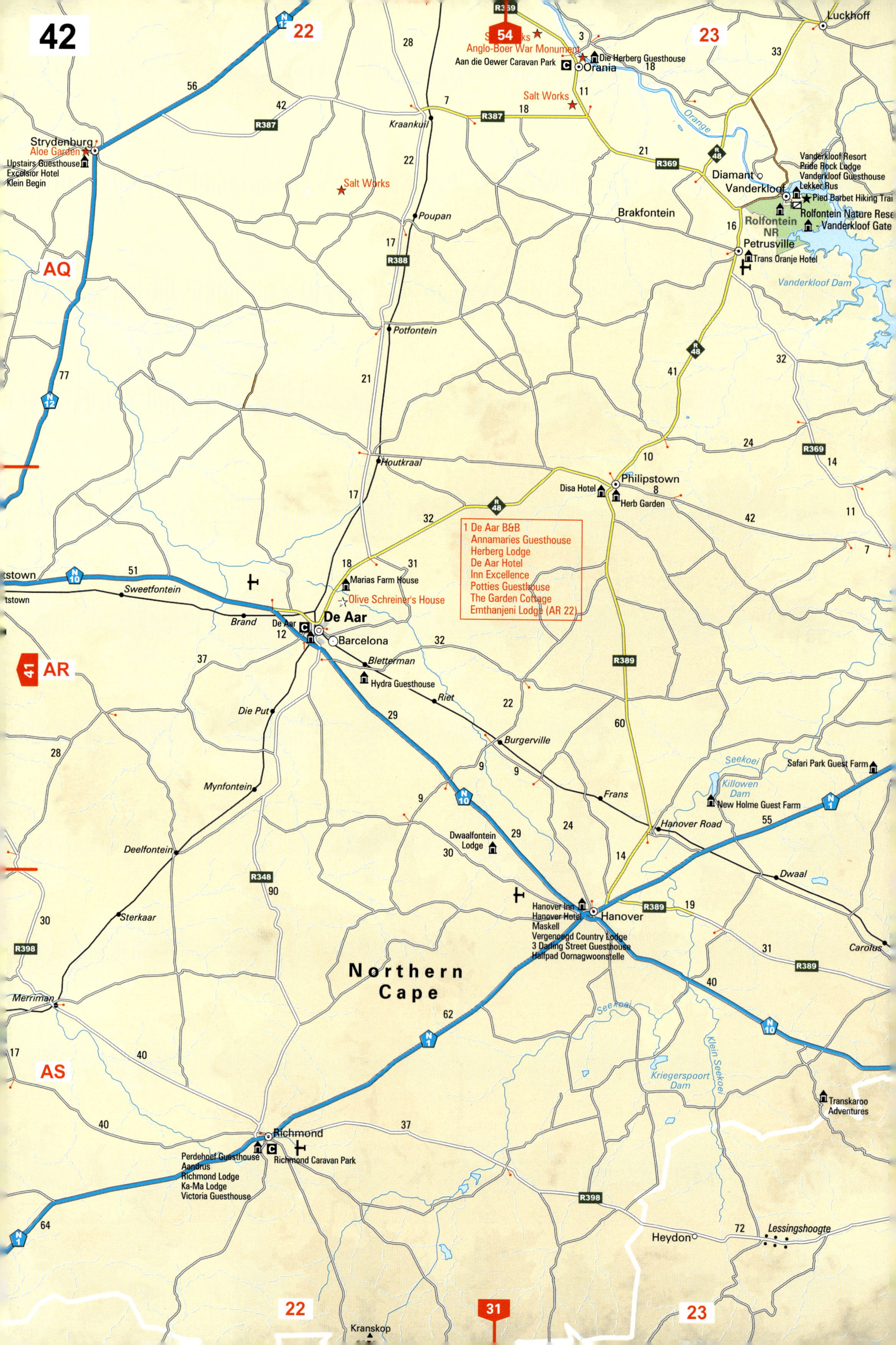

22
23
AQ
AR
AS
41
54
31
Luckhoff
Orania
Die Herberg Guesthouse
Aan die Oewer Caravan Park
Anglo-Boer War Monument
Salt Works
Kraankuil
Strydenburg
Aloe Garden
Upstairs Guesthouse
Excelsior Hotel
Klein Begin
Poupan
Brakfontein
Diamant
Vanderkloof
Vanderkloof Resort
Pride Rock Lodge
Vanderkloof Guesthouse
Lekker Rus
Pied Barbet Hiking Trai
Rolfontein NR
Rolfontein Nature Rese
- Vanderkloof Gate
Petrusville
Trans Oranje Hotel
Vanderkloof Dam
Orange
Potfontein
Houtkraal
Philipstown
Disa Hotel
Herb Garden
1 De Aar B&B
Annamaries Guesthouse
Herberg Lodge
De Aar Hotel
Inn Excellence
Potties Guesthouse
The Garden Cottage
Emthanjeni Lodge (AR 22)
Marias Farm House
Olive Schreiner's House
De Aar
Barcelona
Sweetfontein
Brand
Bletterman
Hydra Guesthouse
Riet
Die Put
Burgerville
Mynfontein
Frans
Seekoei
Killowen Dam
Safari Park Guest Farm
New Holme Guest Farm
Hanover Road
Dwaal
Dwaalfontein Lodge
Deelfontein
Sterkaar
Hanover
Hanover Inn
Hanover Hotel
Maskell
Vergenoegd Country Lodge
3 Darling Street Guesthouse
Halfpad Oornagwoonstelle
Carolus
Northern Cape
Merriman
Kriegerspoort Dam
Klein Seekoei
Transkaroo Adventures
Richmond
Perdehoef Guesthouse
Aandrus
Richmond Lodge
Ka-Ma Lodge
Victoria Guesthouse
Richmond Caravan Park
Heydon
Lessingshoogte
Kranskop

Fauresmith
Jagersfontein
Itumeleng
Charlesville
Kapokbosch
Ranjiesveld Guesthouse
Edenburg
Edenburg Country Lodge
The Green Gables Guesthouse
Riverside
Hartebeestfontein
Boomplaats 1848
Sleutelspoort
Bethulie T&T Guesthouse
Gariep Guesthouse (AR 25)
Gariep Dam Hotel
Forever Resorts - Aventura Gariep
Rooibekkie Guesthouse
Rose Cottage Guesthouse
Green Doors Accommodation (AR 24)
Stables
Karoo Herberg
Middelburg Lodge
Mi Casa Su Casa
Karoo Ouberg Executive Guest Lodge
Cellis Garden Cottage (AS 24)
R704
Krugers
Gomvlei
Tweefontein
Kromellenboog
Driebad
Trompsburg Caravan Park
Trompsburg
Rietpoort Game & Guest Farm
Knibbel & Kool Guesthouse
Phumelela Guesthouse
Beau Vista Country Lodge
Midway Guesthouse
Free State
R717
Lofter
AQ
Philippolis Road
Harte
Blairs Folly
Springfontein Guesthouse
Kuilfontein
Rondefontein Guesthouse
Springfontein
Tiger Canyons Ranch House
Philippolis
Laurens van der Post Memorial Gardens
Karoo Huisie Guesthouse
Philippolis Lodge
Die Volstruisnes Guesthouse
Kanon Guesthouse
Starry Nights Karoo Cottages
Tuindam Ebenhaezer Guesthouse
Waterkloof
Spioenkop Game & Guest Farm
Prior Grange Guest Farm
Boschoek Guest Farm
Dupleston
Garingboom Guest Farm
R715
Slyk
Priors
Boschrand Guest Farm
Boorfontein Guest Farm
Louw Wepener
Picnic Site
Tussen-die-Riviere Game Farm
Spes Bona
Pellissier House and Museum
Bethulie Dam
Bethulie
Oppie Koppie Guesthouse
Hunter's Camp
Orange
Seekoei
Donkerpoort
R701
Ossewatrek 1838
Raptor Ridge
Bush Camp
Gariep Dam NR
Gariep Nature Reserve
Gariep Dam
Oviston West NR
Orange River Lodge
Norvalspont Hotel
Waschbank Game Lodge
Norvalspont
Concentration Camp Cemetery
Orange River Guest Farm & Adventures
Riversmead Caravan Park
R390
Olive
Palmiet
R369
Bastersnek
Van Zylsvlei
Battlefield 1900
Agtertang
Colesberg
Onze Rust
Gariep Dam
Oviston
Lake Gariep Resort
Orange-Fish River Tunnel Entrance Tower
Knapdaar
AR 44
Sunset Chalets
Gables Inn
La Provence Guesthouse
Colesberg Lodge
Merino Inn Hotel
Gallop Inn Lodge
Guinea Fowl Guesthouse
The Barracks Guesthouse
Crane Cottage
Morning Glory Cottage
Komweer Lodge
Oviston NR
Venterstad
Hotel Wild Caravan Park
Winnaarsbaken
Ontspringen
Kuilfontein Stable Cottages
Osfontein
Taalmonument
Burgersdorp
Arundel
Wolwefontein Lodge
Talmon Ephriam Lion Cachet 1901
R390
Eastern Cape
R391
Skietnek 1899
Noupoort
Die Poort
The Don Guesthouse
Bulhoek
Ossewatrek 1838
Henning
Steynsburg
Kai Kai
Stormberg Guesthouse
Black Eagle Ridge
Hartbeesnek
AS
1899
Carlton
Teebus
Lovane
Groot-Brak
Groot-Doringhoek Pass
Moordenaarspoort
Outlet Orange-Fish Tunnel
Molteno Guest Herberg
Schoombee
Middelburg
Rooispruit
Rosmead
R398
KwaNonzame
Klein Brak
Teebus
Groot-Brak
R391
R390
Touch
Tafelberg
Hofmeyr
Teviot
Die Pondokkie
Karoobos Guesthouse
Vlekpoort
Dwarsvlei
Kelly-Patterson Dam
Witkransnek
R401
24
25
32
55

26
56
27
Lord Fraser Guesthouse
Fleetwood Country Inn
Rooyensnek Gate
Mafeteng
Rock Paintin
Birdpark
Welbedacht Dam
Caledon NR
Dereham
Bultfontein
Helvetia
Gomvlei
Tweefontein
Basuto War Memorial 1865
Gen. de Wet's Birthplace
Gelukwaarts
Vanstadensrus
Sepapus Gate
Boesmanskop
Highlands Safari Lodge
Cannibal Caves
Free State
Egmont Dam
Breipaal
AQ
Smithfield Dam
Hartebeesfontein
Lehlaka Conservancy
Smithfield
Smithfield Hotel
Bokmakierie Guesthouse
Pula Victorian Guesthouse
Smithfield Guesthouse
Jacobsdal
Rubida
Makhalengbru
Caledon
Klipplaatsdrif 1839
Mountain View Guesthouse
Die Ou Stal Guesthouse
Country House
Maluti Hotel
The Highlands Guesthouse
Zastron
Wepener
Groenvlei
Dupleston
Bloemendal
Tienfontein Guesthouse
Eeufees
Genadeberg
Letsatsi Private Game Reserve
Rouxville
House 1929
Backpacker's Lodge
Ons Tuiste Guesthouse
Leeubank
Breakaway Trails
Bildemar
Koukraal
Picnic Site
Tussen-die-Riviere Game Farm
Pellissier House and Museum
Spes Bona
Hunter's Camp
Goedemoed
Sanddrif
Anglo-Boer War Monument
Winnaar
Bluegums
Sterkspruit
Brughalte
Hot Sulphur Springs
Herschel
Olive
Freedom Square Memorial Site
Masango
Aliwal North
Buffelspruit Nature Reserve
Tugela
Sterley House B&B
At Home B&B
Mountain View Country Inn
Dukathole
McGarry's Spring Lodge
Lapeng Guest Farm
Aliwal Spa
River Lodge
Queens Terrace
Umtali Gateway Country Inn
Lord Somerset
Saddle Down Lodge
Thaba Nkulu Game Ranch
Beerley
Braamspruit
Lady Grey
Joubert's Pass
Woodlands
Bamboeskloof
Karringmelkspruit
Lupela Lodge
43 AR
Stormberg
Brandkop
Ontspringen
Lekkerdraai
Cacadu
Motkop
Osfontein
Taalmonument
Burgersdorp
J.L. De Bruin Dam
Mzanomhle
De Bruin
Barnard
Vineyard
Clanville
Kwaggaspas
1 34 La Rochelle
The Nook
The Hut
Dusk to Dawn
The Bird Haven (AR 26)
Telemachus
Jamestown
Travellers Lodge
Skulp
Greylings Pass
Rossouw
Killian's Pass
Lower Adamson
Henning
Swempoort
Stormberg
AS
Stormberg 1899
Morristown
Nomonde
Molteno
Molteno Guesthouse
Herberg
Vo̱elvlei
Smuts Pass
Anderson Museum
Dordrecht
Highveld Hotel
Valentines B&B
Washington Guest Farm
Indwe Hotel
Indwe Resort
Indwe
Molteno Dam
Syfergat
Boesmanshoek
Valschfontein
Hazelmere
Halseton
Penhoek Pass
Doringrivier Dam
Hoggs Kloof
Touch the Sky Trail
Sterkstroom
The Stagger Inn
Grootvlei
Tsawulayo
Andriesberg
2106m
Zitapileni
26
33
27
Qoqodala

LESOTHO
Eastern Cape
Semonkong
Mokopung
Nohana
Ketane
Qobong
Mohales Hoek
Phamong
Mphaki
Patlong
Tsoelike
Qacha's Nek
Mafube
Cutting Camp
Sebapala
Tosing
Palmietfontein
Moyeni (Quthing)
Telle Bridge
Ralebona
Rock Paintings
Roamer's Rest
Ongeluksnek
Thaba Chitja
Sigoga
Kinirapoort
Mount Fletcher
Lundin's Nek
Tiffindell Ski Resort
Highest Pass in Eastern Cape
Naudesnek
Tenahead Lodge
Elands Height
Lower Pitseng
Lahlangubo
Rhodes
Naudé's Nek Monument
Moshesh's Ford
New England
Barkly East
Katkop
Pot River Pass
Halcyon Drift
Woodcliffe Cave
Maclear
Ugie
Ntywenka
Barkly Pass
Elliot
Gatberg Wetland
St Cuthberts
Tsolo
Ku-Mayima
Qiba
Cala
Garryowen
Whitmore
Ntibane
Luchaba NP
KD Matanzima
Langdon
Coghlan
Ngcobo
All Saints Nek
Lufuta
Askeaton
Clifford
Langkloof
Otto du Plessis Pass
Forest Station

30
31
58
AQ
AR
AS
45
35
Eastern Cape
KwaZulu-Natal
Sehonghong
Sleeping Beauty Cave
Garden Castle Forest Station
Garden Castle
Swiman
Drakensberg
Bushman's Cave
Giant's Cup
Splashy Fen
Pinelands
Lake Cairn
Old Residency
Himeville
Himeville
Moyeni
Nkumba
Nkelabantwa
Emvuleni
Eaglescliff
Woodford
River Glen
XL Farm
The Banks
Underberg
Underberg Inn
The Swamp NR
Ekuthuleni
Deholm
Bulwer
Reichenau Mill & Mission
Springvale
Sizanenjana
Nkwazela
R617
R612
Silverstreams
Highlands
Penwarn Country Lodge
Bushman's Nek / Nkonkoana
Sehlabathebe
Sehlabathebe Lodge
Sehlabathebe NP
Tsoelike Falls
Taylor's Cottage
New England
Pear Tree Cottages
Glencree Trout Farm
Sarnia
Gala
Makhozeni
Forest Station
Donnybrook
Ndawana
Ranger's Hut
Coleford NR
Coleford
Hlabeni
Creighton
Tsoelike
Glencoe
Balmoral
Riversdale
Kingscote
Gungununu
Fairview
Wembley
Saint Bernards Mountain Lodge
Lake Saint Bernard
Riverside
Qacha's Nek
Ramatselisio's Gate
Altona
Qacha's Nek
Mafube
Ntsikeni Forest Station
Dulini Forest Station
St Bernards
Cabha
Tswereka
Lehlohonolo
Springvale
Dulini
Driefontein
Swartberg
Sterkspruit
Sneezewood Forest Station
Beginsel
Riet
New Amalfi
Singisi
Sneezewood
Roamer's Rest
Matatiele
Matatiele
Aberdeen Farm
Wembley
Franklin
Enguniini
Strallhoek Forest Station
Edendale
Cedarville
Little Bisi
Mountain Lake
Sigoga
Bailden
Dorset
Ben Cairnie Forest Station
Bontrand
Bisi
Cedarberg Guest Farm
Driefontein
Mount Currie NR
Boy Scout War Memorial
Mount Currie
Red Hill
Morulane
Kinirapoort
Adam Kok Memorial Gate
Site of Adam Kok's Laager
Langverwacht Forest Station
Coles Ridge Guesthouse
Kokstad
Karg's Post
Ripplemead
Klipspruit
Stafford's Post
Ingeli Forest Lodge
Mvenyane Forest Station
Stoneybrook Ranch
Bonny Ridge
Bhongweni
Waterloo
Border Forest Station
Mzimkulwana
Deepdale
Somabadi
Palmiet
Rocky Ridge Lodge
Mount Currie Inn
Mooidraai
Harding
Weza
Highlands
Forest Station
Mvenyane
Mkemane
Colonanek
Brooks Nek
Ncome
Mount Fletcher
Mvalweni
Mzintlava
Goxe
Fort Donald
Ndindindi Forest Station
Mjika
Mtamvuna
Lahlangubo
Buffalo Nek Forest Station
Cabazi
Mzimvubu
Rode
Insizwa Forest Station
Mount Ayliff
Ngabeni
Magusheni
Ngabeni
Katkop
Forest Station
Mount Frere
Mncelha
Caba
Ntabankulu
Tsilithwa
Mafusini
Mpemba
Forest Station
Mkumbi
Mgodini
Tina Bridge
Flagstaff
Tsulunca
Ntywenka
R396
Qumbu
Balasi
Holy Cross
Nkozo
Nxuzi
Mtsila
Tsitsa Bridge
Kubedlana
St Cuthberts
Tsolo
Foresters Hut
Kraal of the Paramount Chief
Msikaba
Forest Station
Ngcolora
Coza
Sidwadweni
Stoneyridge
Palmerton
Mbotyi
Mntafufu
Lusikisiki
Cosy Posy
Port Grosvenor
Mzintlava
Ntsubane Forest Station
Angel Falls
Fraser Falls
Mkozi
Lupatana Lodge
Luchaba NP
Mthatha Dam
Nobantu
KD Matanzima
Misty Mount
Libode
Mlengana Pass
Mbotyi
Mbotyi River Lodge
Gemvale
Eden Self Catering Cottages
The Creek Self Catering
Mtambalala Forest Station
Dick King 1842
Port St Johns
Garden Court Mthatha
MTHATHA
Buntingville
Rock of Execution
Tribal Office
Ntshilini
Tombo
Silaka NR
Lloyds
Forest Station
Umngazi River
Hiking Trail
Sikobeni
Zimbane
Ngqeleni
Old Bunting
Mngazana
Sebeni Forest Station
1 Teuleigh
Resthaven
Matatiele Hotel (AQ 30)
2 HMS Bastard Memorial Airfield (AR 31)
3 Barton Elliot Bird Sanctuary (AR 31)
4 Kilimanjaro
The Plane Guesthouse
Travellers Rest
Lidela House
Manora (AR 31)
5 Old Orchard (AR 31)
6 Ivory Palm (AR 31)
7 Protea Hotel Mthatha
Green Park Lodge
Ebony Lodge
Hotel Savoy
The Cottage
7th Heaven (AS 30)
8 The Jetty River Lodge
The Pont Camp Site
Ntaba River Lodge Campsite
Spotted Grunter Resort Lodge
Cremorne Estate Self Catering (AS 31)

1 Inkonka Mbabala Lodges (AQ 32)
2 Indigo Vats (AQ 33)
3 Old Station Facade (AQ 33)
4 Bergthiel House (AQ 33)
5 uShaka Marine World (AQ 33)
6 Dick King's House (AQ 33)
7 Musgrave (AQ 33)
8 Tower College & Memorial Tower (AQ 33)
9 The Moroccan
Shack 22 Guesthouse
Sandcastle Guesthouse
River Gardens
Tradewinds Lodge (AQ 33)
10 Uitspan Campsite
Winkelspruit Caravan Park
Ocean Call Caravan Park (AQ 33)
11 Port Edward Holiday Resort
Hakuna Matata Lodge
Windwood Lodge
Hotel Edwardian
North Gate (AS 32)
12 Protea Hotel - Karridene Caravan Park
ATKV - Natalia Beach Resort
Plett Haven
Wavecrest Resort (AQ 33)
13 Lala Manzi Inn & Dive Charter
Umkomaas Lodge
Aliwal Lodge (AQ 33)
14 Sea Fever Dive Centre
Meridian Dive Centre (AQ 33)
15 Carisford Lodge
Green Point Lodge (AQ 33)
16 Happy Wanderers
Ellingham Park
Vulamanzi
Caravan Cove (AQ 33)
17 Umtwentweni Caravan Resort (AR 32)
18 Mittenwald Camp Site (AR 32)
19 TO Strand
Leisure View Resort (AS 32)
20 Kapenta Bay Hotel
Sharks Den Caravan Park
Milton Hotel (AR 32)
21 Shelly Caravan Park (AR 32)
22 Pure Venom Reptile Park (AR 32)
23 Skyline Nature Reserve (AR 32)
24 Saint Michael's Sands Hotel
Uvongo Caravan Park
Oasis Caravan Park
Eagles Nest Caravan Park (AR 32)
25 Suntide Hotel
Pumlani Caravan Park
Margate Hotel
Dumela Holiday Resort
Postilano Lodge
Sunlawns Hotel
Rock View (AR 32)
26 Ramsgate Holiday Cottages
Ilanga Ntaba Guest Lodge (AR 32)
27 Riverbend Crocodile Farm (AR 32)
28 Mondazur Resort Estate Hotel
Marina Glen Holiday Resort
Paradise Resort (AR 32)
29 Mpenjati NR (AR 32)

10
11
Rosh Pinah
Aaca Mine
Octha Mine
Sendelingsdrif
Sendelingsdrif
Potjiespram
God's Hand
Sendelingsdrif Rest Camp
De Hoop
Fish
Gurib
Orange
Bloeddrift Petroglyphs
De Koei
Koerdegab Pass
Tatasberg
Richtersberg
53
Helskloof Gate
Kokerboomkloof
AN
90
Wondergat & Corneliskilp
4 Wheel Drive & High Clearance Vehicles Only
Aussenkehr Vineyar
Richtersveld National Park
Wondergat
Kuboes
Island Trail
Kuboes Guest House
Brandkaros
Wondergat & Cornellskop Guesthouse
Rosynebos
Fluorspar Valley
Sunvalley
60
Oranjemund
14
Frikkie Snyman Guesthouse
Af-en-Toe Guesthouse
Alexander Bay
Orange River Mouth
Museum
Proposed Richtersveld Community Conservancy
Dolomite Peaks
Eksteenfontein
Kom-Rus-'n-Bietjie
82
Holgat
AO
Historic Stone Mine
Holgatpunt
Lekkersing
Lekkersing Guesthouse
Jakkalsput Bay
Cliff Point
Doringbaai
Lochinvar
Namakwa Mariculture Park
Herring Bay
Witduine
Township Tours
Port Nolloth
Port Nolloth Museum
Gami Goas Guesthouse
Richtersveld Experience Guesthouse
De Duine Self Catering
Scotia Inn Hotel
Kusweg
McDougall's Bay
Beach House Guesthouse
Port Indigo Guesthouse
McDougalls Bay Holiday Resort
Atlantic Ocean
90
R382
Windpoor
Wedge Point
Shifting Dunes
AP
Waaisandduine
Doringbaai
Namaqualand Mines
Buffels
3
Grootmis
Kleinsee
Langbaai
Houthoop Guesthouse
Jakkals Bay
10
36
11
Melkbospunt

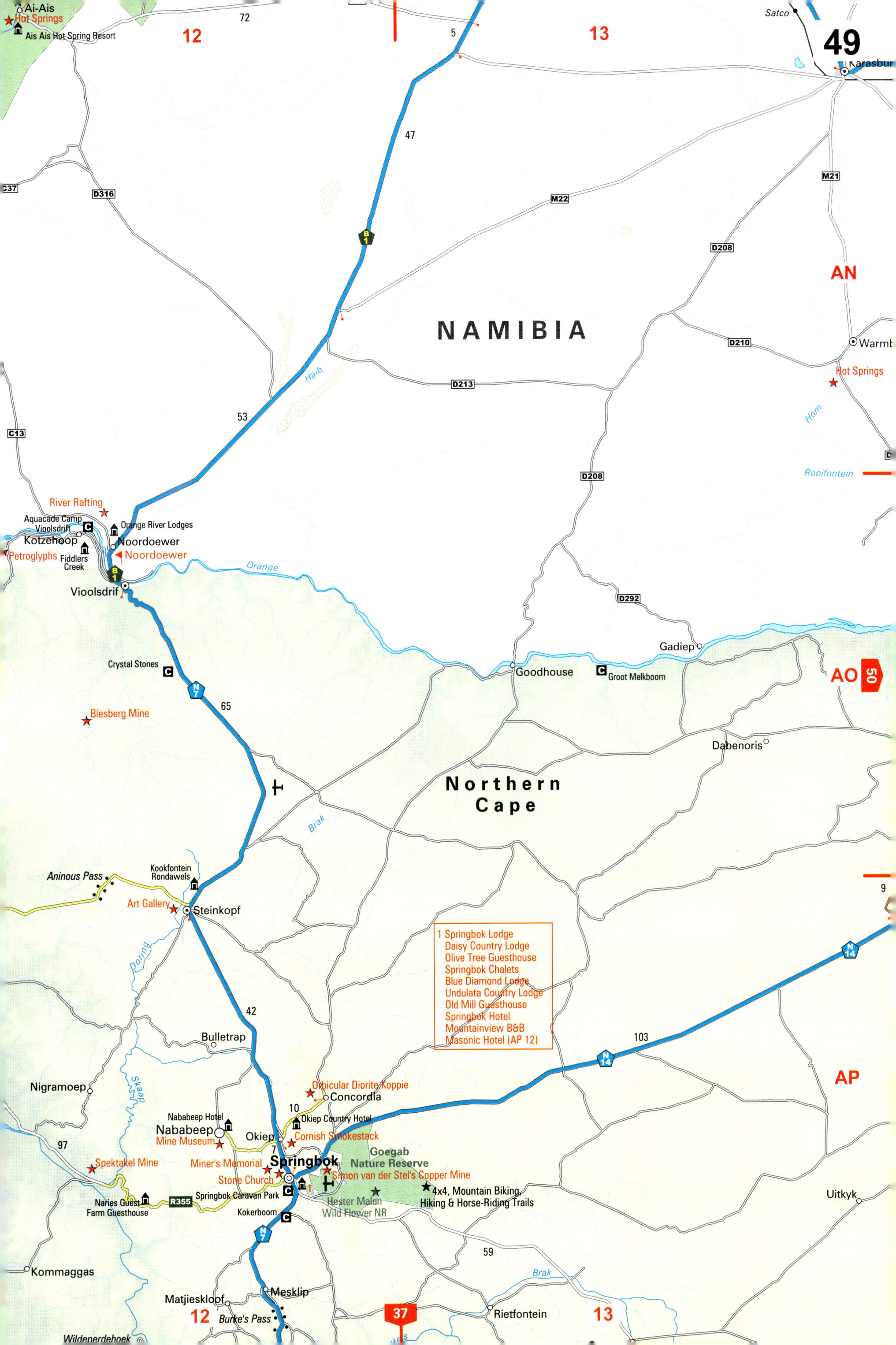

49
NAMIBIA
Northern Cape
Ai-Ais
Hot Springs
Ais Ais Hot Spring Resort
Satco
Karasburg
M21
M22
D316
C37
B1
D208
AN
D210
Warmbad
Hot Springs
Hom
D213
Haib
C13
Rooifontein
River Rafting
Aquacade Camp
Vioolsdrift
Orange River Lodges
Kotzehoop
Noordoewer
Petroglyphs
Fiddlers Creek
Orange
Vioolsdrif
D292
Gadiep
Goodhouse
Groot Melkboom
AO 50
Crystal Stones
N7
Blesberg Mine
Dabenoris
Brak
Kookfontein Rondawels
Aninous Pass
Art Gallery
Steinkopf
Doring
1 Springbok Lodge
Daisy Country Lodge
Olive Tree Guesthouse
Springbok Chalets
Blue Diamond Lodge
Undulata Country Lodge
Old Mill Guesthouse
Springbok Hotel
Mountainview B&B
Masonic Hotel (AP 12)
N14
Bulletrap
Skaap
Nigramoep
Orbicular Diorite Koppie
Concordia
AP
Nababeep Hotel
Okiep Country Hotel
Nababeep
Mine Museum
Okiep
Cornish Smokestack
Goegab Nature Reserve
Spektakel Mine
Miner's Memorial
Springbok
Stone Church
Simon van der Stel's Copper Mine
Naries Guest Farm Guesthouse
R355
Springbok Caravan Park
4x4, Mountain Biking, Hiking & Horse-Riding Trails
Hester Malan Wild Flower NR
Uitkyk
Kokerboom
Kommaggas
Mesklip
Matjieskloof
Burke's Pass
Rietfontein
Wildeperdehoek
37
12
13

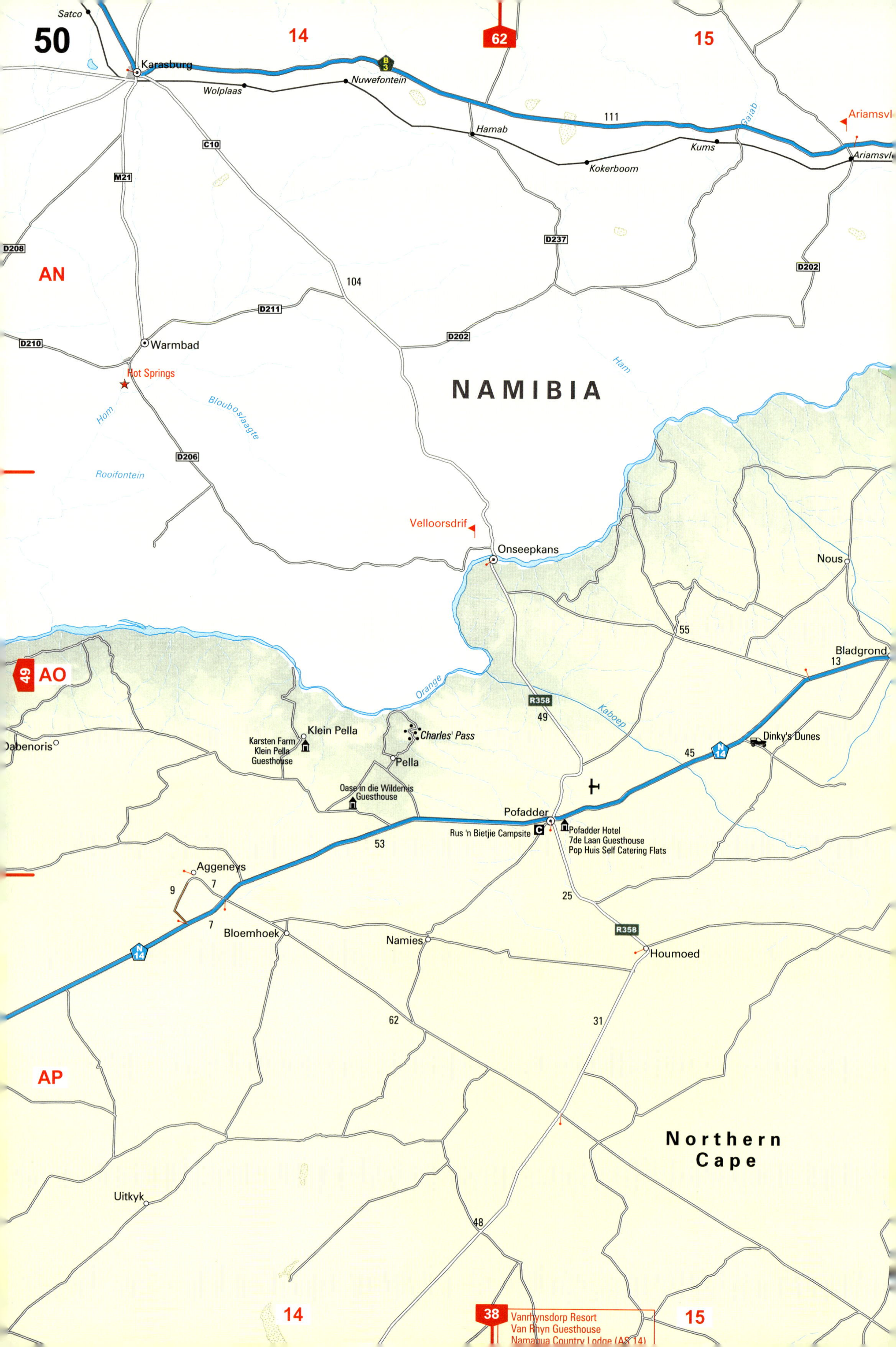

Satco
14
62
15
Karasburg
B3
Nuwefontein
Wolplaas
Ariamsvlei
111
Hamab
Gaiab
Kums
Kokerboom
C10
M21
D237
D202
D208
AN
104
D211
D202
D210
Warmbad
Hot Springs
Ham
NAMIBIA
Hom
Blouboslaagte
D206
Rooifontein
Velloorsdrif
Onseepkans
Nous
55
Bladgrond
13
49
AO
Orange
R358
Kaboep
49
Klein Pella
Charles' Pass
Karsten Farm
Klein Pella
Guesthouse
Dinky's Dunes
45
N14
Pella
Oase in die Wildernis
Guesthouse
Pofadder
Rus 'n Bietjie Campsite
Pofadder Hotel
7de Laan Guesthouse
Pop Huis Self Catering Flats
53
Aggeneys
7
9
7
25
Bloemhoek
Namies
R358
Houmoed
N14
62
31
AP
Northern
Cape
Uitkyk
48
14
38
Vanrhynsdorp Resort
Van Rhyn Guesthouse
15

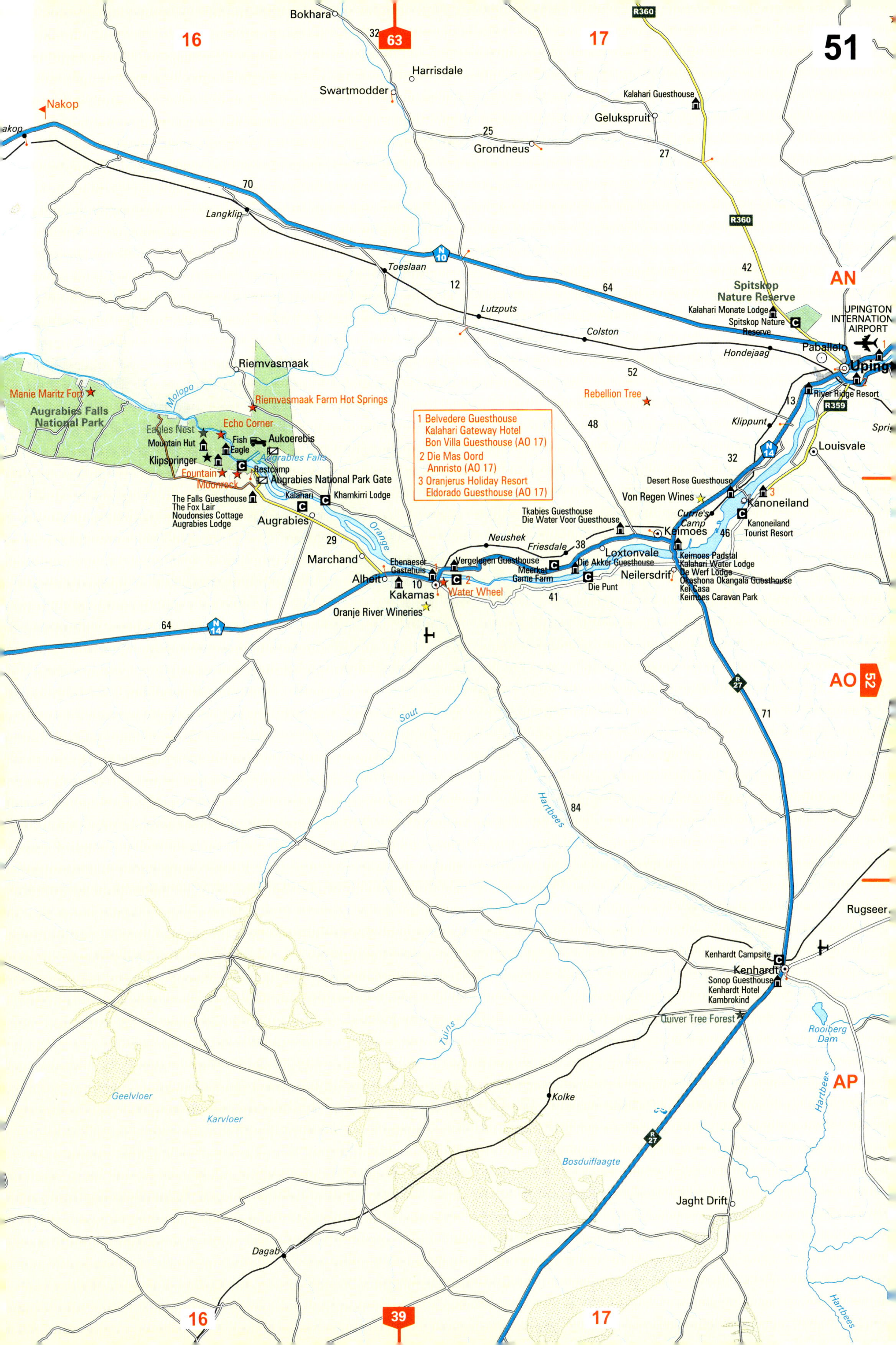

16
17
63
32
Bokhara
Harrisdale
Swartmodder
Nakop
R360
Kalahari Guesthouse
Gelukspruit
25
Grondneus
27
70
Langklip
N 10
Toeslaan
12
64
42
Spitskop Nature Reserve
Kalahari Monate Lodge
Spitskop Nature Reserve
AN
UPINGTON INTERNATIONAL AIRPORT
Lutzputs
Colston
Hondejaag
Paballelo
Upington
Riemvasmaak
Molopo
Manie Maritz Fort
Augrabies Falls National Park
Riemvasmaak Farm Hot Springs
52
Rebellion Tree
River Ridge Resort
R359
13
Klippunt
Louisvale
Echo Corner
Eagles Nest
Mountain Hut
Fish Eagle
Aukoerebis
Augrabies Falls
Klipspringer
Restcamp
Augrabies National Park Gate
Fountain
Moonrock
The Falls Guesthouse
The Fox Lair
Noudonsies Cottage
Augrabies Lodge
Kalahari
Khamkirri Lodge
Augrabies
Orange
29
Marchand
Alheit
1 Belvedere Guesthouse
Kalahari Gateway Hotel
Bon Villa Guesthouse (AO 17)
2 Die Mas Oord
Annristo (AO 17)
3 Oranjerus Holiday Resort
Eldorado Guesthouse (AO 17)
48
N 14
32
Desert Rose Guesthouse
Von Regen Wines
Kanoneiland
Currie's Camp
Kanoneiland Tourist Resort
Tkabies Guesthouse
Die Water Voor Guesthouse
Keimoes
46
Neushek
Friesdale
38
Loxtonvale
Ebenaeser Gastehuis
Vergelegen Guesthouse
Meerkat Game Farm
Die Akker Guesthouse
Neilersdrif
Die Punt
Keimoes Padstal
Kalahari Water Lodge
De Werf Lodge
Okashona Okangala Guesthouse
Kei Casa
Keimoes Caravan Park
10
Kakamas
Water Wheel
41
Oranje River Wineries
64
N 14
R 27
AO
52
71
Sout
Hartbees
84
Rugseer
Kenhardt Campsite
Kenhardt
Sonop Guesthouse
Kenhardt Hotel
Kambrokind
Quiver Tree Forest
Rooiberg Dam
Tuins
Hartbees
AP
Geelvloer
Karvloer
Kolke
R 27
Bosduiflaagte
Jaght Drift
Dagab
Hartbees
16
39
17

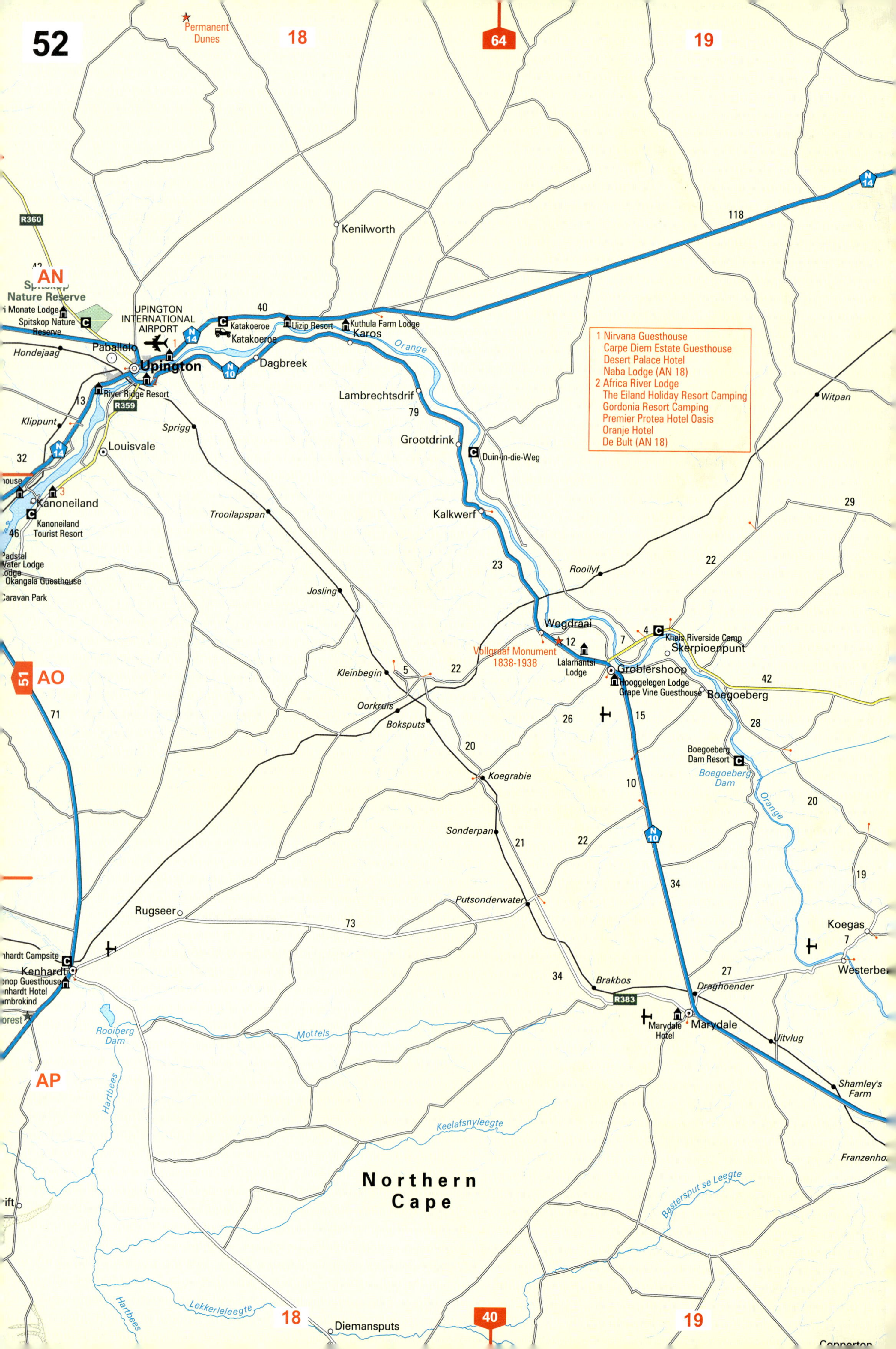

Permanent Dunes
18
64
19
AN
AO
AP
51
Kenilworth
118
UPINGTON INTERNATIONAL AIRPORT
Upington
Paballelo
Hondejaag
Spitskop Nature Reserve
Katakoeroe
Uizip Resort
Kuthula Farm Lodge
Karos
Orange
Dagbreek
Lambrechtsdrif
River Ridge Resort
R359
R360
Klippunt
Louisvale
Sprigg
Kanoneiland
Kanoneiland Tourist Resort
Okangala Guesthouse
Trooilapspan
Grootdrink
Duin-in-die-Weg
Kalkwerf
Josling
Rooilyf
Wegdraai
Vollgraaf Monument 1838-1938
Lalarhantsi Lodge
Groblershoop
Hooggelegen Lodge
Grape Vine Guesthouse
Kheis Riverside Camp
Skerpioenpunt
Boegoeberg
Boegoeberg Dam Resort
Boegoeberg Dam
Witpan
1 Nirvana Guesthouse
Carpe Diem Estate Guesthouse
Desert Palace Hotel
Naba Lodge (AN 18)
2 Africa River Lodge
The Eiland Holiday Resort Camping
Gordonia Resort Camping
Premier Protea Hotel Oasis
Oranje Hotel
De Bult (AN 18)
Kleinbegin
Oorkruis
Boksputs
Koegrabie
Sonderpan
Putsonderwater
Rugseer
Kenhardt
Brakbos
R383
Marydale Hotel
Marydale
Draghoender
Uitvlug
Koegas
Westerberg
Shamley's Farm
Franzenhof
Rooiberg Dam
Mottels
Hartbees
Keelafsnyleegte
Northern Cape
Bastersput se Leegte
Lekkerleleegte
Diemansputs
40

Biki Guesthouse
Mala Lodge
Safari Guesthouse
Ivoor Guesthouse
Olifantshoek
Langberg
Vroeggedeel
Lohatlha
Glosam
Palingpan
Bokkoppie
Beeshoek
Vrolik
Gakarosa
1855m
Mount Carmel Safaris
Rest A While Guesthouse
Daniëlskuil
Dwala Guesthouse
Piet Human Caravan Park
Tlhakalatlou
Owendale
Blinkklip
Silver Streams
Ariesfontein
Lime Acres
Postmasburg
Soetfontein Guest Farm
Bermolli
Bergenaarspad Pass
Witsand
1282m
Roaring Dunes
Papkuil
Klein Papkuil Guesth
Matsap
Koegelbeen Caves
Kalahari Mountain View
Livingstone
Campbell
Griquatown
Mary Moffat Museum
Tula Tula Game Reserve
Northern Cape
Bucklands
Douglas
Orange & Vaal Confluence
Glacial Pavemen
Prans Louts Bridge
Orange
Higg's Hope
Valspan
Niekerkshoop
Diamond Diggings
1 Casa Caballero
Unforgettable Guesthouse
Postmasburg Hotel
Postmasburg Campsite
Belhambra Lodge
Andrisha Motel
Nola's (AN 21)
2 Prieska Hotel
Riverview Country Lodge
Prieska Campsite
Gariep Country Lodge
Die Bos Campsite (AP 20)
1 Dreamriver Guest
Texas Lodge Hote
Transka Holiday F
Prinshof Guestho
2 Sister Henrietta S
3 Five Acres Guest
Bateleur Guestho
4 Protea Hotel - Dia
Garden Court - Kir
Savoy Hotel - Kir
Queens Hotel - Kir
Big Hole Caravan
Bishops Lodge (A
Diklipspoort
eThembeni
Spitskop
Prieska
Tipuana Guesthouse
Uitspanberg
Prieskapoort
Grovèput
Karabee
Keikamaspoort
Redlands
Salt Works
Volop
R385
R325
R309
R313
R357
R369
R62
R31
N14
N10
AN
AO
AP
20
21
41
54
65

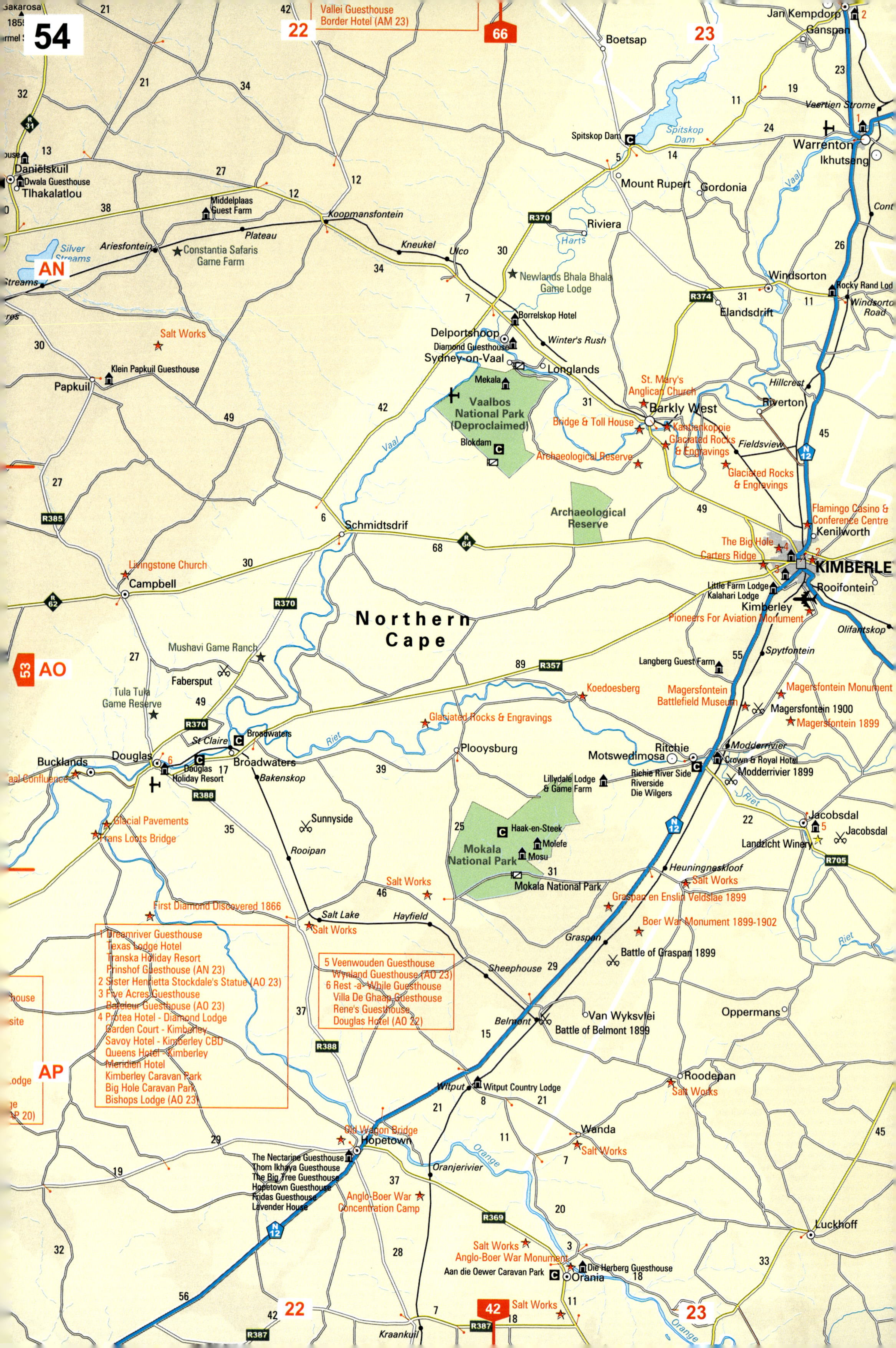

Vallei Guesthouse
Border Hotel (AM 23)
22
66
23
Jan Kempdorp
Ganspan
Boetsap
Spitskop Dam
Spitskop Dam
Vaertien Strome
Warrenton
Ikhutseng
Mount Rupert
Gordonia
Daniëlskuil
Dwala Guesthouse
Tlhakalatlou
Middelplaas Guest Farm
Koopmansfontein
Plateau
Silver Streams
Ariesfontein
Constantia Safaris Game Farm
Kneukel
Ulco
Riviera
Harts
Newlands Bhala Bhala Game Lodge
Windsorton
Rocky Rand Lod
Windsorton Road
Elandsdrift
AN
Streams
Salt Works
Borrelskop Hotel
Delportshoop
Diamond Guesthouse
Sydney-on-Vaal
Winter's Rush
Longlands
Klein Papkuil Guesthouse
Papkuil
Mekala
Vaalbos National Park (Deproclaimed)
St. Mary's Anglican Church
Barkly West
Hillcrest
Riverton
Bridge & Toll House
Kanteenkoppie
Glaciated Rocks & Engravings
Fieldsview
Blokdam
Archaeological Reserve
Glaciated Rocks & Engravings
Vaal
Archaeological Reserve
Flamingo Casino & Conference Centre
Kenilworth
Schmidtsdrif
The Big Hole
Carters Ridge
KIMBERLEY
Livingstone Church
Campbell
Little Farm Lodge
Kalahari Lodge
Rooifontein
Kimberley
Northern Cape
Pioneers For Aviation Monument
Olifantskop
Spytfontein
Mushavi Game Ranch
Langberg Guest Farm
53 AO
Fabersput
Koedoesberg
Magersfontein Battlefield Museum
Magersfontein Monument
Magersfontein 1900
Magersfontein 1899
Tula Tula Game Reserve
Glaciated Rocks & Engravings
St Claire
Broadwaters
Riet
Modderrivier
Ritchie
Motswedimosa
Crown & Royal Hotel
Plooysburg
Buckland
Douglas
Douglas Holiday Resort
Broadwaters
Bakenskop
Richie River Side
Riverside
Die Wilgers
Modderrivier 1899
Lillydale Lodge & Game Farm
Vaal Confluence
Jacobsdal
Jacobsdal
Glacial Pavements
Sunnyside
Haak-en-Steek
Landzicht Winery
Hans Loots Bridge
Molefe
Rooipan
Mokala National Park
Mosu
Heuningneskloof
Salt Works
Salt Works
Mokala National Park
Graspan en Enslin Veldslae 1899
First Diamond Discovered 1866
Salt Lake
Hayfield
Salt Works
Boer War Monument 1899-1902
Graspan
Battle of Graspan 1899
1 Dreamriver Guesthouse
Texas Lodge Hotel
Transka Holiday Resort
Prinshof Guesthouse (AN 23)
2 Sister Henrietta Stockdale's Statue (AO 23)
3 Five Acres Guesthouse
Bateleur Guesthouse (AO 23)
4 Protea Hotel - Diamond Lodge
Garden Court - Kimberley
Savoy Hotel - Kimberley CBD
Queens Hotel - Kimberley
Meridien Hotel
Kimberley Caravan Park
Big Hole Caravan Park
Bishops Lodge (AO 23)
5 Veenwouden Guesthouse
Wyaland Guesthouse (AO 23)
6 Rest -a- While Guesthouse
Villa De Ghaap Guesthouse
Rene's Guesthouse
Douglas Hotel (AO 22)
Sheephouse
Belmont
Van Wyksvlei
Battle of Belmont 1899
Oppermans
AP
Witput
Witput Country Lodge
Roodepan
Salt Works
Wanda
Salt Works
Old Wagon Bridge
Hopetown
The Nectarine Guesthouse
Thom Ikhaya Guesthouse
The Big Tree Guesthouse
Hopetown Guesthouse
Fridas Guesthouse
Lavender House
Oranjerivier
Orange
Anglo-Boer War Concentration Camp
Luckhoff
Salt Works
Anglo-Boer War Monument
Die Herberg Guesthouse
Aan die Oewer Caravan Park
Orania
Salt Works
42
Kraankuil
Orange

Bethsaida Fishing Resort
Over-Hartz Fishing Club
Christiana Recreational Resort
Camelford
Vaal
24
67
25
State
R708
Hertzogville
R59
Bultfontein
Eagles Eye Safari Lodge
Shar Mari's Lodge
Die Dorpshuisie
Middeldeel
AN
R700
Volkspele Monument
Lacoco Inn
Boshoff Hotel
Cobblestones Guesthouse
Toelies Guesthouse
Boshof
Bosmansrus Guest Farm
Boshof Farm Stall
Kareelaagte Guesthouse
Wiets Private Game Reserve
Tswaraganang
Dealesville
R703
Soutpan
Florisbad
Picnic Site
Lapa
Office
Madinokgwe
Predator Park
Krugersdrif Dam
Soetdoring Nature Reserve
Wolwespruit
Modder
Poplar Grove 1900
Perdeberg
Gruisbank Garden of Remembrance
Paardeberg 1900
Driefontein 1900
AO
56
Modigenoeg
Bayswater Lodge
Langehowenpark
BLOEM
Salt Works
Kandirri Guest Lodge
Petrusburg
Bolokanang
Immigrant
De Brug
N8
Castello Guesthouse
Windmill Hotel
Rooidam Pleasure Resort
Women's Monument
Ferreira
Boom van Sames
Free State
1 Koffiefontein (AP 24)
Riet
Ditlhake
Hakuna Matata Guesthouse
The Copper Kettle Guesthouse
Koffiefontein
Uitdraai
Kalkfontein Dam Nature Reserve
Kalkfontein Dam
R706
N6
Tom's Place
Tierpoort
Tierpoort Dam
AP
Austin's Post
Brakfontein
R704
Reddersburg
Sarie Marais Hotel
The Hunters Lodge
Lust Hof Guesthouse
Mooifontein Game Ranch
Fourie
Fouriespruit Dam
Allep
Fauresmith
Kapokbosskerm Guesthouse
Ranjiesveld Guesthouse
Jagersfontein
Itumeleng
Charlesville
Edenburg
Edenburg Country Lodge
The Green Gables Guesthouse
Riverside
Hartebeestfontein
Berg
Sleutelspoort
Boomplaats 1848
43
1 Bethulie T&T Guesthouse
Gariep Guesthouse (AR 25)
2 Gariep Dam Hotel

56
26
27
68
WELKOM
Welkom Airport
Jacobsdal
Game Lodge
Wel-Rie
Au Jordan
Kosmos Guesthouse
Esteranza
Blue Crane Guesthouse
Die Lapa B&B
Hennenman
Die Ou Wingerdstok
Whites
Savanna
Rosendal
Klipfontein
Steynsrus
Ventersburg
Ventersburg Hotel
Die Gewel Guesthouse
Tierfontein
Middeldeel
Vrede
Virginia
Tikwe River Lodge
Amajuba Lodge
Meloding
Merino
Welgeleë
Dagbreek
Sand River Convention 1852
Aldam
Aldam Estate Bushcamp & Lapa
Boating
Picnic Site
Willem Pretorius Resort
Willem Pretorius Game Reserve - South Gate
Willem Pretorius Game Reserve
Allemanskraal Dam
Bultfontein
AN
Theron
Steam Locomotive Museum
Theunissen
Tweefontein Lodge
Affinity Gastehuis
Koffies Lodge
Die Ou Hotel
Erfenis Dam National Reserve
Erfenis Dam
Deelspruit
Danke Schon Guesthouse
Winburg Hotel
Herberg
Winburg Guesthouse
Winburg
Makeleketla
Voortrekker Monument
Hartebeesfontein
Birthplace of Pres. Steyn
Bell's Pass Gastehuis
Tweespruit
Rosendal
Eensgevonden
Houtenbeck
Houtnek
Moemaneng
Sumfra Guesthouse
Valencia Country Lodge
Brandfort
Brandfort War Graves Memorial
Mushroom Valley Dam
Arcadia
Verkeerdevlei Toll Plaza
Verkeerdevlei
Spitskop
Alleman
Gardenia Park
Jacobsdal
Office
Picnic Site
Predator Park
Karee
Lumsden's Horse Monument 1900
55
AO
Glen
Klipfontein
Kgalala
Excelsior
Excelsior Hotel
Moketsi Game Ranch
St. Helena
Voorspoed
1 River of Joy Guesthouse
Wen-Do-Lin B&B
Glen Country Lodge
Plover Cottage
Reinheim (AO 26)
2 Dagbreek Caravan Park
Fakkel Caravan Park (AO 26)
3 Protea Hotel Bloemfontein
Hobbit Boutique Hotel (AO 26)
Bloemfontein
Mooigenoeg
Brandwag
Maselspoort
Boyden Observatory
Raadsaal
Bayswater Lodge
Wild West Holiday Resort
Mockes Dam
Houtnek
Rakhoi
Moroto
BLOEMFONTEIN
Shannon
Tiger River
Oldenburg Lodge & Game Farm
Paradys
Castello Guesthouse
Windmill Hotel and Casino
Rodenbeck
Rooidam Pleasure Resort
Ferreira
Sannaspos
Sepane
Thaba Nchu
Tweespruit
Deno's Place
Westminster
Marseilles
3 Fountains View Lodge
Newberry Dam
Botshabelo
Wilgerboomnek
Montloatse Setlogelo (Groothoek) Dam
Lovedale Dam
Boom van Sameswering
Angling Area
Rustfontein Dam
Rustfontein Dam Nature Reserve
Angling Competition
Yachting
Protea Black Mountain
Maria Moroka Nature Reserve
Nuwe Leeurivier Dam
Thaba Phatshwa
Mabula Lodge
Kommissiepoort
Awimaweh Resort
Balaclava
Rooibult
Rosendal
Tom's Place
Tierpoort Dam
Uysklip
Free State
Meadows
AP
Hobhouse
Koos Taljaard
Frankfort
Dewetsdorp
Hotel de Wet
Voorspoed
Nevada
Reddersburg
Sarie Marais Hotel
The Hunters Lodge
Lust Hof Guesthouse
Rosendal
Mooifontein Game Ranch
Helderhoek Guest Farm
Rooibult
Ts'a-Kholo Lake
Jammerdrif
Lord Fraser Guesthouse
Wepener
Fleetwood Country Inn
Van Rooyensnek Gate
Riverside
Tweespruit
Mafeteng
Rock Paintings
Birdpark
44
Helvetia
Caledon NR
Bultfontein

The Green Door (AL 28)
2 El Shammah Lodge
Khaya i (AL 28)
3 Abrahamskraal Recreation Resort (AK 28)
4 Riverside Hotel & Conference Centre (AK 28)
Emerald River Resort (AK 28)
69
29
28
Groenvlei
Steynsrus
Komspruit
Arcadia
Jas se Spruit
Arlington
Bloemspruit
Shannon
Ooreenkoms
Valsrivier
Vierfontein
Klipfontein
Libertas
Biddulph
Dunlin
Sandhurst Country Lodge
Paul Roux
Senekal
Hendersons Country Lodge
N5 Hotel
Nannies
Anm's Lighthouse
Senekal Municipal Caravan Park
Arizona
Game Lodge
Montevideo
Bloemspruit
Rosendal
Numa Base Camp
Tepelkop
Kranskop
1893m
Moolmanshoek
Marquard
Free State
Amohela Ho Spitskop
Country Retreat
Ben Nevis Cherry
Ben Nevis Cherry Cellar & Guest Farm
Clocolan
Clocolan Hotel
Makoadi Guesthouse
Orsmond Guesthouse
Clocolan Caravan Park
The View Guest Farm
Lions Rest Guest Farm
Peka Bridge
Meulspruit Dam Resort
Fficksburg
Maputsoe Bridge
Maputsoe
Hlotse (Leribe)
Fort
Peka
Corn Exchange
Koenong
Wonderkop
Kolonyama
Rock Paintings
Modderpoort
St Augustine's
Manyatseng
Mamates
Mapoteng
Nokong
Moletsane
Teyateyaneng
Ladybrand
Catharina Brand Museum
Steve Visser
Arcadia
Maseru Bridge
Moshoeshoe's Mountain Fortress
MASERU
Thaba Bosiu
Mazenod
Roma
Mejametalana
Molimo Nthuse Pass
Blue Mountain Pass
Likalaneng
Mohale Dam
LESOTHO
Cheche Pass
Mokhoabong Pass
Thaba-Tseka
Matsieng
Morija
Thaba Putsoa
3095m
Malealea Malealea Lodge
Semonkong
45
1 Highland Inn
Inkwe Lodge
Die Nes
Martelle's Guesthouse
Park Hotel (AN 29)
2 Sunnyside Guest Farm
De Molen Guest Farm (AN 29)
3 Groenhoek Guest Farm
Kiara Lodge (AN 29)
4 Kloof Hiking Trail
Mallen Walk (AN 29)
5 House of Woven Art
Clarens Gallery (AN 29)
6 Lavender Rose
Maluti Mountain Lodge
Camelot Castle Guesthouse
Periwinkle (AN 29)
7 The Morrison Boutique Hotel
Bella Rose Guesthouse
Die Hollandse Woning Guesthouse
The Oregon Cottage
Ficksburg Country Cottage
Highlands Hotel
Thom Park (AO 28)
8 Country Lodge Hotel
Oak Tree Lodge
Casa Romana Guesthouse
Little Rock Resort
Grand Hotel (AO 28)
Danielsrus
Bethlehem
Bohlokong
Petronella Guesthouse
Wolhuterskop Reserve
Loch Athlone
Gerrands Dam
Saulspoort Dam
Pretoriuskloof Bird Sanctuary
Kransfontein
Groenkop
Kestell
AN
Karma Backpackers
Barnea
Jastelle
Graceland Lodge
Noupoortsnek
Highlands Mountain Retreat
Wilgenhof Environmental Education Centre
Sethuthuthu
Golden Gate Highlands NP
Glen Reenen
Brandwag
Phuthaditjhaba
Snymanshoekberg
2468m
Clarens
Bokpoort Holiday Farm
Cathedral Cave
Rhebok Hut
Rhebok Hiking Trail
Holkrans Cave
Monantsa Pass
Castle in Clarens
Rebellie Game Farm
Sefako
Libono
Monontsha
Brandlaagte
La Gratitude
Sun Cottage
Glen Skye Guest Farm
Meiringskloof
Fouriesburg
Arcadia
Carolina Guest Farm
Pumula Guest Farm
Wynford Guest Farm
Foutani Mountain Escape
Lesoba Farm Stay
Oranje Guest Farm
Caledonspoort
Camelrock Lodge
Joel's Drift
Fort Campbell
Generaalsnek
Butha-Buthe
Prehistoric Footprints
Qhobela
Moteng Pass
Khabo
Royal Natal Na
(World Herit
Matlameng
Liqhobong
Pitseng
Kao
Lejone
Katse Dam
Mapholan
AO
58
AP
1 Witsieshoek Mo
2 Cavern Berg Res
3 Mont-Aux-Sourc
4 Dragons Peak (A
5 Dragons Peak Lo
Inkosana Lodge
6 Eland Valley Res
Rest Mount Lod
7 Lake Naverone C
8 Himeville Arms
9 Visitors Centre
10 Drakensberg Bo
11 Ardmore Ceram
12 KwaZulu Weave
13 Voortrekker Mo
14 Gert Maritz 183
15 C aters
16 Good Hope Cave
17 Old Prison Build
18 Fort Durnford (A
19 Barry's Grave 1
20 Mountain Splen
Monk's Cowl C
21 Castle Resort
Castleburn Lodg

30
70
31
AN
AO
57
AP
46
Free State
LESOTHO
Harrismith
Ladysmith
Estcourt
Kruispad
Verkykerskop
Verkykerskop Guesthouse
Mount Pelaan
Glendale
Normandien
Horseshoe
Chelmsford
Klippoort
Hamilton
Cundycleugh
Kransfontein
Groenkop
Aberfeldy
Bird Sanctuary
Kestell
Annie's Guesthouse
Karma Backpackers
Blockhouse
Bushman Paintings
Phomolong
President Brand
Wilgerpark
LaLa Nathi
Cayra
Swinburne
22 Sir Harry's Lodge
Harrismith Inn Hotel
The Gems
Pumula (AN 30)
Kidstone's Memorial 1931
De Beers Pass
Oaklands Manor
Van Reenen
Craigsforth
Driefontein
Hambrook
Colworth
Ngula
Besters
Pepworth
Landaff Oratory
(Smallest Church in SA)
Tea Garden
Van Reenen's Pass
Wyford
Andrew Motel
Second Highest Earth Dam
Wall in the World
Sterkfontein Dam
N.R. Rest Camp
Yachting
Windsurfing
Kerkenberg
Sterkfontein Dam NR
Highlands Mountain Retreat
Golden Gate Highlands NP
Glen Reenen
Brandwag
Holkrans Cave
Phuthaditjhaba
Blue-Gum Bush
Rhebok Hiking Trail
Rhebok Hut
Monontsha
Monontsa Pass
Sefako
Libono
Boschkloof Bay
Picnic Site
Qwantani
Vulture Restaurant & Feeding Scheme
Bushman Cave
Retief Rock
Drifters Inn
Little Switzerland
Oliviershoek Pass
Kaalvoet Vrou
Geluksburg
Green Point
Tugela
Ladysmith
Protea Crown
Siege of Ladysmith
Surprise Hill
Old Stone Fortification
Manchester Fort
Caesar's Camp
Platrand (Wagon)
Carbineer's Grave
War Grave
Mafikeng
Lejoaneng
Cannibal Cave
Rockcliff
Alpine Heath
Jagersrust Guest House
Drakensville Resort
Mont-Aux-Sources
Mahai
Thandanani Craft Village
Tevreden Cheese Farm
Royal Natal National Park
(World Heritage Site)
Thendele
Crow's Nest Cave
World's Fourth Highest Recorded Waterfall
Frog Cave
Tugela Gorge Walk
Singati Cave
Zimisela
Woodstock Dam
Bergville
Rangeworthy Military Cemetery
Nteniwa Bush Camp
Spioenkop 1900
Spioenkop Dam NR
Vulture Hide
Vaalkrans 1900
MIDLANDS TOLL ROUTE
Roosboom
Wenkommando 1838
Blockhouse
Spearman's Military Cemetery
Ambleside Cemetery
Colenso
Mambasa
Kitchener Bridge
Battlefie
Cloustor Field of Remembrance
Chieveley Military Cemetery
Site of Doornkop Laager
Chieveley
Suurlaer
Winterton
Bridge
Church Ruins
Moura
The Palms
Capture of Winston Churchill
Frere
Bloukrans Monumen
Emmaus Mission
Mnweni Cultural Centre
Drakensberg Traverse
Source of the Orange River
Rock Paintings
Sgongweni Cave
Zunckels
Brandkraal
Kelvin Grove
Cayley Lodge
Magangangozi
Loskop
Ardmore
Cathkin Peak 3181m
Didima
Easter Cave
Cathedral Peak
Meteorological Station
Tseketseke
Rainbow Gorge
Drakensberg Sun
Contour Path
Ndedema Gorge
Monk's Cowl
Champagne Sports Resort
Meteorological Station
Agricultural Research Station
Wagendrift NR
Maritz Monument
Vegloer
Greystone
Old Stone Wall
Ntabamhlope
Dalton
Cliffdale
Liqhobong
Mothae
Kao
Champagne Castle 3377m
iNjasuthi Gate
Injasuti
Hillside
Hillside Gate
Battle Cave
Njesuthi Cottage
iNjasuthi Track
Giants Castle Nature Reserve
Upper iNjasuthi Cave
Court House
Rockmount
South Downs
Swiss Manor
Ranger's House (Main Gate)
World's View
Bannerman Hut
Lammergeyer Hide
KwaMkhize
Giant's Lodge
Main Cave
Crane Foundation
Giant's Hutted Camp
Forest Station
Highmoor
Vulture Hide
Giant's Castle Two Huts Hike
The Natal Drakensberg Park
Kamberg
Kamberg Rock Centre
Redcliffe
Ash Cave
Yellowwood Cave
Hiking
Highest Point in Southern Africa
Thabana Ntlenyana 3482m
Lotheni
Root Family Farm
Allendale
Sinclair's Shelter
Cyprus Cave
Fort Nottingham
Lynx Cave
Gelib Tree Hiking Trail
McKenzie Cave
Pingpong Cutting
Vergelegen
Forest Station
Highland Nook
Lower Loteni
Mapholaneng
Mokhotlong
Drakensberg Traverse
Sani Pass Chalets
Sani Pass
Giant's Cup
Police Post
Mkomazana Mountain Cottages
Stepmore
iMpendle
Gomane
Monster Rocks
Mkomazana
Sanu Lodge
Gorge Cave
Spectacle Cave
Bathplug Cave
Giants Cup
Cobham Forest Station
Mzimkhulu Wilderness Area
Ukukhanya
Mkhomazana
Westcliff
Boesmansnek
Pinelands
Lake Cairn
Old Residency
Emvuleni
Garden Castle
Sleeping Beauty Cave
Garden Castle Forest Station
Swiman
Drakensberg
Himeville
Himeville NR
The Swamp NR
Moyeni
Nkumba
Nkelabantwa
Eaglescliff
River Glen
XL Farm
Underberg
Woodford
Ekuthuleni
Deholm
Bulwer
Bushman's Cave
Giant's Cup
Splashy Fen
The Banks
Underberg Inn
Reichenau Mill & Mission
Springvale
Sizanenjana
Nkwazela
Silverstreams
Highlands
Penwarn Country Lodge
Glencree Trout Farm
Nek / Nkonkoana
Sehlabathebe
Sehlabathebe Lodge
Tsoelike Falls
Gala
Sarnia
Sehonghong
Thaba-Tseka
Mantsonyane
Tseka
Linakaneng
Sakeng
Makhapung
Semena River
Bobatsi
Moremoholo
Befali
Bafatsana
Sangebethu
Mokhotlong
Tlaeeng Pass
Marseng
Fanana
Thiolatsi
Tsehlanyane
Fika Patso Dam
Metsimatsho Dam
Kilburn Dam
Driel Dam
Woodstock Dam
Sprookfontein Dam
Diepkloof Dam
Wagendrift Dam
Windsor Dam
Meul
Dwaal
Slang
Vaalbank
Nuwejaar
Wilge
Klip
Sand
Mlambonja
Nsonge
Ifidi
Sithene
Manzana
Bushmans
Mooi
Mlahlangubo
Sani Pass
Mkhomazana
Mzimkhulu
R714
R722
R712
R57
R74
R616
R600
R103
R617
R612
N3
N5
N11
A1
A3
A4
A14
1 Witsieshoek Mountain Resort (AO 30)
2 Cavern Berg Resort (AO 30)
3 Mont-Aux-Sources (AO 30)
4 Dragons Peak (AO 31)
5 Dragons Peak Lodge
Inkosana Lodge (AO 31)
6 Eland Valley Resort
Rest Mount Lodge (AP 31)
7 Lake Naverone (AP 30)
8 Himeville Arms (AP 31)
9 Visitor's Centre (AO 30)
10 Drakensberg Boys Choir School (AO 31)
11 Ardmore Ceramic Art Studio (AO 31)
12 KwaZulu Weavers (AO 31)
13 Voortrekker Memorial (AO 31)
14 Gert Maritz 1838 (AO 31)
15 Crystal Waters (AP 30)
16 Good Hope Cave (AP 31)
17 Old Prison Building (AP 31)
18 Fort Durnford (AO 31)
19 Barry's Grave 1938 (AO 31)
20 Mountain Splendour Eco-Resort
Monk's Cowl Country Club (AO 31)
21 Castle Resort
Castleburn Lodge (AP 31)

For Indexes Please See Page 60
KwaZulu-Natal
Dundee
Glencoe
Fort Mistake
Fort Mistake 1891
Dannhauser
Hattingspruit
Doctor Alden Lloyd NR
Talana Museum
Talana 1899
Van Rooyen
Stanmore
Doringberg
Flint
eMondlo
Calvert
Glückstadt
Ngogweni
Bloubank
Nhlazatshe
uMfolozi
Blood River
Ntabebomvu
Blood River 1838
Prince Imperial Monument 1879
Fort Nembigate
Nondweni
Nqutu
Vant's Drift
Biggarsberg
Karel Landman Monument
Uithoek
Wasbank
Biggarsberg 1900
Himeville Bridge
The Cabins
Elandslaagte
Elandslaagte Dutch Corps Monument
Rorke's Drift 1879
Rorke's Drift
Rorke's Drift Museum
Fugitives' Drift
Fort Northampton
Battlefield of Isandhlwana 1879
Siluthshana
Fort Marshall 1879
Babanango
Fort Evelyn 1879
Dingaan's Kraal
Nsubeni
Mtonjaneni Mount
iTaleni 1838
Fort Prospect
Osborn
Randalhurst
Penny Farthing Country House
Giba
Helpmekaar 1900
Helpmekaar
Camp Buffalo
Harding
Nazareth
Mangeni
Ntanyeni
eTholeni
aMakhasi
eKuvukeni
Valhalla Game Farm
Mozana
Elandskraal
Montrose
Mahlaba
Gordon Memorial 1879
Klipriver
Pomeroy
Fort Pengough 1879
Ndikwe
Qudeni
Nkandla
Witteklei nfontein
Little Niagara Falls
Battle of Tugela Heights
Gxobunyawo
Dinuntuli
Dlolwana
Tugela Ferry
Tugela Gorge
Mbango
Manyiseni
The Ranch
Cetshwayo's Grave
Weenen Game Reserve
Trail Camp
Old Mill & Voortrekker House
Weenen
Beaconview Trail
Umtunzini Picnic Site
Keate's Drift
Ehlanzeni
Jameson Memorial
eNtumeni
Bambatha Police Memorial 1906
Allandale
Fort Thorny
Ntunjambili
Kranskop
Muden
Kranskloof
Ambush Rock 1906
General Louis Botha's Birthplace 1862
Fort Ahrens
Ahrens
Mvozana
Brookhill Farm
Greytown
eNhlalakahle
Merthley Lake
KwaSizabantu Mission
Fort Mtombeni
Mapumulo
oTimati
Mpumulwane
Willow Grange
Willow Grange 1899
Sierra Ranch
Stonehaven Farm
Craigie Burn Nature Reserve
Craigie Burn Dam
Umvoti Valley Nature Reserve
Umvoti Vlei
Mount Alida
Sevenoaks
Treverton College
Weston Agriculture College
Balmoral Monument
Bruntville
MIDLANDS TOLL ROUTE
Rosetta
Karkloof NR
Karkloof Canopy Tours
Bush Willow
Rockwood Forest Lodge
Goodman Household Aviation Monument
Heavenly Hammocks Arts & Crafts
The Hobbit's Hut
York
Dalton
New Hanover
Fawnleas
Shaka's Memorial
Trooper Knight 1906
Nzuze 1906
Aldinville
Shakaskraal
Balgowan
Lions River Trading Post
Umgeni Valley NR
Cascade Shelter
Cramond Farm
Mpolweni
Bon Accord
Albert Falls
Albert Falls NR
Ecabazini
Wartburg
Shuttleworth Weaving
Swissland Cheese
Lidgetton
Culamoya Chimes
The Vukuzenzele
Lavender Co.
Valley of 1000 Hills
Maduna
uMhlali
The Woodturner
Dargle Singisi
Plantation & Picnic Site
Sterlings Wrought Iron
Howick
Merrivale
Hilton College
Hi-Fly Kites
Thulow Lodge
Midmar NR
Midmar Dam
Hilton
Queen Elizabeth Park
PIETERMARITZBURG
Nagle Dam Nature Reserve
Ndwedwe
Hazelmere Resource Reserve
Tongaat
Ballito
NORTH COAST
Ocean Surf
KING SHAKA INTERNATIONAL
Zulu Mpompoment Tourism Experience
World's View
Colenso Mission Station 1854
Geloftekerk
iNanda Farm
Verulam
uMdloti
uMhlanga Lagoon NR
John Williamson
Craiglea
Calderwood Hall & Manor House
KwaMncane
Edendale
Ashburton
Egudwini
Devon
Munywini
Thornville
Camperdown
The Cycads
iNanda
Kranskloof NR
Molweni
KwaMashu
Phoenix
uMhlanga
La Lucia
Glen Ashley
Durban North
Duffs Road
Reservoir Hills
Deepdale
Umhlongonek
Keerom
Cunningham's Castle
Springvale
Mpumalanga
Pinelands
Hammarsdale
Hillcrest
Clermont
Kloof
New Germany
Winston Park
Pinetown
Westville
Minitown
DURBAN
Illovo Nek
Oaks at Byrne Hotel
Watersmeet
Blarney Cottage
Riversdale
Fairview
Leadwood Lodge
Tala Private Game Reserve
Emoyeni
Kwa-Ndengezi
Mariannhill
Dassenhoek
Klaarwater
Queensburgh
Glenwood
Shallcross
The Bluff
Morningside
Richmond
Woodlands
Glenwood
Butu
AN
AO
AP
32
33
71
47
60

34
72
35
AN
AO
AP
59
Swart uMfolozi
Thangami Safari Spa & Mudbath
KwaCeza
Thangami Safari
Bayeni
Sigubudu
Dukumbane
Thanda GR
Zulu Nyala Game Lodge
False Bay Section
Sweetwaters Cottages
Ezulweni Lodge
Dumazulu Village
Hluhluwe
Ubizane Wildlife Reserve
Dugandlovu Lodge
Mzinene Lodge
Bonamanzi Game Reserve
Bushlands
Dumazulu Village
Hluhluwe Game Reserve
Memorial Gate
Hilltop/Mtwazi
Muntulu Bush Lodge
Munyawaneni Bush Lodge
Hluhluwe Dam
eMdoneni Game Farm
Hlabisa
Hluhluwe Imfolozi
Bloubank
Nhlazatshe
uMfolozi
Mahlabathini
Black Mfolozi
iMfolozi Game Park
Bhejane Hide
Sontuli
Gqoyeni
Nselweni
Masinda
Mpila
Nyalazi Gate
Mambeni Gate
Centenary Game Capture Centre
Machibini
Vulamehlo Curio Stall
Mdindini
Mphafa Hide
Shaka's Hunting Pits
Sunseeker Safaris / Emdoneni Lodge
iMfolozi Game Reserve
Nhlozi Game
Fernwood
Lai La Log Cabins Maputal
Dukuduku Forest Reserve
Maphelane Section
Futululu
Sonrooy Lodge
Cane Cutters Estate
Mokana Country Cottages
Mtubatuba
KwaMsane
River View
Lake Eteza Nature Reserve
Teza
Nsubeni
Thandivani
Riverview
uLundi
Mpande's Grave
iLangakazi
Garden Court uLundi
Ondini Cultural Museum
Cetshwayo's Kraal
uLundi Fort
uLundi 1879
Nodwengu
Gengeni Gate
Babanango
Genzagakhona
Dingaan's Kraal
oNdini
Piet Retief's Grave 1838
Umgungundhlovu 1838
Mtonjaneni Mountain
Mtonjaneni Lodge
iTaleni 1838
Fort Prospect and Fort Itala 1901
Khwibi
Munywana
uMunywana
eMakwezini
Osborn
Fort Prospect
Randalhurst
Melmoth
Melmoth Inn
Simunye Cultural Village
Dondotsha
Mabhensa
Ntambanana
KwaMbonambi
Mposa
Nhlabane Lake
Lake Mzingazi
Nkandla
Mblatuze
Fossils
Mpini
Ndundulu
Mfuli Game Ranch
Heatonville
Nkwalini
Protea Hotel Shakaland
Site of Shaka's Kraal
Bhekeshowe Site of Shaka's Kraal
Aloedale Lodge
eMpangeni
Richards Bay Minerals
Dawson's Rock
Picnic Site
Woodpecker Lodge
eNseleni NR
Mzingazi
Five Mile Beach
Richards Bay
Cetshwayo's Grave
Nyawushane
Mvuzane
Vuna
eNtumeni Nature Reserve
eNtumeni
Mamba
Dlinza Forest Nature Reserve
eShowe
Coward's Bush Monument
Ngoye Forest
Felixton
TONGAAT
Richards Bay NR
Cubhu
eSikhawini
British Military Cemetery
Fort KwaMondi
Nonquai Fort 1894
Mlalazi
Mtunzini
Inkwazi Camp
Raffia Palms
Siyaya
Port Durnford
Matigulu
Grave of Tabu R. Dunn
Tongaat
Gingindlovu
uMlalazi Nature Reserve
Mpushini
amatikulu
First American Mission 1836
Dokodweni
Fort Trealork
Mandini
bantu Mission
Fort Mtombeni
Nyoni
Nyathini
Mapumulo
Tugela 1838
TONGAAT
aMatikulu Nature Reserve
oTimati
Tugela
Harold Johnson NR
Tongaat
Tugela Mouth
Tugela Mouth Resort
Mpumulwane
Nonoti
Ultimatum Tree
Fort Pearson
Fort Tenedos
Darnall
Zinkwazi
Zinkwazi Beach
Shaka's Memorial
KwaDukuza (Stanger)
Knight 1906
Aldinville
Mhlali
Chief Albert Luthuli's Grave
uMvoti
Shakaskraal
The Kingdom
Croc Valley Nature Reserve
uMhlali
Sheffield Beach
Salt Rock
Shaka's Rock
Hole in the Wall
Ballito
Tongaat
NORTH COAST TOLL ROUTE
Ocean Surf 1979
KING SHAKA INTERNATIONAL
uMdloti
John Williamson
uMhlanga
La Lucia
Glen Ashley
Durban North
Hills
Minitown
DURBAN
The Bluff
Indian Ocean
1 First Sugar Mill 1851 (AP 34)
2 Dolphin Resort (AP 34)
3 Salt Rock Caravan Park (AP 34)
4 Zululand Tree Lodge (AN 35)
5 Bonamanzi Game Park
Bahati Bush Camp
Izilwone Lodge
Bushbaby Lodge
Lalapanzi Camp (AN 35)
6 Karibu Game Farm (AN 35)
7 Isinkwe Backpackers Bush Camp
Emdoneni Lodge (AN 35)
8 Maputaland Adventures Llala Inn Guest House
Paradiso Guesthouse
Hotel Paradiso
Wendy's Country Lodge
Marula Place
Celtis (AN 35)
9 Eden Park
Monzi (AN 35)
10 Veyane Cultural Village & Backpackers (AN 35)
11 Greenhills Lodge
The Richards Hotel
Protea Hotel The Bay Shore Inn
The Ridge (AO 35)
12 Hilton Manor
Baobab Lodge (AO 35)
13 Hillview Gardens
Golf View Lodge
Carsdale Country
Protea Hotel Empangeni
Raptors Rest (AO 35)
14 Sugar Bay Children's Resort
Ocean Reef Hotel (AP 34)
Interest & Accommodation (See Page 59)
1 Sanctuary Picnic Site (AO 32)
2 Umtombe Picnic Site (AO 32)
3 Nyandu Environmental Tented Camp (AO 3
4 Trail Camp (AO 32)
5 Marrakesh Cheese Farm (AP 32)
6 Michaelhouse School (AP 32)
7 Aladdin's-de-Light Studio (AP 32)
8 Nottingham Road Tourism (AP 32)
9 Hydro (AP 32)
10 Nottingham Road Brewing Co. (AP 32)
11 Hangaboutz Hammocks (AP 32)
12 Nottingham Road (Oldest Hotel in KwaZulu-Natal) (AP 32)
13 Corrie Lynn & Co. (AP 32)
14 Dargle Valley Pottery (AP 32)
15 Thabo's Antiques (AP 32)
16 Lona's Pianos (AP 32)
17 Mandela Monument (AP 32)
18 Historical Village (AP 32)
19 Sakabula Golf Club (AP 32)
20 Cedara Agricultural College (AP 32)
21 Hilton Hotel (AP 32)
22 National Railway Museum (AP 32)
23 Mahatma Gandhi Memorial (AP 33)
24 Sugarmill Casino (AP 33)
25 Steyn's Lodge
Kamnandi Guesthouse
The Hollies (AN 32)
26 The Garden Cottage
Lord Grey Guesthouse
Lady Leuchars (AO 33)
34
35

36 73 37

1 Travel Lodge & Caravan Park
Eden Camp
Sugarloaf Camp
Iphiwa Camp (AN 36)

AN

Indian Ocean

AO

AP

36 37

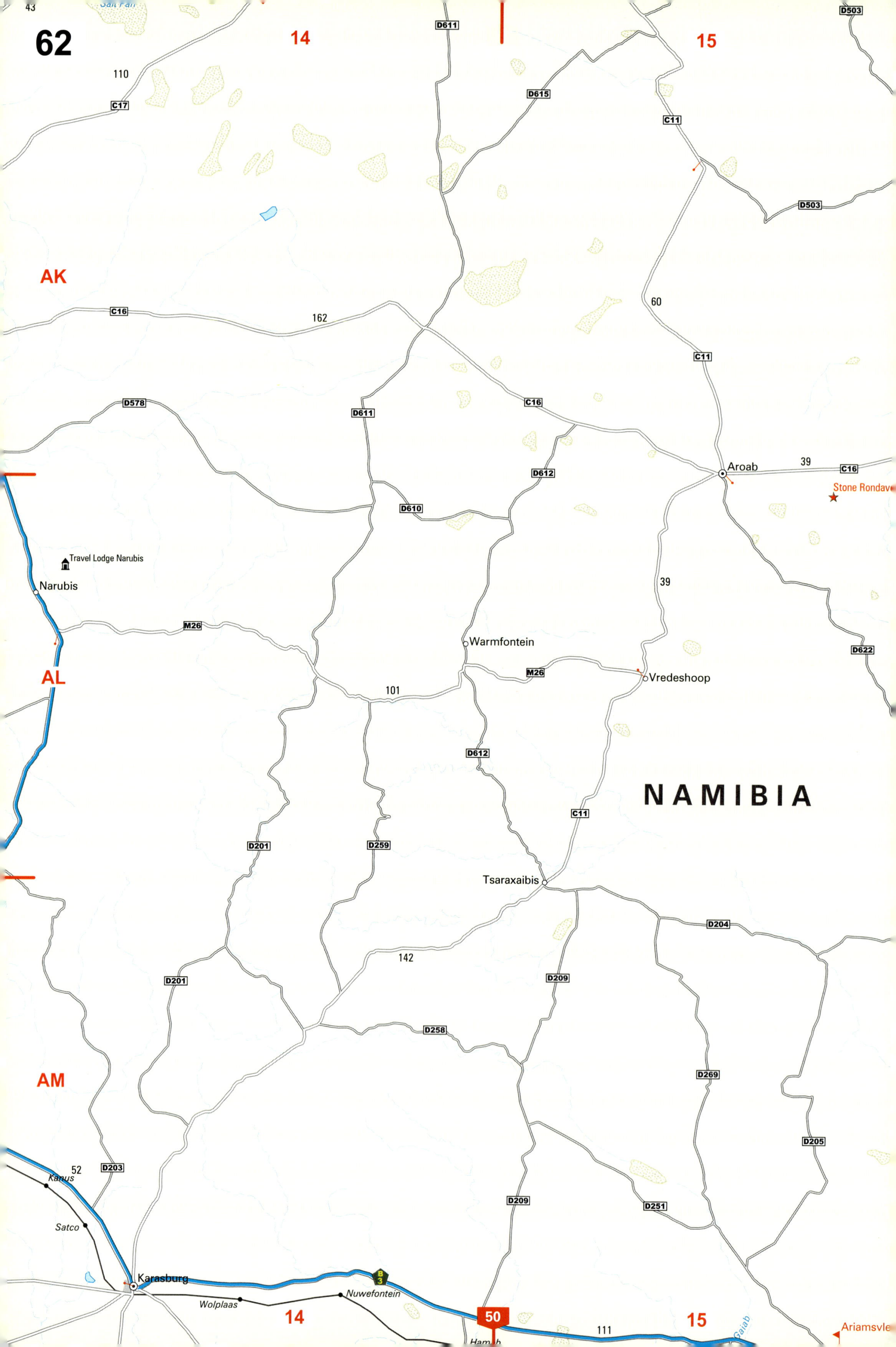

43
14
15
D611
D503
110
C17
D615
C11
D503
AK
60
C16
162
C11
D578
D611
C16
D612
Aroab
39
C16
Stone Rondav
D610
Travel Lodge Narubis
Narubis
39
M26
Warmfontein
D622
AL
101
M26
Vredeshoop
D612
NAMIBIA
C11
D201
D259
Tsaraxaibis
D204
142
D201
D209
D258
D269
AM
D205
52
D203
Kanus
D209
D251
Satco
Karasburg
B3
Nuwefontein
Wolplaas
14
50
15
111
Ariamsvle

16
74
17
!Xaus Lodge
Droëfontein
55
Kieliekrankie
Rooiputs
Kgalagadi Transfrontier Park
Kalahari Gemsbok National Park
Leeuwdril
Two Rivers 07:30 - 16:00
Twee Rivieren
Two Rivers Camp
AK
60
BOTSWANA
Rietfontein
Rietfontein
70
Kalahari Trails Bush Camp
Kalahari
Permanent Dunes
Gemsbok
R31
Permanent Dunes
Bokspits
Molopo Lodge
Andriesvale
Witdraai
Kalahari Sands Guesthouse
63
Permanent Dunes
14
Askham
Kuruman
26
Staansaam
Permanent Dunes
Askham Post Office
Camelthorn
Gemsbokkie Plaashuis
R31
20
R360
22
Cramond
Uitsakpan
Permanent Dunes
AL
64
40
Salt Works
36
Hohlweg
Noenieput
Koopan Suid
Obobogorap
Molopo
Permanent Dunes
Permanent Du
20
Northern Cape
Salt Works
Roopan Guesthouse
Kongapan
Permanent Dunes
Noenieput
Bloupan
Salt Works
Salt Works
Witpan
42
Salt Works
80
Goerapan
Eensaamheidpan
Permanent Dunes
Groot-Witpan
Salt Works
AM
Salt Works
Salt Works
Komkompan
Vrouenspan
Salt Works
Klein-Witpan
Permanent Dunes
Norokeipan
Salt Works
Salt Works
Permanent Dunes
R360
Bokhara
32
Harrisdale
Swartmodder
Kalahari Guesthouse
Nakop
16
51
17
Gelukspruit
25

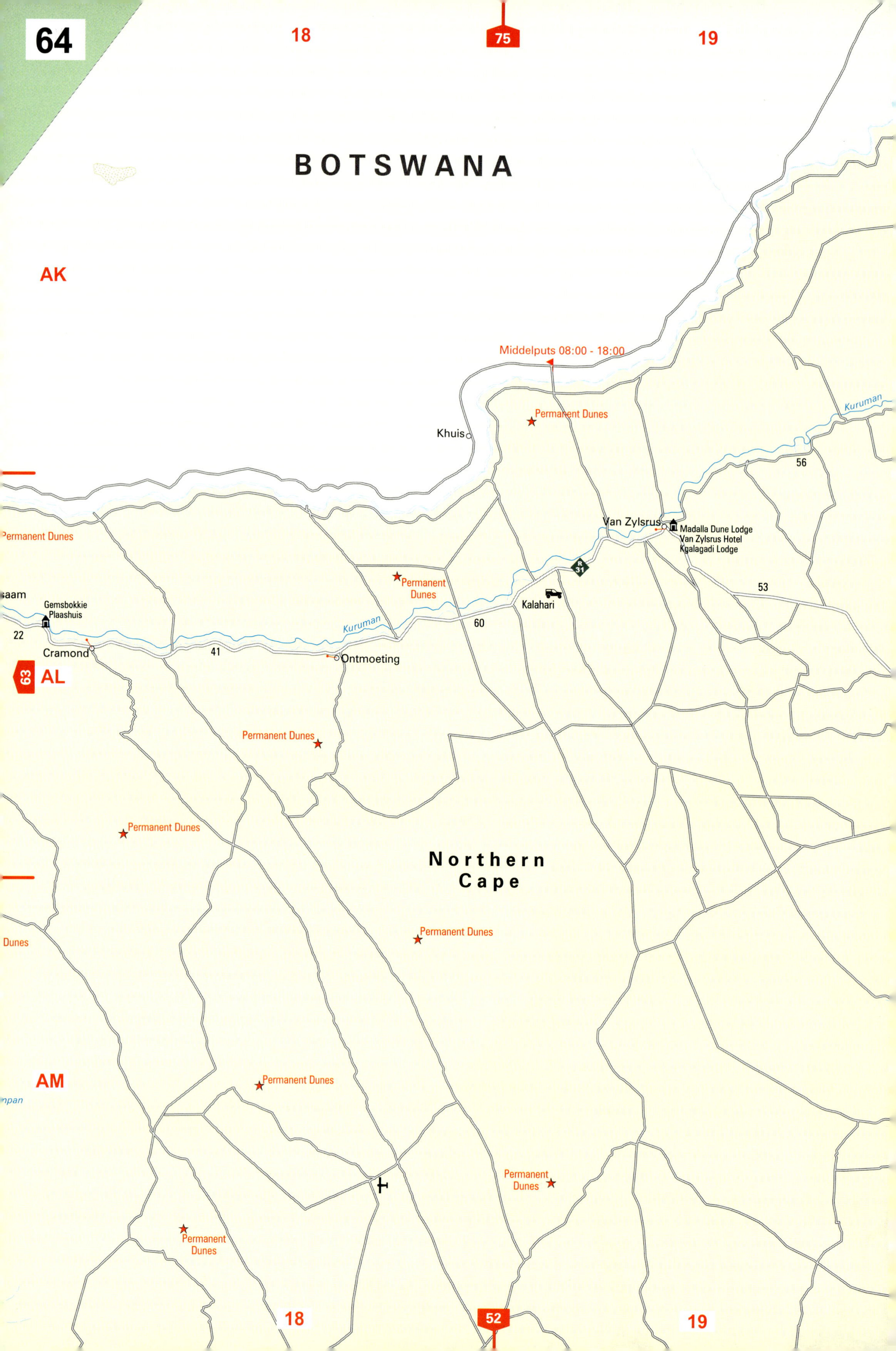
18
75
19
BOTSWANA
AK
Middelputs 08:00 - 18:00
Permanent Dunes
Khuis
Kuruman
56
Van Zylsrus
Madalla Dune Lodge
Van Zylsrus Hotel
Kgalagadi Lodge
Permanent Dunes
R 31
53
saam
Gemsbokkie
Plaashuis
Permanent Dunes
Kalahari
22
Kuruman
60
Cramond
41
Ontmoeting
63
AL
Permanent Dunes
Permanent Dunes
Northern
Cape
Dunes
Permanent Dunes
AM
npan
Permanent Dunes
Permanent Dunes
Permanent Dunes
18
52
19

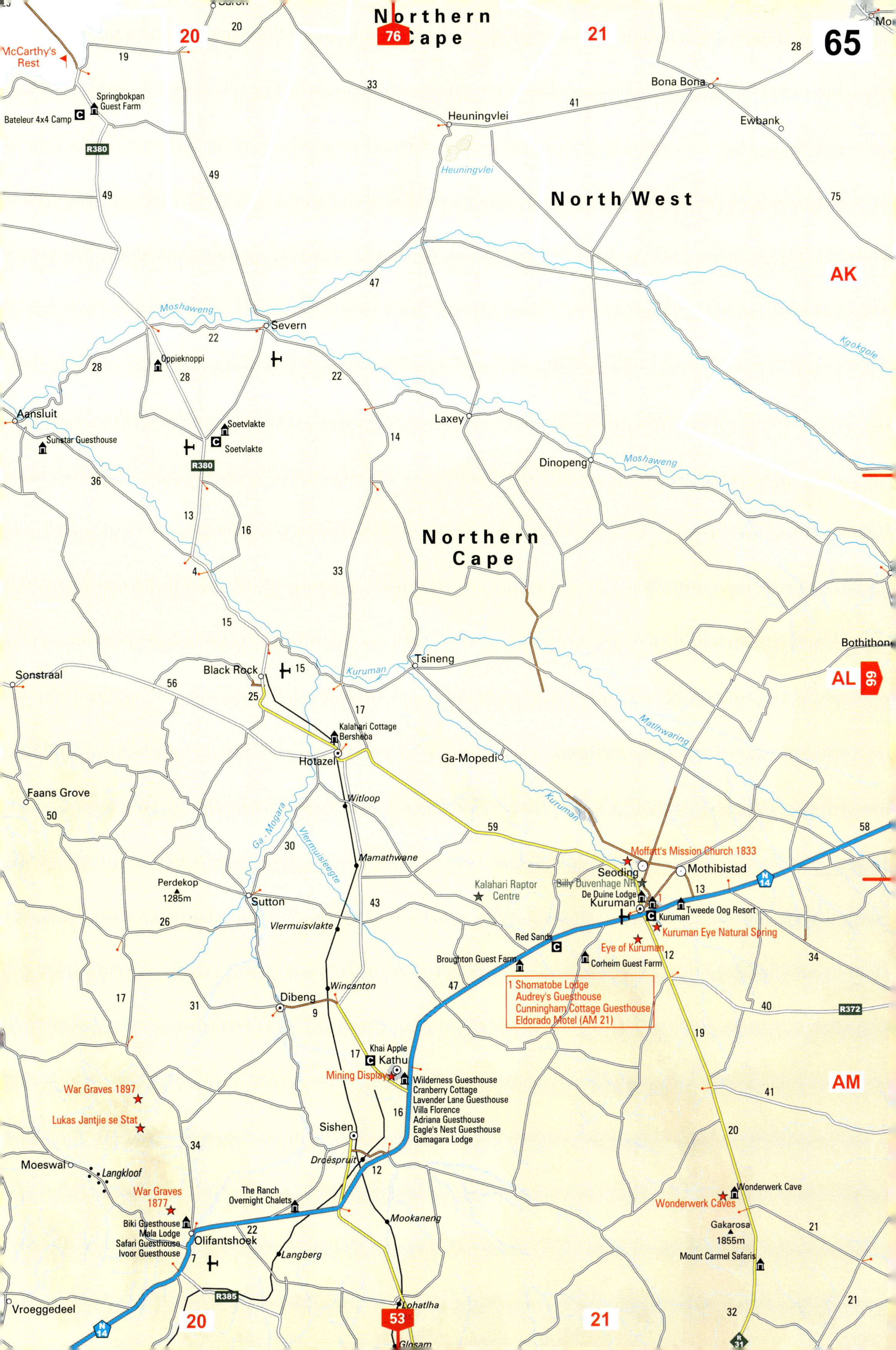
Northern Cape
76
20
21
McCarthy's Rest
Springbokpan Guest Farm
Bateleur 4x4 Camp
R380
Heuningvlei
Bona Bona
Ewbank
North West
AK
Moshaweng
Severn
Oppieknoppi
Aansluit
Sunstar Guesthouse
Soetvlakte
Laxey
Dinopeng
Northern Cape
Kgokgole
Bothithong
Black Rock
Sonstraal
Kuruman
Tsineng
Kalahari Cottage Bersheba
Hotazel
AL
99
Ga-Mopedi
Mathwaring
Faans Grove
Witloop
Ga - Mogara
Vlermuisleegte
Mamathwane
Perdekop 1285m
Sutton
Vlermuisvlakte
Moffatt's Mission Church 1833
Seoding
Mothibistad
Billy Duvenhage NR
Kalahari Raptor Centre
De Duine Lodge
Kuruman
Tweede Oog Resort
Kuruman Eye Natural Spring
Red Sands
Eye of Kuruman
Broughton Guest Farm
Corheim Guest Farm
Wincanton
Dibeng
1 Shomatobe Lodge
Audrey's Guesthouse
Cunningham Cottage Guesthouse
Eldorado Motel (AM 21)
R372
Khai Apple
Kathu
Mining Display
Wilderness Guesthouse
Cranberry Cottage
Lavender Lane Guesthouse
Villa Florence
Adriana Guesthouse
Eagle's Nest Guesthouse
Gamagara Lodge
AM
War Graves 1897
Lukas Jantjie se Stat
Sishen
Moeswal
Langkloof
Droëspruit
War Graves 1877
The Ranch Overnight Chalets
Mookaneng
Wonderwerk Cave
Wonderwerk Caves
Gakarosa 1855m
Biki Guesthouse
Mala Lodge
Safari Guesthouse
Ivoor Guesthouse
Olifantshoek
Langberg
Mount Carmel Safaris
R385
Lohatlha
Vroeggedeel
N14
53
Glosam
R31

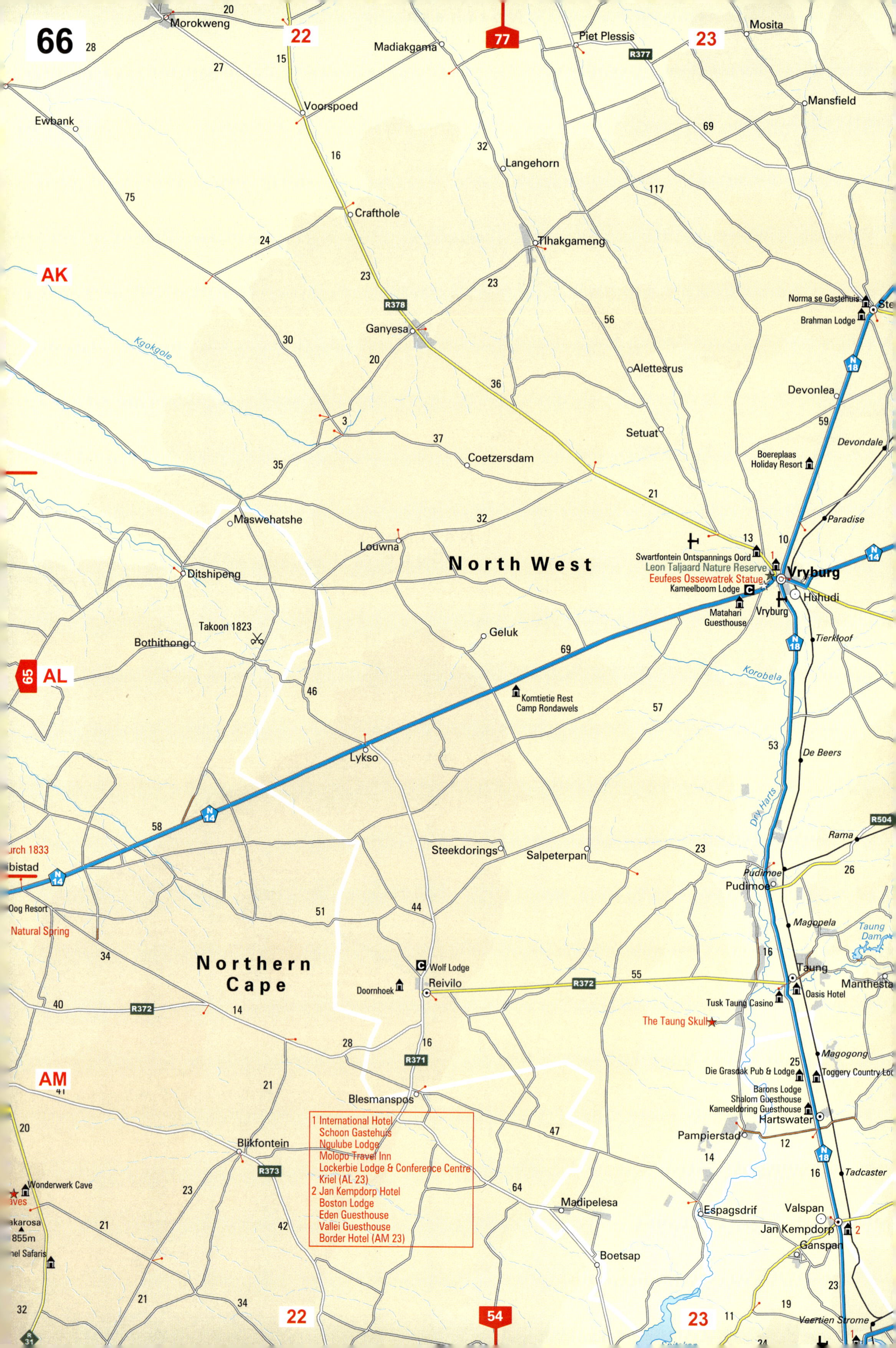

22
77
23
65
AL
54
AK
AM
Morokweng
Madiakgama
Piet Plessis
Mosita
R377
Mansfield
Ewbank
Voorspoed
Langehorn
Crafthole
Tlhakgameng
R378
Ganyesa
Kgokgole
Norma se Gastehuis
Brahman Lodge
N18
Alettesrus
Devonlea
Setuat
Devondale
Coetzersdam
Boereplaas Holiday Resort
Paradise
Maswehatshe
Louwna
North West
Swartfontein Ontspannings Oord
Leon Taljaard Nature Reserve
Eeufees Ossewatrek Statue
Kameelboom Lodge
Vryburg
Huhudi
N14
Ditshipeng
Matahari Guesthouse
Takoon 1823
Bothithong
Geluk
Tierkloof
Korobela
Komtietie Rest Camp Rondawels
Lykso
De Beers
Dry Harts
R504
Steekdorings
Salpeterpan
Rama
urch 1833
ibistad
Pudimoe
Oog Resort
Natural Spring
Magopela
Taung Dam
Northern Cape
Wolf Lodge
Taung
Manthesta
Doornhoek
Reivilo
R372
Oasis Hotel
Tusk Taung Casino
The Taung Skull
R371
Magogong
Die Grasdak Pub & Lodge
Toggery Country Lod
Blesmanspos
Barons Lodge
Shalom Guesthouse
Kameeldoring Guesthouse
Hartswater
Pampierstad
Blikfontein
R373
Tadcaster
Wonderwerk Cave
aves
akarosa
855m
nel Safaris
Madipelesa
Espagsdrif
Valspan
Jan Kempdorp
Ganspan
Boetsap
Vaertien Strome
1 International Hotel
Schoon Gastehuis
Ngulube Lodge
Molopo Travel Inn
Lockerbie Lodge & Conference Centre
Kriel (AL 23)
2 Jan Kempdorp Hotel
Boston Lodge
Eden Guesthouse
Vallei Guesthouse
Border Hotel (AM 23)

Lichtenburg
Lichtenburg Museum
Boikhutso
Cashel Dam
Tau Dam
Maritzani 1900
Mareetsane
Bathobatho
R375
Mooifontein
Setlagole
Kraaipan
Kraaipan 1899
Deelpan
Biesiesvlei
Thabologang
Christie
Harts
Gerdau
Madibogo
Wirsing
Doornbult
Kameel
R507
Geysdorp
Research Station
Office
Barberspan NR
Barberspan Resort
Barberspan Dam
Barberspan
Sannieshof
Pumba's
Vermaas
AK
Doringbult
Bospoort
Mieliebelt
Groot-Harts
Klein-Harts
R377
Salty Waters
Delareyville
Doxa
Mirah
R505
Ouplaas Farm Guesthouse
Werda
Broedersput
Rietpan
Ouplaas Town Guesthouse
Ottosdal
Migdol
North West
Bamboesspruit
Sendelingsfontein
R506
Glaudina
Bamboes
Bona Bona
Hallatt's Hope
Magneet
Berseba
Schweizer-Reneke Monument
Wentzel Dam
Schweizer-Reneke
Ipelegeng
1 Inges Guest House
Feathers Guest Lodge
Wentzel Dam Holiday Resort
Innie Skylte Guesthouse
Mamusa Guest Lodge (AL 24)
Matjesfontein
Dalrene Guesthouse
Bertmaine Guesthouse
Broadbent's Mission
Borobalo Lodge
Drostdy Village Guesthouse
Wolmaransstad
Tswelelang
Witpoort
AL
Leeudoringstad
Amalia
Hester
R504
R502
Makwassie
Peperboom Lodge
Koosfontein
Wolwespruit NR
Boskuil
Aandster
Kingswood
Makwassie
Grasslands
SA Lombaard Lodge
SA Lombard NR
Bloemhof Dam NR
Brandwag
Boitumelong
Bloemhof
Die Hoek
Beyers Pieterse Memorial
Wildhoen
Why Not
Die Oord Resort
Kudaana Guest Lodge
Mimosa Guesthouse
Middeldeel
Bloemhof Dam
AM
Rietgat Game Lodge
Sandveld NR
Britten
Vaal
Hoopstad Hotel
Brinkies Oornag
Tikwana
Hoopstad
Wesselsbron
Wolf Se Gat
Mineral Springs
Utlwanang
Nkolo Spa
Protea Christiana
Christiana
Bethsaida Fishing Resort
Over-Hartz Fishing Club
Meldine Guesthouse
Robyn Guesthouse
Christiana Recreational Resort
Free State
Besemp
Camelford
R708
Tierfontein
Vet
Middeldeel

Lichtenburg
26
79
27
Marcilla Guesthouse
Cozy Nook (AJ 27)
Ga-Ramodingwana
Klerkskraal Dam
Klerkskraal
Leeugatgrot
Kaya Selati Guesthouse
Casa Lumini Guesthouse
Liberty Lodge
Carletonville
El Shaddai Guesthouse
Welverdiend
Christies
Tshing
Ventersdorp
Tlhabologang
Coligny
Taaibosspruit Dam
Bodenstein
Makokskraal
Rietspruit Dam Recreation Resort
Marnel Recreation Resort
Club Amigos
Wawiel Country Lodge
Rietspruit Dam
Naleludi Lodge
Dovesdale
Mesa
Gerdau
AK
Hauptrus
Doringbult
Inyala Game Lodge
Boskop Dam
Klipdrif Dam
Bospoort
North West
Leopard Lilly
Oudewerf Guesthouse
On Golden Pond Guesthouse
Oudrif Riverside Lodge
Agape
Lakeside Caravan Park
Potchefstroomdam Rusoord Caravan Park
Potchefstroom Dam
Modder Dam
Brakspruit
Faan Meintjies NR
Die Bos Oord
Faan Meintjies
Rhebokfontein Camping Grounds
Gunners Memorial 1939-1945
Ikageng
POTCHEFSTROOM (TLOKWE)
Kings Hotel
Willows Garden Court
Magnolia
Rooshoek
Ranch Hotel
Prima Rosa
Hartbeesfontein
Johan Neser Dam
Pickles & Peppers
Eland Safari Lodge
De Rust Lodge
New Machavie
Leeufontein
Koepel Gastehuis
Kiepersol
Barakah Adventure
Venterskroon
Benjoh
Hakuna Matata Adventure
Klerksdorp Dam Pleasure Resort
Bianric Farm Inn Guesthouse
Kemonate Lodge
Ghoma Lodge
Rose Cottage
The Haven Lodge
Aroma Guesthouse
Paulano Guesthouse
La Bonheur Guest Lodge
Foutain Villa Country House
KLERKSDORP
Stilfontein
Thabela Thabeng Mountain Retreat
Suikerbos Nature Resort
Hadeda Creek
Dimalachite Nature Resort
Dominionville
Sendelingsfontein
Maryland Guest Farm
Oord Nebu
Raaswater River Lodge
Rapid Waters Hotel
Wawielpark Holiday Resort
Kanana
Orkney
Orkney Vaal Lion Lodge
Vaal Reefs
Limerick Lodge
Hanzet Distilleerders
Elgro River Lodge
Vredefort
Reizburg
Bona Bona Game Lodge
Reefway Hotel
Costa Do Sol Hotel
Norettes Guesthouse
Scotts Villa Guesthouse
Vredefort Dome (WHS)
St Helena
Vierfontein
Oasis
Spes Bona
AL
Harrisburg
Constantia
1 Sunwa River Lodge
Deep Water Chalets (AL 27)
Witpoort
Kgakala
Leeudoringstad
Hilton
Jan se Plek Guesthouse
Rammulotsi
Viljoenskroon
Roses
Mirage
Paradys
Groenebloem
Middeldeel
Ntlo Ya Baeti
Louvre Guesthouse
Von Abos Guesthouse
Bothaville
Doringpark
Wolwespruit
Wolwespruit NR
Mielliefees Museum
Voorspoed
Rustig
Doornkraal Memorial
Klipfontein
Tweefontein
Free State
Lace Mine Dam
Heuningspruit
Verblyden Guesthouse
Excelsior
Schuttesdraai
Hamilton
Saaiplaas
Hilton
Brandwag
Rosendal
Westleigh
Bayers Pieterse Memorial
Alvira
Hadeda
70 On Reitz
Hacienda Hotel
La Porte Vase
Jukskei Park Vakansie Oord
Kroonpark Vakansie Oord
Maokeng
Kroonstad
Ancona
Cornelia
AM
Middeldeel
Jacobsdal
Paradys
Lechwe Lodge
Allanridge
Prospectors Borehole Monument
Wilgehof
Monyekeng
Kutlwanong
Geneva
Zoutspruit Guesthouse
Wesselsbron Hotel
Wolf Se Gat
Wesselsbron
Odendaalsrus
El-Son-Ne Guesthouse
Die Grasdak Gastehuis
Brunlust Guesthouse
Mimosa Resort
Wonderkop
Besempan
Merino
Bundu Game Lodge
Riebeeckstad
Wel-Rie
Au Jordan
Kosmos Guesthouse
Die Ou Wingerdstok
Saaiplaas
Rosendal
Jacobsdal
Welkom Inn
WELKOM
Thabong
Hennenman
Tierfontein
Esteranza
Blue Crane Guesthouse
Welkom Airport
Whites
Savanna
Klipfontein
Die Lapa B&B
Hennenman
Middeldeel
Steynsrus
26
56
27
Vrede
Virginia
Ventersburg

Roodepoort
JOHANNESBURG
Randfontein
Soweto
Westonaria
Lenasia
Eldorado Park
National Exhibition Centre
Gold Reef City
Germiston
Alberton
Boksburg
Brakpan
Springs
Bedford View
Jan Smuts Park
Gedult
Strubenvale
Welgedacht
Dayeyton
Eloff
Delmas
Sundra
Struisbult
Marievale Bird Sanctuary
Vosloorus
Gauteng
Walkerville
Grasmere
Nigel
Jameson Park
Danie Theron Monument
Fochville
RenGwe Guesthouse
Waenhuis
Henley-on-Klip
Dalesside
Bass Lake
Blockhouse
Springbok
Heidelbergkloof
Blesbok
Duiker
Steenbok
Karreekloof
Eland
Hartbees
Suikerbosrand NR
Transport Museum
Heidelberg
Klipfontein
Meyerton
Rothdene
Riverfront
Midvaal Motor Race Track
Heidelberg 4x4 School and Track
Fortuna Resort
Sebokeng
Arcon Park
Risiville
Sharpeville
Duncanville
Vereeniging
Vanderbijlpark
Holfontein
Balfour
De Hoek
Greylingstad
Village Manor Hotel
Vaal Race Course
Shores of Loch Vaal
Erina Holiday Resort
Abrahamsrust
Viljoensdrif
Sasolburg
Klein Paradys
The Indaba Hotel
Groenewers Pleasure Resort
Rietfontein
Aloe Fjord Resort
Grootvlei
Grootvlei Dam
Dasville
Rapins Paradise Resort
Vaal Marina
Deneysville
Refengkgotso
Rus 'n Bietjie
Rock Island Guesthouse
Gawie De Beer Nature Reserve
KROONVAAL TOLL ROUTE
Kwaggapark
Parys
Tumahole
Wolwehoek
Oranjeville Resort
Metsimaholo
Oranjeville
Jim Fouche Resort
Vaal Dam
Goedegedacht
Rooibult
Qalabotjha
Villiers Resort
Villiers
Niki's Stone House
Shumbalala
Excelsior
Saaiplaas
Kroonheuwel
Dover
Arcadia
Mimosa Park
Weltevrede Lion Farm
Groenvlei
Merino
Cornelia
Blaauwboschbank Nature Reserve
Francolin Creek
Tweefontein
Rooidepoort Dam
Weltevrede Dam
Parys Game Lodge
Caroline's
Koppies
Spitskop
Koppies Dam Nature Reserve
Koppies Dam
Sandersville
Phiritona
Edenburg
Warden
Namahadi
Frankfort
Roosters
Alrines Cottages
Frankfort River Resort
Water Park
Riemland Museum
Heilbron
Vilifees Dam
Rooiwal
Marshall House Country Lodge
Dorpshuis Guesthouse
Villa Bonheun
Syferkuil
Siesta Guesthouse
Zara
Riverside
Pride in Africa
Rooibult
Enkeldoorn
Moratuwa Lodge
Vechtkop
Hoogte
Arcadia
Welkom
Tweefontein
Tweespruit
Edenville
Lions Rest Game Lodge
Tweeling
Free State
Klipfontein
Jacobsdal
Constantia
Groenvlei
Paradys
Saaiplaas
Petrus Steyn
Mamafubedu
Moroka
Blydskap
Prehistoric Stone Huts
Paradys
Eureka
Tweespruit
Mooigelee
Constantia
Reitz
Petsana
Bass Feather Country Lodge
Bayswater
Hadeda Guesthouse
Cherry Cottage
Lindley B&B
Heymans Guesthouse
Theunissen
Paradys
Excelsior
Tweefontein
Eureka
Lindley
Bolivia
Steynsrus Hotel
Allemansnek
Dagbreek
Groenvlei
Steynsrus
Komspruit
Kruisp
Arlington
Danielsrus
Arcadia
Bloemfontein
Shannon
Ooreenkoms
1 Mimosa Garden Resort
Lemon Tree Lodge
The Green Door (AL 28)
2 El Shammah Lodge
Khaya iBhubesi (AL 28)
3 Abrahamsrust Recreation Resort (AK 28)
4 Riverside Hotel & Conference Centre (AK 28)
5 Emfuleni Park (AK 28)
6 Emerald Casino Hotel
Emerald River Resort (AK 28)
AK
AL
AM
28
29
57
70
80

30
81
31
69
AK
AL
AM
58
Delmas
Devon
Leandra
Oban
Kinross
Sunset Lodge
Kinross Inn
Evander
Kriel Aerodrome
Ga-Nala (Kriel)
Riet Dam
Trichardt
Secunda
Kasteel Guesthouse
Grace View Guesthouse
Graceland Casino
Ballynoran Lodge
Umuzi Lodge
Amble Inn Guesthouse
Embalenhle
Leeuwpan Dam
eMzinoni
Bethal
Bethal Aerodrome
Herberg Guesthouse
Bethal Recreation Resort
Die Groen Koei Guesthouse
Davel
Mooivlei
Hendrina
Big Five Guesthouse
Kardoesie Guesthouse
Halfgewonnen
Gloria
Klipfontein
Roodebank
Rhino Lodge
Charl Cilliers
Villieria Country Guesthouse
Greylingstad
Little Glen Guest Farm
Val
Holmdene
Mpumalanga
Maizefield
Morgenzon
Teaksend
Bettiesdam
Twee Dronk Guest Farm
Jonkersdam Resort
Grootdraai Dam
Suidvaal
Standerton
Gecko Guesthouse
Die Kliphuis Guesthouse
River Park
Meyerville
Hawthorne Guesthouse
Sakhile
Ubhibhi
Rinrik Guesthouse
Roberts Drift
Qalabotjha
Villiers
Vrede
Saaiplaas
Bultfontein
De Kuilen
Harvard
Varkensvlei
Platrand
De Vlischa Lodge
Perdekop
Amersfoort
Cornelia
Baptist Church
HIGHVELD TOLL ROUTE
Middeldeel
Tweefontein
Matts
Riverside
Glen Guesthouse
Emanzini Country Resort
Welgevonden Guesthouse
Vrede
Langberg
Little Long Creek
Moreson Ranch
Excelsior
Rietkuil
Fairview Self Catering
Grave of General Joubert
Volksrust
Mahawane Country Resort
Vlakplaas
3 Provinsies
Charlestown
Convention Bridge
Amajuba Mountain 1881
Laingsnek 1881
O'Neill's Cottage
Laingsnek
Middeldeel
Ingogo
Skuinshoogte 1881
Island Water Villa
Bothas Pass
Botha's Pass 1900
Seekoeivlei NR
Sandstone Guesthouse
Cliffdale Hotel
Du Meda
Memel
Sediba Trails
Doornhoek
Camelot Guesthouse
Capricorna Hotel
Free State
Ronderus Guesthouse
Cornelia
Kenilworth
Mullers Pass
Warden
Die Oude Werf Guesthouse
Warden Lodge
Cornelia
Tweefontein
Eureka
Excelsior
Kruispad
Afsluit Guesthouse
Verkykerskop
Verkykerskop Guesthouse
Mount Pelaan
Glendale
Normandien
Horseshoe
Sandford
Chelmsford
Lions Rest Game Lodge
Vaal
Riet
Waterval
Boesman
Blesbok
Leeu
Klip
Wilge
Grootdraai Dam
R547
R548
R580
R545
R550
R546
R103
R543
R722
R714
N17
N3
N11
R35
R38
R39
R50
R23
R34
R42
Free

32
18 Municipal Tourist Lodge
Panorama Rest Camp (AG 33)
Lisbon Hideaway (AG 33)
20 Windmill Wine Shop & Cottages
Böhms Zeederberg Guesthouse (AH 33)
82
Eagles Nest
Tree Lodge
Riverside Chalets (AH 33)
27 White House Lodge (AH 33)
Loch
33
Viewpoint
Hartebeeskop
Oshoek
Ka Daka
Forbes Reef
Witrand
Carlchew
Florence Guest Farm
Warburton
Holnek Game Reserve
Umpuluzi
Chrissiesmeer
Lake Chrissie Lodge
The Church House
Miss Chrissie
Breyten
KwaZanele
Chrissiemeer Dam
Kaiavas
Waverley
Lundzi
Ngwili
MBABANE
Maloyo
Swartwater
Lothair
Metula
Usutu
Bonnie Brook
Luphohlo Dam
Siphocosini
Mlilwane Wildlife Sanctuary
Nondvo
Mlilwane NR
Mhlambanyatsi
Nyonyana
Lojiba
Douglas Dam
Barnyard Lodge
Koolbank
Westoe Dam
Bell's Kop
Ermelo
Holbank
Bhunya
AK
Malkerns
Matsa
Loyengo
Bankkop
Indawo Game Lodge
Grasslands Lodge
Camden
Jericho Dam NR
Jericho Dam
Thole
Magodo
Nerston
Sandlane
Robert Burns Inn
Glen Oak Lodge
Amsterdam
Ossewa Trek 1838
Bushman Paintings
Mankayane
Over-Vaal
Sheepmoor
Sand
Mpama
Morgenstond Dam NR
Morgenstond Dam
Ngwempisi
Towela
Klein-Vaal
Panbult
SWA
Mantola
Iswepe
Mpumalanga
Wildrand
Hlelo
Emahlatini
1 Donna Bella Guesthouse
Hilton Manor Guesthouse
Southfork Guesthouse
De Villas Guesthouse
Hawks Nest (AK 32)
Palm Inn
Waterside Lodge
Eagles Guesthouse
Golden Door Guesthouse
Welgekozen Country Lodge
Cypress Lodge
Sundowner
Bothashoop
Gege
eMkhondo (Piet Retief)
Waterside Lodge
Driefontein
Heyshope Dam
Gude
Anysspruit
Ethandakukhanya
Mineral Baths
Goedgegun
Mahamba
AL
72
Wiel
R543
Wittenberg
Modiman
Mozane
Mzama Royal
Latemanek
Assegaai
Dirkiesdorp
Berbice
Wit
Ntombe
Mabola
Ntombi
Braunschweig
Commondale
Buitenzorg
De Oude Stasie
Weavers Nest
Uitvlugt
Pongola Bush NR
Luneberg
Papale
Wakkerstroom
The Gables
Wetlands Country House & Sheds
Ossewakop
Driefontein
Pandana
Tsakwe
Paulpietersburg
Frischgewaagd
Slang
Grootspruit
Ozwane
Zaaihoek Dam
Groenvlei
Dumbe Paragliding
Wonder (Abandoned Goldmine)
Thalu
Bivane
Kruger Bridge
Natal Spa (Hot Springs)
Doornkraal
Mkuzo
Klipspruit
KwaZulu-Natal
Mpemvana
Mgwabe
Holkrans
Ntshondwe Camp
Womeni
Wasbank
Grand Hotel
Utrecht
Kambula 1879
Nuambuta 1879
Grange
Hlobane
AM
Doring
Dorp
P.L. Uys Memorial
Nsonto
Alpha
Amcordam Resort
Newcastle
Madadeni
Battle of Blood River Poort 1901
Vryheid
Bhekuzulu
Shonalanga Lodge
Stillwater Hotel
The Old Carnegie Museum
Raadsaal and Fort of New Republic
Mpofini Game Lodge
Steilrand
R618
Hilldrop Farmhouse
The Oak Tree
Haggards Hilldrop
Sizweni
Buffels
Scheepersnek
Battle of Scheepersnek 1900
Klipfontein Dam
Brakfontein
Mbabane
Ballengeich
Sediba Trails
Bloodriver
Kingsley
Swart uM
Picnic Site
Boat Club
Flint
Glückstadt
Ntshingwayo Dam
Doringberg
eMondlo
Calvert
Thangami Safari Spa & Mudbath
Dannhauser
Stanmore
Mvunyana
Ngogweni
Hattingspruit
32
59
Blood River
Ntabebomvu
33
Doctor Alden
Thaka

34
83
35
Croydon
Malanoela
Mlawula
Goba
Mailana
Mlawula Ndzindza NR
Hlane Game Sanctuary
Passope
Changalane
MBABANE
Mlilwane Wildlife Sanctuary
Nondvo
Mlilwane NR
Nyonyana
Lojiba
Manzini
Mafutseni
Mpaka
Siteki
Segunduanine
Mau-Dai
AK
Malkerns
Matsapha
MATSAPHA
Loyengo
Hawini
Sidvokodvo
Lubhuku
Mkhaya NR
Nyetane Dam
Hondjandine
Mankayane
Holomi
Siphofaneni
Phuzumoya
SWAZILAND
Van Eck Dam
Big Bend
Catuane
Mantola
Sithobela
Kubutsa
Mboyi
Red Cliffs Picnic Site
Picnic Site
Ndumo GR
Ndumo Wilderness Camp
Bird Hide
Ndumo
Ndumo Hutted Camp
Manyiseni
Hlathikhulu
Maloma
Nsoko
Nkungwini
Shemula Lodge
Ndumu River Lodge
Goedgegun
Mahamba
71
AL
Nhlangano
Shemula
iNgwavuma
Mozane
Mzama Royal Graves
Mhosheni
Mlokolma Royal Graves
Hluti
Hluthi
Mboza
Mthonjeni
Berbice
Onverwacht
Golela
Lavumisa
Mabnada
Shayamoya Lodge
Golela
Inyathi
Ndabeni
Madonela
Pongola
Kortnek
Mvubu
Mpalane Fishing Lodge
Kingholm
Pongolapoort NR
Jozini Dam
Jozini
Tshongwe
Wonder (Abandoned Goldmine)
Mhlangeni
Thalu
Picnic Site
Ithala GR
Doornkraal
Mbizo
Ithala Game Reserve
Louwsburg
Zululand Nyala Lodge
Esikhotheni Lodge
Candover
Nkonkoni
Malobeni
Magudu
Tugam Game Lodge
uBombo
Village & Craft Market
Mantuma
Picnic Site
Ntshondwe Camp
Jacaranda Luxury Hotel
KwaZulu-Natal
Mahlangasi
Emshopi Campsite
Mkuze
Emshopi Campsite
Orpen
Nhlonhlela Bush Lodge
Nzumo Bird Hide
Picnic Site
Nhlonhlela
Mkhuze Game Reserve Rest Camps
Trails Camp
uMkumbi
uMkhuze Section
uMkhumboe Tented Bush Lodge
AM
Alpha
Kranskop
Sizani Lodge
Steilrand
Ngome
Thokazi
Malomeni
Intendele Game Farm
Banghoek Lodge
Baobab Inn
Bayala
Pumalanga NR
Bhumbeni GR
Phinda Resource Reserve
Brakfontein
Zihlakenpele
Kube Yini
Dukumbane
Thanda GR
Nongoma
Swart uMfolozi
Ehlalini Lodge & Lakeview Lodge
False Bay Section
Glückstadt
Zulu Nyala Game Lodge
Sweetwaters Cottages
Ezulweni Lodge
Thangami Safari Spa & Mudbath
KwaCeza
Thangami Safari
Dumazulu Village
Hluhluwe
Dugandlovu
Mzinene Lodge
Ubizane Wildlife Reserve
Hluhluwe Game R
34
60
35
Sigubudu
Hilltop/Mtwazi
Thaka
Sikwebezi
Nkunzana
Msunduzi
Mkuze
Pongola
Spekboom
Mantambe
Mhlatuze
Ngwavuma
Lusutfu
Little Usutu
Mhlatuzane
Mkondo
Mkhondvo
Ndlozane
White Mbuluzi
Mbuluzi
Mkomazane
Mnjoli Dam
Nhlaniwane
Msulutane
Mlawa
Mzinpofu
Mtendekwa
Nhlonga
Sitilo
Mhlumbala
Sihlengeni
Bululwana
Msebe
Mona
Mngeni
Vuna
Rio Mazeminhama
Rio Matilonge
R618
R66
R69

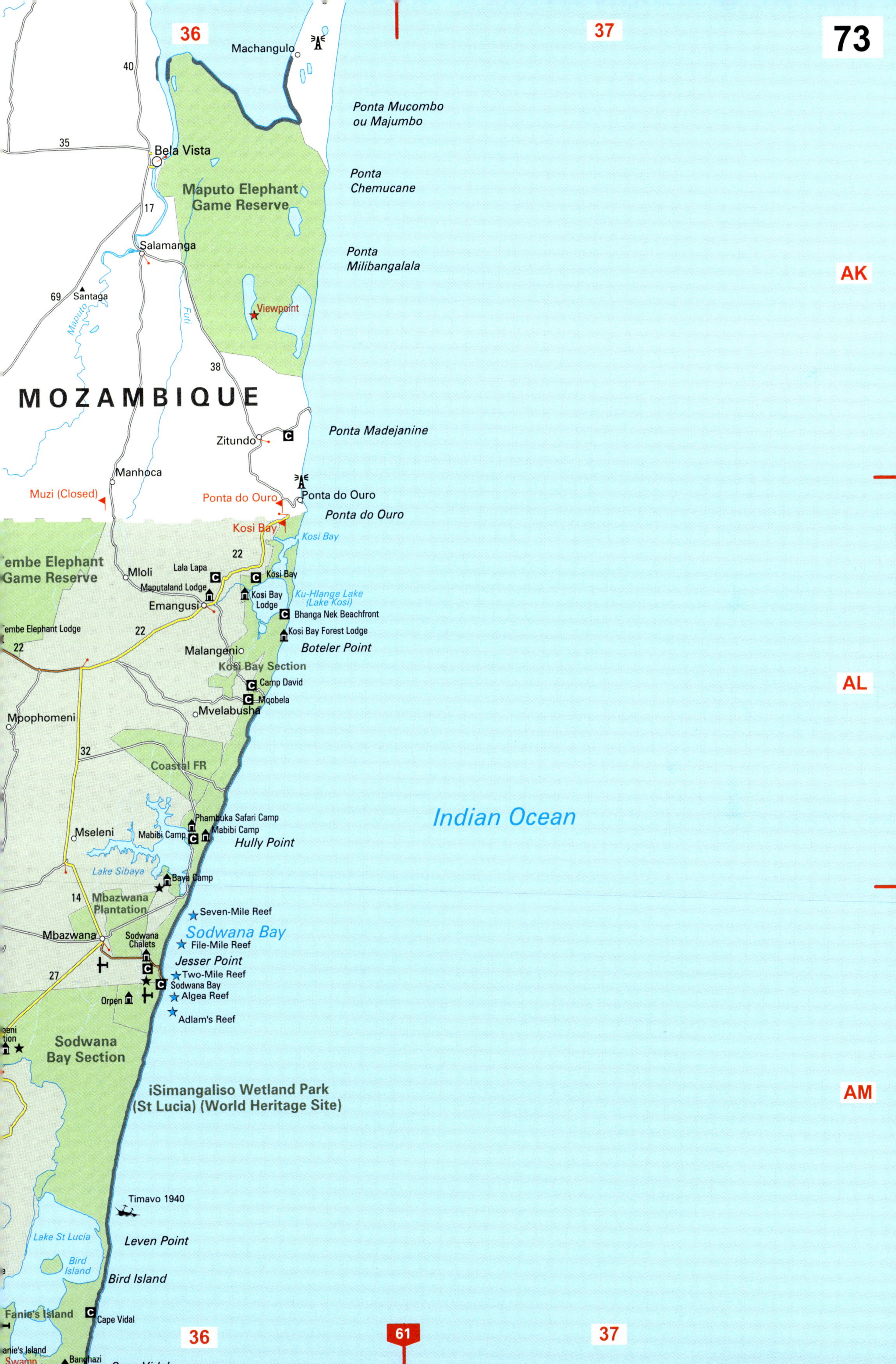
36
37
Machangulo
Ponta Mucombo
ou Majumbo
Bela Vista
Maputo Elephant
Game Reserve
Ponta
Chemucane
Salamanga
Ponta
Milibangalala
Santaga
Maputo
Futi
Viewpoint
MOZAMBIQUE
Zitundo
Ponta Madejanine
Manhoca
Muzi (Closed)
Ponta do Ouro
Ponta do Ouro
Ponta do Ouro
Kosi Bay
Kosi Bay
Tembe Elephant
Game Reserve
Mloli
Lala Lapa
Kosi Bay
Maputaland Lodge
Kosi Bay
Lodge
Ku-Hlange Lake
(Lake Kosi)
Emangusi
Bhanga Nek Beachfront
Tembe Elephant Lodge
Kosi Bay Forest Lodge
Malangeni
Boteler Point
Kosi Bay Section
Camp David
Mqobela
Mvelabusha
Mpophomeni
Coastal FR
Phambuka Safari Camp
Mabibi Camp
Mseleni
Mabibi Camp
Hully Point
Indian Ocean
Lake Sibaya
Baya Camp
Mbazwana
Plantation
Seven-Mile Reef
Sodwana Bay
Mbazwana
Sodwana
Chalets
File-Mile Reef
Jesser Point
Two-Mile Reef
Sodwana Bay
Algea Reef
Orpen
Adlam's Reef
Sodwana
Bay Section
iSimangaliso Wetland Park
(St Lucia) (World Heritage Site)
Timavo 1940
Lake St Lucia
Leven Point
Bird
Island
Bird Island
Fanie's Island
Cape Vidal
Banghazi
Swamp
AK
AL
AM
61
36
37

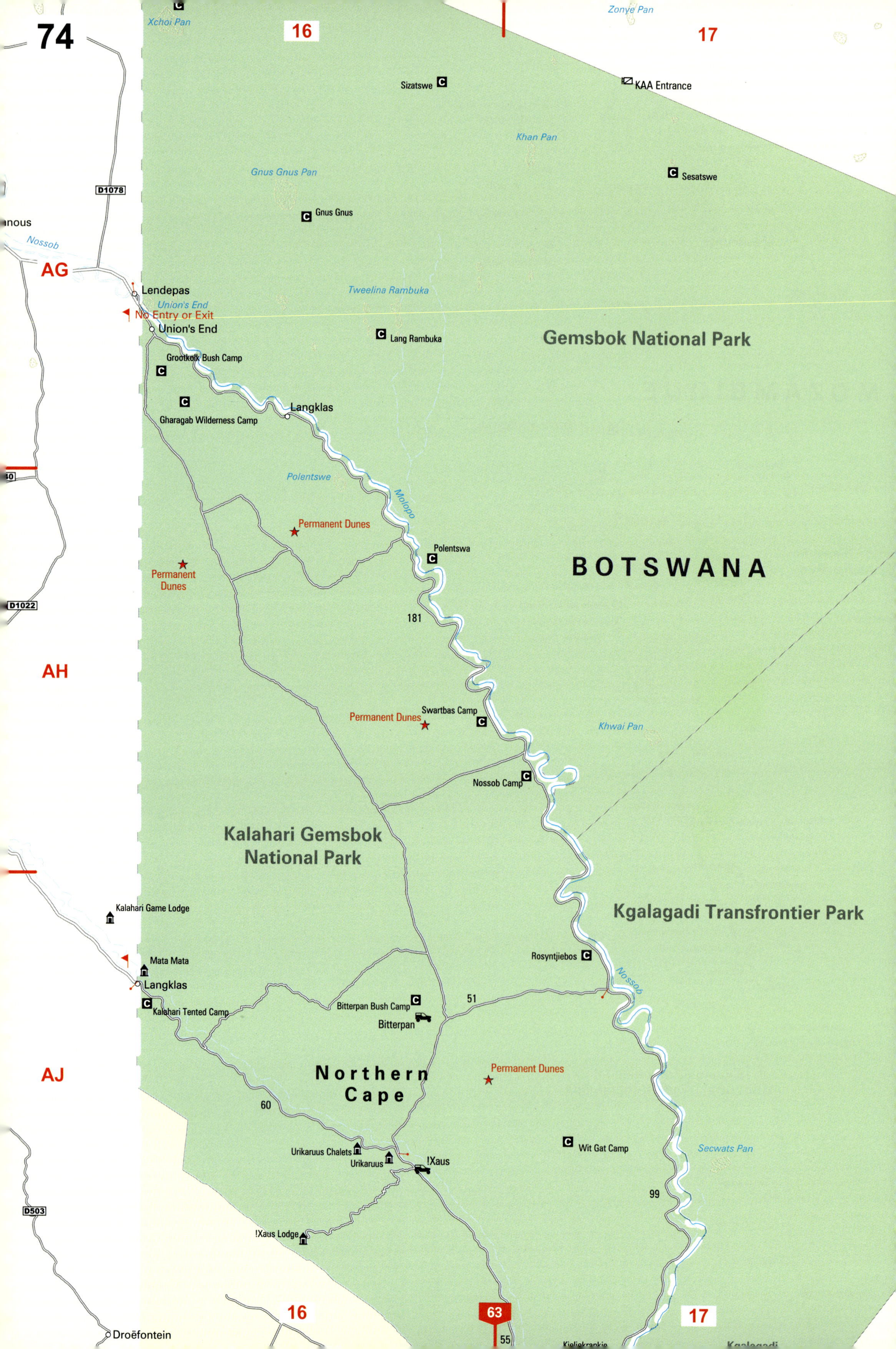

16
17
Xchoi Pan
Zonye Pan
Sizatswe
KAA Entrance
Khan Pan
Sesatswe
Gnus Gnus Pan
Gnus Gnus
D1078
Nossob
AG
Lendepas
Union's End
No Entry or Exit
Union's End
Tweelina Rambuka
Lang Rambuka
Gemsbok National Park
Grootkolk Bush Camp
Gharagab Wilderness Camp
Langklas
Polentswe
Molopo
Permanent Dunes
Polentswa
BOTSWANA
Permanent Dunes
D1022
181
AH
Permanent Dunes
Swartbas Camp
Khwai Pan
Nossob Camp
Kalahari Gemsbok National Park
Kgalagadi Transfrontier Park
Kalahari Game Lodge
Mata Mata
Langklas
Kalahari Tented Camp
Rosyntjiebos
Nossob
Bitterpan Bush Camp
51
Bitterpan
AJ
Northern Cape
Permanent Dunes
60
Wit Gat Camp
Urikaruus Chalets
Urikaruus
!Xaus
Secwats Pan
D503
99
!Xaus Lodge
16
63
17
Droëfontein
55

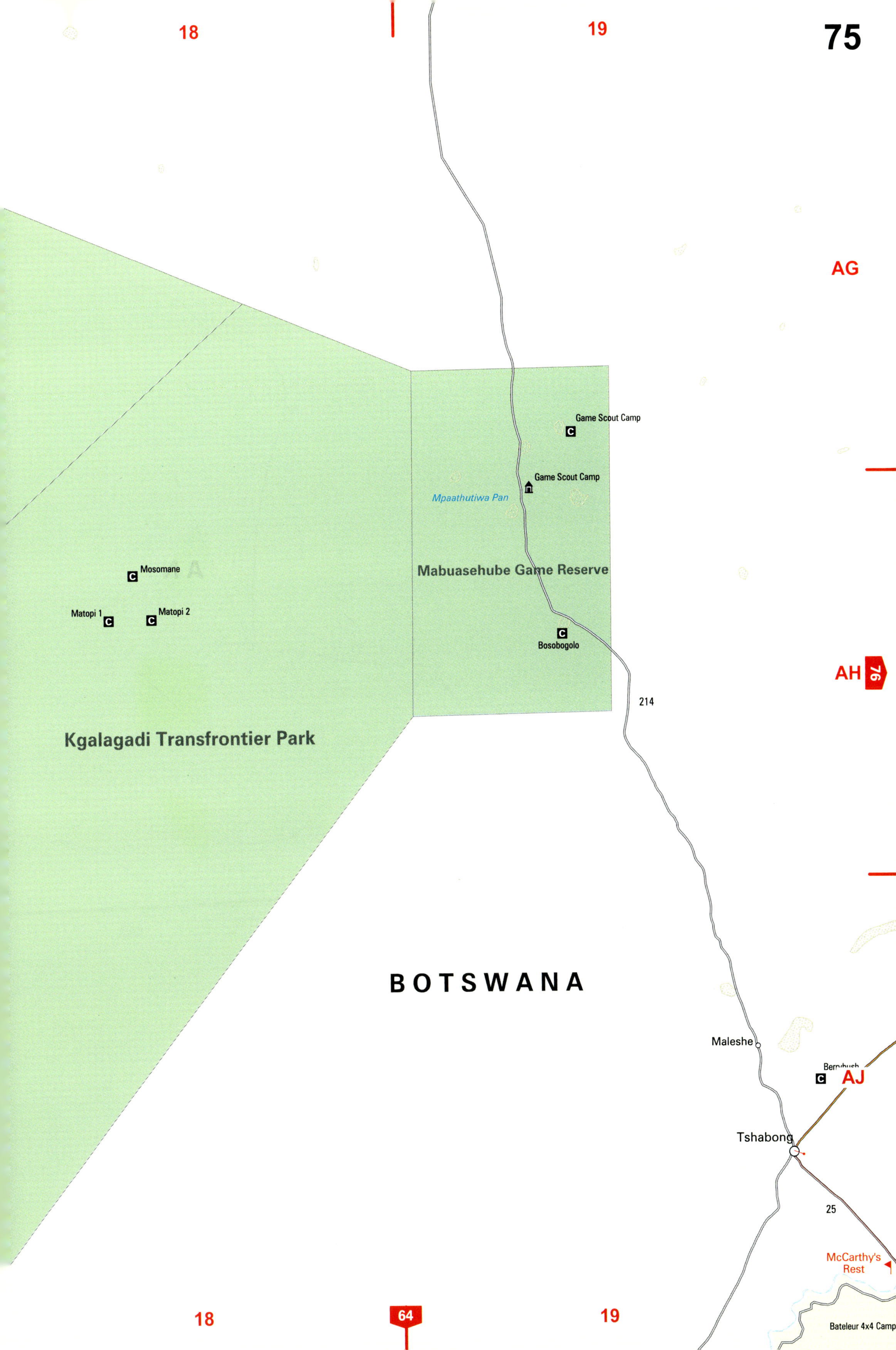
18
19
AG
AH
76
AJ
Game Scout Camp
Game Scout Camp
Mpaathutiwa Pan
Mabuasehube Game Reserve
Bosobogolo
214
Mosomane
Matopi 1
Matopi 2
Kgalagadi Transfrontier Park
BOTSWANA
Maleshe
Tshabong
25
McCarthy's Rest
Bateleur 4x4 Camp
18
64
19

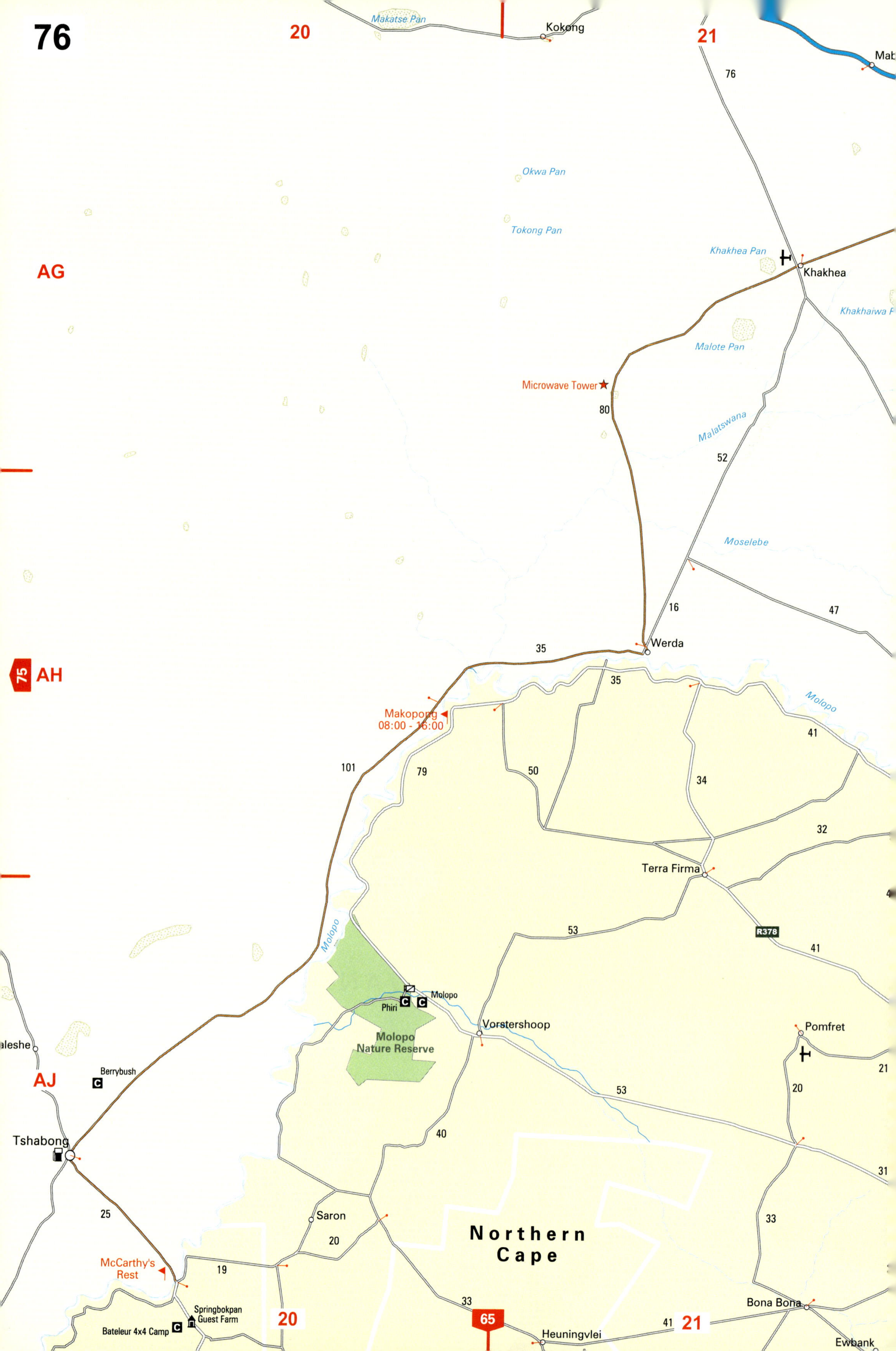
20
21
Makatse Pan
Kokong
Mat
76
Okwa Pan
Tokong Pan
AG
Khakhea Pan
Khakhea
Khakhaiwa P
Malote Pan
Microwave Tower
80
Malatswana
52
Moselebe
16
47
Werda
35
35
Molopo
75
AH
Makopong
08:00 - 16:00
41
101
79
50
34
32
Terra Firma
R378
53
41
Molopo
Molopo
Phiri
Molopo Nature Reserve
Vorstershoop
Pomfret
aleshe
Berrybush
AJ
21
20
53
40
Tshabong
31
25
Saron
33
20
Northern Cape
McCarthy's Rest
19
Springbokpan Guest Farm
Bateleur 4x4 Camp
20
33
65
Heuningvlei
41
21
Bona Bona
Ewbank

22
23
A2
40
Sekoma Pan
Sekoma
50
Tshinka Pan
Mine
80
Jwaneng
Cezar Hotel
Mokala Lodge
AG
143
Khwekhwe Pan
Tswaing Pan
Selokolela
BOTSWANA
Sita Pan
AH
78
86
55
Moselebe
Bray 08:00 - 16:30
Bray
Sekhutlane
38
Molopo
37
11
12
10
Moloporivier
Boshoek
17
7
Vergeleë
Gen. C.R. de Wet 1914
25
35
Mabule
Phitshane-Molopo
07:30 - 16:30
59
Senlac
6
R375
Labera
Tshidilamolomo
8
Setlagole
19
Tosca
16
41
22
9
19
AJ
16
Gemsbokvlakte
Logageng
17
50
1 Sundown G
Bougainville
Scott's Mar
Lakeside (A
33
R378
27
Setlagole
North West
30
Mareetsane
27
15
20
Morokweng
Mosita
Piet Plessis
20
Madiakgama
R377
15
26
27
Mansfield
66
69

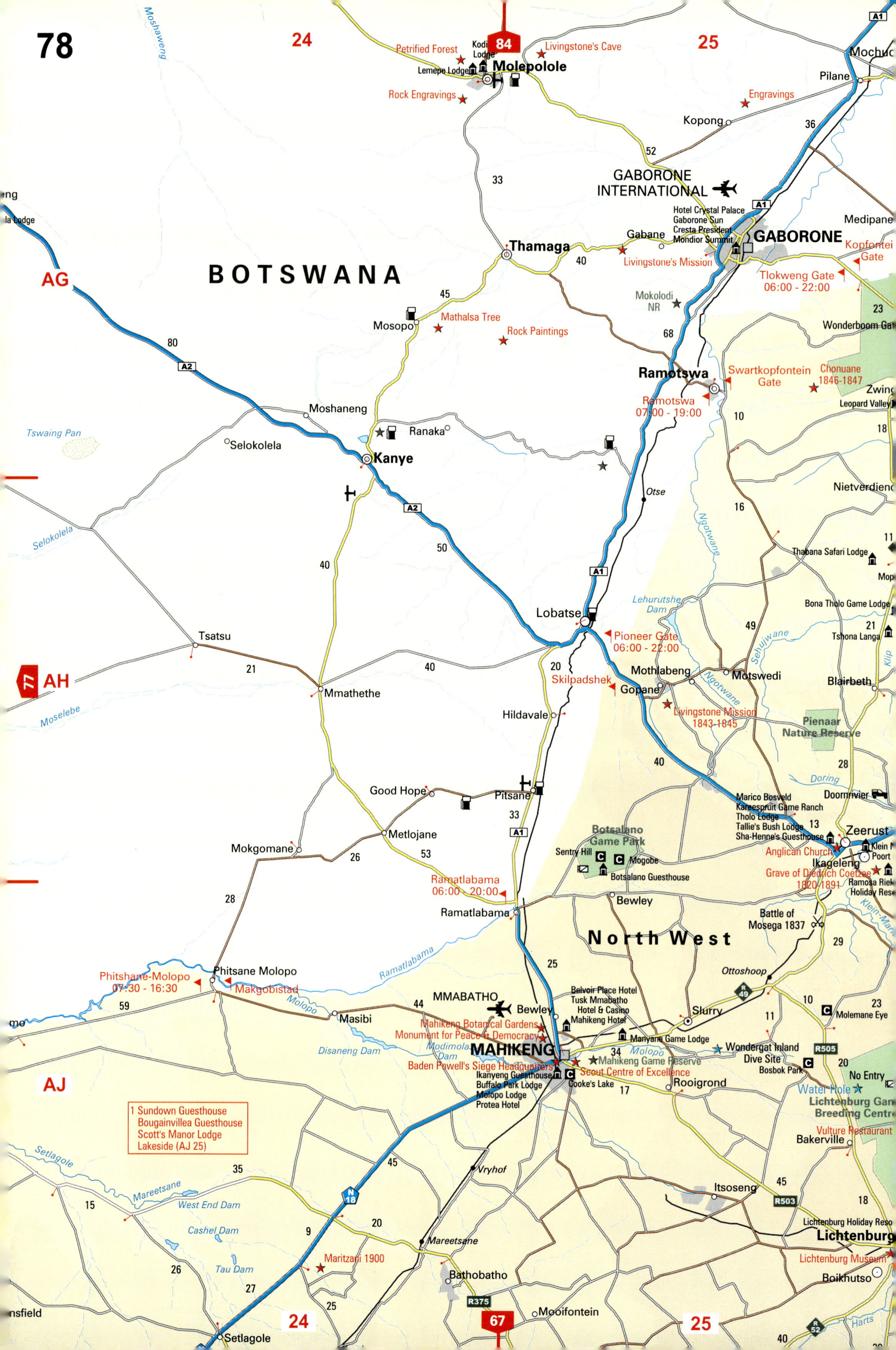
BOTSWANA
North West
Molepolole
Petrified Forest
Kodi Lodge
Lemepe Lodge
Livingstone's Cave
Rock Engravings
Engravings
Kopong
Pilane
Mochudi
GABORONE INTERNATIONAL
GABORONE
Hotel Crystal Palace
Gaborone Sun
Cresta President
Mondior Summit
Gabane
Medipane
Kopfontein Gate
Tlokweng Gate 06:00 - 22:00
Thamaga
Livingstone's Mission
Mokolodi NR
Wonderboom Gate
Mosopo
Mathalsa Tree
Rock Paintings
Ramotswa
Ramotswa 07:00 - 19:00
Swartkopfontein Gate
Chonuane 1846-1847
Leopard Valley
Moshaneng
Tswaing Pan
Selokolela
Ranaka
Kanye
Otse
Nietverdiend
Thabana Safari Lodge
Ngotwane
Lehurutshe Dam
Bona Tholo Game Lodge
Tshona Langa
Lobatse
Pioneer Gate 06:00 - 22:00
Tsatsu
Mmathethe
Moselebe
Skilpadshek
Gopane
Mothlabeng
Motswedi
Blairbeth
Sehujwane
Livingstone Mission 1843-1845
Pienaar Nature Reserve
Hildavale
Doring
Doornrivier
Good Hope
Pitsane
Marico Bosveld
Kareespruit Game Ranch
Tholo Lodge
Tallie's Bush Lodge
Sha-Henne's Guesthouse
Zeerust
Klein Poort
Anglican Church
Ikageleng
Grave of Diedrich Coetzee 1820-1891
Ramosa Riek
Holiday Res
Metlojane
Mokgomane
Botsalano Game Park
Sentry Hill
Mogobe
Botsalano Guesthouse
Ramatlabama 06:00 - 20:00
Ramatlabama
Bewley
Battle of Mosega 1837
Klein-Marico
Ottoshoop
Ramatlabama
Phitshane-Molopo 07:30 - 16:30
Phitsane Molopo
Makgobistad
Molopo
MMABATHO
Bewley
Belvoir Place Hotel
Tusk Mmabatho Hotel & Casino
Mahikeng Hotel
Slurry
Molemane Eye
Masibi
Mahikeng Botanical Gardens
Monument for Peace & Democracy
Manyane Game Lodge
Disaneng Dam
Modimola Dam
MAHIKENG
Molopo
Mahikeng Game Reserve
Wondergat Inland Dive Site
Bosbok Park
Baden Powell's Siege Headquarters
Ikanyeng Guesthouse
Buffalo Park Lodge
Molopo Lodge
Protea Hotel
Cooke's Lake
Scout Centre of Excellence
Rooigrond
No Entry
Water Hole
Lichtenburg Game Breeding Centre
1 Sundown Guesthouse
Bougainvillea Guesthouse
Scott's Manor Lodge
Lakeside (AJ 25)
Vulture Restaurant
Bakerville
Setlagole
Vryhof
Mareetsane
West End Dam
Itsoseng
Cashel Dam
Tau Dam
Mareetsane
Maritzani 1900
Lichtenburg Holiday Resort
Lichtenburg
Lichtenburg Museum
Bathobatho
Boikhutso
Mooifontein
Harts
Setlagole
AG
AH
AJ
24
25
84
67
77

Limpopo
North West
Thabazimbi
Rustenburg
Derdepoort
Sikwane
Sikwane 06:00 - 18:00
Derdepoort Gate
Madikwe Game Reserve
Madikwe River Lodge
Sesobe Mission
Molatedi Gate
Molatedi
Molatedi Dam
Kaya se put
1899-1900
Silent Valley
Atherstone Nature Reserve
Oostermoed
Dwaalboom
Ganskuil
Dwarsberg
Silkaatskop
Silkaatskop Monument
Bulskop 1530m
Middelwit
Biersspruit
Biersspruit Dam
Northam
Shonalang Lodge
Grobs Lodge
Mawala Lodge
Tussenin
Koppie Alleen Guesthouse
Thaba Tholo Eco-park
Marula Game Lodge
Badger Bush
Jabulani Lodge
Sweet Home Mountain Lodge
Smokey Mountain
Thaba Nkwe Bushveld Inn
Oasis
Bonanza
Echo Mountain Inn
Ben Alberts Nature Reserve
Motsomi Lodge
Mongatane Lodge
Impangele Guesthouse
Camel Thorn Lodge
Blinkwater Lodge
Mabeskraal
Mabalstad
Mogwase
Pilanesberg Game Reserve
Bakgatla
Metswedi
Kololo
Mankwe
Manyane
Iron Age Site
Tshukudu
Bakubung
Kwa Maritane
Bosele
Houwater Dam
Sun City / Lost City
Ledig
Ostrich Farm
Paul
Finfoot Lake Reserve
Vaalkop Dam
Vaalkop Dam NR
Laboheme NR
Kwa Tidimalo
Atlanta Holiday Resort
Motshikiri
Straatsdrif
Skuinsdrif
Riekertsdam
Pella
Lindleyspoort
Rametsi Eco Lodge
Rusverby
Marico Bosveld Dam
Marico Bosveld Nature Reserve
Doornkraal Guesthouse
4 Seasons
Woodbine
Groot Marico
Battle of Kleinfontein
Lourie Guesthouse
Botshabelo Guesthouse
Groot Marico Bosveld Lodge
Stille Waters Guest Farm
River Still Guesthouse
Up The Creek
Swartruggens
Red Chilli Inn
Africa Dreams Game Lodge
Wondermere
Lead Mine
Twinbrook
Millvale
Koster Dam
Reagile
Koster
Harmony Guesthouse
Iwamanzi Lodge
Over Tuin
Dessing
Derby
Megani Private Game Reserve
Bulls in the Bush Lodge
Boshoek
Keder Lodge
Boekenhoutfontein 1873
Phokeng
Ga-Luka
Bospoort Dam
God's Window Holiday Resort
Tlholego Eco Village
Ananda
Rustenburg Kloof
Orion Safari Hotel
Rustenburg Nature Reserve
Bush Willows
Wigwam Hotel
Bleskop
Marikana
Modderfontein Guesthouse
Westwinds
Bergheim
Olifantsnek Dam
Matlopeng Retreat Lodge
Aasvoëlkraans
Jabula Manzi
Magaliesberg Nature Area
Utopia Nature Resort
ATKV
Mountain Park Sanctuary
Sekelele
Wind in the willows
Bergbries
Boons
Grootpan
Rietpan Guesthouse
Swartplaas
Ga-Ramodingwana
Christies
Klerkskraal
Klerkskraal Dam
Leeugatgrot
1 Palm Lodge
Casa Mia
Cumari Guesthouse
Marcilla Guesthouse
Cozy Nook (AJ 27)
Dennekruin Vakansieoord
Fyndraai Hengel Oord
Roodekopjes
Roodekopjes Dam
Mothabeng Guesthouse
No Entry
26
85
27
68
AG
AH
AJ
80

28
86
29
AG
AH
79
AJ
69
Limpopo
North West
Gauteng
Welgevonden Game Reserve
Modikela
Tlopi
Bontle
Makoti's Nest Bush Camp
Marakeli
Towers Gate
Rra-Ditau Game Lodge
Boschoff Guesthouse
Mongatane Lodge
Impangele Guesthouse
Smokey Mountain
Nkwe Bushveld Inn
Oasis
Bonanza
Echo Mountain Inn
Thabazimbi
Camel Thorn Lodge
Kololo Game Reserve
Nyala Lodge
Equus Horse Safaris
Matlabas
Sterkstroom
Waterkruin
Rankins Lodge
Rhenosterpoort
Rankin's Pass
Rhenosterpoort Guesthouse
Dabchick Wildlife Reserve & Conservancy
Daeraad
River Valley Guesthouse
Bundu Lodge
Little 5 Guesthouse
Mashudu Lodge
Klein-Sand
Alma
Veldslag
Sand
Loubad
Loubad Resort
Nylstroom Lodge
Mineral Springs
Lekkerrus Holiday Resort
Libertas
Bothania Hill Holiday Resort
Vanalphensvlei
Serendipity Eco Trails
Tempel
Warmbaths
Avuxeni Spa
Olifantspoort
Donkerpoort Dam
Thaba Kwena Crocodile Farm
Weesgerus Holiday Resort
Modimolle(Nylstroom)
Phagameng
Middelfontein
Strijdom House & Reformed Church
Thaba Kgatla Lodge
Klein Paradys
Kranskop
Holme Park
Spa Vista
Forever Resorts
KRANSKOP TOLL ROAD
Pendleberry Grove Family Holiday Resort
Bela-Bela(Warmbaths)
Blockhouse
Sondela Nature Reserve
Bela-Bela
Settlers
Willem
Hot Mineral Springs
Mabalingwe Game Reserve
Mabula
Pumbali
Koro-Koro Safari Lodge
Mbizi Caravan Lodge
Shakama Game Farm
Zebula Resort and Spa
Kaya-Ingwe
Mabula Game Reserve
Vaalwater
Ra-Molopo Lodge
Rooiberg
Ukuthula Lodge
Sunflower
Letlabo Private Nature Reserve
Kunkuru Private Bush Lodge
Leeupoort
Koedoeskop
Calali Bush Lodge
Blinkwater
Blinkwater Lodge
Crocodile
Tussenin
Koppie Alleen Guesthouse
Northam
Mawala Lodge
Inibos Lodge
Nooitgedacht
Riet
Karee
Maririetsa
Radium
Leonie
Moretele
Borakalalo Game Reserve
Pitjane
Phudufudu
Klipvoor Dam
Assen
Atlanta Holiday Resort
Pienaarsrivier
Pienaars
Plat
Rust de Winter
Tshukudu Lodge
Genius Loci Game Ranch
Rust de Winter Nature Reserve
Kigeli Nature Spa
Rust de Winter Dam
The Carousel Entertainment Centre
Motshikiri
Atlanta
Kopana Wilderness Retreat
Tolwane
Kutswane
Apies
Vaalkop Dam
Kokoriba Resort
Laboheme NR
Kwa Tidimalo
Vaalkop Dam NR
Shongololo
Beestekraal
Jericho
Moegatle Lodge
Dikhololo Lodge
Veekraal
Nyala Nature Reserve
Hartebeeshoek NR
Dube Private Game Reserve
Dennekruin Vakansie Oord
Fyndraai Hengel Oord
Roodekopjes
Roodekopjes Dam
Mothabeng Guest Lodge
Klein Paradys
Brits
Bethanie
Pansdrif
Hartland Bush Camp
Temba
Babelegi
Tswaing Meteorite Crater and Museum
Tswaing
Winterveld
Tswaing NR
Hammanskraal
De Rust
Mongena Lodge
Butjani Bush Lodge
Lama-Lama Game Reserve
Bokenhout
Iquana
Morula Sun
Mabopane
Leeuwkloof Valley Conservancy
Kiasoma
Bobbejaansberg Mine
Little Eden Private Reserve
Ga-Rankuwa
Bospoort Dam
Sonop
Brits
De Wildt
Bon Accord
Roodeplaat Dam NR
Roodeplaat
Roodeplaat Dam
Overvaal Resort
Cullinan
Onderstepoort
Doornpoort
Rustenburg
Bleskop
Marikana
Maroelakop
Miracle Waters Inland Dive Site
Vredesboom
Cable Way
De Wildt Cheetah Research Centre
Hartbeespoort
Snake Park
Tunnel
Aquarium
Zanandi
Kosmos
QUAGGA
Mamelodi
PRETORIA
National Zoo
Sammy Marks Museum
Eden dal
Premier Diamond Mine
Rayton
Diamond Hill
Willows
Marikana
Magaliesberg Nature Area
Modderfontein Guesthouse
Utopia Nature Resort
ATKV
Buffelspoort Dam
Omaramba Holiday Resort
Mamagalie Lodge
Westwinds
Magaliespark
Hartbeespoort Dam
Atteridgeville
Hennops Offroad Trail
Voortrekker Monument
Magaliesberg Conference Centre
Valhalla
Cullinan Ramps
McCarthy 4x4 Club Rhino Park
Mountain Park Sanctuary
Battle of Nooitgedacht
Skeerpoort
Lesedi Cultural Village
Winsome Valley
Centurion
Lion Camp
Rietvlei Dam
Hartbeeshoek Game Reserve
Rhenosterspruit NR
Rietfontein
Magaliesberg Nature Area
Hartbeeshoek Satellite Tracking Station
Hartebeesthoek Tracking Station
Jan Smuts House
Rietvlei NR
Clover Hill Resort
Maanhaarrand
John Ness NR (Private)
The Cradle
Diepsloot NR
Diepsloot
Hekpoort
Old Fort (Barton's Folly)
LANSERIA
Midrand
Die Hoek
Lovers Rock
Magaliesburg
Rainbow Trout Farm
Wonder Caves
Halfway House
Bergbries
Greensleeves
Kyalami
Tembisa
Bapsfontein
Wind in the willows
Sterkfontein Caves
Fourways
Land Rover Experience
Old Kromdraai Gold Mine
Ngongama
Proranda Pleasure Resort
Krugersdorp
Randburg
Kempton Park
Protea Eco-Adventures
Ngonyama Lion Lodge
Sandton
The Brightwater Common
Krugersdorp Game Reserve
Edenvale
O.R. TAMBO INTERNATIONAL
Benoni
Daveyton
Eloff
Roodepoort
Randfontein
JOHANNESBURG
Bedford View
Boksburg
Jan Smuts Park
Blesbok
Murray
Sundra
Welgedacht
National Exhibition Centre
Gold Reef City
Germiston
Geduld
Strubenvale
Springs
Soweto
Alberton
Eldorado Park
R101
R516
R576
R511
R566
R513
R514
R573
R560
R512
R563
R562
R564
R558
R559
R554
R555
R515
N1
N4
N12
N14
N3
M1

Limpopo
Mpumalanga
Marble Hall
Groblersdal
Middelburg
Mhluzi
EMALAHLENI (WITBANK)
KwaGuqa
Ogies
Delmas
Bronkhorstspruit
Roedtan
Mookgophong (Naboomspruit)
Dennilton
Siyabuswa
Hendrina
Loskop Dam Game Reserve
Flag Boshielo Dam
Witbank Dam
Fort Merensky
Fort Weber 1878
Battle of Sekhukhuneland
Battle of Bronkhorstspruit 1880
1 Ekandustria Ramps (AJ 30)
AG
AH
AJ
30
31
70
82
87

Limpopo
Mpumalanga
MBOMBELA (NELSPRUIT)
Mashishing (Lydenburg)
Emgwenya (Waterval Boven)
eNtokozweni (Machadodorp)
eMakhazeni (Belfast)
eManzana (Badplaas)
Dullstroom
Barberton
Sabie
Graskop
Pilgrims Rest
Hazyview
White River
Burgersfort
Steelpoort
Ohrigstad
Carolina
Kaapsehoop
Josefsdal Songimvelo Game Reserve
Pot & Plough (AF 32)
6 Magoebaskloof Ruskamp
Lodge (AF 32)
39 Elandskrans Hiking Trail (AJ 32)
40 Crane Creek Hiking Trail (AJ 32)
1 Kwa-Mbili (AG 33)
2 Kapama (AG 33)
3 Hongonyi Game Lodge (AG 33)
4 Jackalberry (AG 33)
5 Phelwana Game Lodge (AG 33)
6 Pezulu Tree House (AG 33)
7 Mbabaat Safari Lodge (AG 33)
8 Heybrook Country Lodge (AJ 32)
9 Come Together Guest Farm (AJ 33)
10 Nelspruit Holiday Resort (AJ 33)
11 Brohem Farm Lodge (AJ 33)
12 Hops Hollow Country House (AH 33)
13 Campsite and Guesthouses (AG 33)
14 Summit Lodge (AG 33)
15 Pilgrim's Rest (AG 33)
16 Zur Alten Mine (AG 33)
17 West Lodge
Panorama Rest Camp (AG 33)
18 Municipal Tourist Lodge
Panorama Rest Camp (AG 33)
19 Lisbon Hideaway (AG 33)
20 Windmill Wine Shop & Cottages
Böhms Zeederberg Guesthouse (AH 33)
21 Riverside Cottages
Rock-A-Bye
Hazyview Cabanas (AH 33)
22 Chili Pepper Lodge (AH 33)
23 Aan De Vliet
Lions Rock
Hippo Hollow
Gecko Lodge (AH 33)
24 Kruger Park Lodge
Shingalana Guesthouse (AH 33)
25 Chestnut Country Lodge
Eagles Nest
Haus Kopatsch (AH 33)
26 Fern Tree Lodge
Glass Bungalows
Riverside Chalets (AH 33)
27 White House Lodge (AH 33)
28 Sulphur Springs (AJ 32)
29 Jock of the Bushveld Trek 1885 (AG 33)
30 Old Diggings (AG 33)
31 Graskop Gorge (AG 33)
32 Jock of the Bushveld 1885 (AG 33)
33 Sabie Mineral Springs (AH 33)
34 Hot Air Balloon Launch Site (AH 33)
35 Alkmaar 4x4 Trail (AH 33)
36 Ou Kraal Rest Camp
Rex's Ranch (AJ 32)
37 Therans Rest Camp
Marysvale Rest Camp
Forever Resorts (AJ 33)
38 Gods Window (AG 33)

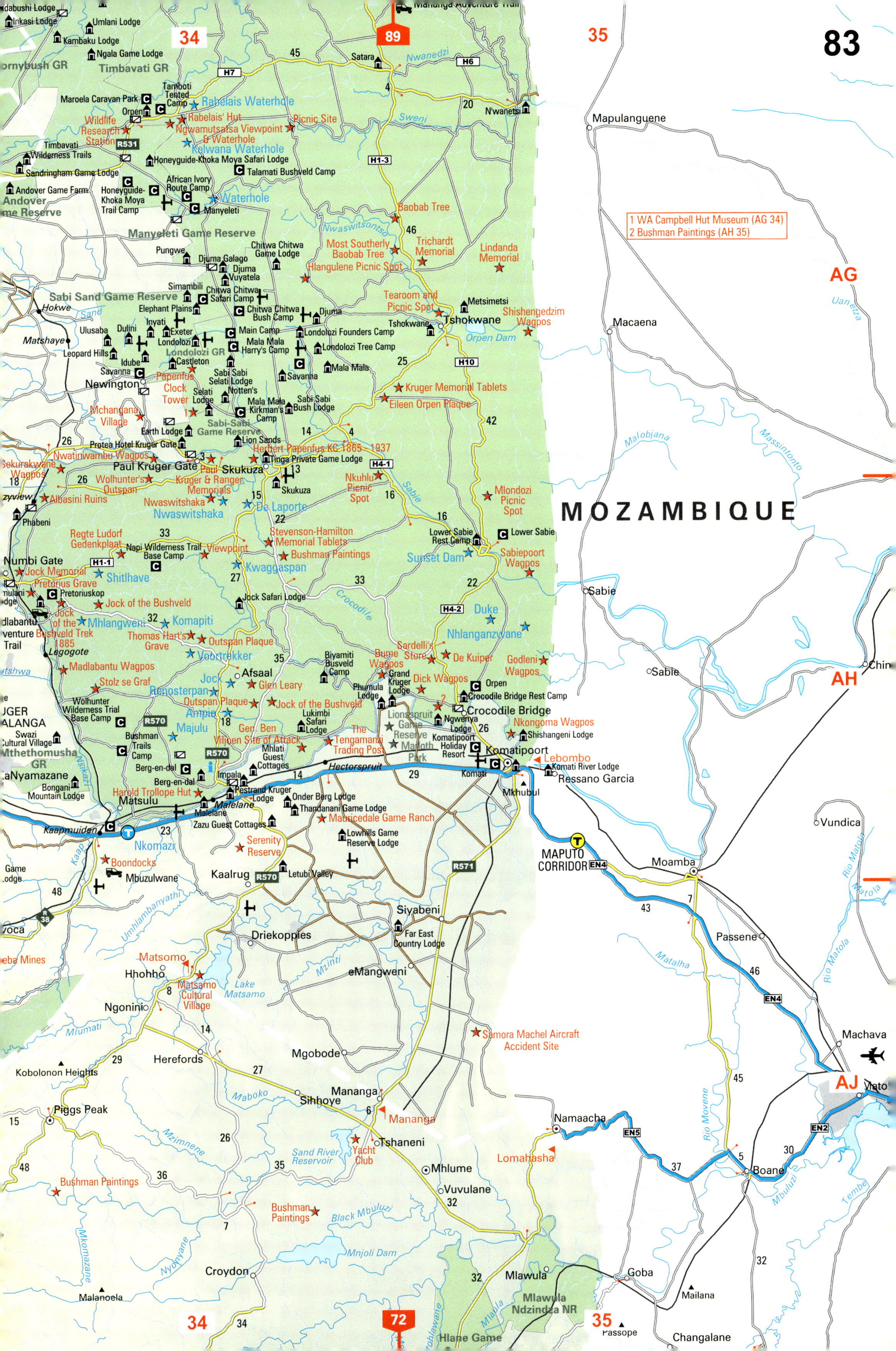
MOZAMBIQUE
1 WA Campbell Hut Museum (AG 34)
2 Bushman Paintings (AH 35)
Kruger Memorial Tablets
Skukuza
Lower Sabie
Crocodile Bridge
Komatipoort
Ressano Garcia
MAPUTO CORRIDOR
Moamba
Boane
Namaacha
Piggs Peak
Matsamo
Mapulanguene
Macaena
Sabie
Tshokwane
Satara

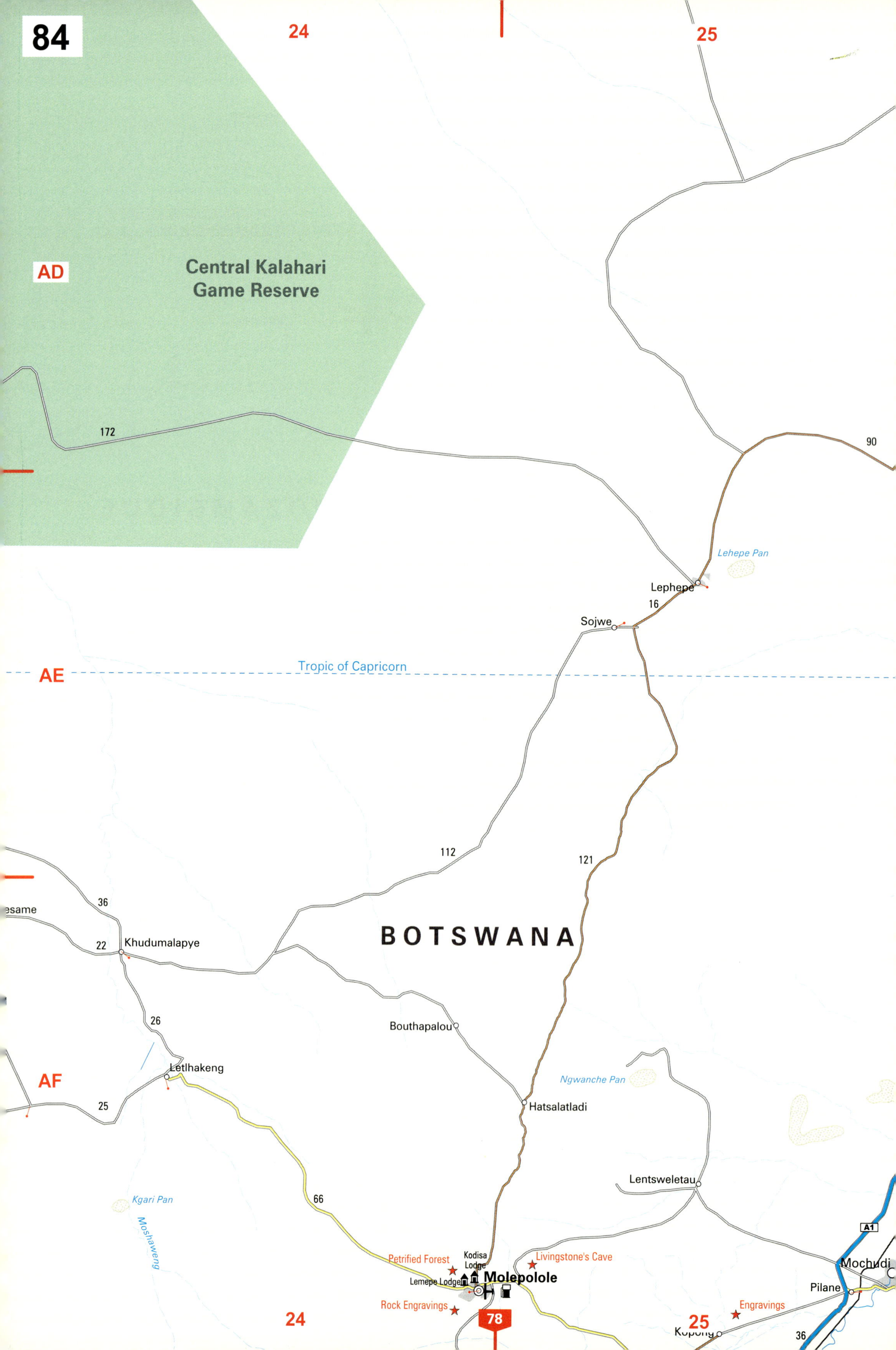
24
25
AD
Central Kalahari
Game Reserve
172
90
Lehepe Pan
Lephepe
16
Sojwe
AE
Tropic of Capricorn
112
121
36
esame
22
Khudumalapye
BOTSWANA
26
Bouthapalou
Letlhakeng
AF
25
Ngwanche Pan
Hatsalatladi
Lentsweletau
Kgari Pan
Moshaweng
66
A1
Petrified Forest
Kodisa
Lodge
Livingstone's Cave
Mochudi
Lemepe Lodge
Molepolole
Pilane
Rock Engravings
Engravings
24
78
25
36

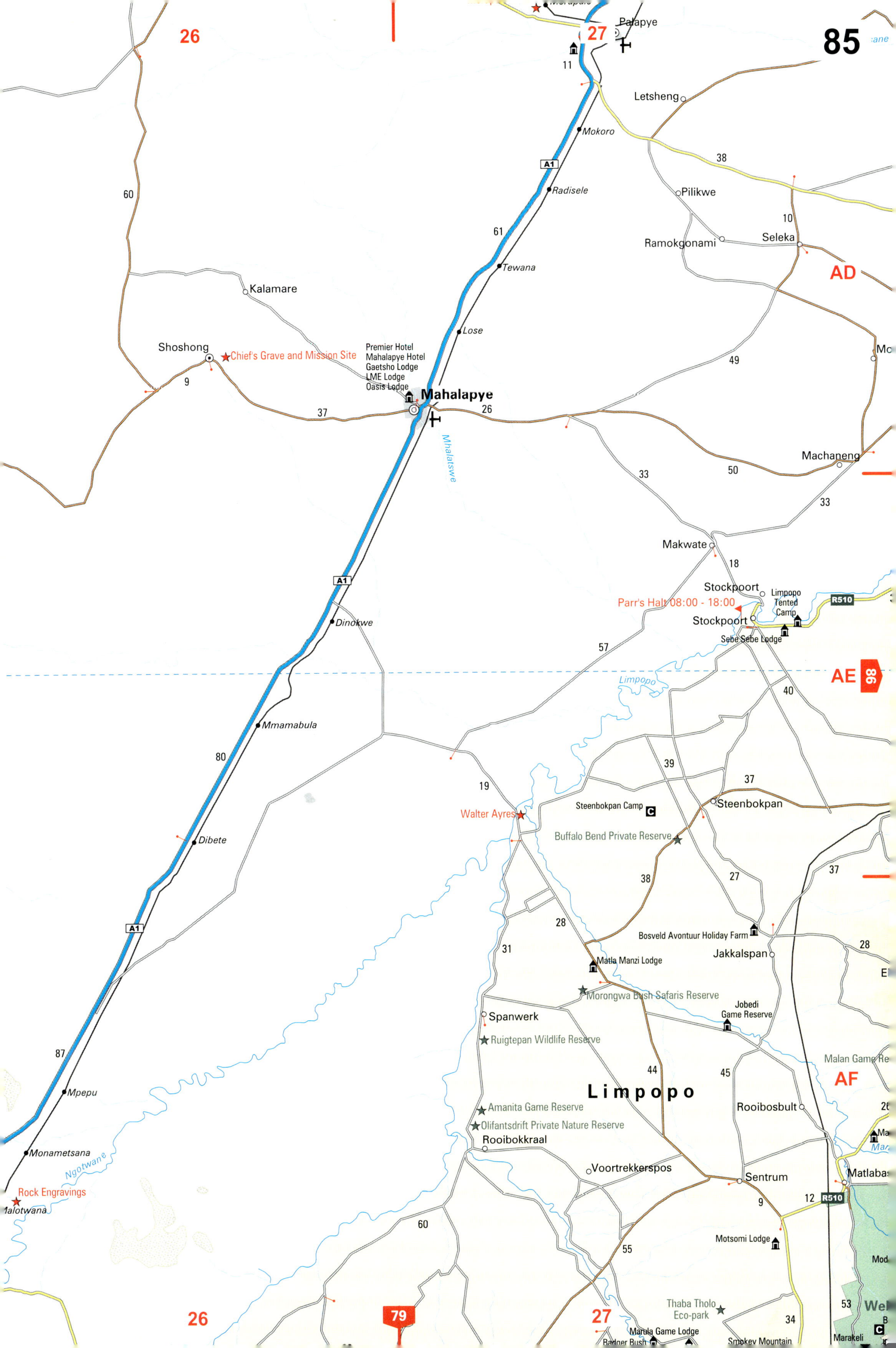
26
27
AD
AE
86
AF
79
Palapye
Letsheng
Mokoro
A1
Radisele
Pilikwe
Ramokgonami
Seleka
Tewana
Kalamare
Lose
Shoshong
Chief's Grave and Mission Site
Premier Hotel
Mahalapye Hotel
Gaetsho Lodge
LME Lodge
Oasis Lodge
Mahalapye
Mhalatswe
Machaneng
Makwate
Stockpoort
Limpopo Tented Camp
Parr's Halt 08:00 - 18:00
Sebe Sebe Lodge
R510
Dinokwe
Limpopo
Mmamabula
Steenbokpan Camp
Steenbokpan
Walter Ayres
Buffalo Bend Private Reserve
Dibete
Bosveld Avontuur Holiday Farm
Jakkalspan
Matla Manzi Lodge
Morongwa Bush Safaris Reserve
Jobedi Game Reserve
Spanwerk
Ruigtepan Wildlife Reserve
Malan Game Re
Limpopo
Rooibosbult
Mpepu
Amanita Game Reserve
Olifantsdrift Private Nature Reserve
Rooibokkraal
Monametsana
Ngotwane
Voortrekkerspos
Matlabas
Sentrum
Rock Engravings
Malotwana
Motsomi Lodge
Thaba Tholo Eco-park
Marula Game Lodge
Badger Bush
Smokey Mountain
Marakeli
Mokoro
Moro
Mahalapye
Ma
Wel

BOTSWANA
Limpopo
Maunatlala
Lotsane
Moeng
Sesulelo Mine
Lerala
Seleka
Sherwood
Martin's Drift 08:00 - 22:00
Grobler's Bridge
Mokobeng
Machaneng
Tom Burke
Bua Nnete
Bushmen Safari Camp Lodge
Marnitz
Marnitz Mini Town
Dale Luxury Lodge
Gaseleka
Beauty
Magenta Game Farm
Babala Lodge
Monte Christo
Limpopo Tented Camp
Sebe Sebe Lodge
Oranjefontein
Leeuwfontein Guesthouse
Tropic of Capricorn
Ons Hoop
De Kuile Accommodation
Lephalale (Ellisras)
Wildfig
Palm Park Hotel
Golf Course
Voëlparadys
Sheppard's Tree Lodge
Onverwacht
Molalatau
Steenbokpan
Afguns
Ntwane Game Farm
D'Nyala Game Reserve
Amsterdam Game Lodge
Villa Nora
Lamave Game Ranch
Thaba Monati Game Lodge
Zingela Game Farm
Overyssel
Marken
Tambotie Gastehuis
Bergsig Game Lodge
Alkantrant
Touchstone Game Ranch
Lapalala Nature Reserve
Lapalala Wilderness Game Reserve
Mogalakwenastroom
Zanzibar 08:00 - 16:00
Ruins
Usutu
Kopersspruit
Moshate Ranch Reserve
Zazoe Xperience Game Farm
Maasstroom
Al Te Ver Game Farm
Naga Game Lodge
Mareba Game Lodge
Swartwater
Lapland Game Farm
Zingela Game Ranch
Wag-'n-Bietjie Guest Farm
Bosveld Oase
Tolwe
African Hornbill Safaris Game Farm
Wonderkop NR
Baltimore
Bosveld Skerm Guesthouse
Woudkop
Phuduhudu Game Farm
Hard Times Game Farm
Eulalie Game Ranch
Steilwater
Steilloopbrug (Rebone)
Uitzicht
Groesbeek
Mokamole
Melkrivier
Waterberg Natuurpraal Holiday Resort
Aloe Ridge Game Lodge & Camp
Bokland
Emaweni Game Lodge
Witwater Lodge
Waterberg Game Park
Eagle Lodge
Sediba Lodge
Shenzi Safari Ranch
Tswana Game Farm
Kukama Game Farm
Mokolo Dam Game Reserve
Mokolo Dam
Mokolo Dam NR
Leopard Lodge & The Cubs
Kudu Canyon Game Farm
Elmeston
Jakkalspan
Jobedi Game Reserve
Malan Game Reserve
Panda Haven Game Farm
The Owl & Quill
Bushveld Retreat Resort
Ribbok
Hermanusdorings
Waterberg Farmstay
Taaibos Avonture
Rooibosbult
Manzi Game Lodge
Hainshaven Game Farm
Sentrum
Matlabas
Marakele National Park
Vaalwater
Thaba Meetse Game Ranch
In Africa Safaris
River Valley Guesthouse
Bundu Lodge
Little 5 Guesthouse
Daeraad
Vier-en-Twintig Riviere
Thaba Ya Tholo Bush Camp
Palala
Motsomi Lodge
Modikela
Tlopi
Nyala Lodge
Kololo Game Reserve
Equus Horse Safaris
Mashudu Lodge
Welgevonden Game Reserve
Bontle
Makoti's Nest Bush Camp
Marakeli
Waterkruin
Rankins Lodge
Rhenosterpoort
Alma
Smokey Mountain
Klein-Sand
Vanalphensvlei
Mineral Springs
Lekkerrus Holiday Resort
Libertas
Bothania Hills
Mokolo
Tambotie
Lephalala
Riet
Malmanies
Poer se Loop
Bulge
Mamba
Platbos
Sterkstroom
Matlabas
Dwars
Rietbokvlei
Sterk
AD
AE
AF
R510
R572
R561
R518
N11
R33
28
29
90
80
85

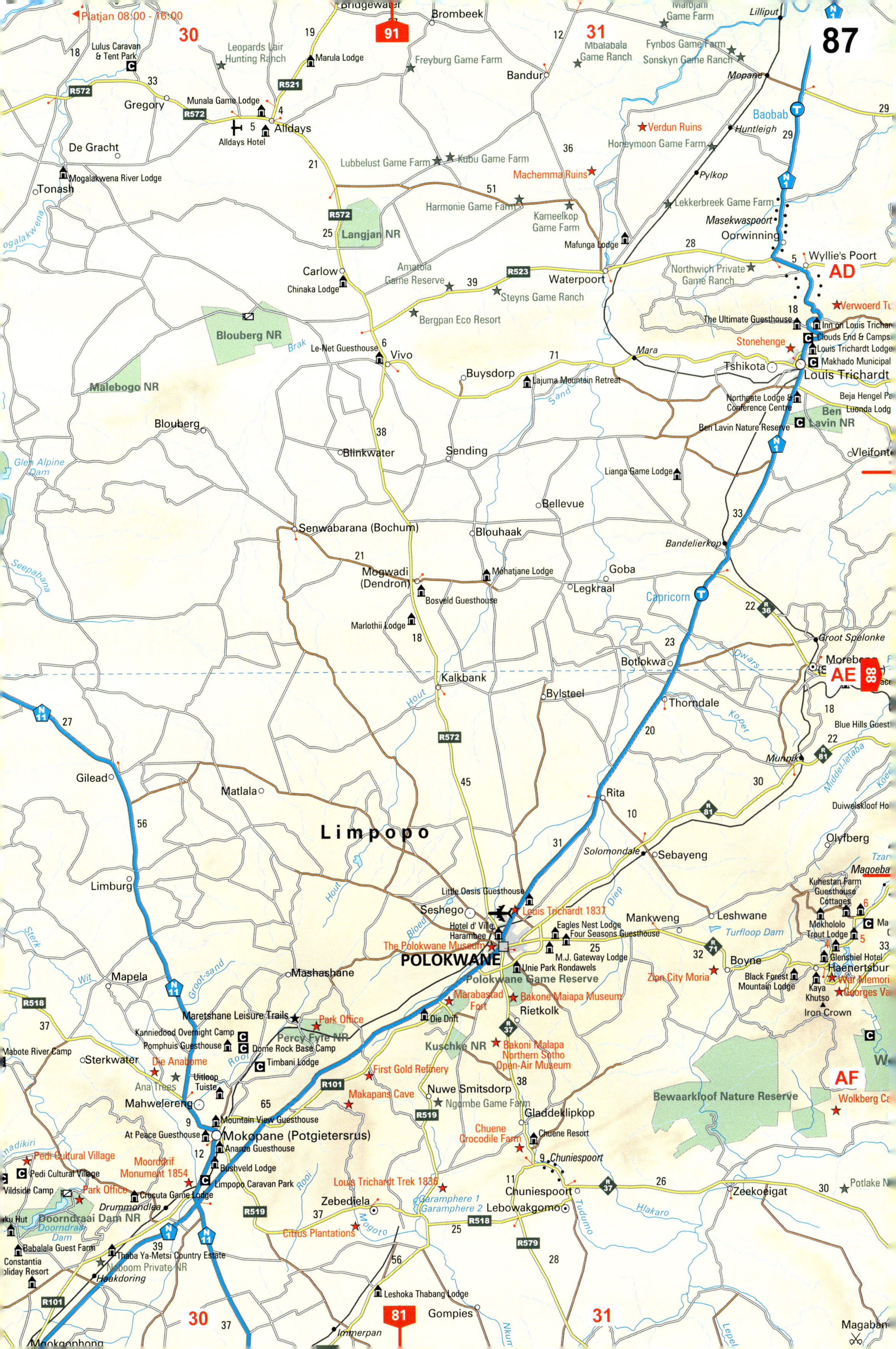
Platjan 08:00 - 16:00
30
31
91
Bridgewater
Brombeek
Lulus Caravan & Tent Park
Leopards Lair Hunting Ranch
Marula Lodge
Freyburg Game Farm
Mbalabala Game Ranch
Fynbos Game Farm
Sonskyn Game Ranch
Lilliput
Bandur
Mopane
Gregory
Munala Game Lodge
Alldays
Alldays Hotel
De Gracht
Baobab
Verdun Ruins
Huntleigh
Honeymoon Game Farm
Mogalakwena River Lodge
Tonash
Lubbelust Game Farm
Kubu Game Farm
Machemma Ruins
Pylkop
Harmonie Game Farm
Kameelkop Game Farm
Lekkerbreek Game Farm
Masekwaspoort
Oorwinning
Langjan NR
Mafunga Lodge
Wyllie's Poort
Carlow
Chinaka Lodge
Amatola Game Reserve
Waterpoort
Northwich Private Game Ranch
AD
Steyns Game Ranch
Bergpan Eco Resort
Verwoerd Tunnel
The Ultimate Guesthouse
Inn on Louis Trichardt
Clouds End & Campsite
Louis Trichardt Lodge
Makhado Municipal
Blouberg NR
Le-Net Guesthouse
Vivo
Mara
Stonehenge
Tshikota
Louis Trichardt
Buysdorp
Lajuma Mountain Retreat
Malebogo NR
Northgate Lodge & Conference Centre
Beja Hengel Park
Luonda Lodge
Ben Lavin NR
Ben Lavin Nature Reserve
Blouberg
Glen Alpine Dam
Blinkwater
Sending
Vleifontein
Lianga Game Lodge
Bellevue
Senwabarana (Bochum)
Blouhaak
Bandelierkop
Mogwadi (Dendron)
Mohatjane Lodge
Goba
Legkraal
Bosveld Guesthouse
Capricorn
Marlothii Lodge
Groot Spelonke
Morebeng
Botlokwa
AE
88
Kalkbank
Bylsteel
Thorndale
Blue Hills Guesthouse
Gilead
Munnik
Matlala
Rita
Duiwelskloof
Limpopo
Solomondale
Sebayeng
Olyfberg
Magoebaskloof
Limburg
Little Oasis Guesthouse
Kuhestan Farm Guesthouse Cottages
Seshego
Louis Trichardt 1837
Leshwane
Hotel d' Ville
Harambee
Eagles Nest Lodge
Mankweng
Four Seasons Guesthouse
Turfloop Dam
Mokhololo Trout Lodge
The Polokwane Museum
POLOKWANE
M.J. Gateway Lodge
Unie Park Rondawels
Boyne
Glenshiel Hotel
Haenertsburg
Polokwane Game Reserve
Zion City Moria
Black Forest Mountain Lodge
Kaya Khutso
War Memorial
Georges Valley
Mapela
Mashashane
Marabastad Fort
Bakone Malapa Museum
Rietkolk
Iron Crown
Maretshane Leisure Trails
Park Office
Percy Fyfe NR
Die Drift
Kanniedood Overnight Camp
Pomphuis Guesthouse
Dome Rock Base Camp
Kuschke NR
Bakoni Malapa Northern Sotho Open-Air Museum
Mabote River Camp
Sterkwater
Die Anabome
Timbani Lodge
Uitloop
Tuiste
First Gold Refinery
AF
Ana Trees
Nuwe Smitsdorp
Bewaarkloof Nature Reserve
Makapans Cave
Wolkberg Caves
Mahwelereng
Ngombe Game Farm
Gladdeklipkop
Mountain View Guesthouse
At Peace Guesthouse
Mokopane (Potgietersrus)
Ananza Guesthouse
Chuene Crocodile Farm
Chuene Resort
Pedi Cultural Village
Moorddrif Monument 1854
Bushveld Lodge
Chuniespoort
Limpopo Caravan Park
Louis Trichardt Trek 1836
Vildside Camp
Park Office
Crocuta Game Lodge
Chuniespoort
Zeekoeigat
Potlake NR
Drummondlea
Zebediela
Garamphere 1
Garamphere 2
Lebowakgomo
Doorndraai Dam NR
Doorndraai Dam
Citrus Plantations
Babalala Guest Farm
Thaba Ya-Metsi Country Estate
Constantia Holiday Resort
Nyl-boom Private NR
Haakdoring
Leshoka Thabang Lodge
Gompies
81
Magabane
Immerpan
Mookgophong

Lilliput
32
Baobab Private Nature Reserve
92
Sagole Spa
Serena
Limpopo
33
Kruger National Park
Riamana Lodge
Forever Resorts
Tshipise
Nwanedi GR
Mopane
Aventura Tshipise
Bushbaby Lodge
Honnet GR
Protea Hotel Nwanedi
Nwanedzi Dam
Gundi Mutsiwa
Baobab
Huntleigh
Witsand Waterhole
Golwe
Punda Maria Camp
Coetser Waterhole
Punda Maria Gate
Mhinga
Nzhelele Dam
Dzata Ruins
Lake Fundudzi
Orwinning
AD
Wyllie's Poort
Nzhelele
R523
Mutshindudi
Sidou Lodge
R524
Xigalo
Thohoyandou
Eagles Rest Caravan Park
Verwoerd Tunnels
Ultimate Guesthouse
Inn on Louis Trichardt
The Goose & Labrador
Stonehenge
Clouds End & Campsite
Louis Trichardt Lodge
Luvuvhu
Mavamba
Malamulele
Phugwane
Tshikota
Makhado Municipal
Khaya Guesthouse
Lalani Lodge
Tshakhuma
Ratombo
Louis Trichardt (Makhado)
Albasini Dam
Levubu
Northgate Lodge & Conference Centre
Beja Hengel Paradys
Albasini Dam
Hippo Park Lodge
Ben Lavin NR
Luonda Lodge
Shiluvari Lakeside Lodge
Borchers
Lavin Nature Reserve
Elim
Vuwani
Muswani
Kojalingo
Shangoni
Mambedi Country Lodge
Vleifontein
R578
Nsami Dam
Mhangys Rock Resort
Amukelani Caravan And Fishing Camp
Babangu
Ha-Magoro
Midletaba Resort
Oasis Lodge
Xisaka Guesthouse
Giyani
Mopani Guesthouse
Middel-Letaba Dam
Mamaila
Nsama
Nwanedzi
Groot Spelonke
Nkomo
African Ivory Route Camp
Lornadawn Dam
Hildreth Ridge
Morebeng (Soekmekaar)
AE
87
Magnab Lodge
Meg's Place
Molototsi
Klein-Letaba
Byashishi
Limpopo
Dzumeri
Blue Hills Guesthouse
Mooketsi
Brandboontjies
Ga-Modjadji
Modjadji NR
Modjadji Palms (Cycads)
R529
Eiland
Mineral Springs
Eiland Spa & Eco Park
Mahlangeni
Munnik
Middel-Letaba
Koedoes
Modjadjiskloof (Duiwelskloof)
Duiwelskloof Holiday Resort
Modjadjiskloof Road Camp
Maleketla
Hans Merensky NR
La Cotte
Gecko Lodge
Stonehaven Lodge
Olyfberg
Politsi
Tzaneen Dam
Magoebaskloof
Die Stoep
Hlangana
Ndzalama Wildlife Reserve
Kuhestan Farm Guesthouse Cottages
Lavenir Manor Guesthouse
Ivory Tusk Lodge
Bushveld
Tzaneen
Tzaneen Country Lodge
De Neck Private NR
Mulati
Lulekani
Leshwane
Tamboti Lodge
Maxims Guesthouse
Satvik Backpackers
Mashutti Country Lodge
Letsitele
Mokhololo Trout Lodge
Magoebaskloof Getaway
Flamboyant Guesthouse
Turfloop Dam
R528
Kings Walden Lodge
Mountain Glen Guesthouse
Mulati
Glenshiel Hotel
Haenertsburg
Namakgale
Phalaborwa
Boyne
War Memorial
Baobab Tree
Gravelotte
Selati River Lodge
Inge Park
Black Forest Mountain Lodge
Georges Valley
New Agatha Plantation
Leisitele
Thabina
Leydsdorp
Ga-selati
Selati Game Reserve
Kaya Khutso
Iron Crown
R526
San Wild Game Farm
Cycad Reserve
Wolkberg NR
Pidwa Wilderness Reserve
Tintshaba Game Lodge
Tulani
Mfubu
AF
Nature Reserve
Pioneer Graves
Ofcolaco
Makutsi Conservancy
Darisandi
Wolkberg Caves
The Downs
Makalali Resource Reserve
Mica
Ramulutsi's Grave
Trichardtsdal
Nyati safari Lodge
Legalameetse NR
Sorabi Rock Lodge
Edeni
Tantis Game Lodge
1 Baobab Tree (AF 33)
2 Khamai Reptile Park (AF 33)
3 Swadini Reptile Park (AF 33)
4 Cheerio Farm Trout Fishing Lodge Stanford Lake Lodge (AF 32)
5 Magoebaskloof Hotel Pot & Plough (AF 32)
6 Magoebaskloof Ruskamp Mountain Lodge (AF 32)
Makutsi Safari Farm
Balule NR
Klaserie NR
Ingwe Game Lodge
Hippo Pools
Mohlabetsi Safari Lodge
Tremisana Game Lodge
Klaserie NR
Mohlapitse
R525
Ekutheleni
Phuza Moya
Lissataba
Zeekoeigat
Potlake Nature Reserve
Blyde Olifants Conservancy
Tshukudu Bush Lodge
Dithaba Game Lodge
Mokwalo White Lions
Motse
Monsoon Gallery
Boulders
Hoedspruit
EASTGATE
Dublin Farm Cottages
Thekwane Arts & Crafts
Loerie Guest House
Raptor's Lodge
Landela Lodge
Thornybush Lodge
Diphuti
Kokkariba
Clivia Cottage
Kapama GR
Chapungu Lodge
Penge
The Trading Post
Otters Den
Manoutsa Park
Manoutsa Park
Zuleika Country House
R531
Elephant Inn
Ruimte
Gwala Gwala
J.G. Strijdom Tunnel
Hoedspruit Cheetah Project
Mariepsig
Lerato
Marepe Lodge
Buffalo Camp
Madumu Boma
32
82
Kwa Thabeng
33
Magabaneng
Moopetsi
Duiwel
Old Coach Road
Trackers
Hoedspruit Cheetah Project
Nikkis

MOZAMBIQUE
Great Limpopo Transfrontier Park
Parque Nacional do Limpopo
Parque Nacional de Banhine
Kruger National Park
Limpopo
Umbabat NR
Timbavati GR
Tropic of Capricorn
Mapai
Dothole
Regua
S. Jorge de Limpopo
Vimioso
Combom
Lagoa Nova
Massingir
Barragem de Massingir
Ndunzi
Giriyondo
Letaba
Engelhard Dam
Olifants
Balule
Roodewaal
Satara
N'wanetsi
Mapulanguene
Shingwedzi
Kanniedood Dam
Mopani
Mooi Plaas
Boulders
Shimuwini Bushveld Camp
Lonely Bull
Bateleur Bushveld Camp
Northern Plains Adventure Trail
Nonokani Adventure Trail
Mananga Adventure Trail
Masorini Museum
Mamba
Ingwelala
Kings Camp
Motswari Game Lodge
Gomo Gomo Game Lodge
Tanda Tula
Umlani Lodge
Kambaku Lodge
Ngala Game Lodge
Ndabushi Lodge
Inkasi Lodge
Maroela Caravan Park
Orpen
Tamboti Tented
Babalala Picnic Place
Baobab Hill
Picnic Site
Middelvlei Waterhole
Jumbo Waterhole
Nwanetsi Waterhole
Marhumbyeni Waterhole
Shivhulani Waterhole
Ntomeni Waterhole
Frasers Rus Waterhole
Shidlayengwenya Waterhole
Bowkers Kop Waterhole
Olifantsbad Waterhole
Nkokodzi Waterhole
Silver Vis Waterhole
Red Rocks Waterhole
Lamont Waterhole
Nwarihlanggari Waterhole
Boyela Waterhole
Magamba Waterhole
Mandadzidzi Waterhole
Nkovakulu Waterhole
Mazanje Waterhole
Mashikhiri Waterhole
Kremetart Waterhole
Limpopo
Singuedeze
Shingwidzi
Shisha
Letaba
Shimuwini Dam
Elefantes
Pumeni Dam
Nwanedzi
Sweni
Mazimechopes
Ngwamutsatsa Viewpoint
Wildlife Research
Thornybush GR
AD
AE
AF
34
35
93
83
H1-7
H1-6
H1-5
H1-4
H14
H-9
H7
H6

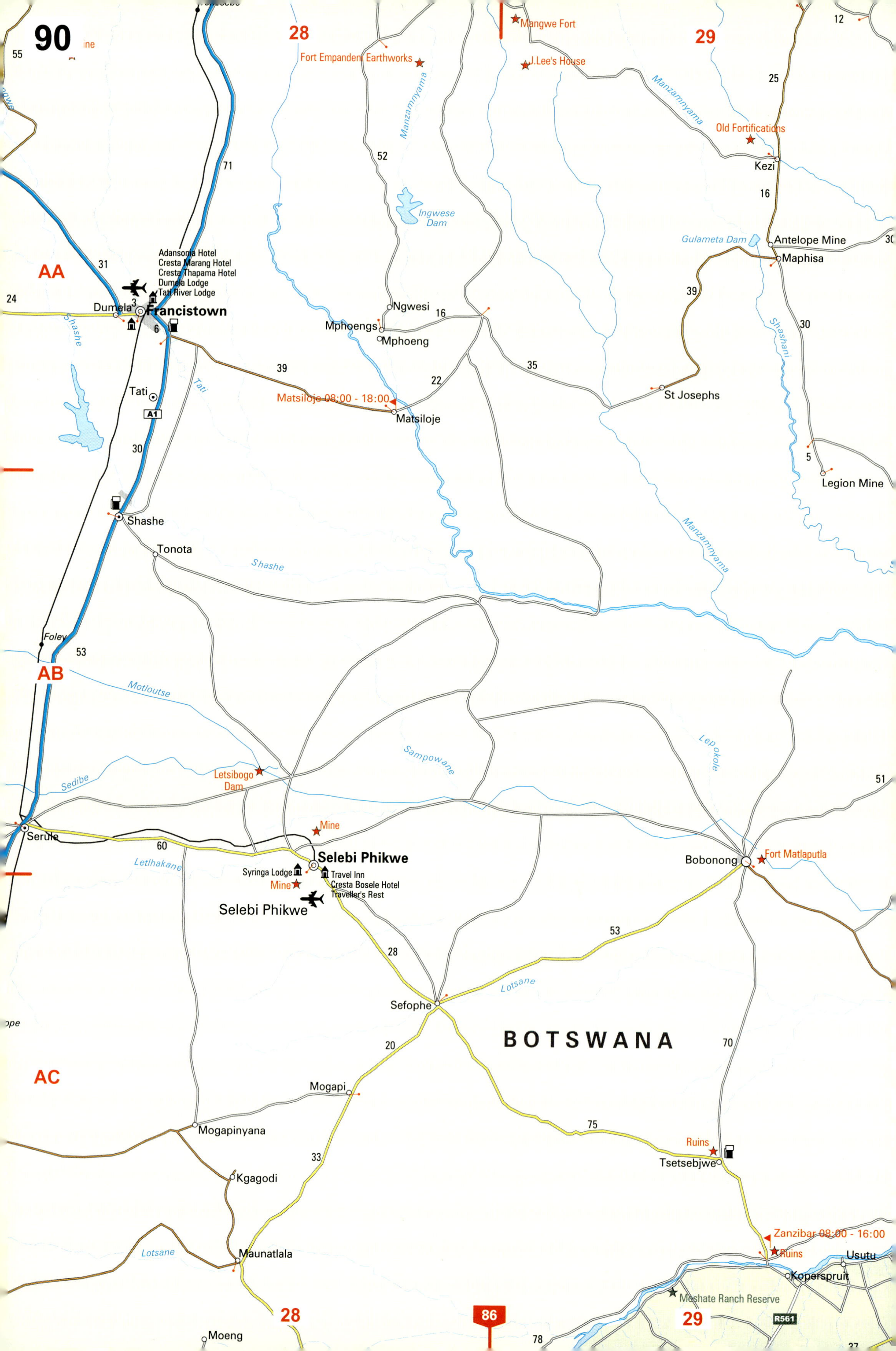
28
Fort Empandeni Earthworks
Mangwe Fort
J.Lee's House
29
Manzamnyama
Old Fortifications
Kezi
Ingwese Dam
Gulameta Dam
Antelope Mine
Maphisa
AA
Adansonia Hotel
Cresta Marang Hotel
Cresta Thapama Hotel
Dumela Lodge
Tati River Lodge
Dumela
Francistown
Shashe
Ngwesi
Mphoengs
Mphoeng
Tati
A1
Matsiloje 08:00 - 18:00
Matsiloje
St Josephs
Shashani
Legion Mine
Shashe
Tonota
Foley
AB
Motloutse
Sedibe
Letsibogo Dam
Sampowane
Lepokole
Serule
Mine
Selebi Phikwe
Syringa Lodge
Travel Inn
Cresta Bosele Hotel
Traveller's Rest
Bobonong
Fort Matlaputla
Letlhakane
Lotsane
Sefophe
BOTSWANA
AC
Mogapi
Mogapinyana
Kgagodi
Ruins
Tsetsebjwe
Zanzibar 08:00 - 16:00
Ruins
Usutu
Maunatlala
Lotsane
Kopersspruit
Meshate Ranch Reserve
R561
28
Moeng
29

86

ZIMBABWE
Limpopo
Gwanda
Colleen Bawn
West Nicholson
Silalabuhwa
Masase
Chegat
Makwe Dam
Ruins
Mchelu Cave National Monument
Cave of Hands
Pioneer Crossing
Tamba
Makado
Taula
Guyu
Manama
Hwali
Mazunga
Semolale
Tuli
Fort Tuli
Tuli Safari Area
Pioneer Memorial
Giraffe Petroglyph
1 Maloutswa Game Hide (AC 31)
2 Little Muck Game Hide (AC 30)
Nottingham Dam
Northern Tuli Conservation Area
Tuli Lodge
Mashatu Lodge
Rhodes Drift Lodge
Limpopo Forest
Vhembe Wilderness Camp
Leokwe Restcamp
Museum & Interpretation Centre
Mapungubwe National Park
Tshugulu Lodge
Little Muck Lodge
Mopanie Camp
Rakwena Crocodile Farm
Reptile Footprints
Ratho Bush Camp
Pont Drif 08:00 - 16:00
Dongola Ranch
Klein Bolayi Game Lodge
Beitbridge
Nancefield
Kuzingela Safaris Game Farm
Char-Man Game Farm
Elephant Trunk Tree
Mmamagwe Ruins
Ostrolenka Lodge & Game Farm
Evangelina Game Lodge
Evangelina
Muvhuyu Lodge
Kamkusi
Oasis Lodge
Baines' Drift
Dumukwa Lodge
Bivack Game Lodge
Platjan 08:00 - 16:00
Bridgewater
Brombeek
Mafojani Game Farm
Lilliput
Lulus Caravan & Tent Park
Leopards Lair Hunting Ranch
Marula Lodge
Freyburg Game Farm
Mbalabala Game Ranch
Fynbos Game Farm
Sonskyn Game Ranch
Bandur
Mopane
Gregory
Alldays
Baobab
Huntleigh
Verdun Ruins
Shashe
Tuli
Insiza
Umzingwani
Bubi
R572
R521
A6
N1
AA
AB 92
AC
30
31
87

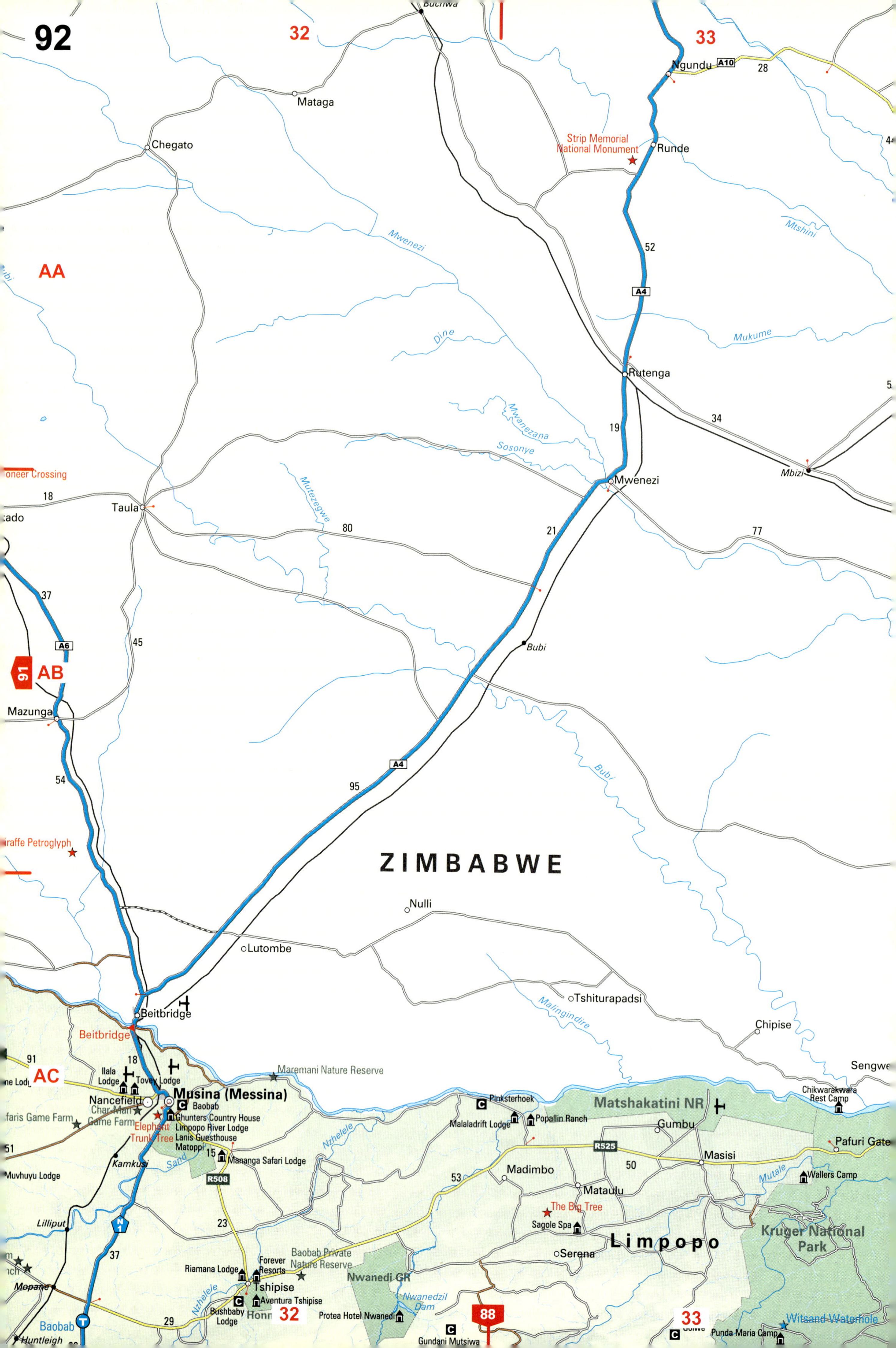

32
33
Buchwa
Ngundu
A10
28
Mataga
Chegato
Strip Memorial National Monument
Runde
Mtshini
52
A4
AA
Mwenezi
Dine
Mukume
Rutenga
Mwanezana
Sosonye
19
34
Pioneer Crossing
Mutezegwe
Mwenezi
Mbizi
18
Taula
80
21
77
37
A6
45
Bubi
91
AB
Mazunga
A4
Bubi
54
95
Giraffe Petroglyph
ZIMBABWE
Nulli
Lutombe
Tshiturapadsi
Malingindire
Beitbridge
Beitbridge
Chipise
Sengwe
91
18
AC
Ilala Lodge
Tovey Lodge
Maremani Nature Reserve
Pinksterhoek
Chikwarakwara Rest Camp
Nancefield
Musina (Messina)
Baobab
Char-Mari Game Farm
Ghunters Country House
Limpopo River Lodge
Lanis Guesthouse
Matoppi
Elephant Trunk Tree
Malaladrift Lodge
Popallin Ranch
Matshakatini NR
Gumbu
15
Mananga Safari Lodge
Sand
Nzhelele
R525
Pafuri Gate
Masisi
Kamkusi
50
Muvhuyu Lodge
R508
53
Madimbo
Mataulu
Mutale
Wallers Camp
The Big Tree
Lilliput
23
Sagole Spa
Kruger National Park
N1
Limpopo
37
Serena
Baobab Private Nature Reserve
Forever Resorts
Riamana Lodge
Nwanedi GR
Mopane
Tshipise
Aventura Tshipise
Nwanedzi Dam
Nzhelele
Bushbaby Lodge
32
88
33
Protea Hotel Nwanedi
Witsand Waterhole
Baobab
29
Huntleigh
Gundani Mutsiwa
Punda Maria Camp

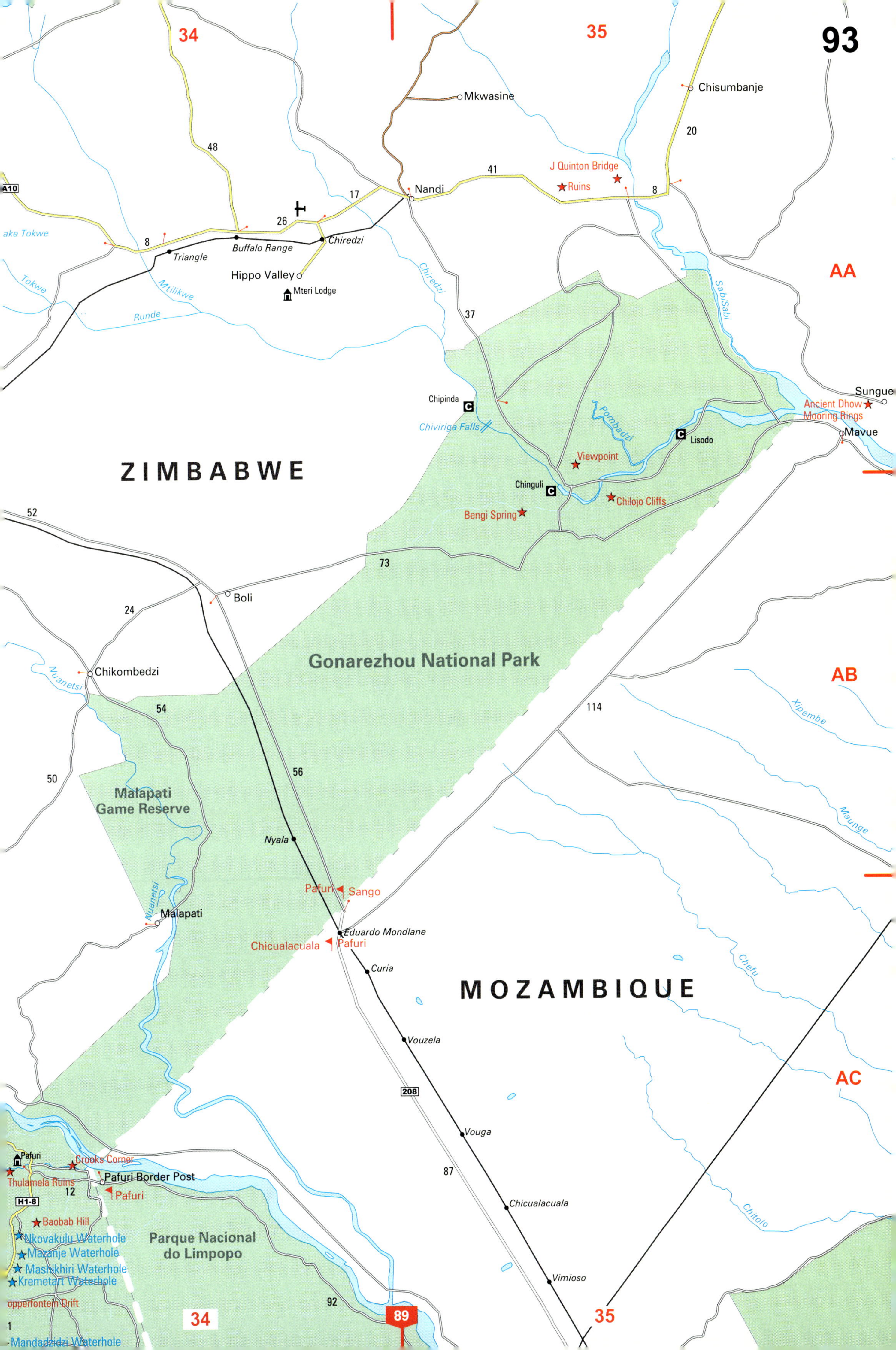

34
35
Mkwasine
Chisumbanje
20
48
J Quinton Bridge
Ruins
8
41
Nandi
17
A10
26
Chiredzi
Buffalo Range
Triangle
8
ake Tokwe
Hippo Valley
Mteri Lodge
Tokwe
Mtilikwe
Runde
Chiredzi
37
Sabi
Sabi
AA
Sungue
Ancient Dhow
Mooring Rings
Mavue
Chipinda
Chivirira Falls
Pombadzi
Lisodo
Viewpoint
ZIMBABWE
Chinguli
Chilojo Cliffs
Bengi Spring
52
73
Boli
24
Chikombedzi
Nuanetsi
Gonarezhou National Park
AB
Xipembe
54
114
50
56
Malapati
Game Reserve
Maunge
Nyala
Pafuri
Sango
Malapati
Nuanetsi
Eduardo Mondlane
Chicualacuala
Pafuri
Curia
MOZAMBIQUE
Chefu
Vouzela
208
AC
Vouga
Pafuri
Crooks Corner
Thulamela Ruins
Pafuri Border Post
12
Pafuri
87
H1-8
Baobab Hill
Nkovakulu Waterhole
Mazanje Waterhole
Mashikhiri Waterhole
Kremetart Waterhole
Parque Nacional
do Limpopo
Chicualacuala
Chitolo
Vimioso
92
89
34
35
1
Mandadzidzi Waterhole

CAPE TOWN

Western Cape

CAPE TOWN

ATLANTIC OCEAN

Table Bay

M 250 500

Mouille Point
Granger Bay
Green Point
Three Anchor Bay
Sea Point
Fresnaye
Tamboers kloof
Schotsche Kloof
Malay Quarter
De Waterkant
Victoria & Alfred Waterfront
Foreshore
Zonnebloem (District Six)
Devil's Peak Estate
Vredehoek
Oranjezicht
Gardens
Camps Bay
LION'S RUMP
TABLE MOUNTAIN
DEVIL'S PEAK
Signal Hill 350m
Noon Gun
Green Point Common
Three Anchor Bay Sports Ground
Company's Garden
Gardens Football Ground
De Waal Park
Molteno Reservoir
Mocke Reservoir
Victoria Basin
Alfred Basin
Robinson Dock
Duncan Dock
Granger Bay
Breakwater

Mouille Point Lighthouse
Viewpoint
Parking
Cape Peninsula University of Technology (Granger Bay Campus)
Granger Bay Yacht Club
Cape Town Stadium
Fort Wynyard
Theatre@ The Pavilion
Somerset
Telkom Exploratorium
UCT Graduate School of Business
Weekend Market
Cape Medical Museum
Victoria Wharf
Buses to City
Ferryman's Tavern
Quay Four
Helicopter Flights
Nelson Mandela Gateway to Robben Island
Waterfront Clocktower Precinct
Two Oceans Aquarium
Art & Craft Market
Waterfront Theatre School
Waterfront Residential Marina
Cruise Ship Berths
Library
De Goede Verwachting Museum
Cape Town International Convention Centre
Incomplete Flyover
Diaz Statue
Tulbagh Square
Martin Melck House
Heritage Square
Riebeeck Square
Van Riebeeck Statue
Thibault Square
Artscape
Bo-Kaap Museum
Barnard Memorial
Greenmarket Square
Old Town House
Golden Acre
Inter-City Bus Terminus & Information
Civic Centre
Flower Market
Cape Town Railway Station
Fruit & Vegetable Market
Grand Parade
City Hall
Castle of Good Hope
Long-Distance Minibus' Terminals
St George's Cathedral
SA Library
Supreme Court
Houses of Parliament
City Library
Good Hope Centre
Magistrates' Court
District Six Museum
Long Street Turkish Baths
De Tuynhuys
SA Museum Planetarium
Bertha Statue
Automobile Association
National Art Gallery
Rust en Vreugd
Cape Town Holocaust Centre
Labia Cinema
New Holland Publishing
State Archives
Cape Peninsula University of Technology
Gardens Shopping Centre
Wembley Square
Cape Town Fire Station
Welgemoed
Waterfront
Cape Town Medi-Clinic
Booth Memorial Hospital
Pump House
Leeuwenhof & Bo-Tuin
Carlucci's Restaurant
Champers Restaurant
Yum Restaurant
Fresnaye Sports Club
Sea Point Pavilion

5 km Walkway
Western Blvd / Helen Suzman Blvd
Main
High Level
Signal Hill Hiking Trail
Table Bay Boulevard
Buitengracht
Long
Strand
Adderley
Darling
Orange
Kloof Nek
De Waal
Upper Orange

SEE INSET

TO PAARL
TO CAPE TOWN INTERNATIONAL AIRPORT
TO NEWLANDS
TO CAMPS BAY/HOUT BAY

6 61 62 60 3

TABLE MOUNTAIN NATIONAL PARK

Km 3 6

Thermopylae 1899
Table Bay
TO MALMESBURY
Canal Walk
Athens 1865
SA Seafarer 1966
Lighthouse
Victoria & Alfred Waterfront
R27
M5
N1
M7
TO BELLVILLE
Cape Town Stadium
Noon Gun
Cape Town International Convention Centre
Three Anchor Bay
Sea Point
SIGNAL HILL
N1
R102
GrandWest Casino
Bantry Bay
Lion's Head
670m
Castle of Good Hope
N2
SA Astronomical Observatory
Clifton Bay
Camps Bay
M6
Camps Bay
Cable Car
Rhodes Memorial
N2
Theatre on the Bay
TABLE MOUNTAIN
Devil's Peak 1001m
TO CAPE TOWN INTERNATIONAL AIRPORT / SOMERSET WEST
Het Huis te Kraaiestein 1698
Bellsfontein Kramat
Orion's Cave
TWELVE APOSTLES
Kirstenbosch National Botanical Garden
Antipolis 1977
Boshof Gateway
M5
M17
Ouderkraal
M6
Table Mountain National Park
Van Riebeeck's Hedge
Kenilworth Race Course
M9
Llandudno Bay
Little Lion's Head
World of Birds
Romelia 1977
436m
M63
CONSTANTIABERG
Alphen 1714
Maynardville Open Air Theatre
Sandy Bay
Constantia
M41
Ouder Schip
Suther Peak 614m
Groot Constantia 1685
Maori 1909
Boss 400
Hout Bay
Mariner's Wharf
The Leopard
M42
M3
M41
M5
Karbonkelberg Sanctuary Zone
Hout Bay
Constantiaberg
928m
The Lonely Bridge
Rondevlei
Zeekoevlei
Duiker Island
West Fort 1781
M6
Elephant's Eye Cave
Astor
Vulcan Rock
Katzmaru 1970
Spotty Dog
Rondevlei Bird Sanctuary
Die Josie
Tokai Forest
Chapman's Peak 592m
Higher Steenberg Peak
M4
M5
Chapman's Point
537m
Muizenberg Cave
R310
Noordhoek Toll Booth
Silvermine 1687
M6
Silvermine Nature Reserve
Muizenberg
ATLANTIC OCEAN
Chapman's Bay
Tunnel Cave
Peer's Cave
Neptune's Corner
Rhodes Cottage
Kalk Bay Cave
Tidal Lagoon
Kakapo 1900
Trappies Caves
Klein Slangkop Point
Kommetjie Bay
M65
Fish Hoek
False Bay
Slangkop Point
M65
Fish Hoek Bay
Kommetjie Lighthouse
Rooikrans 364m
Else Peak 303m
Skeleton Rock
Clan Munroe 1905
Slangkop 174m
Else Bay
The Anchor
Hartenberg Circa 1730
M4
Simon's Town
Clan Stuart 1914
Table Mountain National Park
Lighthouse
Roman Rock
Die Eiland
Simon's Bay
Phoenix 1829
Witsand Bay
Camel Rock
Red Hill 256m
Just Nuisance Statue
Schuster's Bay
Schusterskraal
Simonsberg 548m
SWARTKOP MOUNTAINS
Bonteberg 227m
M4
Miller's Point
Lookout Post
Dassiekop 314m
Menskop Point
M65
Olifantsbos Bay
Olifantsbos Cottage
Viewpoint
Smitswinkel Bay
Thomas T Tucker 1942
Judas Peak 319m
Blaasbalk Cave
Nolloth 1965
Table Mountain National Park
Old Cannon
Phyllisia 1968
Kommetjieberg
Da Gama Monument 1497
Bordjiesrif
Hoek van Bobbejaan
114m
Dias Monument 1488
107m
Tania 1972
Matroosskop
Bloubergstrand
GROOT-BLOUBERG
Viewpoint
Rooikrans
Platboom Bay
Viewpoint
Lighthouse
Cape Point
Cape of Good Hope
Shir-Yib 1970

KIRSTENBOSCH NATIONAL BOTANICAL GARDEN

Kirstenbosch National Botanical Garden
TO SKELETON GORGE
Yellowwood Trail
Skeleton
Stinkwood Trail
Nursery Stream
Fynbos Walk
Reservoirs (No Access)
Proteas
Braille
Education Centre
Smuts Track
Fynbos Walk
Buchus
Toilets
Garden Centre
Gate 2 Garden Centre Entrance
Proteas
Ericas
Bookshop
Parking
The Koppie
Lecture Hall
Irrigation Dam (No Entry)
Cycads
Toilets
Tea Room
Lawn
Pearson House
Xhosa Hut
Water-wise Garden
Colonel Bird's Bath
Window
TO CAPE TOWN
Useful Plants
Fragrance Garden
Peninsula Garden
Vlei Garden
NBI Admin Office
Pearson's Grave
Toilets
Medicinal Plants
Mathew's Rockery
Garden Vygies
Pond
Silver Tree Restaurant & Deli
Sculpture Garden
Nedbank Lodge
Fynbos Lodge
Seed Orchard
Restios
Concert Stage
Annuals
Info & tickets
Parking
Van Riebeeck's Hedge
Gate 1 Visitor's Centre Entrance
Toilets
M63
Coffee Shop
Church of the Good Shepherd
TO HOUT BAY
Gate 3 Rycroft Entrance
Conservatory
Visitor's Centre
Liesbeek
Bookshop
Gift Shop
Nursery (no entry)
Rhodes Drive
M63
Toilets
Garden Office
Rhodes Drive
Parking
Klaassen's Road
The Garden is open all year
08:00 – 19:00 (Sept to Mar)
08:00 – 18:00 (Apr to Aug)

BLOEMFONTEIN

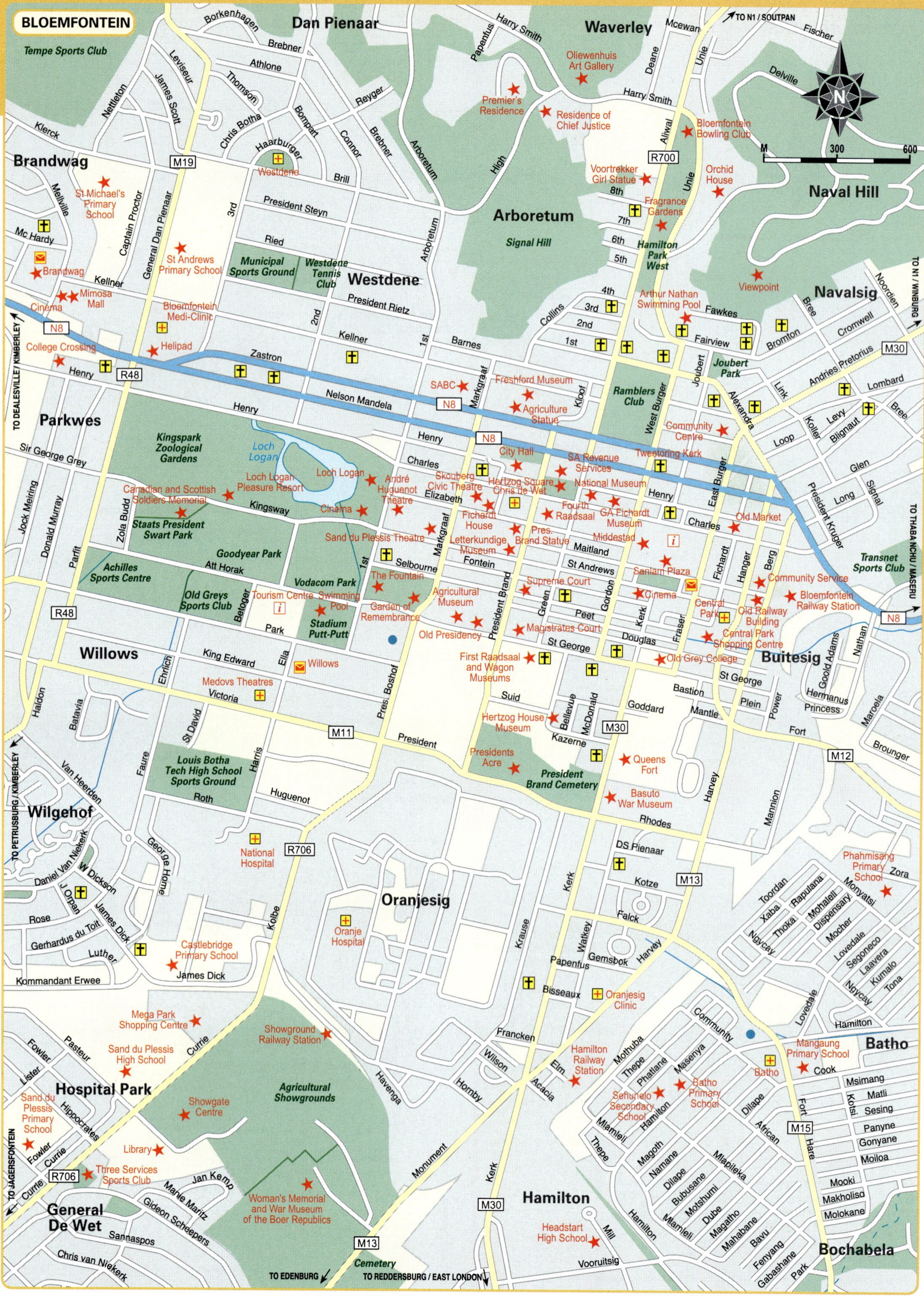

Free State

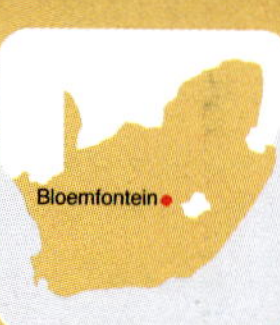

BLOEMFONTEIN

Dan Pienaar
Waverley
Brandwag
Westdene
Arboretum
Signal Hill
Naval Hill
Navalsig
Parkwes
Willows
Wilgehof
Oranjesig
Hospital Park
General De Wet
Hamilton
Batho
Bochabela
Buitesig

Tempe Sports Club
Oliewenhuis Art Gallery
Premier's Residence
Residence of Chief Justice
Bloemfontein Bowling Club
Voortrekker Girl Statue
Orchid House
Fragrance Gardens
Hamilton Park West
Arthur Nathan Swimming Pool
Viewpoint
Joubert Park
Ramblers Club
St Michael's Primary School
St Andrews Primary School
Municipal Sports Ground
Westdene Tennis Club
Westdene
Brandwag
Cinema
Mimosa Mall
Bloemfontein Medi-Clinic
College Crossing
Helipad
Freshford Museum
SABC
Agriculture Statue
Community Centre
Tweetoring Kerk
Kingspark Zoological Gardens
Loch Logan
Loch Logan Pleasure Resort
André Huguenot Theatre
Skouberg Civic Theatre
Hertzog Square Chris de Wet
City Hall
SA Revenue Services
National Museum
Fourth Raadsaal
GA Fichardt Museum
Fichardt House
Pres. Brand Statue
Middestad
Old Market
Canadian and Scottish Soldiers Memorial
Staats President Swart Park
Sand du Plessis Theatre
Letterkundige Museum
Sanlam Plaza
Transnet Sports Club
Community Service
Bloemfontein Railway Station
Achilles Sports Centre
Goodyear Park
Vodacom Park
The Fountain
Supreme Court
Cinema
Central Park
Old Railway Building
Central Park Shopping Centre
Old Greys Sports Club
Tourism Centre
Swimming Pool
Stadium Putt-Putt
Garden of Remembrance
Agricultural Museum
Magistrates Court
Old Presidency
Old Grey College
First Raadsaal and Wagon Museums
Willows
Medovs Theatres
Hertzog House Museum
Presidents Acre
President Brand Cemetery
Queens Fort
Basuto War Museum
Louis Botha Tech High School Sports Ground
National Hospital
Oranje Hospital
Phahamisang Primary School
Castlebridge Primary School
Oranjesig Clinic
Mega Park Shopping Centre
Showground Railway Station
Sand du Plessis High School
Hamilton Railway Station
Mangaung Primary School
Batho
Batho Primary School
Sehunelo Secondary School
Agricultural Showgrounds
Showgate Centre
Sand du Plessis Primary School
Library
Three Services Sports Club
Woman's Memorial and War Museum of the Boer Republics
Headstart High School
Cemetery

N1 N8 M19 R48 R700 M30 M11 M12 M13 R706 M15

TO N1 / SOUTPAN
TO N1 / WINBURG
TO THABA NCHU / MASERU
TO DEALESVILLE / KIMBERLEY
TO PETRUSBURG / KIMBERLEY
TO JAGERSFONTEIN
TO EDENBURG
TO REDDERSBURG / EAST LONDON

M 300 600

DURBAN

TO KING SHAKA INTERNATIONAL AIRPORT
TO DURBAN NORTH
TO NORTH COAST
TO N2
TO PIETERMARITZBURG
TO UMBILO INDUSTRIAL
TO SOUTH COAST
TO USHAKA MARINE WORLD

M 250 500

INDIAN OCEAN
Bay of Plenty
Bay of Natal

Windermere
Stamford
Greyville
Kingsmead
Central
Congella
Point

Durban Preparatory School
Windermere Shopping Centre
Moses Mabhida Stadium
King's Park Olympic Swimming Pool
Water World
Village Green
Animal Farm
German School
Little Chelsea
Clarence Primary School
Durban Drive-In
Durban Bowling Club
Queen's Tavern
Game City Shopping Centre
Bechet Training College
Royal Durban Golf Course
Durban Railway Station
Parking
Durban Fire Station
Magistrates' Court
Mangrove Beach Shopping Centre
Snake Park
Minitown
Amphitheatre
Baseball Park
Hoy Park
Greyville Race Course
DLI Hall
Municipal Sports Ground
Superior College of Education
St Augustine Primary School
Futura Secondary School
St Anthony's Catholic Private Aided School
DUT (ML Sultan Campus)
Orient Islamic Educational Institution
Currie's Fountain Sports Ground
Durban Girls' School
Department of Transport
St Adens
Central Fire Station
DUT (Steve Biko Campus)
Traffic Department
Old Fort Clinic
Archie Gumede
Old Fort & Warrior's Gate
Kingsmead Cricket Ground
SABC
UNISA
Durban Jewish Club
Exhibition Hall
Durban Indoor Sports Centre
Conservation Centre
KwaMuhle Museum
Exhibition Centre
Inkosi Albert Luthuli International Convention Centre & Arena
Library
Paddling Pools
Funworld
Victoria Park
Stable Theatre
Surat Hindoo Primary School
Buses
Central Park
South Plaza Market
The Workshop Shopping Centre
Varsity School
Whyallis Camera Museum
Berea Rd Railway Station
Victoria Street Market
Juma Musjid Mosque
African Art Centre
Durban Academy of Learning
Medwood Gardens
History Museum
Lancet Clinic
Muthi Market
Durban Chest Clinic
West Street Cemetery
St James College
Damelin College
Francis Farewell Gardens
City Hall
Natal Playhouse Theatre
Cambridge College
GA Riches Building
City Market
Botha Gardens
Durdoc Clinic
Quadrant House
The Wheel Shopping Complex
Trampolines
Little Top Theatre
Durban University of Technology
Victoria Embankment
Dick King Statue
Maritime Museum
Da Gama Clock
Department of Customs & Excise
Addington
Point Clinic
Pleasure Cruises
Point Yacht Club
Supreme Court
Old House Museum
Albert Park Clinic
Albert Park
Royal Natal Yacht Club
Gardiner St Jetty
BAT Centre Museum
Small Craft Harbour
Sugar Terminal

Oasis Beach
Battery Beach II
Battery Beach I
Snake Park Beach
Somtseu Road Pier
Bay of Plenty Pier
North Beach
North Beach Pier
Dairy Beach Pier
Dairy Beach
Wedge Beach
West St Jetty
South Beach
Yacht Mole
Wilson's Wharf
Fish Wharf
Fishing Boat Jetty
Sugar Wharf
Ocean Terminal
R Berth
Q Berth
P Berth
T Berth
H Berth
L Berth
G Berth

Springfield
Montpelier
Gordon
Claribell
Churchill
Millar
Poynton
Madeline
Florida
Eighth North
Seventh North
Mckenzie
Harvey
Linkway
Bishop
Roadknight
Heathrow
Shepstone
Guildford
12th
11th
Clarence
Lilian Ngoyi
Silver
Steel
Oldham
Ivy
Umgeni
Walls
Henwood
Sandile Thusi
Currie
Holstead Gdns
Problem Mkhize
10th
9th
Avondale
7th
6th
5th
4th
3rd
Florida
Lennox
Findlay
Oblate
Linze
St Marys
Mathews Meyiwa
Gladys Mazibuko
Linden
Esselmont
Haden
Mitchell
Second
Fir
Walkers
Kent
Daly
Kolling
Marriott
Milner
Madras
John Zikhali
DLI
Osborne
Fynn
Gladys Manzi
May
Jeff Taylor
Newmarket
Ascot
Epsom
Mansel
Derby
Carlisle
Ismail C Meer
Maude
Charlotte Maxeke
Grey
Fountain
Ingcuce
M I Sultan
Market
Cross
Steve Biko
Alice
Chris Ntuli
David Webster
Short
Dr Goonam
Bertha Mkhize
Bond
Denis Hurley
Joe Slovo
Soldiers Way
Wyatt
Durnford
Prior
Bram Fischer
Samora Machel
Walnut
Stanger
Florence Nzama
K E Masinga
Somtseu
Sandown
Sol Harris
Sylvester Ntuli
Playfair
Snell Parade
Molyneux
Pavilion Tce
Pedestrian Walk
Frobisher
Baumann
Boscombe
Foster
Serridge
Lower Marine Parade
O R Tambo Parade
North
Morrison
West
Hunter
John Milne
East
Milne
South
Sea View
Palmer
Mahatma Gandhi
Kearsney
Farewell
Monty Naicker
Commercial
Union
Dr Pixley Kaseme St
Peck
Anton Lembede
Gull
Mazeppa
Roy
Timber
Creek
Gilligan
Cato
Masobiya Mdluli
Mulberry
Keeler
Brighton
Beatty
Grenville
Gillespie
Sturdee
Rochester
Rutherford
Pickering
Dr Langalibalele Dube
Bay Terrace
Ocean
Erskine
Shearer
Masonic
Prince
Jewitts
Hospital
Ripley
South Beach
Bell
Quayside
Shepstone
Canongate
Douglas
Milton
Acorn
Julius Nyerere
Brook
Joseph Nduli
Alexandra
Park
Davis
Theatre
Convent
Broad
L N Singh
Dullah Omar
Beach
Salmon
Fenton
Hermitage
Parry
Bay
Church
Dorothy Nyembe
Mona
Jonsson
Mills
Kitchener
Albany
Acutt
Lancers
University
Richards
College
Maud Mfusi
McArthur
Diakonia
Lloyd
Benningfield
Mutual
Che Guevara
Cuckoo
Albert Luthuli Highway
Maydon
Richard Walne
Boatman's
Leuchars
Maydon Wharf
Sunlight
Lever
Northern Freeway
Battery Beach
NMR
M4
M8
M12
M13
M15
M17
N3
R102

KwaZulu-Natal

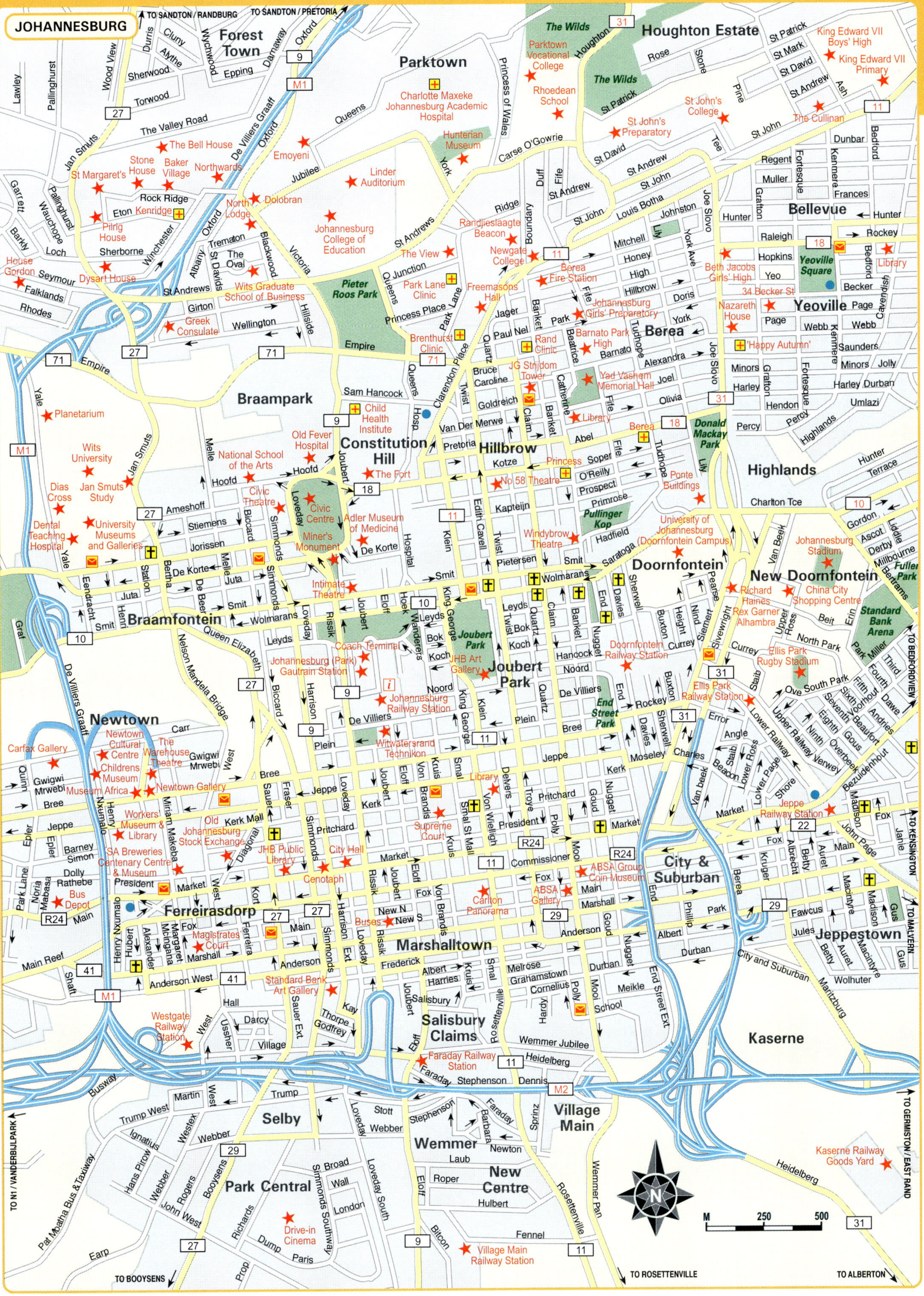

JOHANNESBURG

TO SANDTON / RANDBURG
TO SANDTON / PRETORIA
Forest Town
Parktown
Houghton Estate
The Wilds
Parktown Vocational College
Rhodean School
King Edward VII Boys' High
King Edward VII Primary
St John's College
St John's Preparatory
The Cullinan
Charlotte Maxeke Johannesburg Academic Hospital
Hunterian Museum
The Bell House
Stone House
Baker Village
Northwards
Emoyeni
Linder Auditorium
St Margaret's
Kenridge
Dolobran
North Lodge
Pilrig House
Johannesburg College of Education
Randjieslaagte Beacon
Newgate College
The View
Dysart House
House Gordon
Wits Graduate School of Business
Pieter Roos Park
Park Lane Clinic
Freemasons Hall
Berea Fire Station
Beth Jacobs Girls' High
Bellevue
Yeoville Square
Library
Yeoville
34 Becker St
Nazareth House
Greek Consulate
Brenthurst Clinic
Rand Clinic
Johannesburg Girls' Preparatory
Barnato Park High
Berea
'Happy Autumn'
JG Strijdom Tower
Yad Vashem Memorial Hall
Braampark
Planetarium
Child Health Institute
Constitution Hill
Old Fever Hospital
Hillbrow
Berea
Donald Mackay Park
Highlands
Wits University
National School of the Arts
The Fort
Princess
No 58 Theatre
Ponte Buildings
Jan Smuts Study
Dias Cross
Civic Theatre
Civic Centre
Adler Museum of Medicine
Pullinger Kop
University of Johannesburg (Doornfontein Campus)
Dental Teaching Hospital
University Museums and Galleries
Miner's Monument
Windybrow Theatre
Johannesburg Stadium
Doornfontein
New Doornfontein
Fuller Park
Intimate Theatre
Richard Haines
China City Shopping Centre
Standard Bank Arena
Rex Garner Alhambra
Braamfontein
Joubert Park
Coach Terminal
JHB Art Gallery
Doornfontein Railway Station
Ellis Park Rugby Stadium
Johannesburg (Park) Gautrain Station
Joubert Park
Ellis Park Railway Station
Johannesburg Railway Station
End Street Park
Newtown
Carfax Gallery
Newtown Cultural Centre
The Warehouse Theatre
Childrens Museum
Witwatersrand Technikon
Museum Africa
Newtown Gallery
Library
Jeppe Railway Station
Workers' Museum & Library
Old Johannesburg Stock Exchange
Supreme Court
SA Breweries Centenary Centre & Museum
JHB Public Library
City Hall
ABSA Group Coin Museum
City & Suburban
Cenotaph
ABSA Gallery
Bus Depot
Carlton Panorama
Ferreirasdorp
Buses
Jeppestown
Magistrates' Court
Marshalltown
Standard Bank Art Gallery
Salisbury Claims
Kaserne
Westgate Railway Station
Faraday Railway Station
Selby
Village Main
Wemmer
New Centre
Kaserne Railway Goods Yard
Park Central
Drive-in Cinema
Village Main Railway Station
TO BEDFORDVIEW
TO KENSINGTON
TO MALVERN
TO GERMISTON / EAST RAND
TO N1 / VANDERBIJLPARK
TO BOOYSENS
TO ROSETTENVILLE
TO ALBERTON
M 250 500
N

JOHANNESBURG RING ROAD

Gauteng

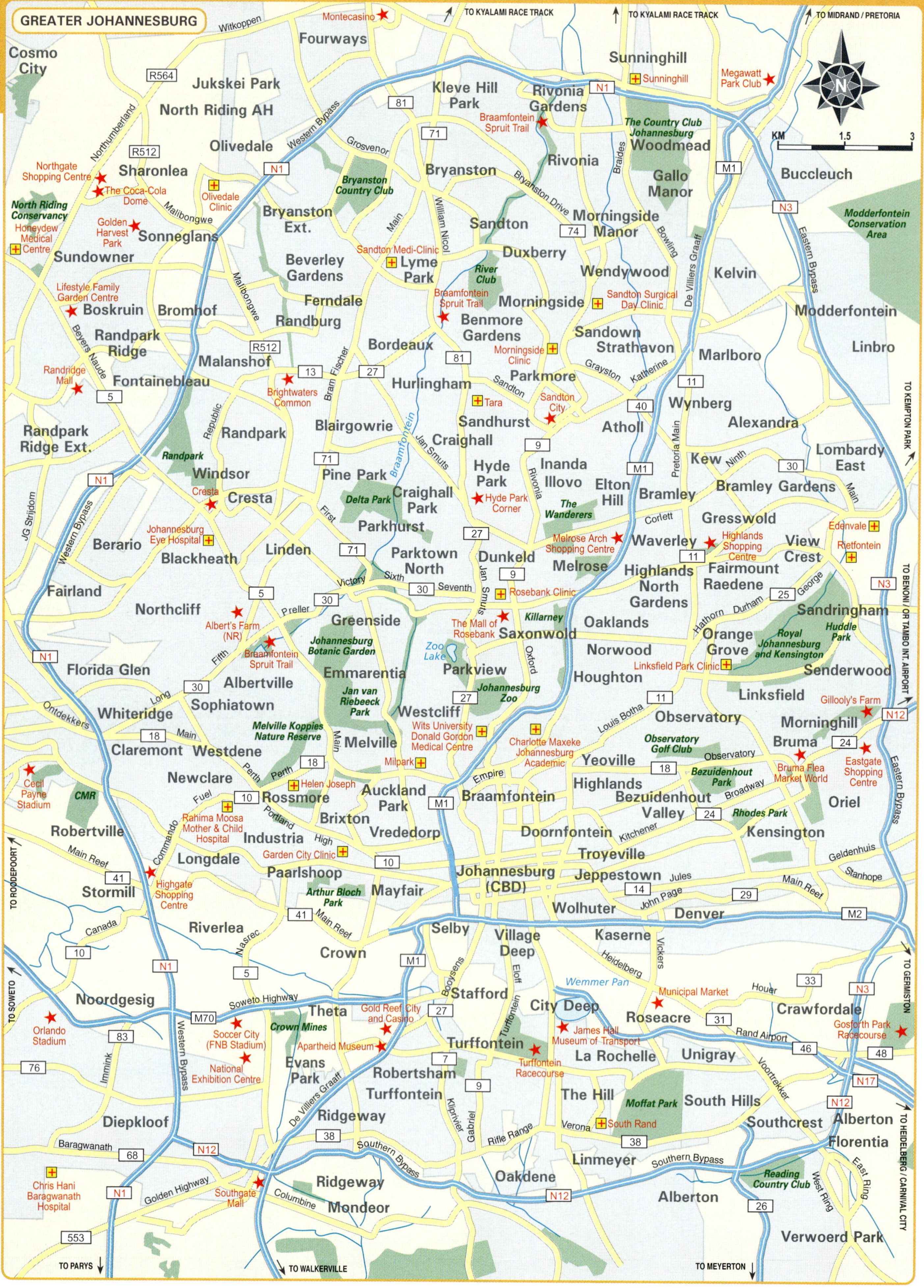

GREATER JOHANNESBURG

TO KYALAMI RACE TRACK
TO KYALAMI RACE TRACK
TO MIDRAND / PRETORIA
Montecasino
Witkoppen
Fourways
Cosmo City
R564
Jukskei Park
Kleve Hill Park
Rivonia Gardens
N1
Sunninghill
Sunninghill
Megawatt Park Club
North Riding AH
81
Braamfontein Spruit Trail
The Country Club Johannesburg
Woodmead
KM 1.5 3
Northumberland
Western Bypass
71
R512
Olivedale
Grosvenor
Rivonia
Braides
M1
Buccleuch
Northgate Shopping Centre
Sharonlea
N1
Bryanston
Gallo Manor
The Coca-Cola Dome
Olivedale Clinic
Bryanston Country Club
Bryanston Drive
N3
North Riding Conservancy
Malibongwe
Bryanston Ext.
William Nicol
Morningside Manor
Modderfontein Conservation Area
Honeydew Medical Centre
Golden Harvest Park
Sonneglans
Main
Sandton
74
Bowling
Eastern Bypass
Sundowner
Beverley Gardens
Sandton Medi-Clinic
Lyme Park
Duxberry
De Villiers Graaff
Malibongwe
River Club
Wendywood
Kelvin
Lifestyle Family Garden Centre
Ferndale
Braamfontein Spruit Trail
Morningside
Sandton Surgical Day Clinic
Modderfontein
Boskruin
Bromhof
Randburg
Benmore Gardens
Sandown
Beyers Naude
Randpark Ridge
Bordeaux
Strathavon
Linbro
R512
Malanshof
81
Morningside Clinic
Marlboro
Bram Fischer
13
27
Parkmore
Grayston
Katherine
Randridge Mall
Fontainebleau
Brightwaters Common
Hurlingham
Sandton
11
TO KEMPTON PARK
5
Tara
Sandton City
Wynberg
Republic
Sandhurst
40
Alexandra
Randpark Ridge Ext.
Randpark
Blairgowrie
Braamfontein
Jan Smuts
Craighall
Atholl
Pretoria Main
9
Lombardy East
Randpark
71
Hyde Park
Inanda
Kew
Ninth
30
Windsor
Pine Park
Rivonia
Illovo
Elton Hill
M1
Main
N1
Cresta
Cresta
Hyde Park Corner
The Wanderers
Bramley
Bramley Gardens
JG Strijdom
Delta Park
Craighall Park
Western Bypass
First
Corlett
Gresswold
Johannesburg Eye Hospital
Parkhurst
27
Edenvale
Berario
Melrose Arch Shopping Centre
Waverley
Highlands Shopping Centre
View Crest
Blackheath
Linden
71
Parktown North
Dunkeld
Rietfontein
11
Melrose
Highlands North Gardens
Fairmount
Victory
Sixth
9
Raedene
George
TO BENONI / OR TAMBO INT. AIRPORT
Fairland
5
30
Seventh
Jan Smuts
Rosebank Clinic
25
N3
30
Durban
Northcliff
Preller
Greenside
Killarney
Oaklands
Hathorn
Sandringham
Albert's Farm (NR)
The Mall of Rosebank
Saxonwold
Orange Grove
Royal Johannesburg and Kensington
Huddle Park
Johannesburg Botanic Garden
Braamfontein Spruit Trail
Zoo Lake
Norwood
N1
Fifth
Oxford
Linksfield Park Clinic
Senderwood
Florida Glen
Albertville
Emmarentia
Parkview
Houghton
30
Long
Johannesburg Zoo
Linksfield
Jan van Riebeeck Park
11
Gillooly's Farm
Whiteridge
Sophiatown
Westcliff
Louis Botha
Observatory
Ontdekkers
27
N12
Morninghill
Melville Koppies Nature Reserve
Wits University Donald Gordon Medical Centre
Charlotte Maxeke Johannesburg Academic
18
Main
Melville
Observatory Golf Club
Bruma
24
Claremont
Westdene
Main
Yeoville
Observatory
Eastgate Shopping Centre
Milpark
Empire
18
Bezuidenhout Park
Bruma Flea Market World
Cecil Payne Stadium
18
Perth
Perth
Helen Joseph
Highlands
Eastern Bypass
Newclare
Fuel
10
Auckland Park
Braamfontein
Bezuidenhout Valley
Broadway
Oriel
CMR
Rossmore
M1
24
Rhodes Park
Rahima Moosa Mother & Child Hospital
Portland
Brixton
Robertville
Industria
High
Vrededorp
Doornfontein
Kitchener
Kensington
Commando
TO ROODEPOORT
Main Reef
Garden City Clinic
Longdale
10
Troyeville
Geldenhuis
41
Paarlshoop
Johannesburg (CBD)
Jeppestown
Jules
Stanhope
Highgate Shopping Centre
Stormill
Arthur Bloch Park
Mayfair
14
29
Main Reef
John Page
41
Main Reef
Wolhuter
Denver
M2
Riverlea
Selby
Canada
Nasrec
Village Deep
Kaserne
10
Crown
Vickers
TO GERMISTON
N1
M1
Heidelberg
TO SOWETO
5
Boeysens
Eloff
Wemmer Pan
33
Noordgesig
Stafford
Municipal Market
Houer
N3
Soweto Highway
Theta
Gold Reef City and Casino
City Deep
M70
27
Turffontein
Roseacre
Crawfordale
Crown Mines
31
Gosforth Park Racecourse
Orlando Stadium
Soccer City (FNB Stadium)
Western Bypass
James Hall Museum of Transport
Rand Airport
83
Apartheid Museum
Turffontein
La Rochelle
Unigray
46
48
Evans Park
7
National Exhibition Centre
Turffontein Racecourse
Voortrekker
76
Robertsham
N17
Immink
De Villiers Graaff
9
The Hill
Moffat Park
South Hills
Turffontein
N12
Kliprivier
Gabriel
Alberton
Diepkloof
Ridgeway
Southcrest
Verona
South Rand
TO HEIDELBERG / CARNIVAL CITY
38
Rifle Range
38
Florentia
Baragwanath
N12
Southern Bypass
68
Linmeyer
Southern Bypass
East Ring
Chris Hani Baragwanath Hospital
Southgate Mall
Ridgeway
Oakdene
Reading Country Club
N1
Golden Highway
Columbine
N12
Alberton
West Ring
Mondeor
26
Verwoerd Park
553
TO PARYS
TO WALKERVILLE
TO MEYERTON

SANDTON/ROSEBANK & MIDRAND

KYALAMI RACE TRACK
Witkoppen
Cambridge Crossing Shopping Centre
The Square Shopping Centre
KYALAMI RACE TRACK
Sunninghill Shopping Centre
TO MIDRAND / PRETORIA
Megawatt Park Club
Sunninghill
Waterval Islamic Institute
N1
Norscot
Bryanston East
Petervale
Cowley
Petervale Shopping Centre
Sunninghill
Witkoppen
N1
Western Bypass
Epson Downs
William Nicol
Sloane
Mount
Kleve Hill Park
12th
Rivonia
Rivonia Gardens
Main
Sloane Square
81
Braamfontein Spruit Trail
Cambridge
12th
The Country Club Johannesburg
Plymouth
Woodmead
Buccleuch
71
Bryanston Wedge
Post House
Bryanston
Rivonia Centre
Rivonia Strip
Bowling
Woodmead
Woodmead Value Market
M1
Eastern Bypass
Bryanston East
Grosvenor
Bryanston
Rivonia
Rivoland
Canterbury
Dunwoody Shopping Centre
Eastern Service
Bryanston Country Club
St James
Riverside Shopping Centre
The Cloisters
Mutual Mews
Gallo Manor
Makro
N3
Grosvenor Crossing
Maps & Travel
Rivonia Junction
Woodlands
Bryanston
Eccleston
St Audley
Bryanston
Rivonia
TO KEMPTON PARK
Hobart Road
Morning Glen Shopping Centre
Kelvin
Curzon
Main
Clonmore
William Nicol
Riverclub Centre
Morningside Manor
Bowling
90 on Rivonia Shopping Centre
Southway
Homestead
Old Kilcullen
Ballyclare
Fairway
Northway
Kensigton "B"
Sandton Medi-Clinic
Lyme Park
Bryanston Shopping Centre
Duxberry
74
The Wedge Shopping Centre
Bowling
Wendywood
Kelvin Village Shopping Centre
River Club
Coleraine
Morningside Shopping Centre
Southway
Kelvin
Peter
Coatchmans Crossing
Bram Fischer
Ferndale
Morningside
West South
Wendywood Shopping Centre
Sandton Surgical Day Clinic
South
Braamfontein Spruit Trail
Grosfam
Benmore
Rivonia
Marlboro
Randburg Square Shopping Centre
Nicolway Centre
South
Adrienne
Main
Benmore Gardens
Sandown
Marlboro
Zina
Randburg
Bordeaux
Kent
Morningside Clinic
Park More Shopping Centre
North
Grayston Shopping Centre
Strathavon
81
St Andrews
Piazza Shopping Centre
27
Garden
Grayston
Katherine
Vasco Da Gama
13
Main
Parkmore
Greyston
Rivonia
11
Jan Smuts
Hurlingham
Sandton
West
Sandton Square
Boundary Lane
Village Walk
40
Wynberg
Alexandra
Sandton City
Tara Care And Rehabilitaion Centre
Athole
Waterfall
Sandton
(Sandton)
Andries South
Pretoria Main
Vasco Da Gama
Sandhurst
Empire
Bram Fischer
Blairgowrie
The Valley Centre
William Nicol
Atholl
Wynberg
Blairgowrie Shopping Centre
Conrad
Oxford
9
Inanda
M1
Craighall
Jan Smuts
Craig Park Centre
Sandhurst Centre
Forest
Freeway Shopping Centre
2nd
Ninth
71
Pine Park
Hyde Park
Kew
Rivonia
Illovo
Central
Bramley Gardens
Braamfontein
South
Boundary
Athol
Sensory Trail
The Colony
Hyde Park Corner
3rd
Bramley
Elton Hill
Bramley Gardens Shopping Centre
Delta Park
Hyde Square
Illovo Square Shopping Centre
Wanderers Cricket Ground
Corlett
Corlett City
Craighall Park
Melrose Arch Shopping Centre
View Crest
The Wanderers
Capri Shopping Centre
Gresswold
Dunkeld West Shopping Centre
Thrupps Shopping Centre
First
27
Bompas
Balfour Park Shopping Centre
Northview
Queens Place Shopping Centre
71
Victory Park
12th
Corlett
Park Gallery Shopping Centre
Scott
The Terrace Shopping Centre
Waverley
11
Parktown North
Dunkeld
Birdhaven Shopping Centre
James & Ethel Gray Park
De Villiers Graaff Motorway
Highlands Centre
Athol
Keith Flemming Park
Parkhurst
1st West
3rd
9
Melrose
Woodyatt
Fairmount
Victory
Sixth
Jan Smuts
Highlands North
Fairmount Shopping Centre
Gleneagles
30
Seventh
Rosebank Clinic
Glenhove
Raedene
30
Greenside
Chester
Rosebank Mall
25
Constantia Shopping Centre
Oaklands Shopping Centre
Orchids
Norwood Mall
Durham
Barry Hertzog
Killarney
Saxonwold
Hathorn
Greenway
11th
Oaklands
11th
Royal Johannesburg and Kensington
Zoo Lake
Cotswold
Ivy
Orange Grove
N
Oxford
Central
9th
M 300 600
Jan Smuts
Green Hill
8th
M1
Norwood
Iris
9th
Johannesburg Botanic Garden
11
Osborn
Linksfield Park Clinic
Riviera
Houghton
8th
Club
Parkview
Louis Botha
Emmarentia
Johannesburg Zoo
Green Hill
27
Killarney Mall
TO N1
2nd
Linksfield

102 PRETORIA

Gauteng

PRETORIA

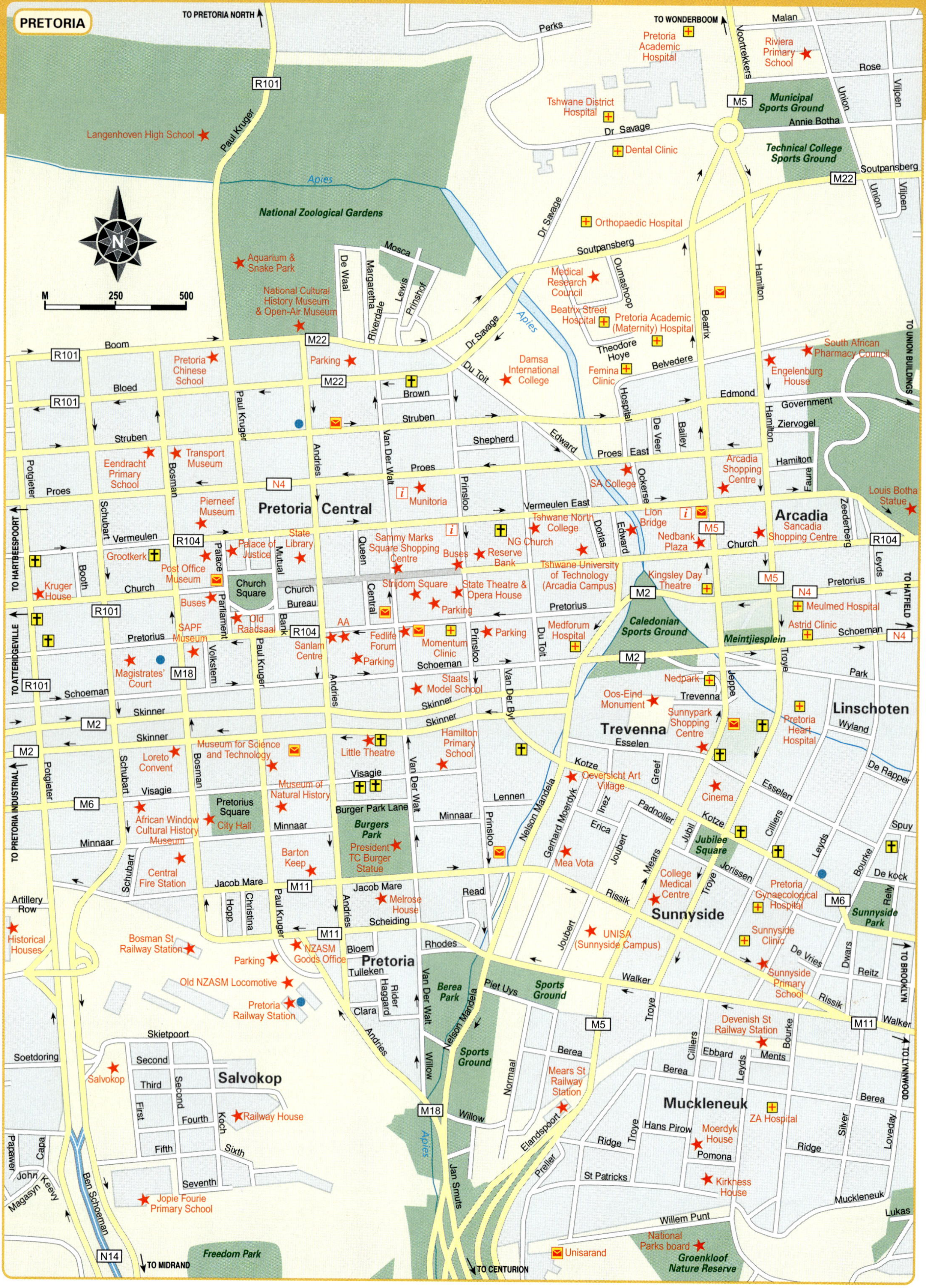

TO PRETORIA NORTH
TO WONDERBOOM
Malan
Perks
Pretoria Academic Hospital
Riviera Primary School
Rose
Vootrekkers
Viljoen
Union
R101
M5
Municipal Sports Ground
Annie Botha
Tshwane District Hospital
Dr Savage
Technical College Sports Ground
Dental Clinic
Langenhoven High School
Paul Kruger
Apies
M22
Soutpansberg
National Zoological Gardens
Orthopaedic Hospital
Dr Savage
Soutpansberg
Mosca
Aquarium & Snake Park
De Waal
Margaretha
Lewis
Prinshof
Medical Research Council
Oumashoop
Hamilton
M 250 500
National Cultural History Museum & Open-Air Museum
Riverdale
Dr Savage
Beatrix Street Hospital
Pretoria Academic (Maternity) Hospital
Beatrix
TO UNION BUILDINGS
Boom
M22
Theodore Hoye
South African Pharmacy Council
R101
Pretoria Chinese School
Parking
Du Toit
Damsa International College
Femina Clinic
Belvedere
Engelenburg House
Bloed
M22
Brown
Hospital
Edmond
R101
Government
Struben
Hamilton
Ziervogel
Struben
Shepherd
Edward
De Veer
Bailey
Eendracht Primary School
Transport Museum
Proes
East
Arcadia Shopping Centre
Hamilton
Potgieter
Proes
Bosman
Andries
Van Der Walt
Prinsloo
Ockerse
SA College
Fehrsen
Louis Botha Statue
Pierneef Museum
N4
Pretoria Central
Munitoria
Vermeulen East
Tshwane North College
Lion Bridge
Arcadia
TO HARTBEESPOORT
Schubart
Vermeulen
State Library
Queen
Sammy Marks Square Shopping Centre
NG Church
Dorfas
Edward
Nedbank Plaza
M5
Sancadia Shopping Centre
Zeederberg
R104
Grootkerk
R104
Palace of Justice
Mutual
Buses
Reserve Bank
Tshwane University of Technology (Arcadia Campus)
Church
Leyds
Booth
Post Office Museum
Palace
Church Square
Church
Kingsley Day Theatre
M5
Pretorius
TO HATFIELD
Kruger House
Church
Bureau
Central
Strijdom Square
State Theatre & Opera House
M2
N4
Buses
Parking
Pretorius
Meulmed Hospital
R101
Old Raadsaal
Bank
AA
Medforum Hospital
Caledonian Sports Ground
Astrid Clinic
Schoeman
TO ATTERIDGEVILLE
Pretorius
SAPF Museum
Parliament
R104
Fedlife Forum
Momentum Clinic
Prinsloo
Parking
Du Toit
Meintjiesplein
N4
Magistrates' Court
M18
Volkstem
Paul Kruger
Sanlam Centre
Parking
Schoeman
Van Der Byl
M2
Park
R101
Schoeman
Andries
Staats Model School
Nedpark
Troye
Jeppe
Skinner
Skinner
Oos-Eind Monument
Trevenna
Linschoten
M2
Skinner
Skinner
Hamilton Primary School
Trevenna
Sunnypark Shopping Centre
Pretoria Heart Hospital
Wyland
M2
Loreto Convent
Museum for Science and Technology
Little Theatre
Esselen
Potgieter
Visagie
Kotze
Oeversicht Art Village
Greef
De Rapper
TO PRETORIA INDUSTRIAL
Schubart
Bosman
Visagie
Van Der Walt
Lennen
Esselen
M6
Visagie
Museum of Natural History
Burger Park Lane
Nelson Mandela
Inez
Padnoller
Cinema
Pretorius Square City Hall
Minnaar
Burgers Park
Minnaar
Gerhard Moerdyk
Erica
Kotze
Cilliers
Spuy
Minnaar
African Window Cultural History Museum
Prinsloo
Jubilee Square
Leyds
President TC Burger Statue
Joubert
Mears
Jubil
Bourke
Central Fire Station
Barton Keep
Mea Vota
Jorissen
De kock
Schubart
Jacob Mare
M11
Jacob Mare
Troye
College Medical Centre
Pretoria Gynaecological Hospital
Artillery Row
Hopp
Christina
Paul Kruger
Andries
Melrose House
Read
Rissik
M6
Reitz
Sunnyside Park
Historical Houses
Scheiding
Sunnyside
Bosman St Railway Station
M11
Joubert
UNISA (Sunnyside Campus)
Sunnyside Clinic
TO BROOKLYN
Parking
NZASM Goods Office
Bloem
Rhodes
De Vries
Dwars
Pretoria
Tulleken
Reitz
Old NZASM Locomotive
Berea Park
Piet Uys
Sports Ground
Walker
Sunnyside Primary School
Rissik
Pretoria Railway Station
Rider Haggard
Van Der Walt
Clara
Troye
Walker
Andries
M5
Devenish St Railway Station
M11
Skietpoort
Nelson Mandela
Cilliers
Ebbard
Bourke
Soetdoring
Sports Ground
Berea
Ments
TO LYNNWOOD
Second
Salvokop
Willow
Normaal
Mears St Railway Station
Berea
Leyds
Berea
Third
Second
Salvokop
Muckleneuk
ZA Hospital
First
Fourth
Koch
Railway House
M18
Willow
Elandspoort
Papawer
Capa
Fifth
Sixth
Apies
Ridge
Troye
Hans Pirow
Moerdyk House
Silver
Ridge
Loveday
John
Keevy
Ben Schoeman
Pomona
Jan Smuts
Preller
Magasyn
Seventh
St Patricks
Kirkness House
Jopie Fourie Primary School
Muckleneuk
Lukas
Willem Punt
National Parks board
N14
TO MIDRAND
Freedom Park
TO CENTURION
Unisarand
Groenkloof Nature Reserve

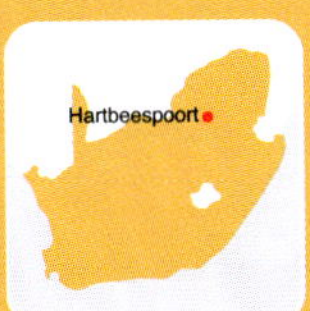

Hartbeespoort

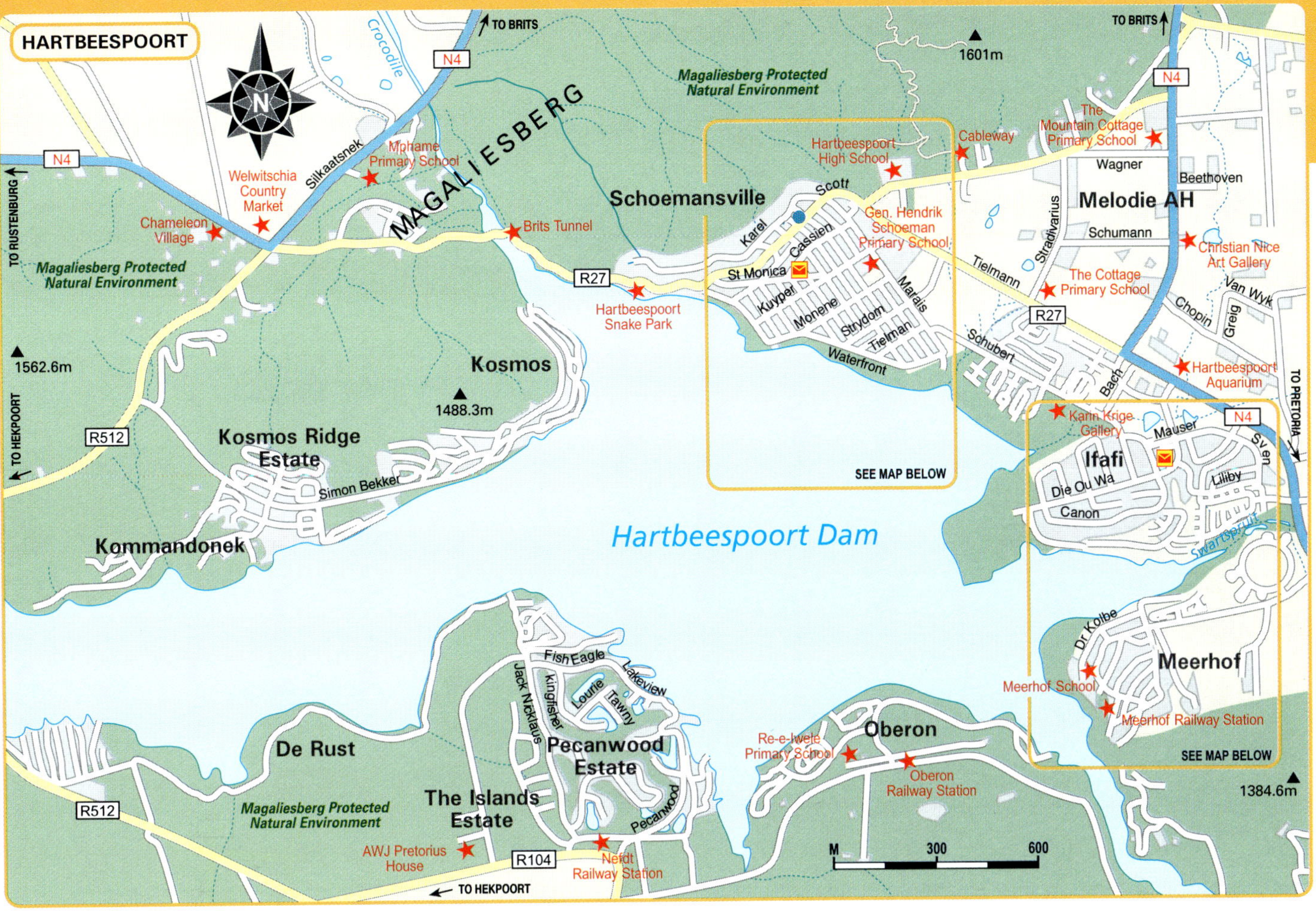

HARTBEESPOORT
N
TO BRITS
N4
Crocodile
MAGALIESBERG
Magaliesberg Protected Natural Environment
1601m
TO BRITS
The Mountain Cottage Primary School
Wagner
Beethoven
Melodie AH
Schumann
Christian Nice Art Gallery
Van Wyk
Chopin
Greig
Tielmann
The Cottage Primary School
Stradivarius
R27
Schubert
Bach
Hartbeespoort Aquarium
TO PRETORIA
Cableway
Hartbeespoort High School
Scott
Gen. Hendrik Schoeman Primary School
Schoemansville
Karel
Cassien
St Monica
Kuyper
Monene
Strydom
Marais
Tielman
Waterfront
SEE MAP BELOW
Silkaatsnek
Mphame Primary School
Welwitschia Country Market
Chameleon Village
Brits Tunnel
Magaliesberg Protected Natural Environment
TO RUSTENBURG
R27
Hartbeespoort Snake Park
1562.6m
Kosmos
1488.3m
TO HEKPOORT
R512
Kosmos Ridge Estate
Simon Bekker
Kommandonek
Hartbeespoort Dam
Karin Krige Gallery
N4
Mauser
Sven
Ifafi
Die Ou Wa
Liliby
Canon
Swart Spruit
Dr Kolbe
Meerhof
Meerhof School
Meerhof Railway Station
SEE MAP BELOW
1384.6m
Fish Eagle
Lakeview
Jack Nicklaus
Kingfisher
Lourie
Tawny
Pecanwood Estate
Pecanwood
De Rust
The Islands Estate
Magaliesberg Protected Natural Environment
R512
AWJ Pretorius House
R104
Neidt Railway Station
TO HEKPOORT
Re-e-lwele Primary School
Oberon
Oberon Railway Station
M 300 600

SCHOEMANSVILLE
Magaliesberg Protected Natural Environment
Hartbeespoort High School
R514
TO N4
Cemetery
Scott
Kerk
Marais
R27
Tielmann
TO IFAFI
Lakeview Conference Centre
Karel
Karlson
Cassien
Malan
Hertzog
Baldwin
Harrington
Van Velden
Blue Ivy Art Gallery
Silver Hills Scratch Patch
Gen. Hendrik Schoeman Primary School
Strydom
TO RUSTENBURG
R27
St Monica
Dalcos Shopping Centre
Marais
Tolstoi
Elizabeth
Kuyper
Meintjies
Devalera
Monene
Malan
Hertzog
Waterfront
Viviers
Danie
Schoemansville
Schubert
Strydom
James
Tielman
Waterfront
Waterfront
Oewer Yacht Club
Hartbeespoort Dam
N
M 300 600

IFAFI & MEERHOF
TO SCHOEMANSVILLE
Bach
Karin Krige Gallery
Magaliesberg Protected Natural Environment
Die Ou Wa
N4
Mauser
Sven
Amanda
Leemeforf
Bottlenek
Kleinste
Geweer
Dam
Dam
Howitzer
Cannon
Boem
Charl
Madeleine
Lincoln
TO PRETORIA
Canon
Long Tom
Die Ou Wa
Liliby
Cemetery
Buskruit
Baobab
Ifafi
Powder
British Military Site
Mopane
Marula
Bush Willow
Canon
Middle Stone Age Site
Kingfisher
Bloem South
Fish Eagle
Hartbeespoort Dam
Boem
Dr Kolbe
Findley
Bain
Jan Smuts
Meerhof
Louis Botha
Deneys Reitz
Findley
Dr Popper House (Good Shepherd Retreat Centre)
Meerhof Primary School
Mentz
Hendrik Schoeman
Meerhof Café and Steam Pump
Lincoln
Meerhof Railway Station
Cloister
James
Jean Botha
Meerhof Train Bridge
N
M 300 600

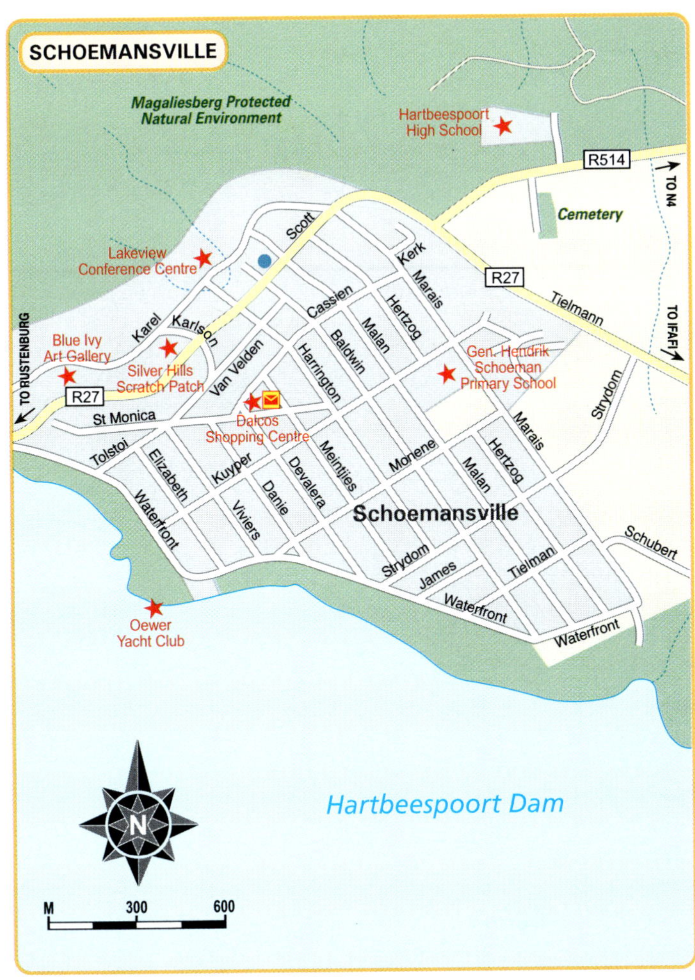

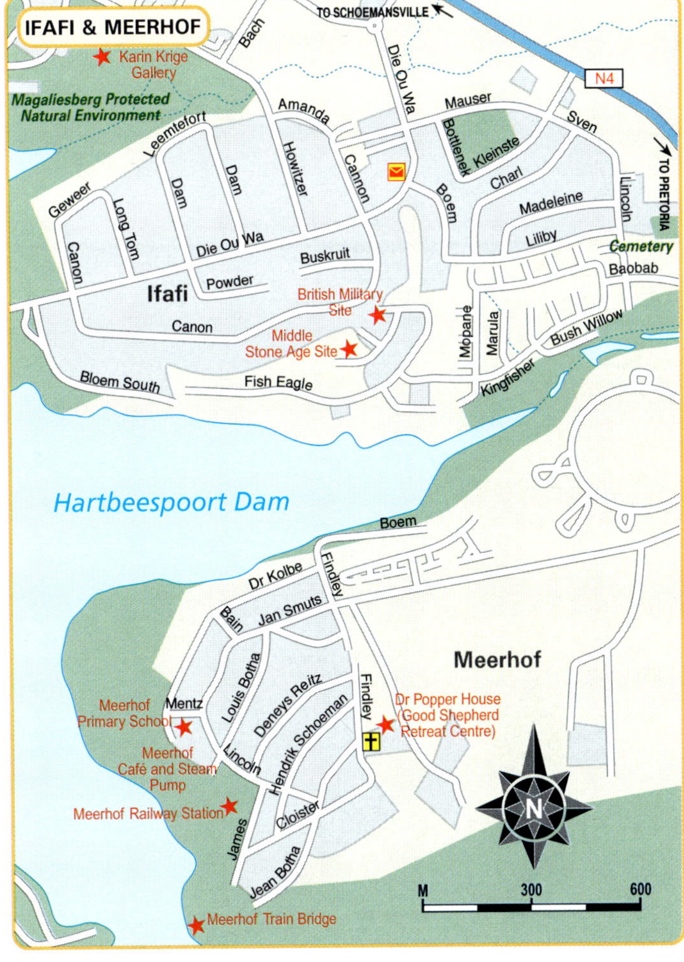

WEST RAND REGION

Gauteng

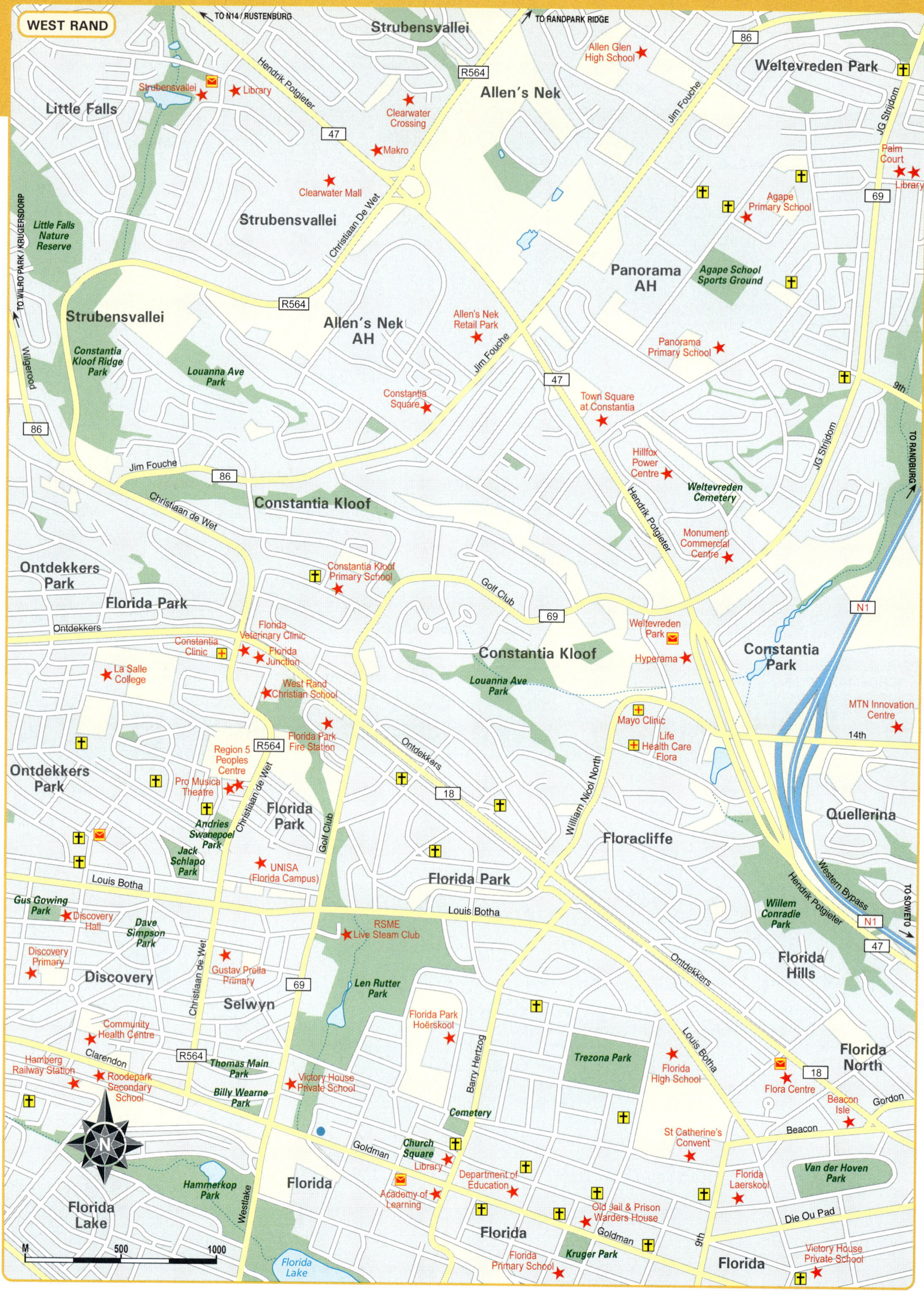

WEST RAND

TO N14 / RUSTENBURG
TO RANDPARK RIDGE
TO WILRO PARK / KRUGERSDORP
TO RANDBURG
TO SOWETO

Strubensvallei
Little Falls
Strubensvallei
Library
Hendrik Potgieter
Clearwater Crossing
Makro
Clearwater Mall
Strubensvallei
Christiaan De Wet
Little Falls Nature Reserve
R564
Allen's Nek
Allen Glen High School
Weltevreden Park
Jim Fouche
JG Strijdom
Palm Court
Library
Agape Primary School
Panorama AH
Agape School Sports Ground
Strubensvallei
Constantia Kloof Ridge Park
Louanna Ave Park
Allen's Nek AH
Allen's Nek Retail Park
Jim Fouche
Constantia Square
Panorama Primary School
Town Square at Constantia
9th
Wilgerood
Jim Fouche
Christiaan de Wet
Constantia Kloof
Hillfox Power Centre
Weltevreden Cemetery
Hendrik Potgieter
Monument Commercial Centre
JG Strijdom
Ontdekkers Park
Florida Park
Ontdekkers
Constantia Kloof Primary School
Golf Club
Florida Veterinary Clinic
Constantia Clinic
Florida Junction
La Salle College
West Rand Christian School
Constantia Kloof
Louanna Ave Park
Weltevreden Park
Hyperama
Constantia Park
N1
MTN Innovation Centre
14th
Mayo Clinic
Life Health Care Flora
Florida Park Fire Station
Region 5 Peoples Centre
Pro Musica Theatre
Ontdekkers Park
Andries Swanepoel Park
Jack Schlapo Park
Florida Park
Golf Club
Ontdekkers
William Nicol North
Floracliffe
Quellerina
UNISA (Florida Campus)
Florida Park
Louis Botha
Gus Gowing Park
Discovery Hall
Dave Simpson Park
Louis Botha
RSME Live Steam Club
Western Bypass
Willem Conradie Park
Florida Hills
Discovery Primary
Discovery
Gustav Preller Primary
Selwyn
Len Rutter Park
Florida Park Hoërskool
Ontdekkers
Louis Botha
Community Health Centre
Clarendon
Hamberg Railway Station
Roodepark Secondary School
Thomas Main Park
Billy Wearne Park
Victory House Private School
Barry Hertzog
Trezona Park
Florida High School
Florida North
Flora Centre
Beacon Isle
Gordon
Beacon
Cemetery
St Catherine's Convent
Goldman
Church Square
Library
Department of Education
Academy of Learning
Hammerkop Park
Florida
Westlake
Florida Lake
Old Jail & Prison Warders House
Goldman
Florida Laerskool
Van der Hoven Park
Die Ou Pad
9th
Florida
Florida Primary School
Kruger Park
Florida
Victory House Private School
Florida Lake
M 500 1000
N
86
47
R564
69
47
86
86
69
R564
18
69
R564
N1
47
18

EAST RAND

TO KEMPTON PARK
Kempton City
Kempton Park Hospital
Agape Primary School
Festive Mall
Boston City Campus
Kempton Square
Library
Long
Voortrekker
Kempton Park
Kempton Park Golf Course
Zuurfontein Cemetery
Elim Clinic
Ice Rink
Park Plaza
Arwyp Medical Centre
Central
Spartan
Kempton Park Medicross Centre
Shoprite
Park
Albertross
Plane
Lemoen
Forge
Steel
Derrick
Rigger
Cresslawn
Fitter
Cresslawn Primary School
Kempton Park Fire Station
West St Cemetery
Kempton Park Primary School
Harvard
Spartan School
Public Pools
Zuurfontein
Spartan
Green
SPCA
Newton
Loper
Kelvin
Household
Spoorlyn
Pretoria
Gladiator
Marauder
Albertina Sisulu Freeway
Rhodesfield
Meteor
Serena
Brussels
Marie Linde
Kiewiet
Kimmerling
Rhodesfield High School
Director
Vanacht
Gewel
Anson
Croydon
Jacobia Loots
André Greyvenstein
Isando
Electron
Melt Brink
Twin Oaks Conference Centre
Brewery
TO EDENVALE
Purtin
Foundary
Monteer
Isando
Anvil
Diesel
Quality
Isando Railway Station
Jones
Moregloed
Barbara
Klopper Park
Kruin
Klopper Park Hall
Emperor's Palace Hotel Casino Convention Resort
Griffiths
Siswe School
Kruinhof
Jet Park
Elandsfontein Rail
Transnet Sports Secondary School
Web
Patrick
Innes
Malcolm Moodie
Amber
Serenade
Henville
Kraft
Carlos Rolfes Lake
Kelly
Jansen
North Reef
Rustivia
Yaldwyn
Tudor
Rudo Nell
Sand Ham
Bisset
Transvaal
1st
Marlands
4th
5th
6th
East Rand Christian Academy
Ravensklip
Witfield
Pine
Main
Denne
North Rand
Trade Centre
Hughes Exts
East Rand Value Mall
TO BOKSBURG
Bonaero
Aeroparque
Bonaero Park Primary School
JBM Hertzog
Aldergrove
Atlas
Bonaero Park
Aero
Laguardia
OR Tambo International Airport
M 250 500
Springbok
Fire Protection Association Training College
Yaldwyn
Ridge
Spar
Bartlett Exts
Trichardts
Bardene Exts
Wild Waters
View Point
Key Largo
East Rand Trade Square
Dunswart
Birkenhead Centre
Flora Farm
North Rand
East Rand Galleria
K90 Centre
Boksburg Medicross Centre
East Rand Mall
Leon Ferreira Training Centre
Rietfontein
Jensen Park
Edgar

ADELAIDE ALICE

ALEXANDER BAY ALIWAL NORTH

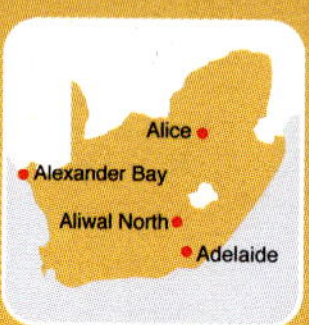

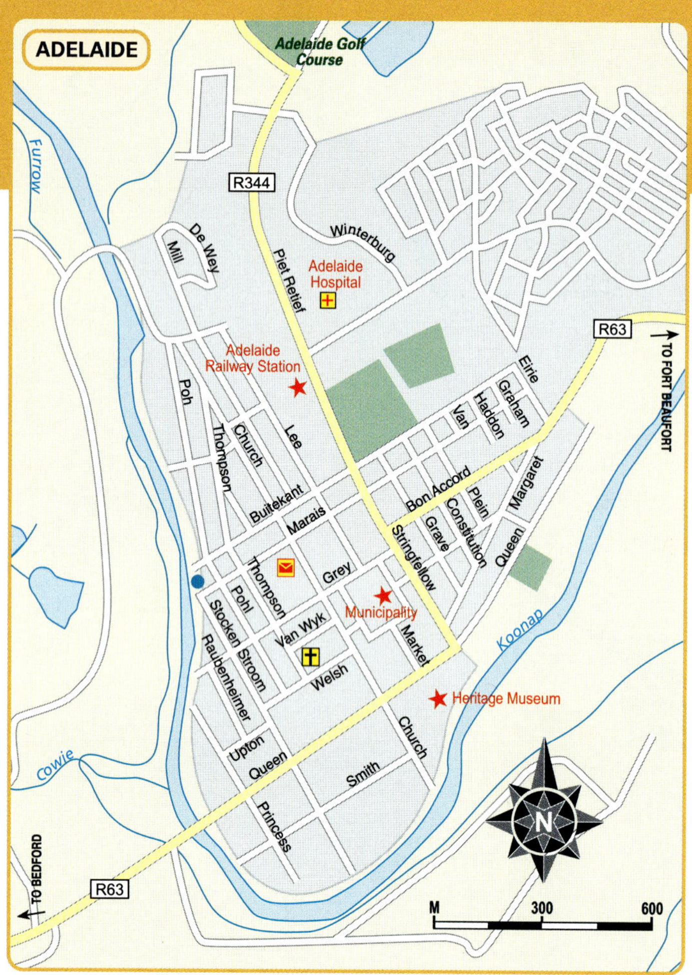

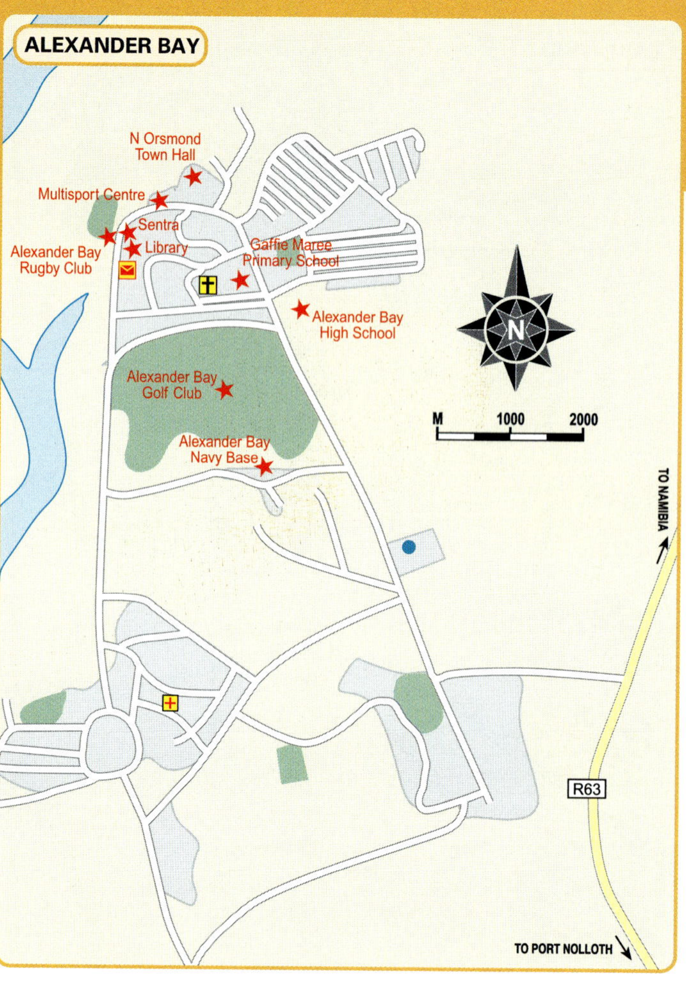

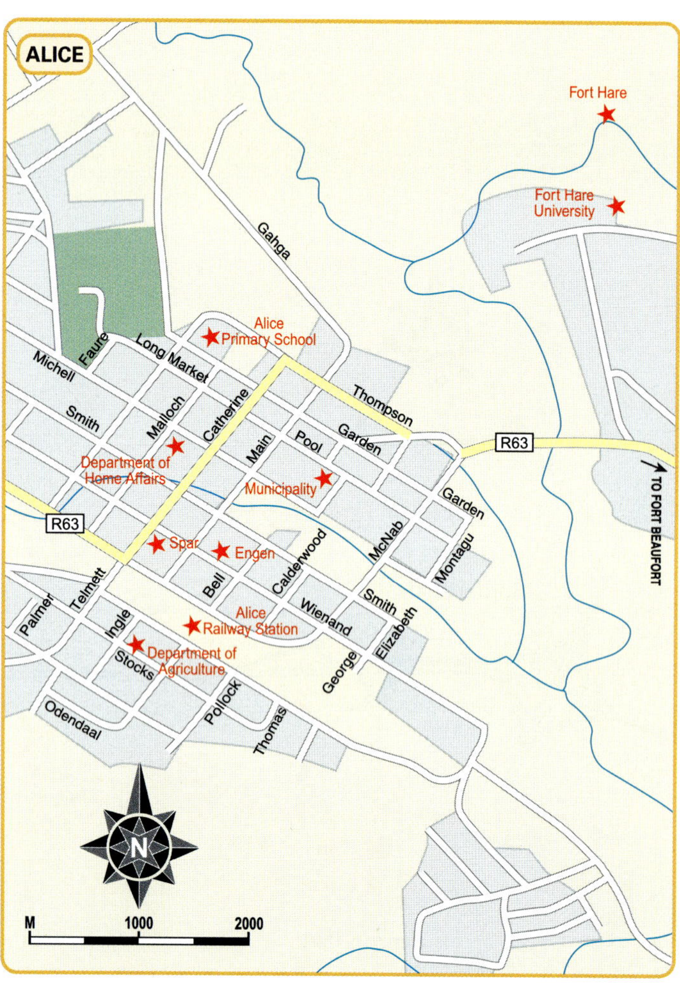

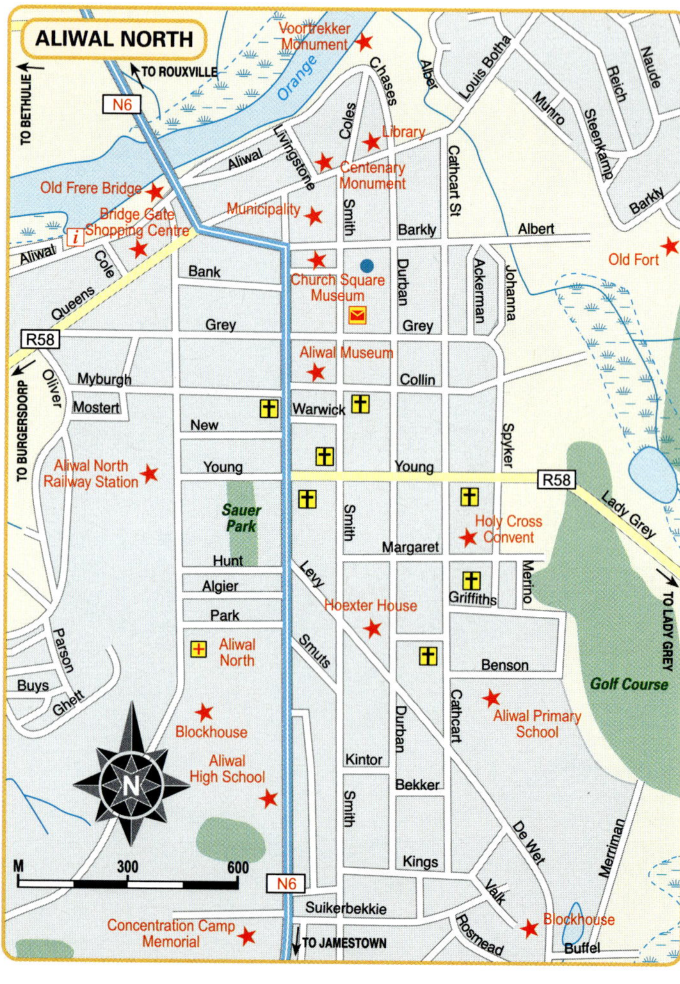

Barberton
Ballito
aManzimtoti
Ashton

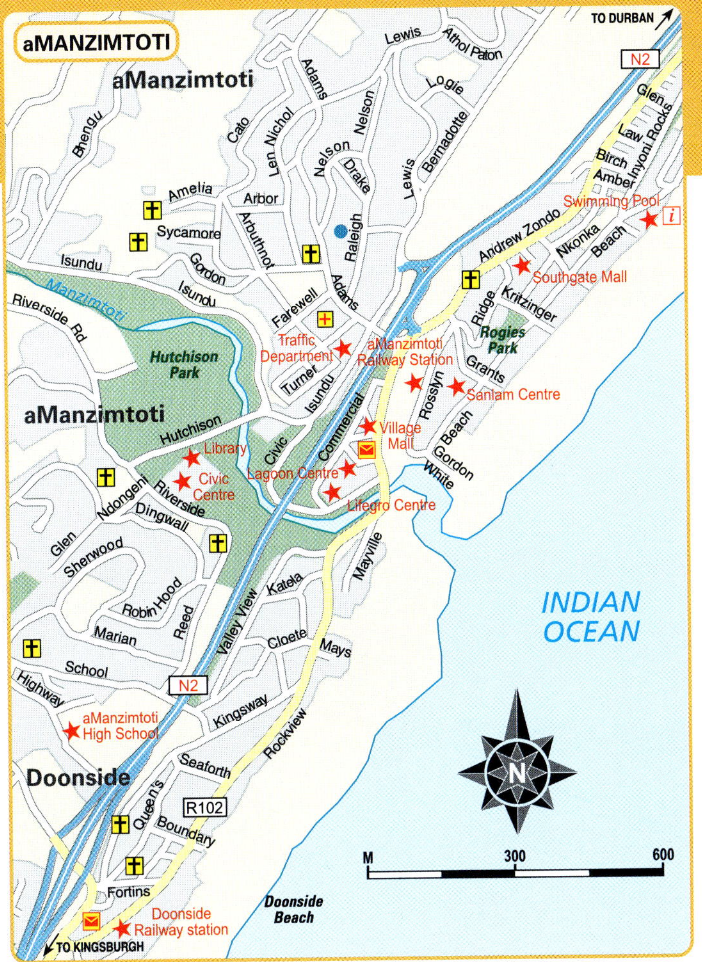

aMANZIMTOTI
aManzimtoti
TO DURBAN
N2
Lewis
Athol Paton
Logie
Adams
Bernadotte
Nelson
Drake
Cato
Len Nichol
Bhengu
Glen
Law
Invoni Rocks
Birch
Amber
Amelia
Arbor
Sycamore
Arbuthnot
Raleigh
Andrew Zondo
Swimming Pool
Nkonka
Beach
Isundu
Gordon
Southgate Mall
Manzimtoti
Farewell
Kritzinger
Riverside Rd
Ridge
Rogies Park
Traffic Department
aManzimtoti Railway Station
Hutchison Park
Turner
Grants
Sanlam Centre
Rossyn
Hutchison
Commercial
Village Mall
Beach
Library
Civic
Civic Centre
Lagoon Centre
Gordon
White
Ndongeni
Riverside
Dingwall
Lifegro Centre
Glen
Sherwood
Robin Hood
Reed
Valley View
Katela
Mayville
Marian
Cloete
Mays
School
Highway
N2
INDIAN OCEAN
aManzimtoti High School
Kingsway
Rockview
Doonside
Seaforth
Queen's
R102
Boundary
M 300 600
Fortins
Doonside Railway station
Doonside Beach
TO KINGSBURGH

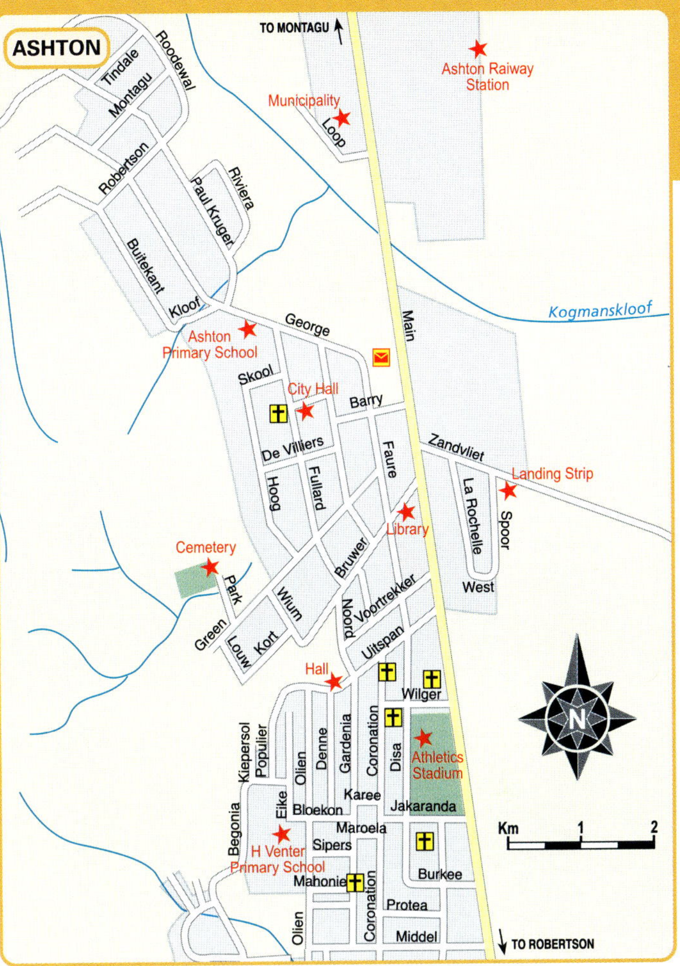

ASHTON
TO MONTAGU
Tindale
Montagu
Roodewal
Ashton Raiway Station
Municipality
Loop
Robertson
Paul Kruger
Riviera
Buitekant
Kloof
Kogmanskloof
Main
Ashton Primary School
George
Skool
City Hall
Barry
De Villiers
Zandvliet
Faure
Fullard
Hoog
Landing Strip
La Rochelle
Spoor
Library
Cemetery
Park
Bruwer
West
Wium
Noord
Voortrekker
Green
Louw
Kort
Uitspan
Hall
Wilger
Kiepersol
Populier
Olien
Denne
Gardenia
Coronation
Disa
Athletics Stadium
Eike
Bloekon
Karee
Jakaranda
Begonia
Maroela
Km 1 2
H Venter Primary School
Sipers
Mahonie
Burkee
Protea
Olien
Coronation
Middel
TO ROBERTSON

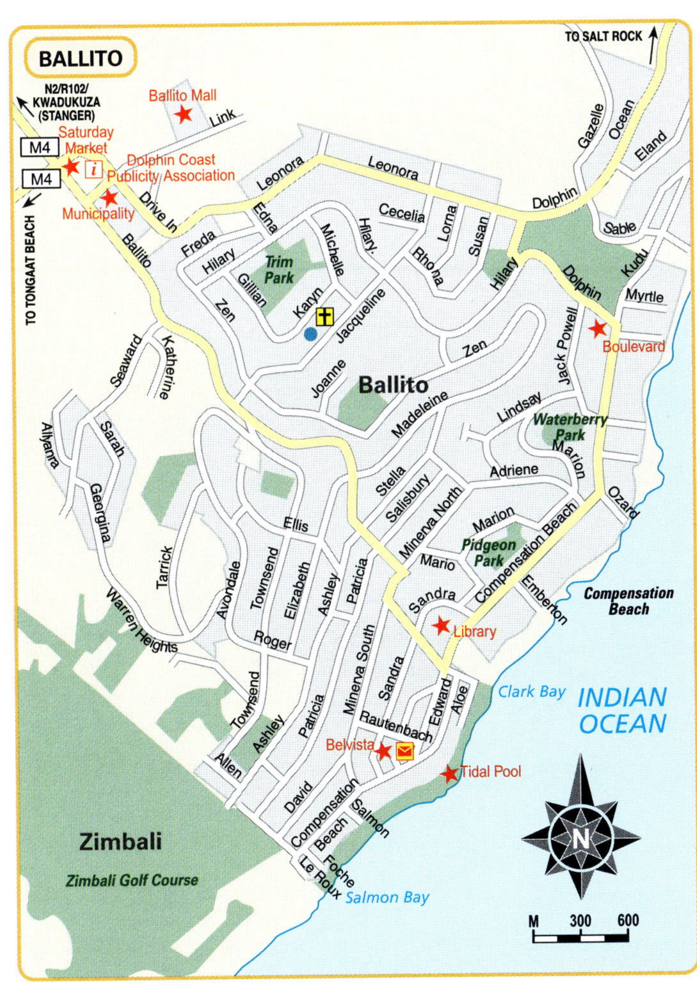

BALLITO
TO SALT ROCK
N2/R102/ KWADUKUZA (STANGER)
Ballito Mall
Link
M4
Saturday Market
Dolphin Coast Publicity Association
M4
Municipality
Drive In
Leonora
Leonora
Gazelle
Ocean
Eland
TO TONGAAT BEACH
Ballito
Freda
Hilary
Edna
Cecelia
Lorna
Susan
Dolphin
Sable
Kudu
Gillian
Trim Park
Michelle
Hilary
Rhona
Hilary
Dolphin
Myrtle
Zen
Karyn
Jacqueline
Jack Powell
Boulevard
Seaward
Katherine
Joanne
Zen
Ballito
Madeleine
Lindsay
Waterberry Park
Alyana
Sarah
Marion
Stella
Adriene
Georgina
Salisbury
Minerva North
Marion
Ozard
Ellis
Mario
Pidgeon Park
Compensation Beach
Tarrick
Avondale
Townsend
Elizabeth
Ashley
Patricia
Sandra
Emberton
Compensation Beach
Warren Heights
Roger
Library
Townsend
Minerva South
Sandra
Edward
Aloe
Clark Bay
INDIAN OCEAN
Ashley
Patricia
Rautenbach
Allen
Belvista
Tidal Pool
David
Compensation
Salmon
Beach
Zimbali
Foche
Le Roux
Salmon Bay
Zimbali Golf Course
M 300 600

BARBERTON
TO NOORDKAAP
M 250 500
President
Breda
Loveday
Sheba
Coronation Park
Alexandra
Munro
Van der Merwe
TO BOTHASNEK
Adams
Pretorius
Bank
Barberton Shopping Centre
Nourse
Peacock
Barberton Hospital
Eureka Shopping Centre
Grauman
Williams
Tate
General
Van der Bijl
Louw
Town Hall, Jock of the Bushveld Statue
Shoprite
Barberton Museum
Harris
Wagner
Halder
Blockhouse
De Villiers
Bank
Natal
Rimers Creek
Lee
Stanley
De Kaap Stock Exchange
Lewis & Marks Building
Belhaven House Museum
Fernlea House
Crown
Pilgrims
Reef
De Kock
Judge
Globe Tavern
Keller Park
Carolina
Krause
Bowness
Stopforth House
Barberton Primary School
Hambridge
Russel
Aerial Cableway
Stopforth
President
Indigenous Tree Park

BARRYDALE BELA-BELA (Warmbaths) BEAUFORT WEST BELLVILLE

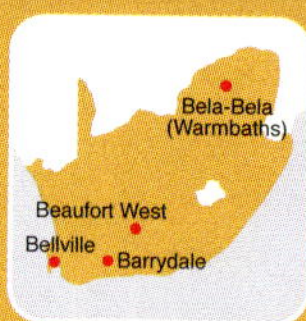

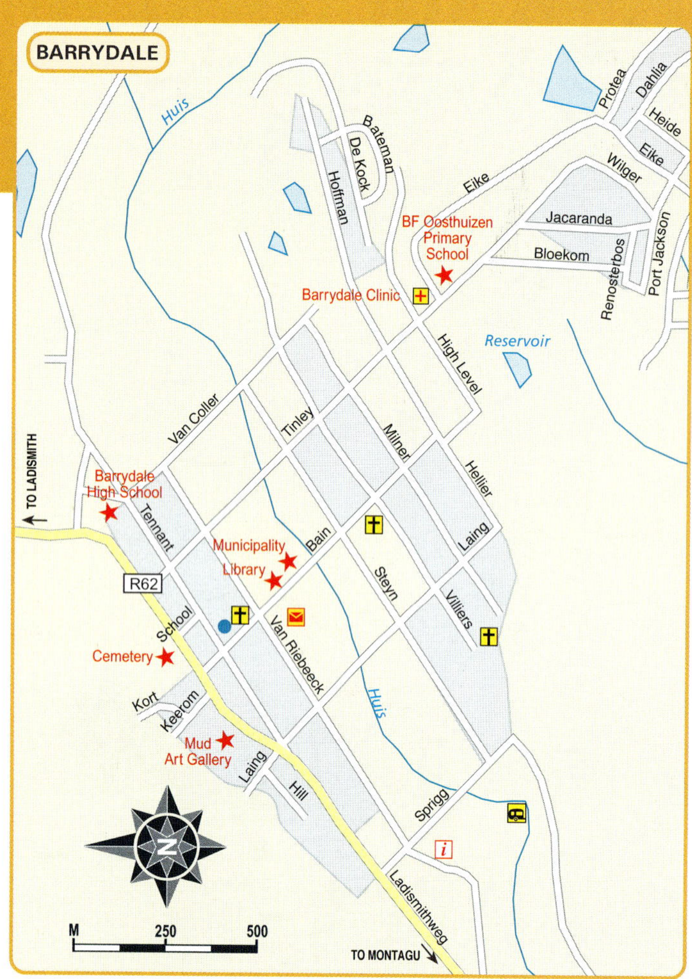

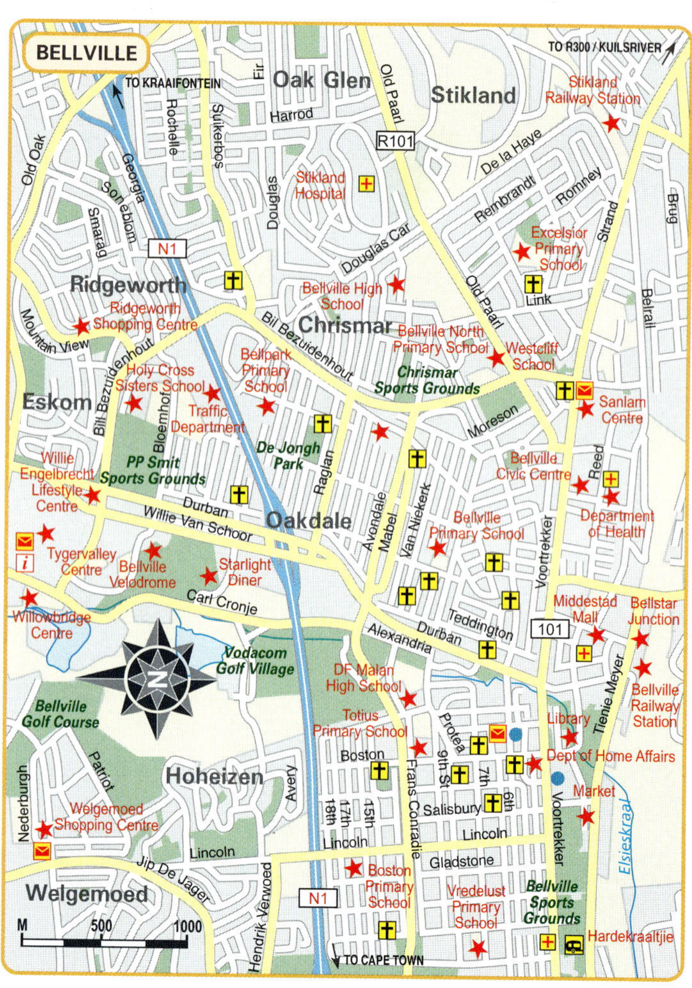

BENONI

TO N3 / KEMPTON PARK
Brandwag High School
Wordsworth High School
Airfield
Northmead Primary School
Northmead Club
McDowell Park
Benoni Veterinary Hospital
Damelin (Benoni Campus)
Danie Taljaard Park
Didakos Christel Primary School
Whitehouse
Northmead Railway Station
Kleinfontein Lake
Civic Lake
Lakeview Medical Clinic
Nestadt Park
Lakeside Mall
Benoni Traffic Department
Library
Ekurhuleni Development Planning
Lee Road Primary School
Lee Road High School
Hyperama
Walmsley Park
Swimming Pool
St Columba's Primary School
SARS
Benoni
Day Clinic Lakeview
Department of Home Affairs
Plaza
Benoni Educational College
Verkenner Primary School
New Kleinfontein
Curtis Park
Glynwood Hospital
Benoni Magistrate Courts
Glynwood Shopping Centre
Willowmoore Park
Benoni Municipal Sports Club
MOTH Club
Benoni Railway Station
Willowmoore High School
Benoni South
TO BOKSBURG
TO WITBANK
TO BRAKPAN
N12
R29
R23
44
M 250 500

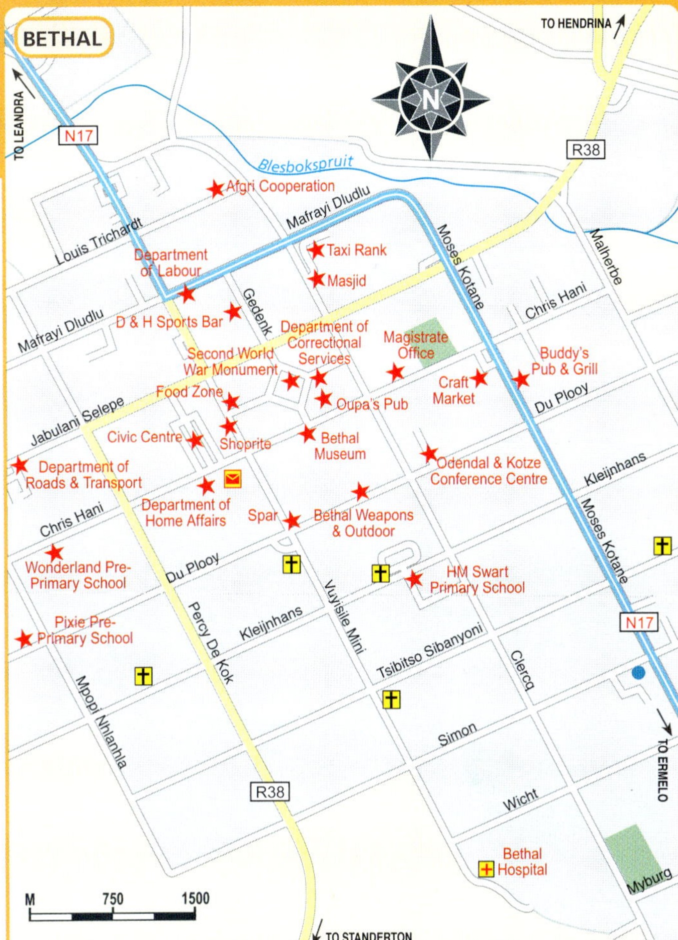

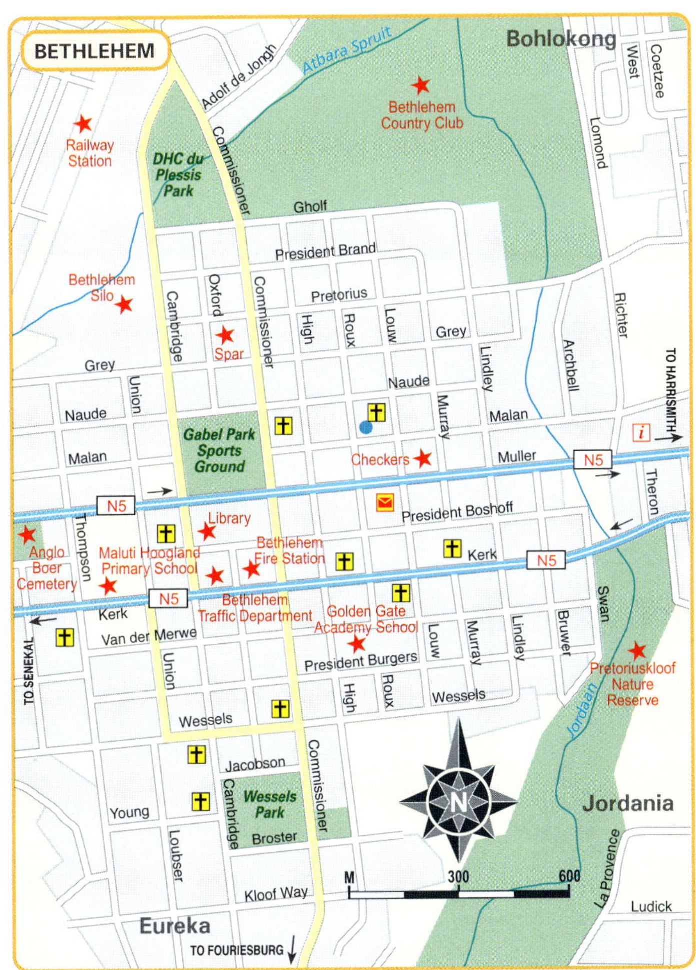

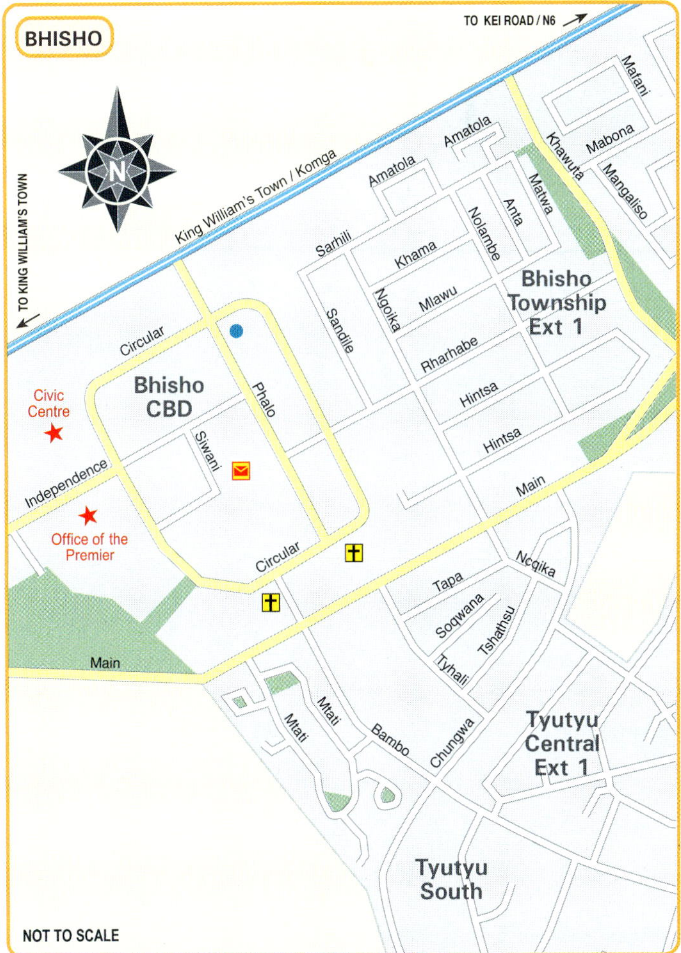

BOTHAVILLE BRANDFORT BRAKPAN BREDASDORP

BOTHAVILLE

TO KROONSTAD
R30
Bothaville Golf Club
TO ALLANRIDGE / ODENDAALSRUS
TO ORKNEY / KLERKSDORP
Recreation Area
Bothaville Railway Station
Bothaville Clinic
Municipality
Library
Spar
Bothaville Tennis Club
Mieliehoofstad Museum
Bothaville High School
Eben Dönges Primary School
Meyerhof
Sewage Disposal Works
Voortrekker
Botha
Oberholzer
Van Riebeeck
Muller
Van der Ligen
Mark
Steyn
Preller
Kerk
Theron
Smith
Van Abo
Coetzer
Sapsford
Station
Castiglioni
Bukes
Carey
Symonds
Garden
Van Zyl
Bank
River
Brand
President
Sering
Stinkhout
Kameeldoring
Mimosa
Taaibos
Karee
Olienhout
Suikerbos
Kiaat
Bloekom
M 300 600

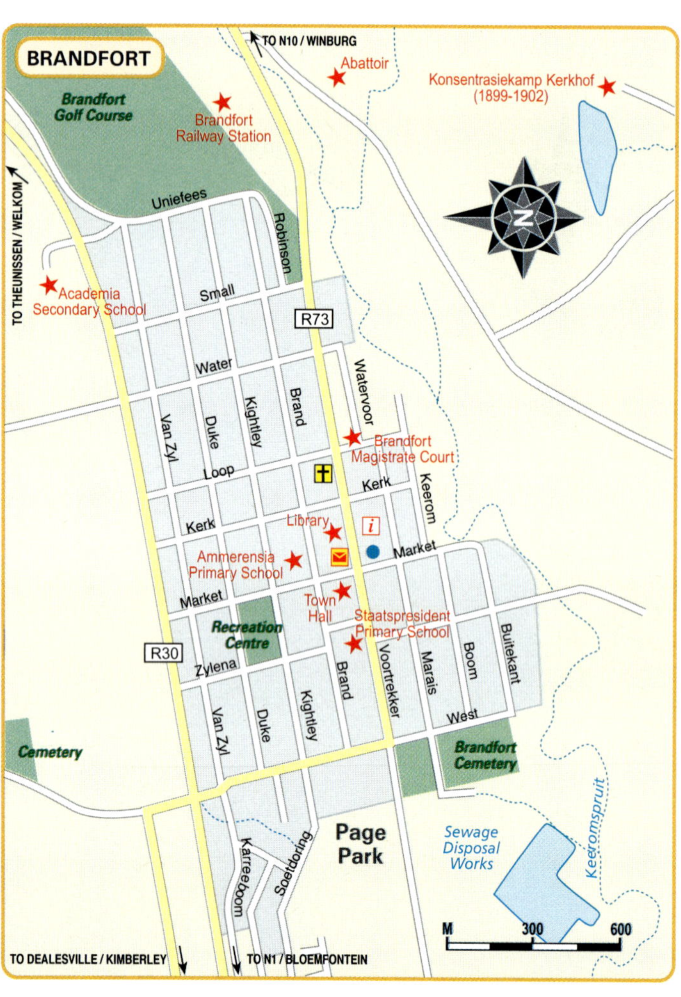

BRITS
Brits Correctional Services
Swimming Pool
Brits High School
Arend Plaza
Brits Hospital
Safari Plaza
Brits Medi Clinic
Academy for Christian Education
Madibeng LM Municipal Office
Brits Magistrate Court
Shoprite
Brits Fire Station
Primindia
Brits Primary School
Priminda Railway Station
Central Secondary School
TO THABAZIMBI
TO HARTBEESPOORT / N4 (PRETORIA)

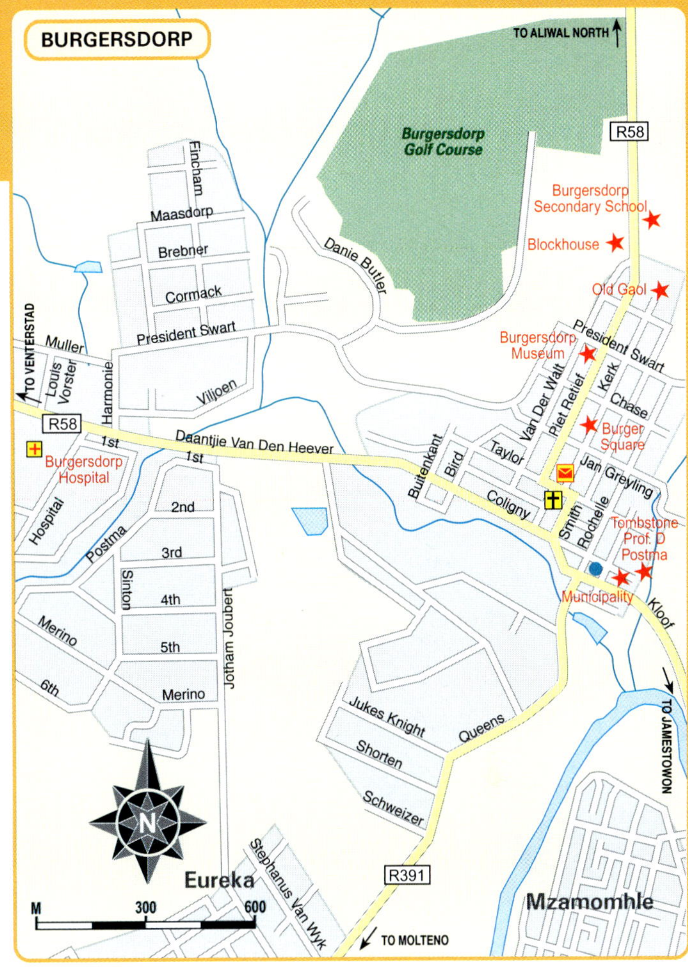
BURGERSDORP
TO ALIWAL NORTH
Burgersdorp Golf Course
Burgersdorp Secondary School
Blockhouse
Old Gaol
Burgersdorp Museum
Burger Square
Tombstone Prof. D Postma
Municipality
Burgersdorp Hospital
Eureka
Mzamomhle
TO VENTERSTAD
TO JAMESTOWN
TO MOLTENO

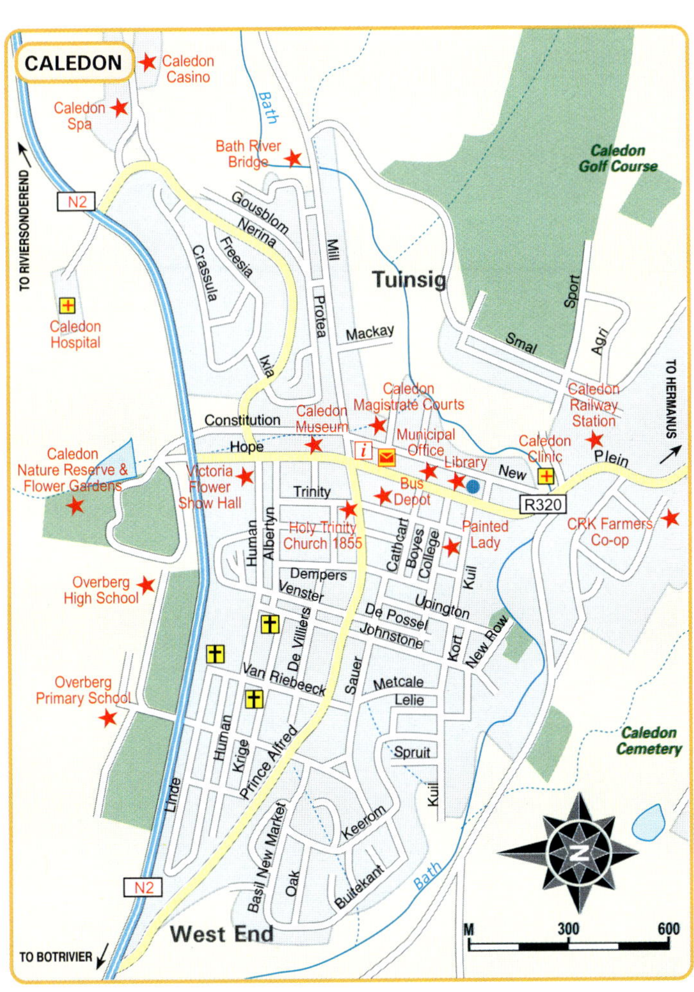
CALEDON
Caledon Casino
Caledon Spa
Bath River Bridge
Caledon Golf Course
Tuinsig
Caledon Hospital
Caledon Museum
Caledon Magistrate Courts
Municipal Office
Library
Caledon Clinic
Caledon Railway Station
Caledon Nature Reserve & Flower Gardens
Victoria Flower Show Hall
Bus Depot
Holy Trinity Church 1855
Painted Lady
CRK Farmers Co-op
Overberg High School
Overberg Primary School
Caledon Cemetery
West End
TO RIVIERSONDEREND
TO HERMANUS
TO BOTRIVIER

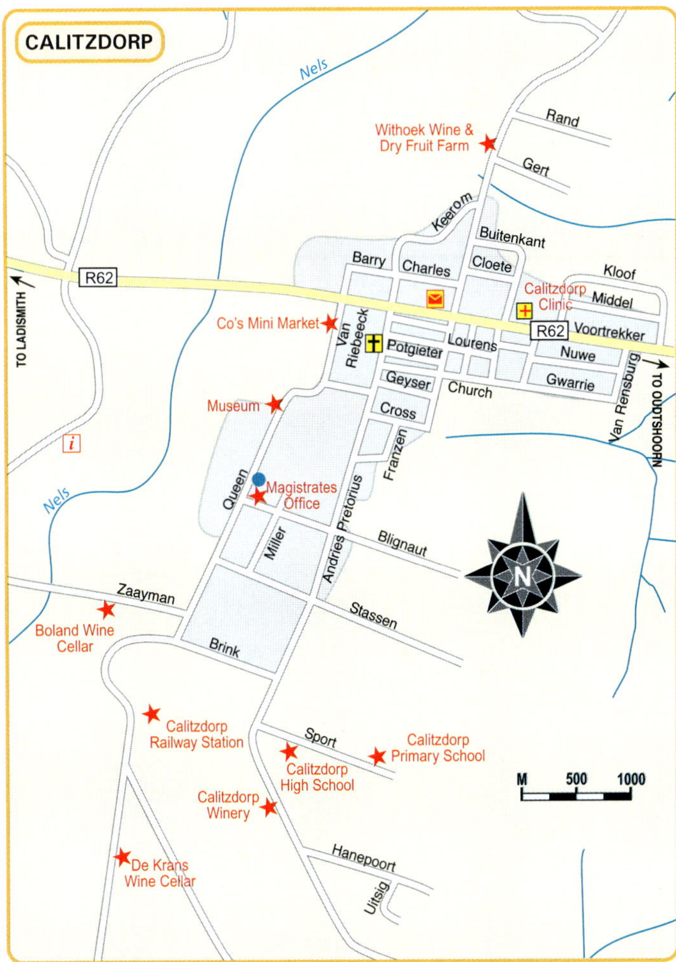
CALITZDORP
Withoek Wine & Dry Fruit Farm
Calitzdorp Clinic
Co's Mini Market
Museum
Magistrates Office
Boland Wine Cellar
Calitzdorp Railway Station
Calitzdorp High School
Calitzdorp Primary School
Calitzdorp Winery
De Krans Wine Cellar
TO LADISMITH
TO OUDTSHOORN

CALVINIA CARLETONVILLE

CAMPS BAY CARNARVON

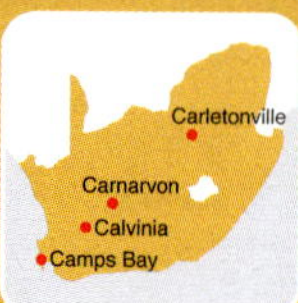

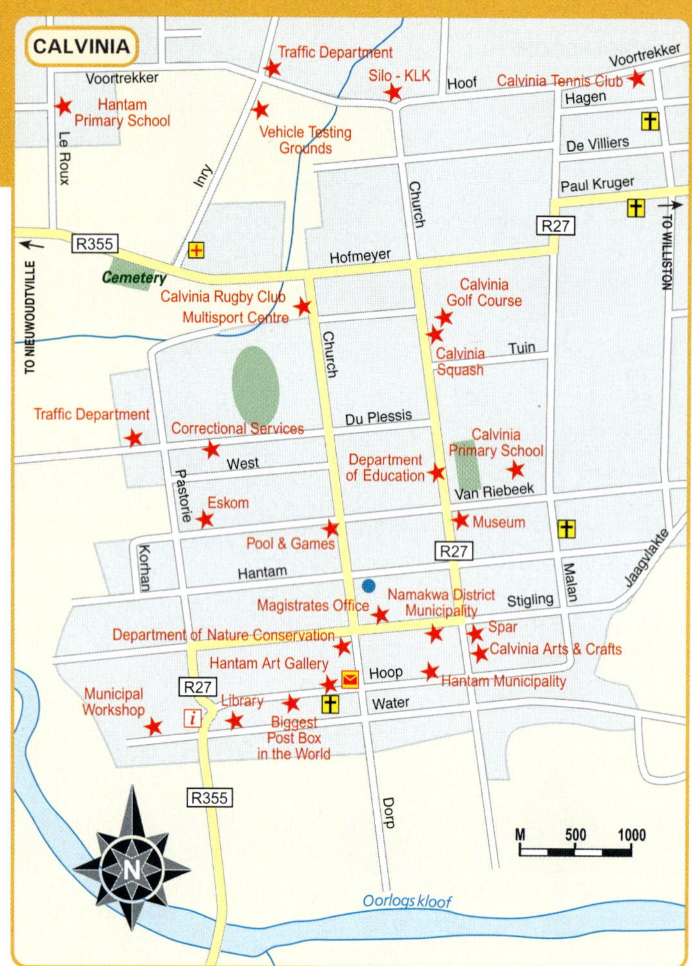

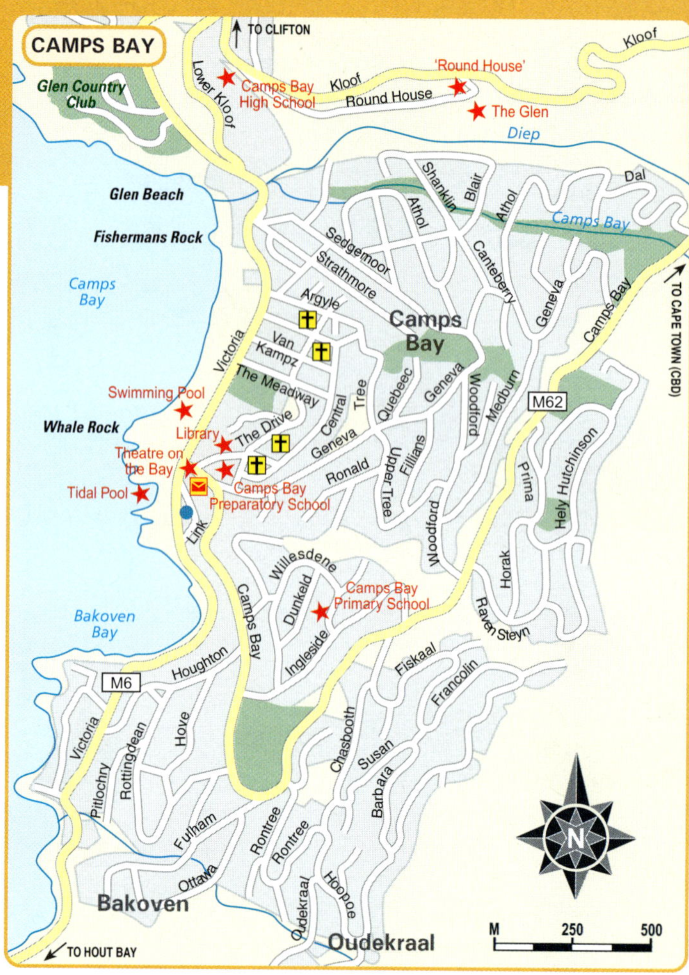

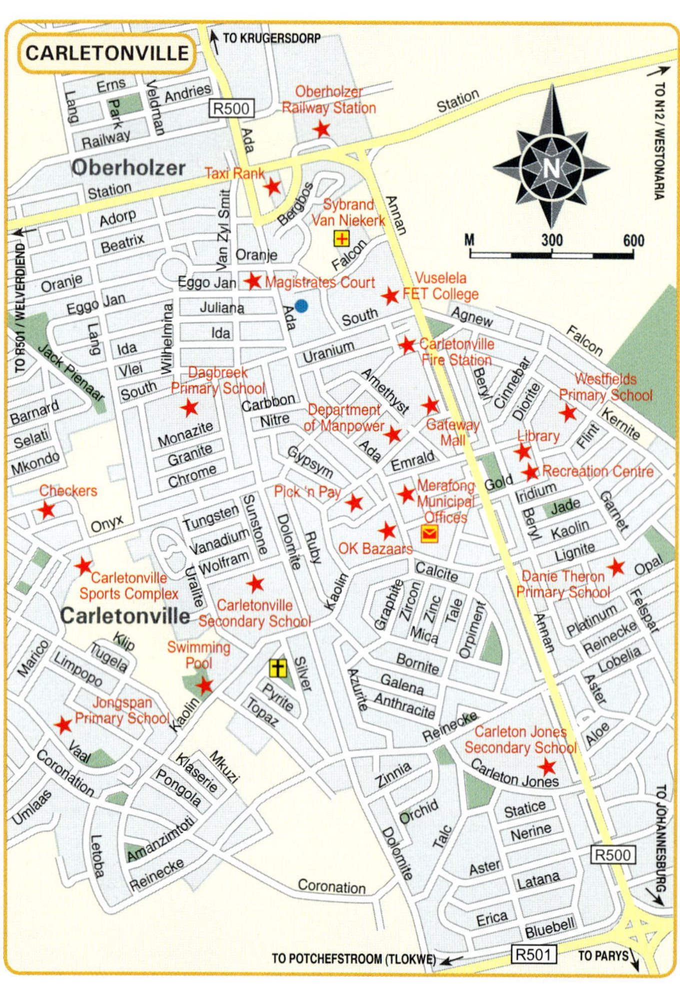

CAROLINA

TO MACHADODORP
Volkskool Carolina
Pinsloo
Church
R36
Hamman
Van Riebeeck
Combrink
R33
TO WONDERFONTEIN
Voortrekker
Viljoen
Duvenage
Hugo
Joubert
APK
Traffic Department
Smit
Carolina Municipal Clinic
Carolina Combined School
Grobler
Care Cross Clinic
Magistrates Office
Cardinaal
Versveld
Carolina Railway Station
Spar
Shoprite
Ubuntu Medical Plaza
Albert Luthuli LM
TO BADPLAAS
Church
Breytenbach
R38
Middel
Market
Steyn
Power Save
Lange
Department of Public Works
R38
Hugo
Correctional Services
R33
R36
Carolina Hospital
Niekerk
Coetzee
Goud
Agri Corporation
Du Toit
TO WARBURTON
TO BREYTON
N
M 250 500

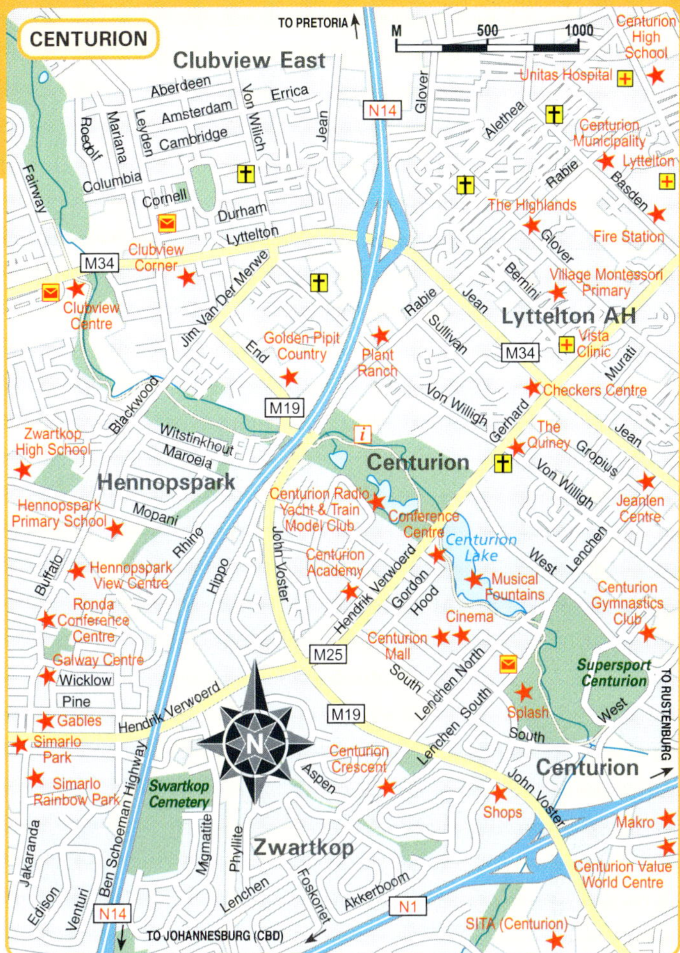

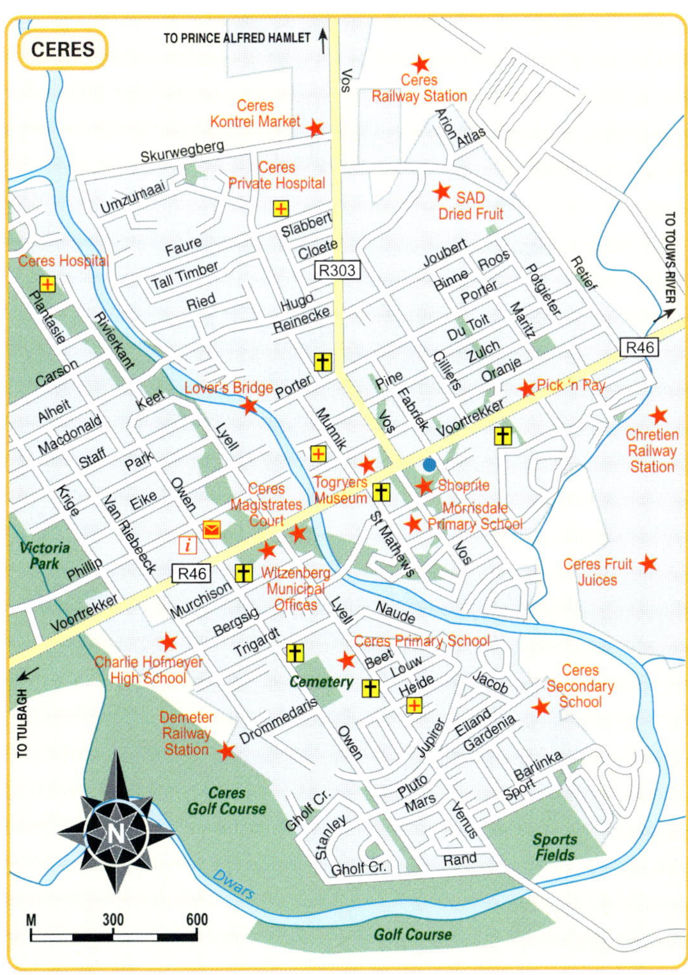

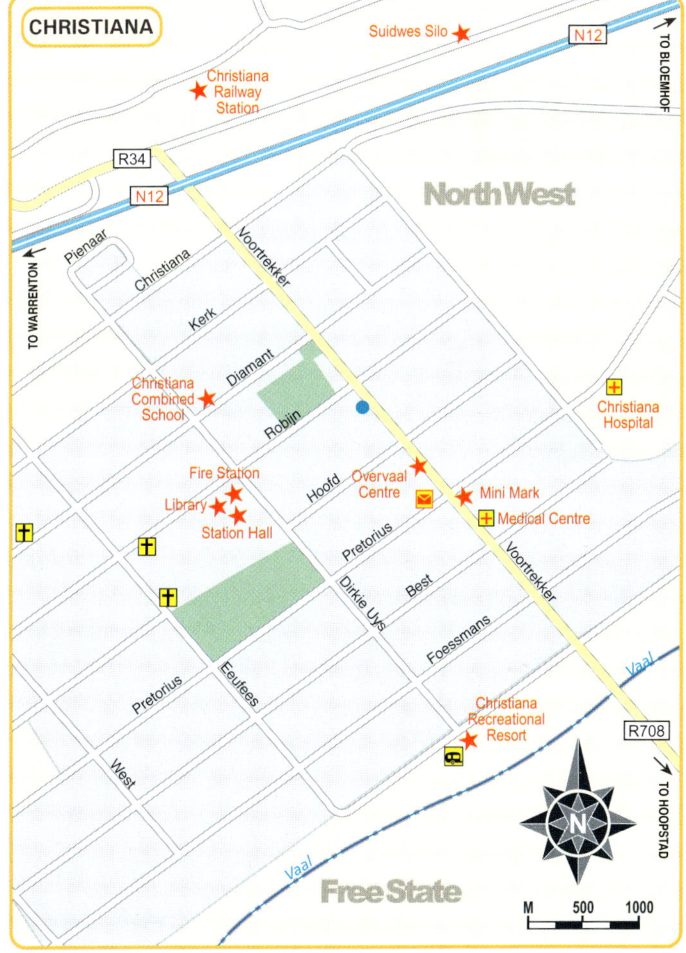

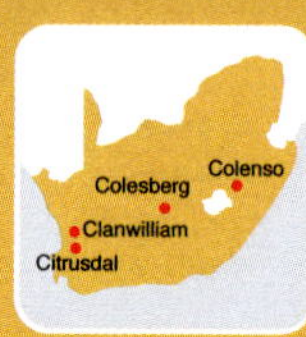

Colesberg
Colenso
Clanwilliam
Citrusdal

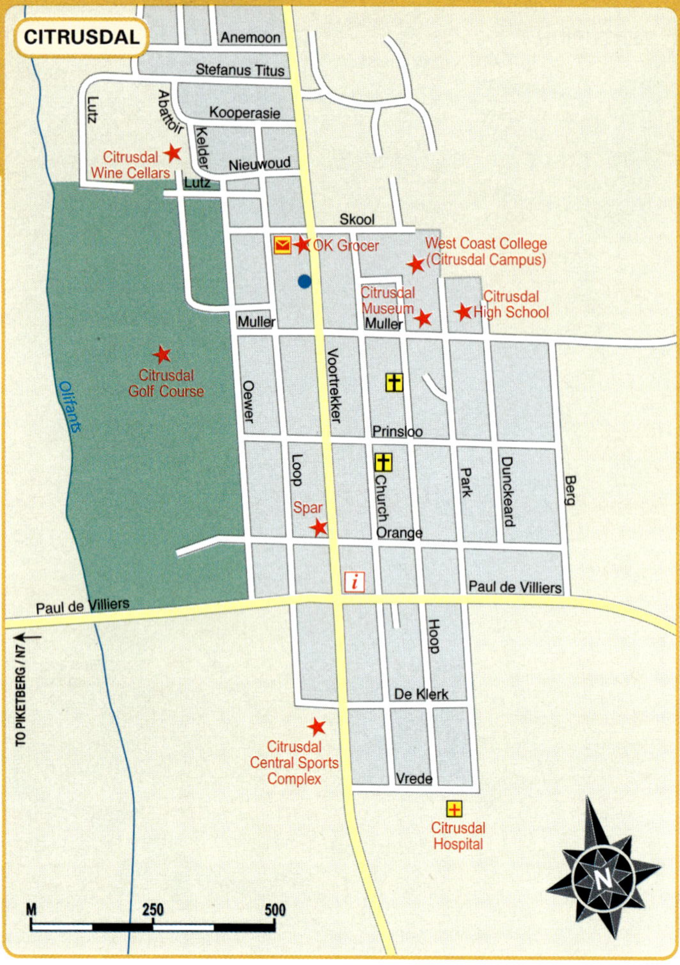

CITRUSDAL
Anemoon
Stefanus Titus
Kooperasie
Lutz
Abattoir
Kelder
Nieuwoud
Citrusdal Wine Cellars
Skool
OK Grocer
West Coast College (Citrusdal Campus)
Citrusdal Museum
Citrusdal High School
Muller
Citrusdal Golf Course
Olifants
Oewer
Voortrekker
Prinsloo
Loop
Church
Park
Dunckeard
Berg
Spar
Orange
Paul de Villiers
Hoop
De Klerk
Citrusdal Central Sports Complex
Vrede
Citrusdal Hospital
TO PIKETBERG / N7
M
250
500
N

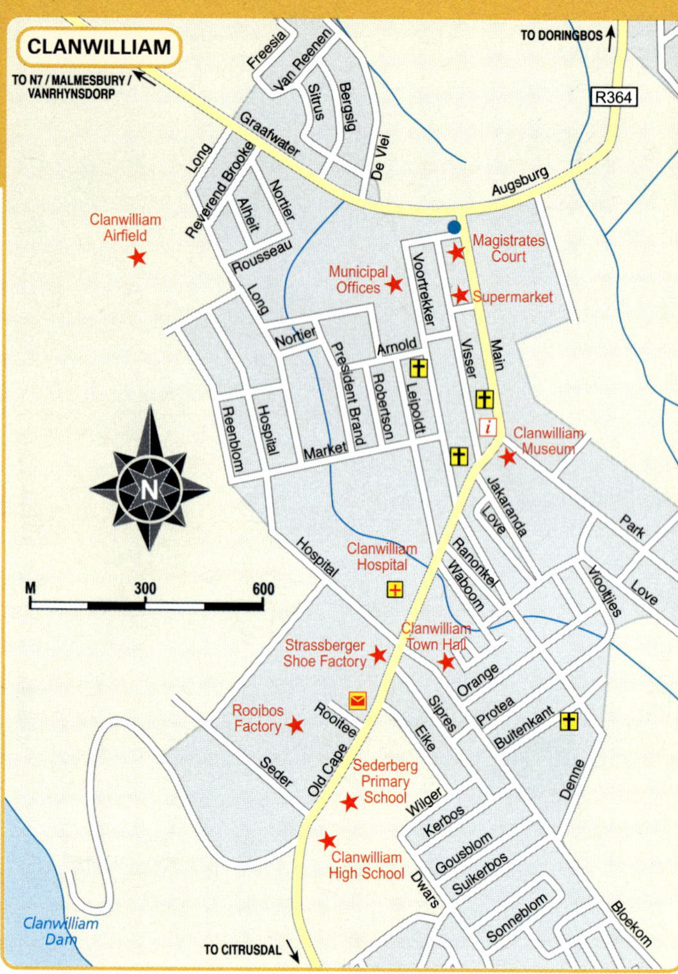

CLANWILLIAM
TO N7 / MALMESBURY / VANRHYNSDORP
TO DORINGBOS
R364
Freesia
Van Reenen
Sitrus
Bergsig
Graafwater
De Vlei
Augsburg
Long
Reverend Brooke
Alheit
Nortier
Clanwilliam Airfield
Rousseau
Magistrates Court
Municipal Offices
Supermarket
Voortrekker
Arnold
President Brand
Robertson
Leipoldt
Visser
Main
Reenblom
Hospital
Market
Clanwilliam Museum
Jakaranda
Love
Park
M
300
600
N
Clanwilliam Hospital
Ranonkel
Waboom
Vooltjies
Clanwilliam Town Hall
Strassberger Shoe Factory
Orange
Sipres
Protea
Buitenkant
Rooibos Factory
Rooitee
Elke
Seder
Old Cape
Sederberg Primary School
Wilger
Kerbos
Denne
Clanwilliam High School
Gousblom
Suikerbos
Dwars
Sonneblom
Bloekom
Clanwilliam Dam
TO CITRUSDAL

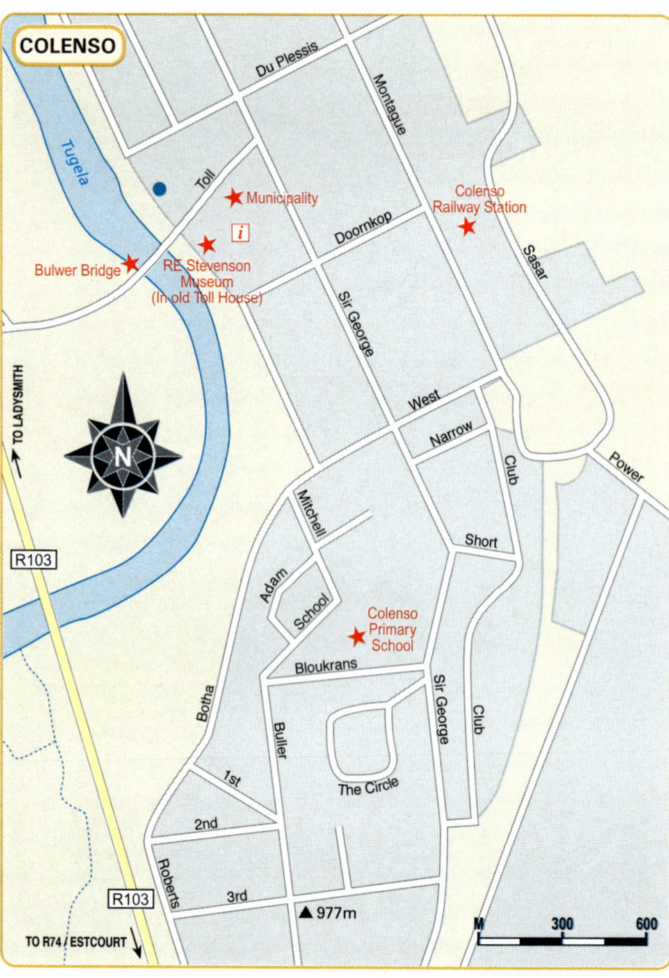

COLENSO
Du Plessis
Montague
Tugela
Toll
Municipality
Colenso Railway Station
Doornkop
Sasar
Bulwer Bridge
RE Stevenson Museum (In old Toll House)
Sir George
West
Narrow
Club
Power
TO LADYSMITH
N
Mitchell
Short
R103
Adam
School
Colenso Primary School
Bloukrans
Botha
Buller
Sir George
Club
The Circle
1st
2nd
Roberts
3rd
977m
R103
TO R74 / ESTCOURT
M
300
600

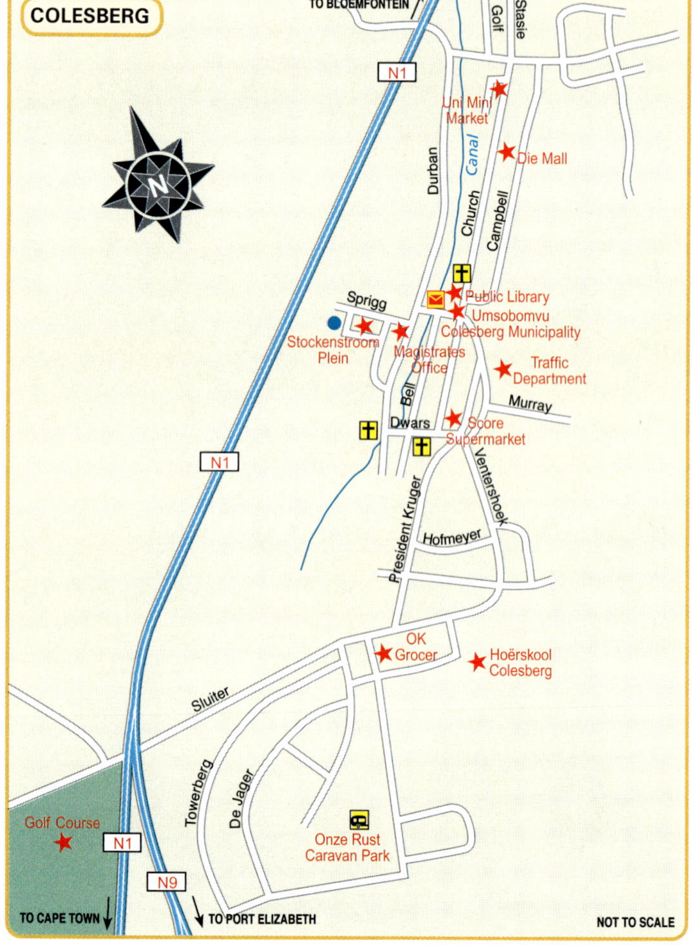

COLESBERG
TO BLOEMFONTEIN
Golf
Stasie
N1
Uni Mini Market
Die Mall
Canal
Durban
Church
Campbell
N
Sprigg
Public Library
Umsobomvu Colesberg Municipality
Stockenstroom Plein
Magistrates Office
Traffic Department
Bell
Murray
Dwars
Score Supermarket
N1
Ventershoek
President Kruger
Hofmeyer
OK Grocer
Hoërskool Colesberg
Sluiter
Towerberg
De Jager
Golf Course
N1
Onze Rust Caravan Park
N9
TO CAPE TOWN
TO PORT ELIZABETH
NOT TO SCALE

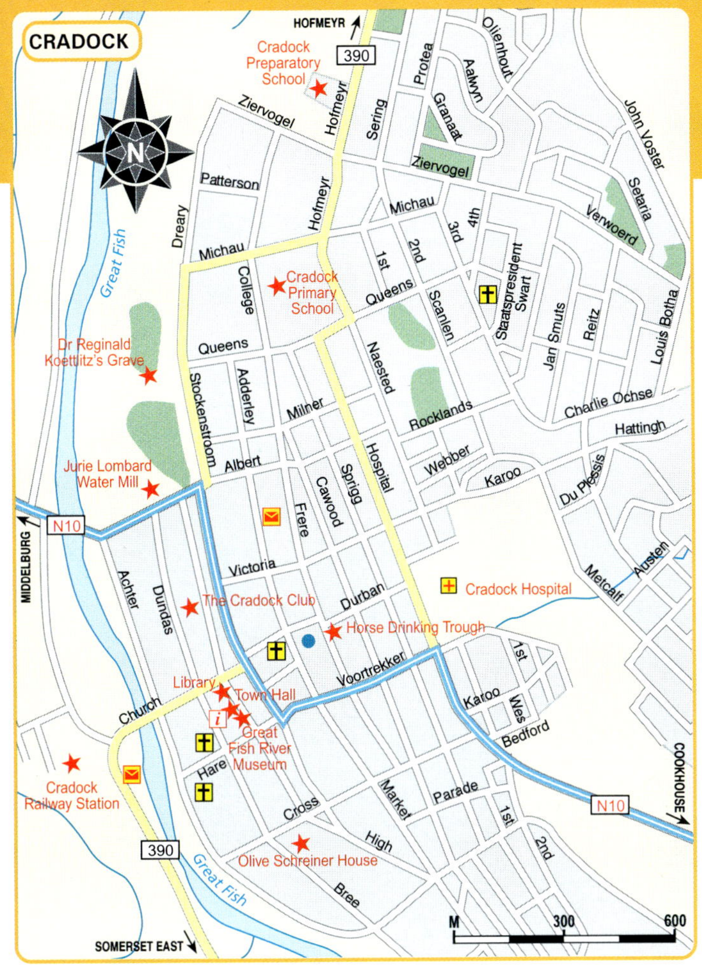
CRADOCK
HOFMEYR
390
Cradock Preparatory School
Ziervogel
Hofmeyr
Sering
Protea
Granaat
Aakyn
Olienhout
John Vorster
Setaria
Verwoerd
Ziervogel
Patterson
Dreary
Michau
Michau
4th
3rd
2nd
1st
Hofmeyr
Great Fish
College
Cradock Primary School
Queens
Scanlen
Staatspresident Swart
Jan Smuts
Reitz
Louis Botha
Dr Reginald Koettlitz's Grave
Queens
Adderley
Stockenstroom
Milner
Naested
Rocklands
Charlie Ochse
Hattingh
Jurie Lombard Water Mill
Albert
Hospital
Sprigg
Cawood
Frere
Webber
Karoo
Du Plessis
N10
MIDDELBURG
Achter
Dundas
Victoria
Durban
Metcalf
Austen
Cradock Hospital
The Cradock Club
Horse Drinking Trough
Voortrekker
1st
Library
Town Hall
Church
Great Fish River Museum
Karoo
Wes
Bedford
Hare
Cradock Railway Station
Cross
Market
Parade
1st
2nd
N10
COOKHOUSE
390
High
Olive Schreiner House
Great Fish
Bree
SOMERSET EAST
M
300
600

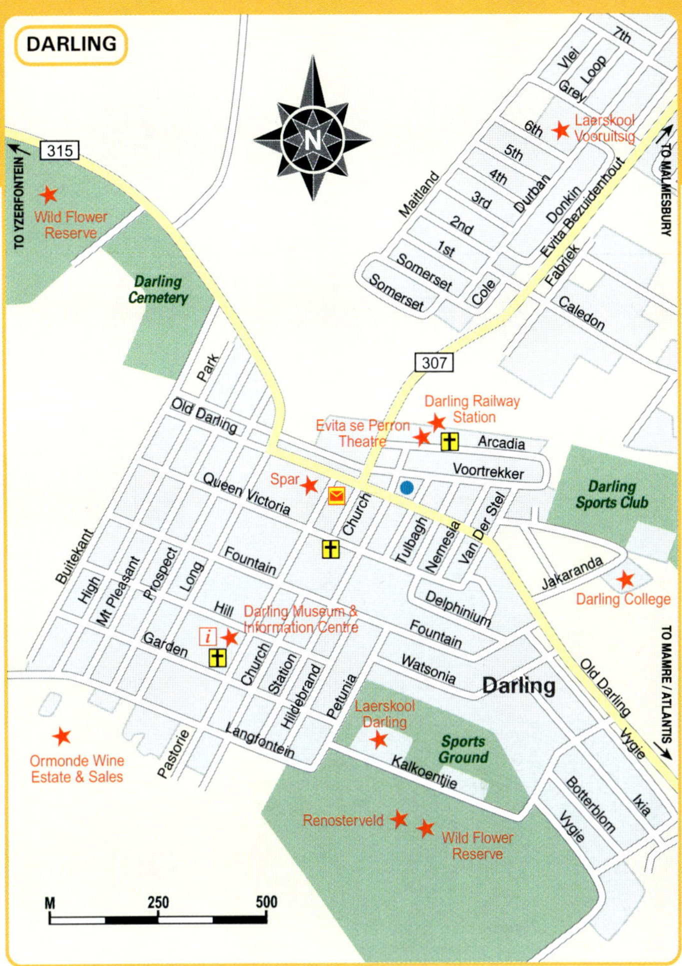
DARLING
7th
Vlei
Loop
Grey
Laerskool Vooruitsig
6th
5th
4th
3rd
2nd
1st
Maitland
Durban
Donkin
Evita Bezuidenhout
TO MALMESBURY
Somerset
Somerset
Cole
Fabriek
Caledon
315
TO YZERFONTEIN
Wild Flower Reserve
Darling Cemetery
307
Park
Old Darling
Darling Railway Station
Evita se Perron Theatre
Arcadia
Voortrekker
Spar
Queen Victoria
Church
Tulbagh
Nemesia
Van Der Stel
Darling Sports Club
Buitekant
High
Mt Pleasant
Prospect
Long
Fountain
Jakaranda
Darling College
Hill
Darling Museum & Information Centre
Delphinium
Fountain
Garden
Church
Station
Hildebrand
Petunia
Watsonia
Darling
TO MAMRE / ATLANTIS
Old Darling
Vygie
Laerskool Darling
Sports Ground
Langfontein
Pastorie
Kalkoentjie
Ormonde Wine Estate & Sales
Botterblom
Vygie
Ixia
Renosterveld
Wild Flower Reserve
M
250
500

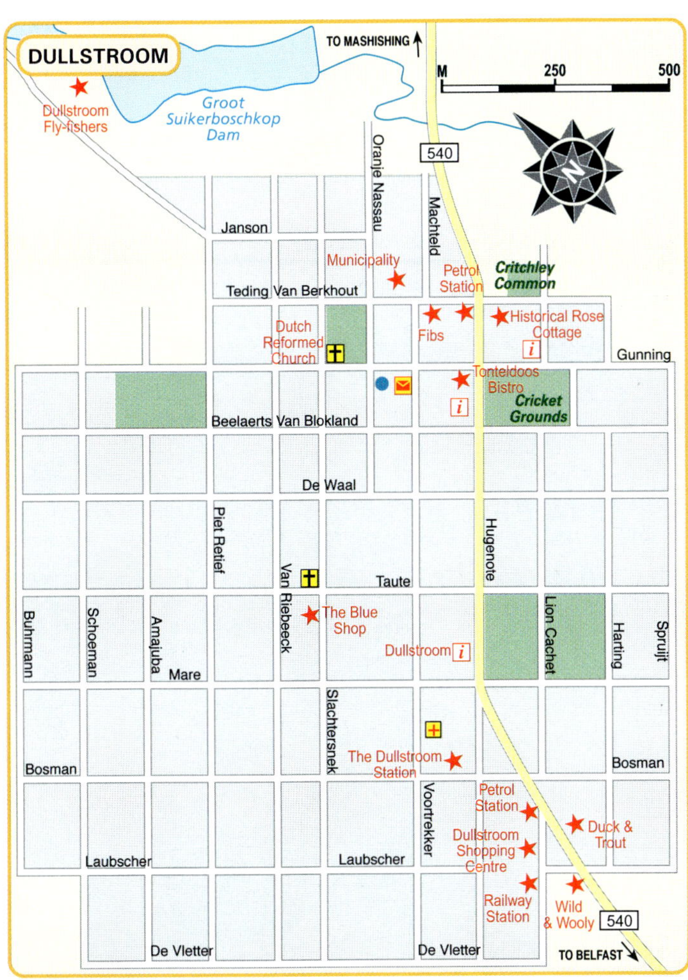
DULLSTROOM
TO MASHISHING
Dullstroom Fly-fishers
Groot Suikerboschkop Dam
M
250
500
540
Oranje Nassau
Machteld
Janson
Municipality
Petrol Station
Critchley Common
Teding Van Berkhout
Dutch Reformed Church
Fibs
Historical Rose Cottage
Gunning
Tonteldoos Bistro
Cricket Grounds
Beelaerts Van Blokland
De Waal
Piet Retief
Hugenote
Van Riebeeck
Taute
The Blue Shop
Dullstroom
Lion Cachet
Harting
Sprujit
Buhrmann
Schoeman
Amajuba
Mare
Slachtersnek
Bosman
Bosman
The Dullstroom Station
Voortrekker
Petrol Station
Duck & Trout
Dullstroom Shopping Centre
Laubscher
Laubscher
Railway Station
Wild & Wooly
540
De Vletter
De Vletter
TO BELFAST

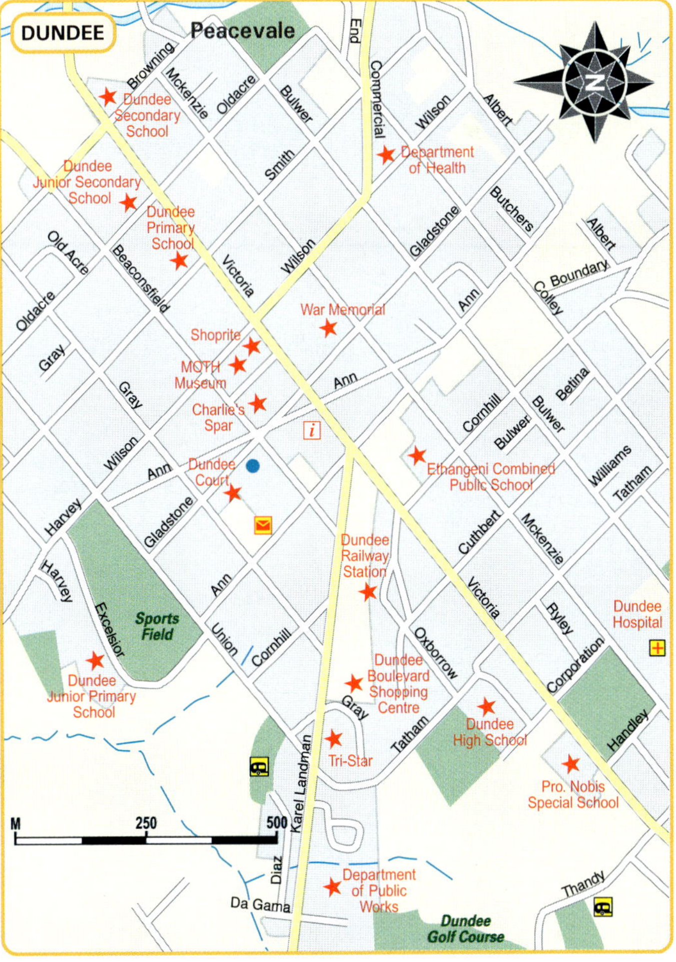
DUNDEE
Peacevale
End
Browning
Mckenzie
Oldacre
Bulwer
Commercial
Wilson
Albert
Dundee Secondary School
Smith
Department of Health
Dundee Junior Secondary School
Dundee Primary School
Butchers
Old Acre
Beaconsfield
Victoria
Wilson
Gladstone
Albert
Boundary
Colley
Oldacre
Gray
War Memorial
Ann
Shoprite
MOTH Museum
Ann
Gray
Charlie's Spar
Cornhill
Betina
Bulwer
Bulwer
Wilson
Ann
Dundee Court
Ethangeni Combined Public School
Williams
Tatham
Harvey
Gladstone
Mckenzie
Cuthbert
Harvey
Dundee Railway Station
Ann
Victoria
Excelsior
Sports Field
Union
Cornhill
Oxborrow
Ryley
Dundee Hospital
Corporation
Dundee Junior Primary School
Dundee Boulevard Shopping Centre
Gray
Tatham
Dundee High School
Handley
Tri-Star
Pro. Nobis Special School
Karel Landman
M
250
500
Diaz
Department of Public Works
Da Gama
Thandy
Dundee Golf Course

116 EAST LONDON ERMELO

eMPANGENI eSHOWE

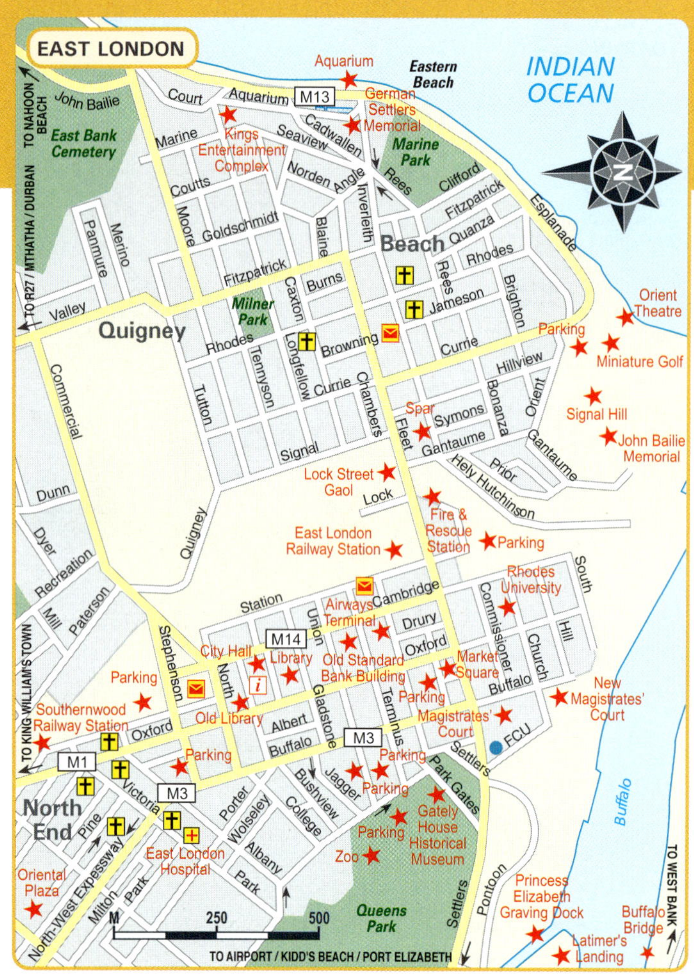

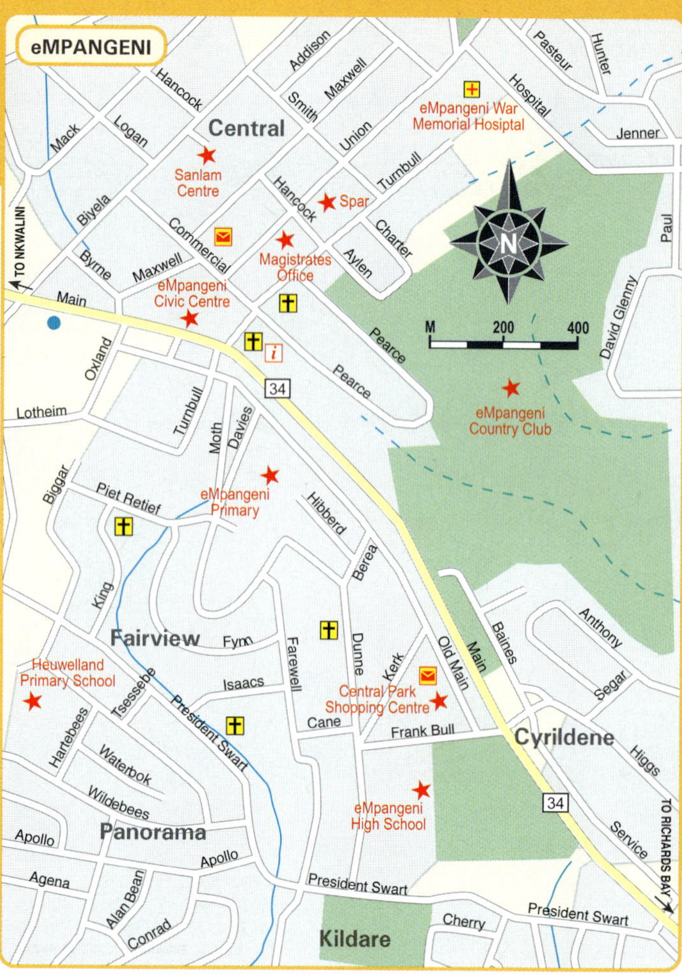

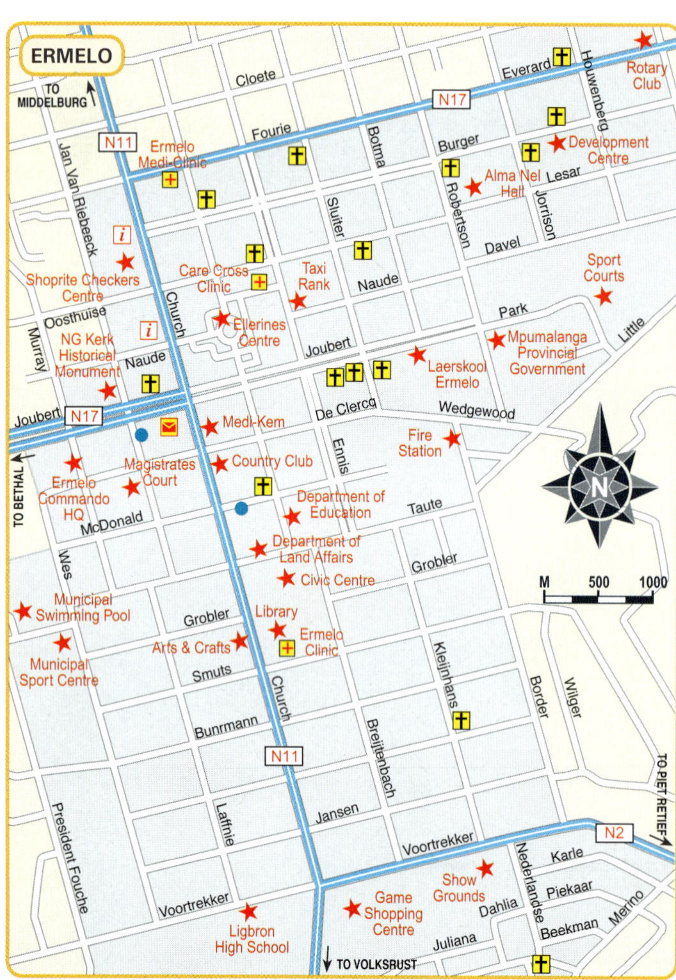

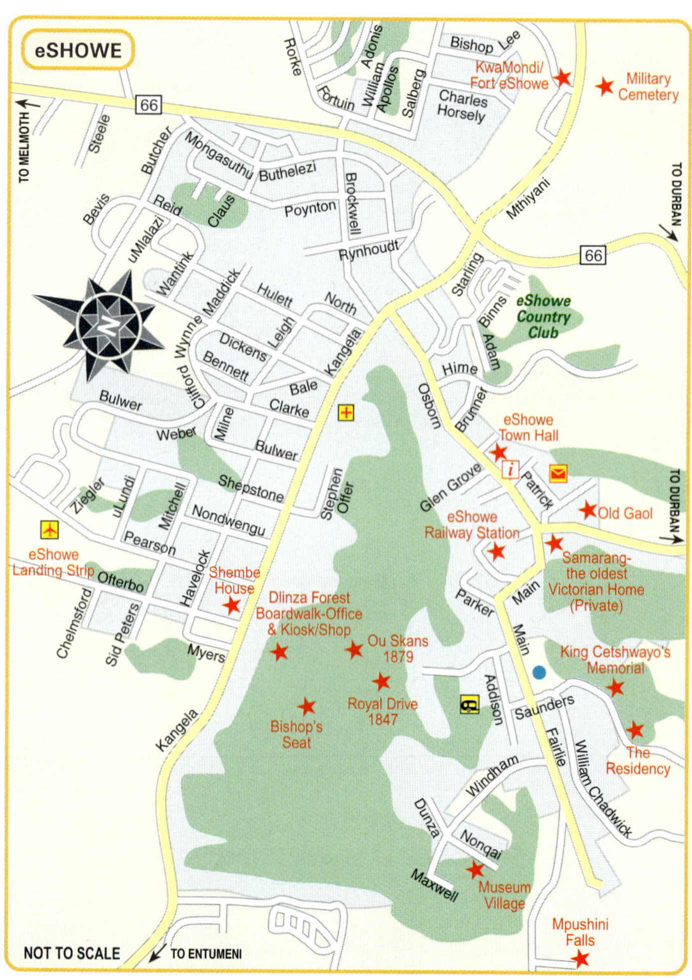

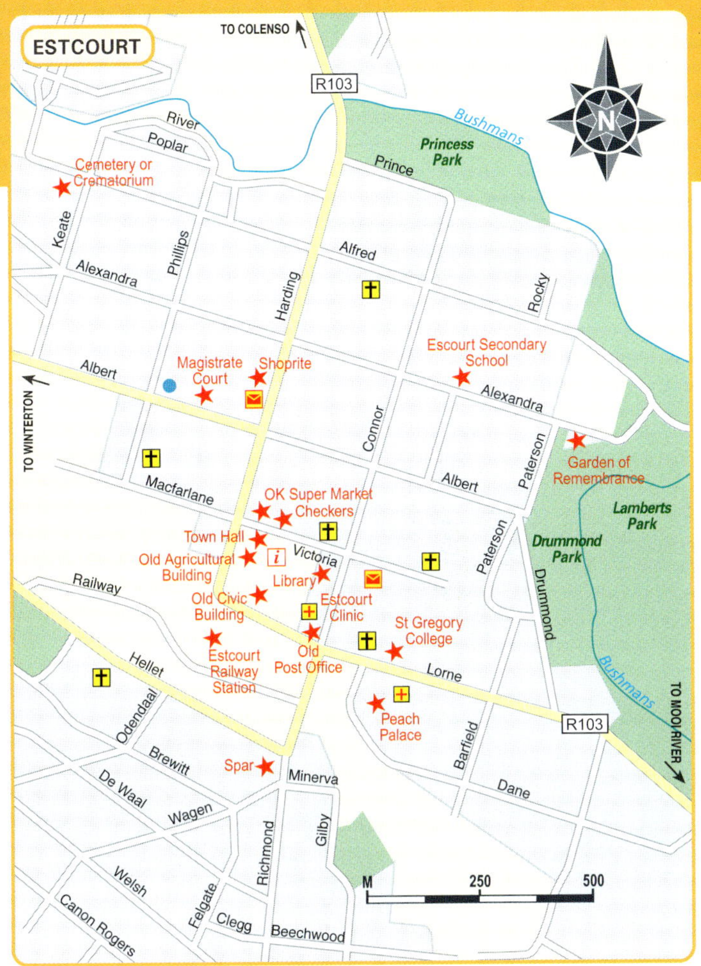
ESTCOURT
TO COLENSO
R103
Princess Park
Bushmans
Cemetery or Crematorium
Magistrate Court
Shoprite
Escourt Secondary School
Garden of Remembrance
Lamberts Park
Drummond Park
OK Super Market
Checkers
Town Hall
Old Agricultural Building
Library
Old Civic Building
Estcourt Clinic
St Gregory College
Estcourt Railway Station
Old Post Office
Peach Palace
Spar
TO WINTERTON
TO MOOI RIVER
R103
M 250 500

FICKSBURG
TO FOURIESBURG
Ficksburg Country Club
Quantum Primary School
Ficksburg Railway Station
Ficksburg Primary School
Cemetery
Hennie De Wet Park Sports Grounds
Town Hall
Ficksburg Museum
Shoprite
Ficksburg High School
TO CLOCOLAN
Phutholoha District Hospital
TO MAPUTSOE
Caledon Park Primary School
M 300 600

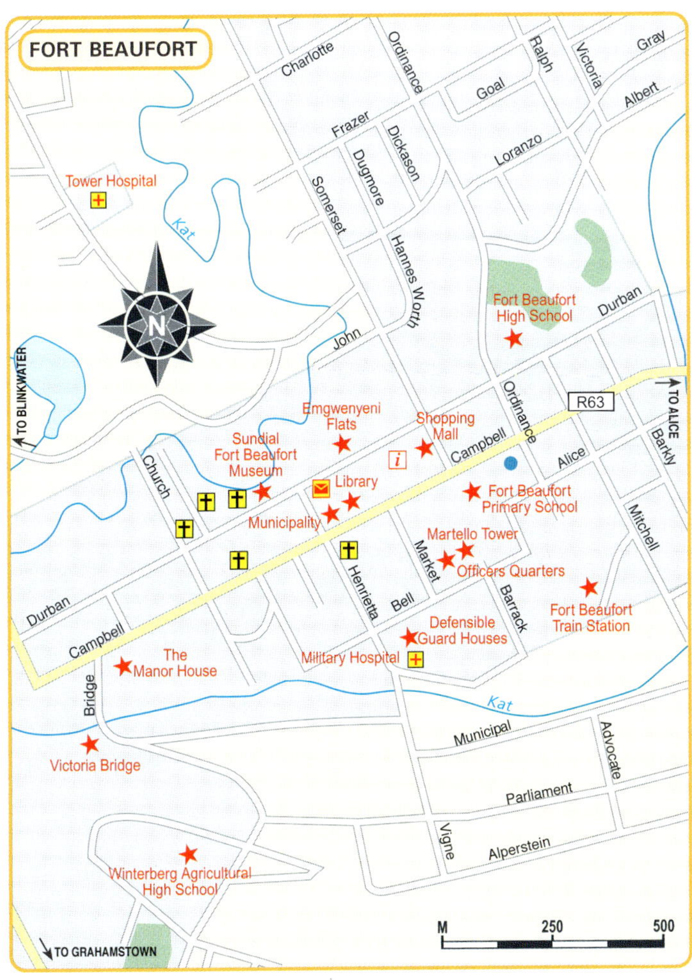
FORT BEAUFORT
Tower Hospital
Kat
Fort Beaufort High School
TO BLINKWATER
R63
TO ALICE
Emgwenyeni Flats
Shopping Mall
Sundial Fort Beaufort Museum
Library
Municipality
Fort Beaufort Primary School
Martello Tower
Officers Quarters
Fort Beaufort Train Station
Defensible Guard Houses
Military Hospital
The Manor House
Victoria Bridge
Winterberg Agricultural High School
TO GRAHAMSTOWN
M 250 500

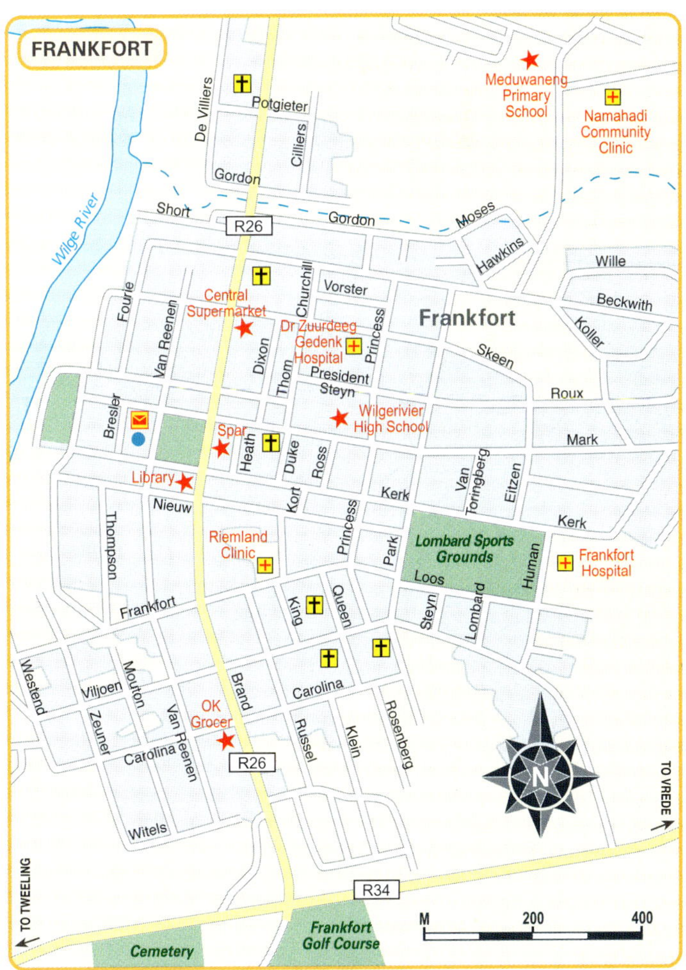
FRANKFORT
Meduwaneng Primary School
Namahadi Community Clinic
Wilge River
R26
Frankfort
Central Supermarket
Dr Zuurdeeg Gedenk Hospital
Wilgerivier High School
Spar
Library
Riemland Clinic
Lombard Sports Grounds
Frankfort Hospital
OK Grocer
R26
R34
TO VREDE
TO TWEELING
Cemetery
Frankfort Golf Course
M 200 400

FRANSCHHOEK GEORGE

GANSBAAI GERMISTON

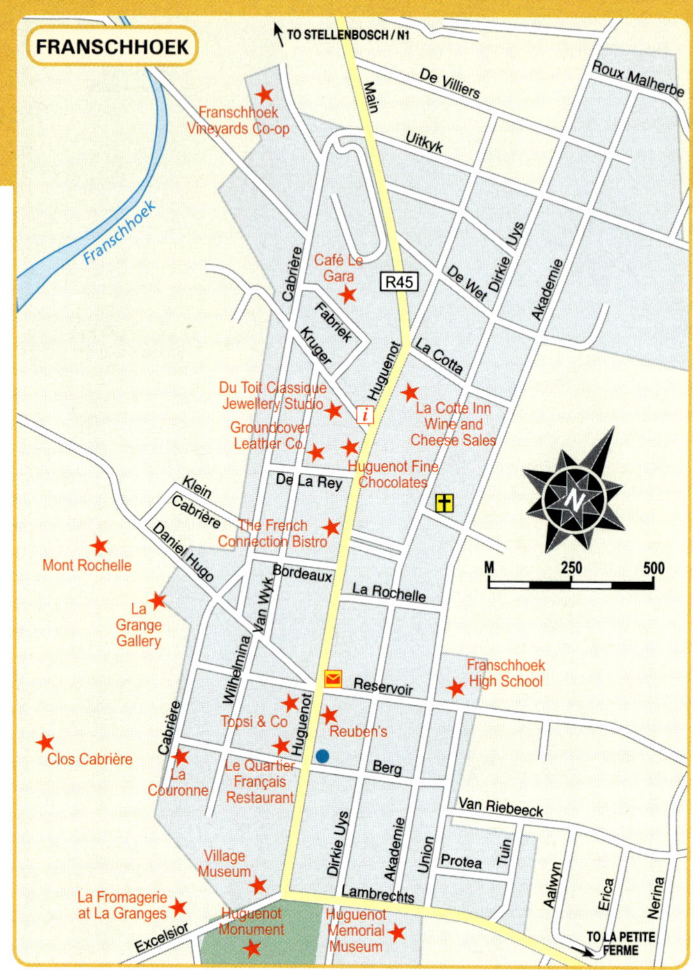

GINGINDLOVU
GRAAFF-REINET
GLENCOE
GRABOUW

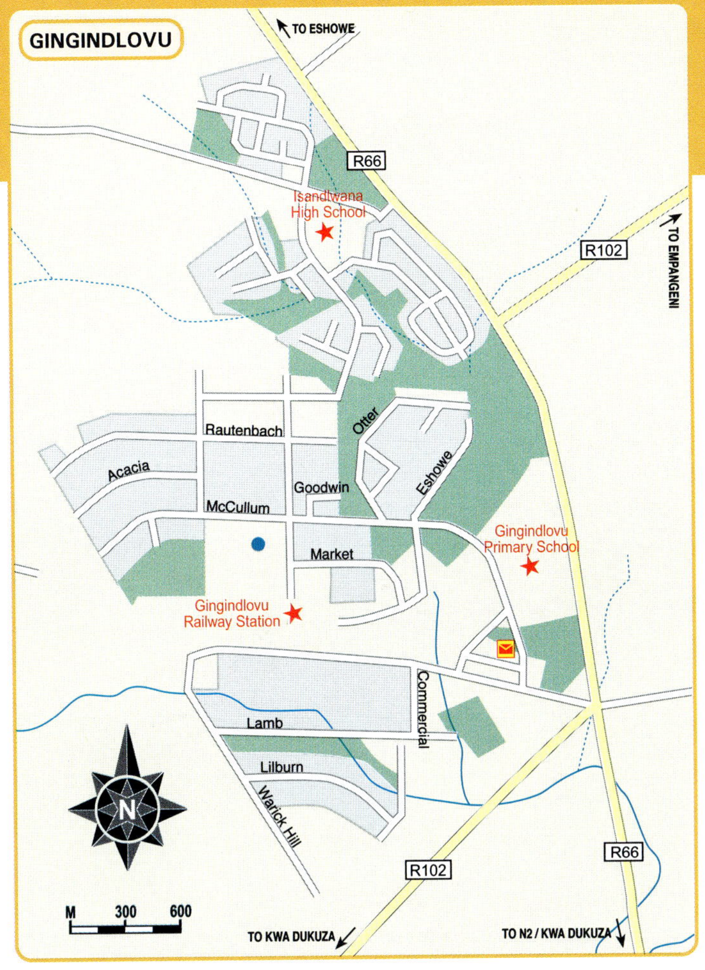

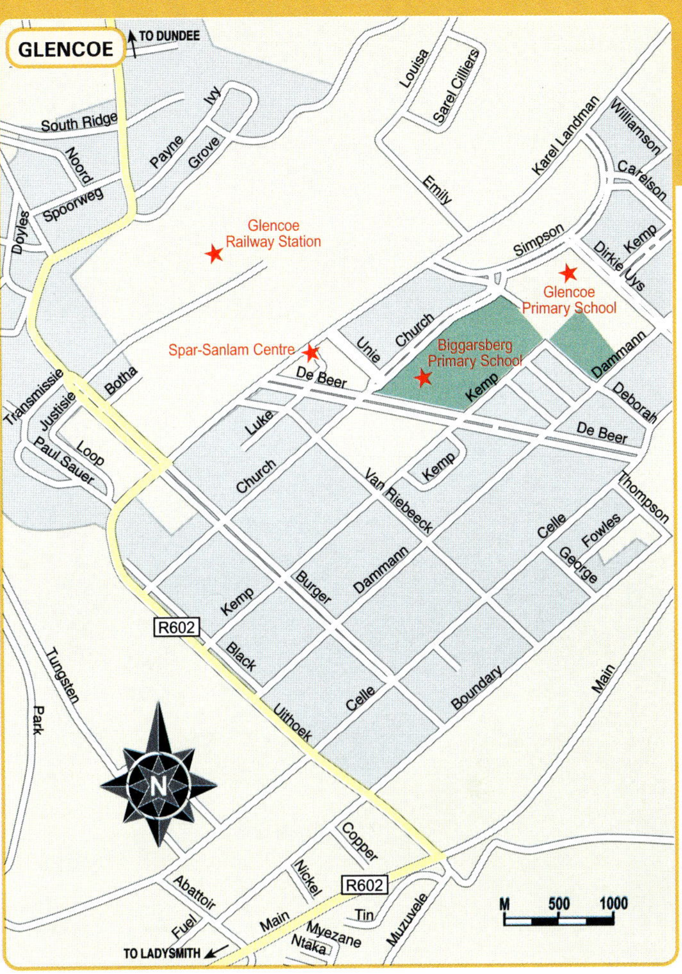

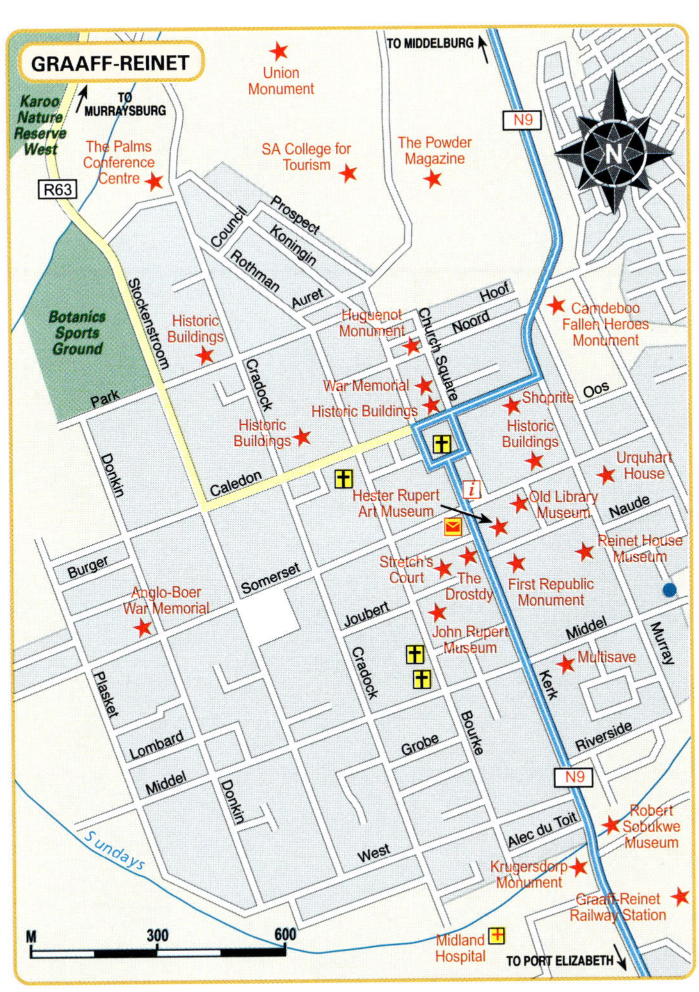

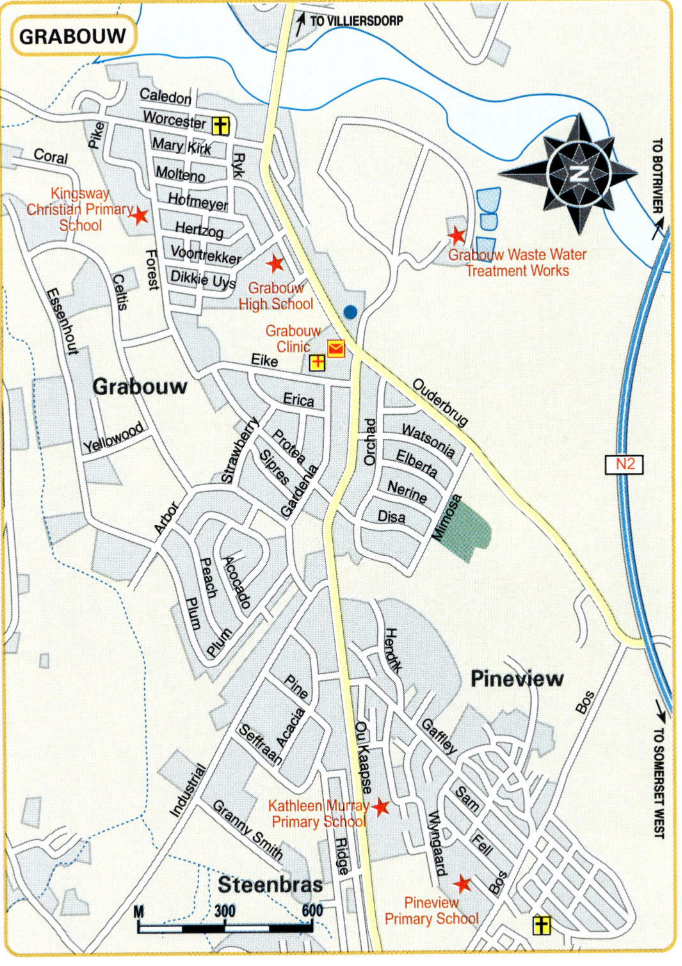

GRASKOP GREYTOWN

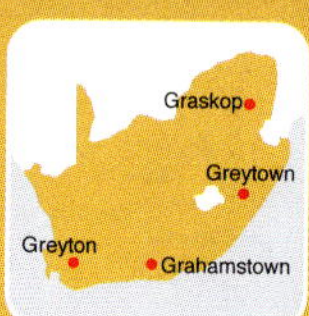

GRAHAMSTOWN

Oatlands
Albany Bowling Club
Slater
Kingswood College Secondary School
St Aidans
Miller
Oatlands
Henry
Charles
Lansdowne
Kingswood College Primary School
Burton
Caldecott
Fordyce
Constitution
Speke
Napier
Roberts
Anderson
Worcester
Holland
Grant
Carlisle
Hodges
TO BEDFORD / N10
Oatlands Preparatory School
Spring
Settlers Day Hospital
TO FORT BEAUFORT / FORT BROWN
St Andrew's College
Rose
Luke
Fire Station
Cawood
Cobden
Pepper Grove Mall
Hill
Knight
High
Baillie
African
New
Observatory Museum
Shaw Chapel
Allen
Cuyler
Sephton
Link
South African Institute for Biodiversity
Anglo African St Clinic
Anglo African
Cathedral Church
Beaufort
Grahamstown Municipal Clinic
Dundas
The Odean
Prince Alfred
Scotts
Library
Bathurst
Market Square
Hemming
Library
Howse
West
Drostdy Gateway
High
Thomson
Huntley
The Cock
Somerset
Victoria Girls' Primary School
St Bartholomew
Mill
Rhodes University
Albany Museum
Montagu
Nelson
Market
Victoria Girls' High School
Chase
History Museum
Cross
Lucas
Provost Prison
Johan Carinus Art Centre
Whitnall
Webbs (Hillsview)
Lawrence
Shepperson
St Peter's Campus
Donkin
Rae
Market
Cathcart
Makana Botanical Gardens
Somerset
Robinson
Hillsview
Darling
TO PEDDIE / KING WILLIAM'S TOWN
Grey
Fort Selwyn
PJ Olivier High School
Hillsview
1820 Settlers National Monument
Douglas Reservoir
Makana Municipal Campsite/Caravan Park
Grahamstown Bypass
TO PORT ELIZABETH
N2
Mountain
M 300 600

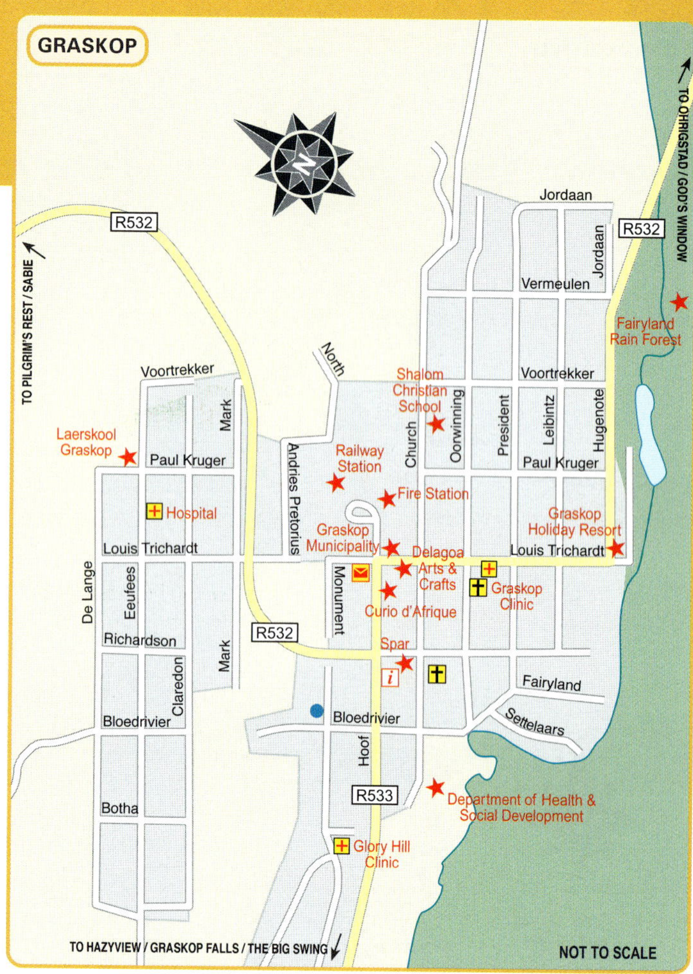

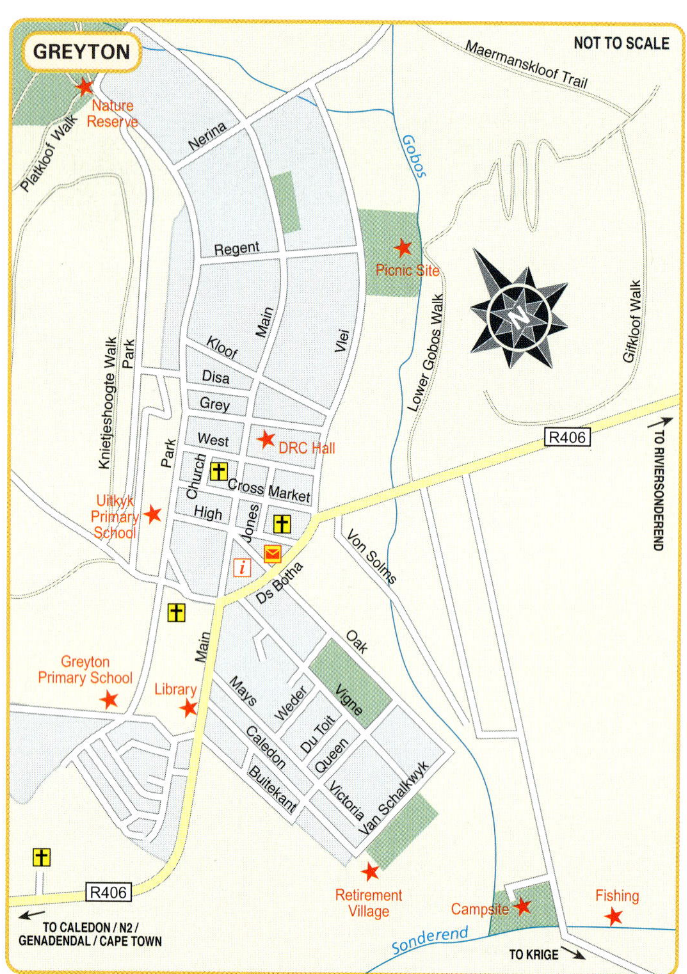

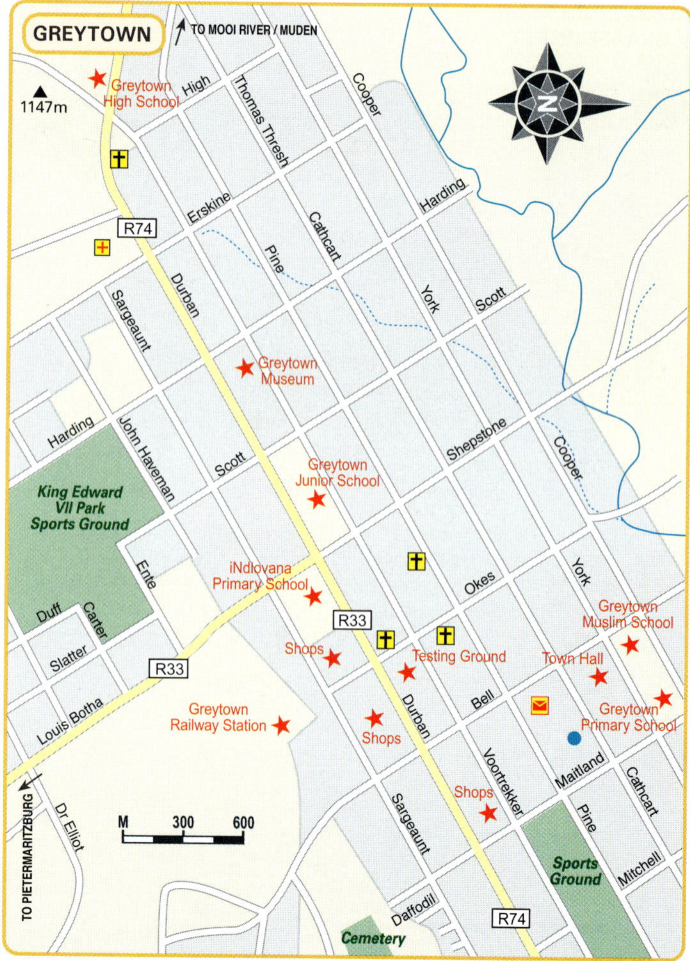

GRIQUATOWN HARRISMITH HARDING HARTENBOS

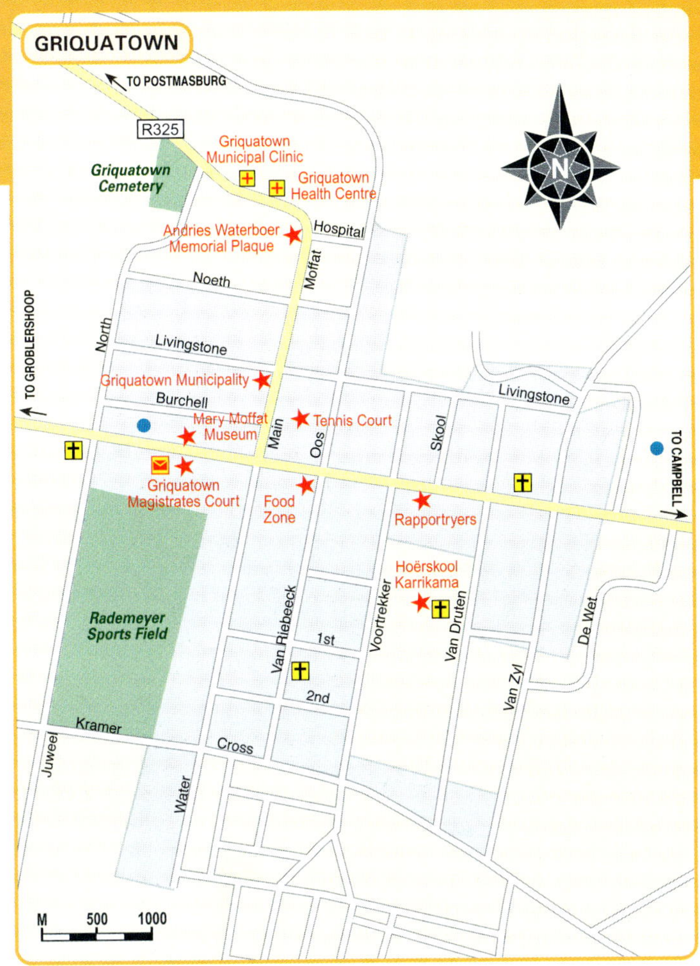

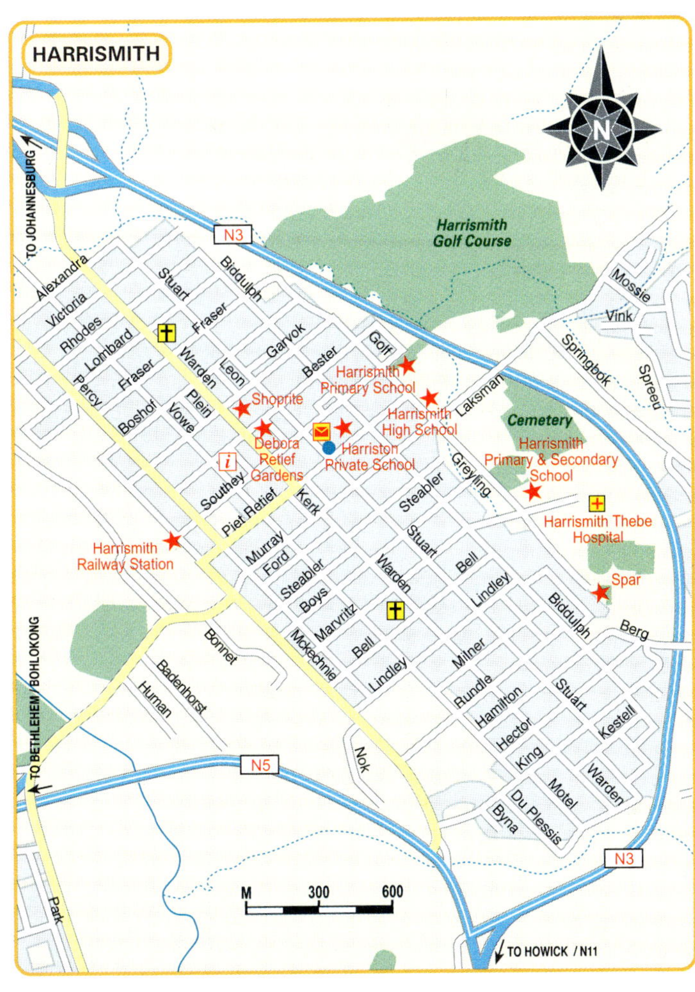

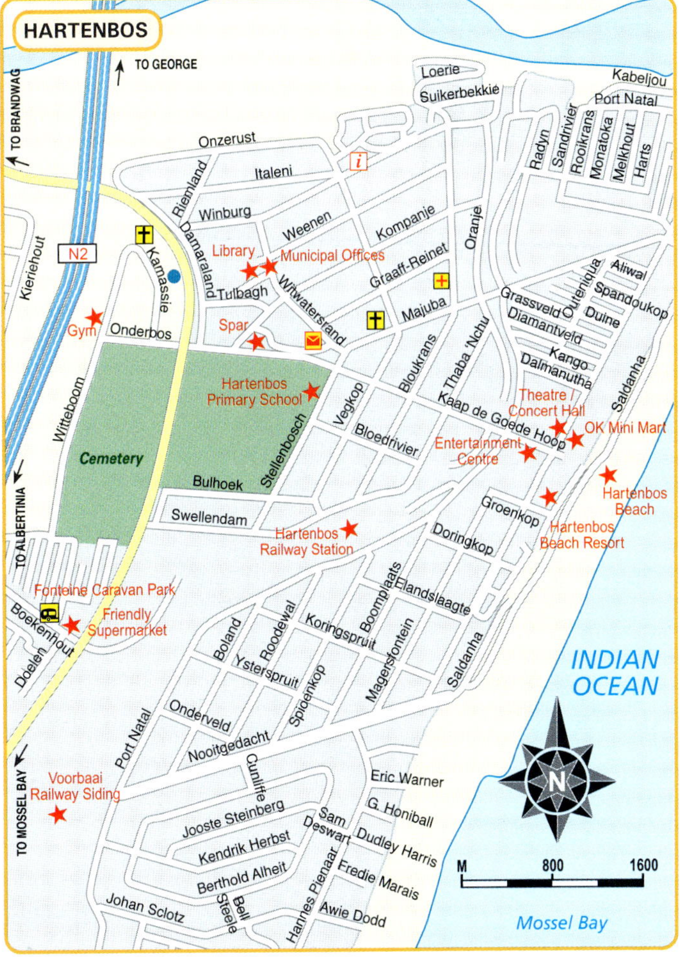

Hazyview
Heidelberg
Heilbron
Heidelberg

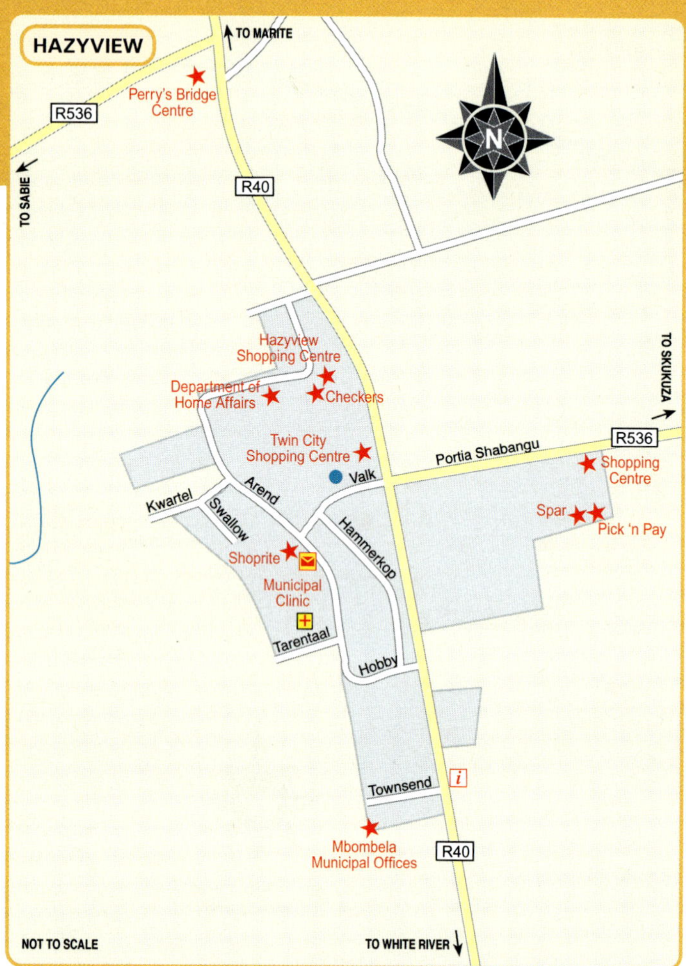
HAZYVIEW
TO MARITE
R536
Perry's Bridge Centre
TO SABIE
R40
TO SKUKUZA
Hazyview Shopping Centre
Department of Home Affairs
Checkers
Twin City Shopping Centre
Portia Shabangu
R536
Shopping Centre
Valk
Kwartel
Arend
Swallow
Spar
Pick 'n Pay
Hammerkop
Shoprite
Municipal Clinic
Tarentaal
Hobby
Townsend
Mbombela Municipal Offices
R40
NOT TO SCALE
TO WHITE RIVER

HEIDELBERG (GAUTENG)
TO BENONI
Kloof Cemetery
Kloofspruit
R23
The Victorian Shopping Centre
Jordaan
Marais
Louw
Pretorius
Begeman
Laerskool Volkskool
Van der Westhuizen
Library
Ueckermann
Jacobs
A.G. Visser Bust
NGK Klipkerk
Strydom
Du Preez
Berg
Fenter
Town Hall
Maré
R42
Hospitaal
Suikerbosrand Municipal Clinic
Ueckermann Municipal Clinic
Van der Westhuizen
Begeman
Unie
H.F. Verwoerd
Voortrekker
60 Strydom St
Heidelberg Hospital
Merz
Traffic Department
Fraser
Graham
Von Geusau
Smit
Harvey
Van Der Steen
Sipresboom
Blokkomboom
Van Driel
Blyth
Schoeman
Apsey
Marshall
Rissik
Oasis Shopping Centre
Freeman
TO VEREENIGING / MEYERTON
M 300 600
Heidelberg Primary School
Sager
Simla
Community Hall
Library
Shalimar Ridge Municipal Clinic
Chris
Reitz
Albert
TO DENEYSVILLE

HEIDELBERG (WESTERN CAPE)
Muir
Van Eeden
De Jager
Meyer
Heidelberg Railway Station
Heidelberg High School
Ford
Van Aardt
Kleinhans
Swimming Pool
Murray
De Villiers
Heidelberg Golf Club
Louw
Raal
Heidelberg Municipality
Niekerk
Krige
Reitz
Van Riebeeck
Spar
Swart
Fourie
Uys
Buitekant
Eksteen
Rainer
TO RIVERSDALE
Middelton
Uys
Marais
N2
Haig
High
Lilly
Lilly
Kloof
Mission
Church
M 800 1600
Newton
Olimpic
Barlow
Schierhout
Yuong
Geldenhuys
Gamble
Helm
Roberts
Johansen
King
Kairos Secondary School
Malva
TO SWELLENDAM

HEILBRON
TO SASOLBURG
Petunia
Haarlem
Sandersville
Sandersville Community Hall & Clinic
Moeweni
Molsepe
Xaba
Mololo
Poho
R57
Schoeman
Willemse
Sandersville Combined School
Concentration Camp Cemetery
Mopgotsi
Molebela
Sibeko
Phiritone Community Hall
M 250 500
Hull
Wentworth
Steyn
Vegkop
Tiente Grobler
Pierce
Els
Bree
Plein
Ringer
Potgieter
Botha
Steil
Loubser
Parradys
Boitumelong Primary School
Landmark
Cilliers
Eendracht Heilbron Volkskool
Kerk
Heil
Heilbron
Oranje
Jacobs
Tanner
Luyt
Heil
Els
Plein
R57
TO PARYS
Leahy
Oranje
Hospital
Library
Via Felix
Tokollo District Hospital
Myron
Heilbron Railway Station
Heilbron Civic Centre
Tucker
Bree
Raubenheim
Pienaar
Spoor
Gilbert
Greenman
Nicol
Pierce
School of Destiny Combined School
Lamprecht
Stoffel Nel
Raubenheim
Heilbron Golf Club
Heilbron High School
Bree
TO KROONSTAD
Bree
1st
8th
Sonneblom
Swart
9th
2nd
3rd
7th
TO PETRUS STEYN

HERMANUS
TO GANSBAAI
Walker Bay
Cliff Path
Eastcliff
Mitchell
Hermanus High School
Moffat
Mcfarlane
Stemmet
Main
Nichol
Maffat
Musson
Luyt
Lord Roberts
Village Square Shopping Centre
Old Harbour Museum
Perlemoen Hatchery
Castle Rock
Whale Crier
Library
Magnolia
Hermanus Primary School
Dirkie Uys
Aberdeen Shopping Centre
Paterson
Long
Victoria Square Shopping Centre
Steenbok
Mossie
Harmony
Overstrand Municipality
Bird
Hermanus Accommodation Centre
Gearings Point
Robin
Albertyn
R43
INDIAN OCEAN
Fourie
Flower
Church
Marine
Fick's Pool
Flora
Main
Smuts
Cliff Path
Duiker
De Goede
Armagh
Westcliff
Fynbos Park
Hermanus Medi-Clinic Hospital
TO CAPE TOWN
M 300 600

HIBBERDENE
TO DURBAN
N2
Main
TO PORT SHEPSTONE
Hooper
Hooper
901
R102
David
Santa Barbara
Aubrey
Catalina
Minerva
Hibberdene Railway Station
Bermuda
Town Hall
Capri
St Ives
Marlin
Baracuda
Tahiti
Bermuda
Riviera Highway
Capri
Hibberdene Village Shopping Centre
Hibberdene
Happy Days
INDIAN OCEAN
Mzimayi
R102
Casuarina
Woodgrange
Simpson
M 300 600

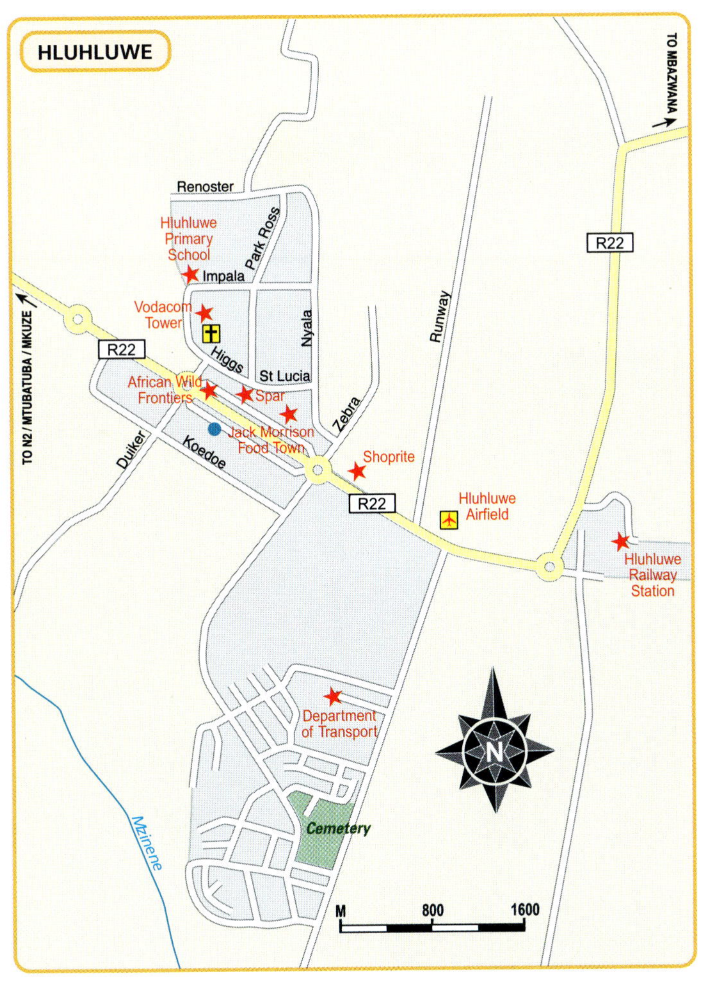
HLUHLUWE
TO MBAZWANA
Renoster
Hluhluwe Primary School
Park Ross
Impala
R22
Runway
Vodacom Tower
Nyala
TO N2/ MTUBATUBA / MKUZE
R22
Higgs
St Lucia
African Wild Frontiers
Spar
Zebra
Jack Morrison Food Town
Duiker
Koedoe
Shoprite
R22
Hluhluwe Airfield
Hluhluwe Railway Station
Department of Transport
Cemetery
Mzinene
M 800 1600

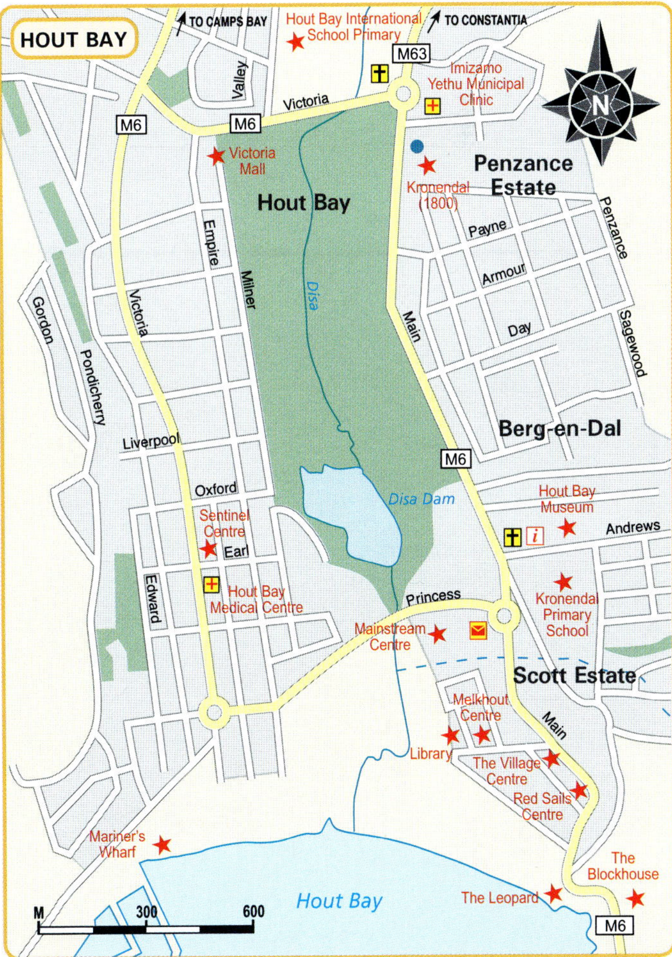
HOUT BAY
TO CAMPS BAY
Hout Bay International School Primary
TO CONSTANTIA
M63
Imizamo Yethu Municipal Clinic
Valley
Victoria
M6
M6
Victoria Mall
Penzance Estate
Kronendal (1800)
Hout Bay
Payne
Penzance
Empire
Armour
Gordon
Milner
Disa
Day
Victoria
Main
Sagewood
Pondicherry
Liverpool
Berg-en-Dal
M6
Oxford
Disa Dam
Sentinel Centre
Hout Bay Museum
Earl
Andrews
Edward
Hout Bay Medical Centre
Kronendal Primary School
Princess
Mainstream Centre
Scott Estate
Melkhout Centre
Main
Library
The Village Centre
Red Sails Centre
Mariner's Wharf
The Blockhouse
Hout Bay
The Leopard
M 300 600
M6

HOWICK JEFFREYS BAY HUMANSDORP KENTON-ON-SEA

HOWICK

TO RIETVLEI
TO N3 / MOOI RIVER
TO N3 / PIETERMARITZBURG
Gush
Paddock
Main
Holmes
Patterson
Symmonds
Mare
R103
Philpott
Shops
Dicks
Clarendon
Memory
Shopping Centre
Dewar
Market
Bell
Main
Falls
Ridge
Alexandra
Swimming Pool
Somme
Pick 'n Pay
Harvard
Goddard Park
Eagle's Nest
Athlone
Bell
Shepstone
Howick Clinic
Memorial
Spar
Howick Falls Museum
Polo
Park
Crafts Southern Africa
Rhodes
Berea
Morling
Howick Falls
Harvard
Exchange
Nduna Mills
Howick CHC
uMgeni
Rylands
Howick Senior Primary School
Howick Junior Primary School
Theed
Injoloba High School
Berea
Power
R103
Winston
Ridge
Campbell
Main
Howick Golf Course
Rosebank
Gazala
Tobruk
Meadow
Victory
Monty
Hillbrow
Aloe
Woodburn
M 300 600

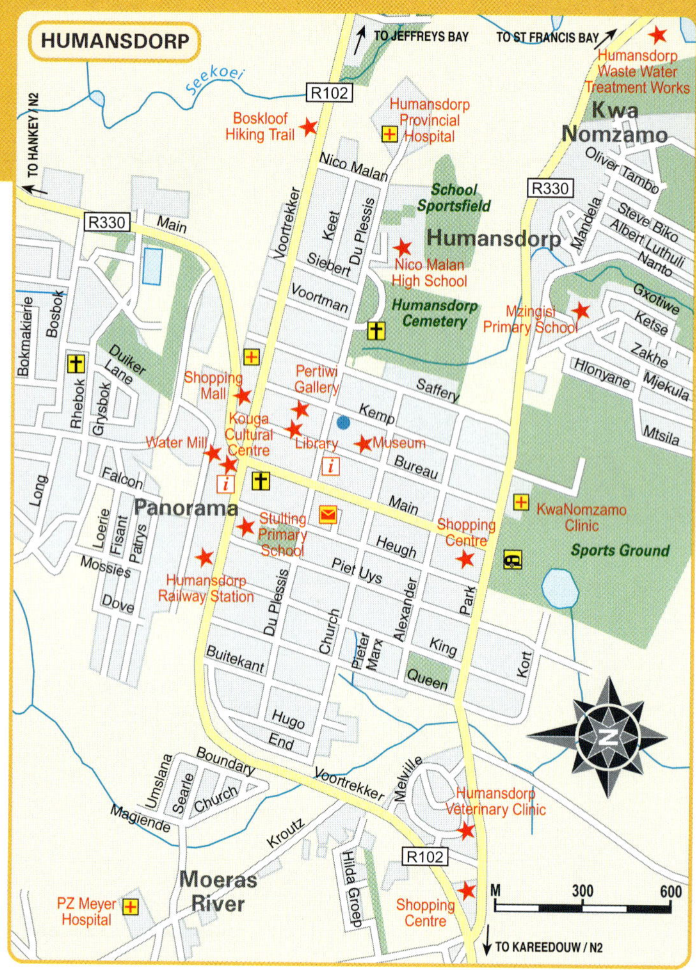

JEFFREYS BAY

Wavecrest
TO PORT ELIZABETH / N2
TO PORT ELIZABETH / N2
Bottlebrush
Poplar
Cedar
Da Gama
Tecoma
Noorsekloof Mall
Seetuin
Oleander
Tambotie
Waratah
Noorsekloof
Keurboom
Inside Point
Olienhout
Combretum
Blackwood
Fever Tree
Eike
Silver-tree
Magnolia
Spindle
Dr AD Keet
Mimosa
The Point
Snowdrop
Whale & Dolphin Lookout Point
Wattle
Blombos
Kruisbessie
Waboom
Impossibles
Noorsekloof Rd
Dogwood
Noorskloofpunt
Super Tubes
Dogwood
Leadwood
Karee
Myrtle
Noorsekloof Nature Reserve
Dr BB Keet
Cinema
Boneyards
Leadwood
Wavecrest
Myrtle
Saffron
Magna Tubes Trio
Beach Break
Broom
Koedoe
Mopane
Acorn
Olive
Myrtle
Waterkant
Magna Tubes
Jeffreys Bay Country Club
Gazelle
Sable
Ferreira Town
Protea
Disa
Oribi
Petunia
Tulip
Azalea
Da Gama
TO HUMANSDORP / R330 / N2
Aandblom
INDIAN OCEAN
Tulip
Dolly Varden
St Francis
Uys
Pick 'n Pay Centre
Angelwings
Heide
Mossel
Dresden
Petal
C-Place
De Reyger
Sandkasteel
Seekoei Nature Reserve
Nautilus
Ancilea
Solen
Jeffreys
Da Gama
Diaz
Goede Hoop
Library
Surf Museum
Friendly Grocer
Village Market
Koraal
Main Beach
Woltemade
Diaz
TO ASTON BAY
St Croix
Shell Museum
M 400 800

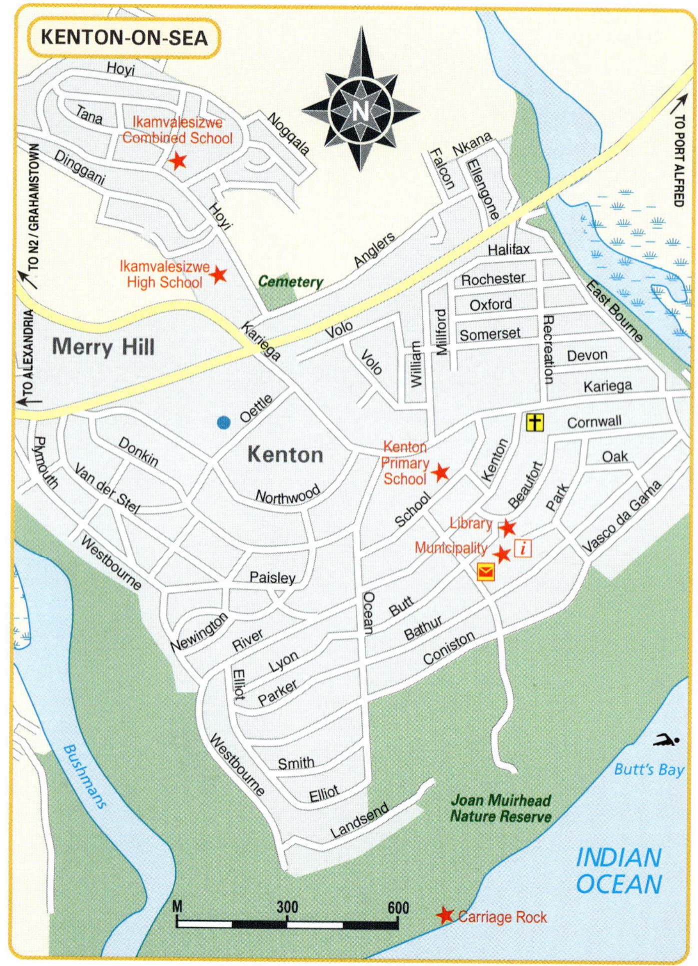

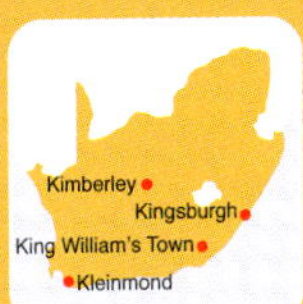
Kimberley
Kingsburgh
King William's Town
Kleinmond

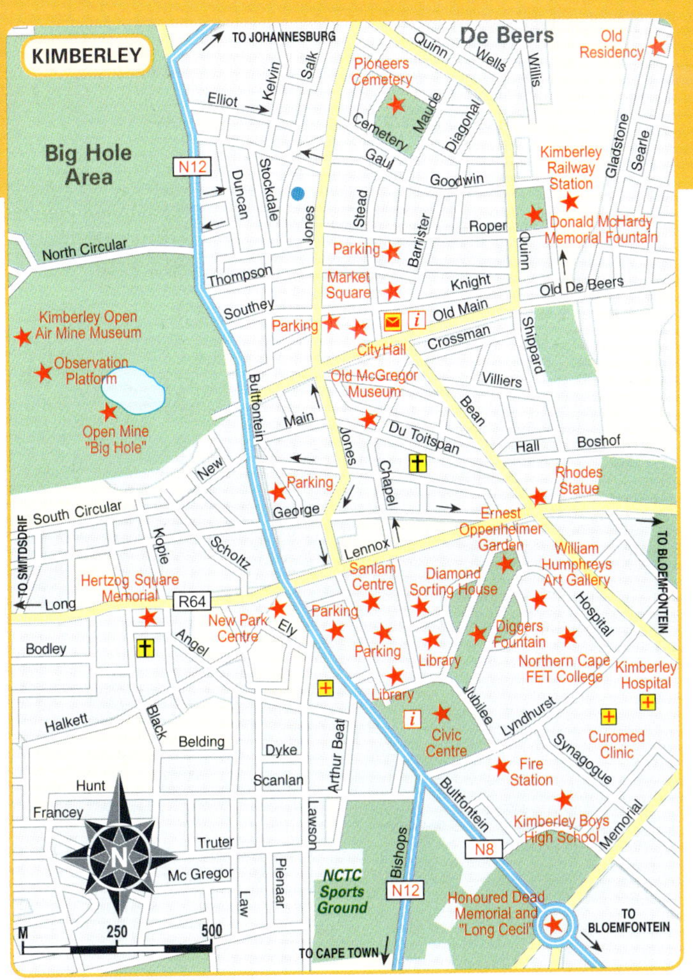
KIMBERLEY
TO JOHANNESBURG
De Beers
Old Residency
Pioneers Cemetery
Big Hole Area
N12
Kimberley Railway Station
Donald McHardy Memorial Fountain
North Circular
Parking
Market Square
Old De Beers
Old Main
City Hall
Kimberley Open Air Mine Museum
Observation Platform
Old McGregor Museum
Open Mine "Big Hole"
Du Toitspan
Villiers
Hall
Boshof
Rhodes Statue
South Circular
George
Lennox
Ernest Oppenheimer Garden
William Humphreys Art Gallery
TO SMITSDRIF
TO BLOEMFONTEIN
Hertzog Square Memorial
R64
Long
Sanlam Centre
Diamond Sorting House
New Park Centre
Diggers Fountain
Northern Cape FET College
Kimberley Hospital
Library
Bodley
Halkett
Belding
Dyke
Scanlan
Civic Centre
Curomed Clinic
Fire Station
Hunt
Francey
Truter
Mc Gregor
Kimberley Boys High School
N8
NCTC Sports Ground
Honoured Dead Memorial and "Long Cecil"
TO BLOEMFONTEIN
TO CAPE TOWN
M 250 500

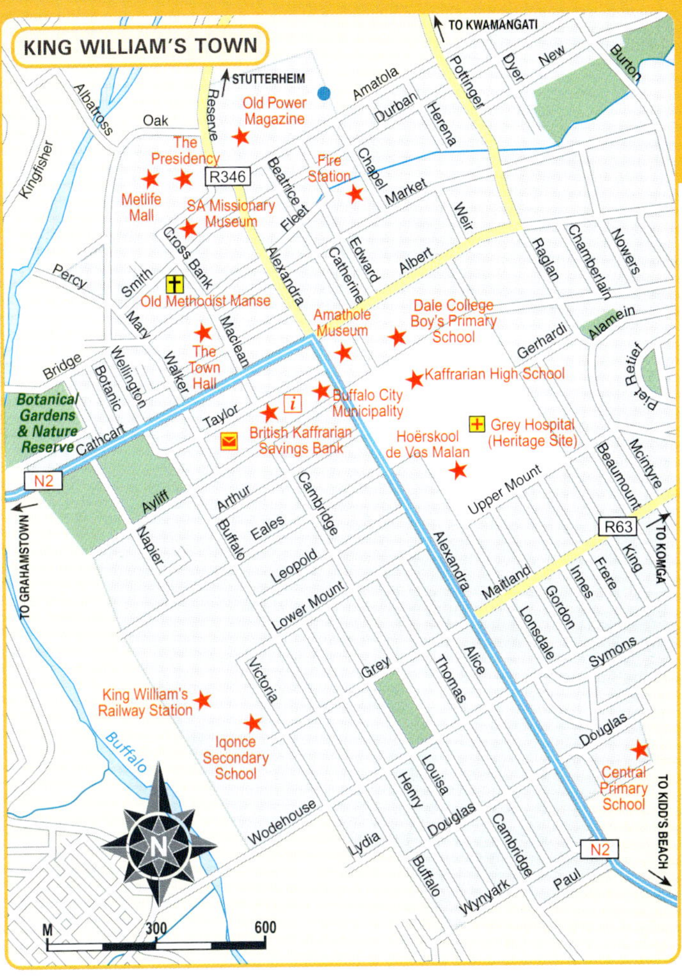
KING WILLIAM'S TOWN
TO KWAMANGATI
STUTTERHEIM
Old Power Magazine
The Presidency
R346
Metlife Mall
SA Missionary Museum
Fire Station
Old Methodist Manse
Amathole Museum
Dale College Boy's Primary School
The Town Hall
Buffalo City Municipality
Kaffrarian High School
Botanical Gardens & Nature Reserve
British Kaffrarian Savings Bank
Hoërskool de Vos Malan
Grey Hospital (Heritage Site)
N2
R63
TO KOMGA
TO GRAHAMSTOWN
King William's Railway Station
Iqonce Secondary School
Central Primary School
TO KIDD'S BEACH
N2
M 300 600

KINGSBURGH
Doon Heights
TO DURBAN
N2
Warner Beach Senior Primary School
Little Manzimtoti
Warner Beach
R102
Warner Beach Railway Station
Warner Beach Museum
Winklespruit Bowling Club
Illovo Glen
Warner Beach Junior Primary School
INDIAN OCEAN
Kingsburgh
St Winifred's Beach
N2
St Winifreds
Triangle Park
Plowman Park
Warner Beach
R102
aManzimtoti Testing Ground
Winklespruit Lifesaving Clubhouse
Astra Park
Municipality
Natal Sharks Board
Winklespruit Beach
R603
TO HIBBERDENE
M 300 600

KLEINMOND
TO BOTRIVIER
Kleinmond Golf Course
M 300 600
Kogel Park Clinic
Laerskool Kleinmond
Spar
Overstrand Municipality
ATLANTIC OCEAN
Kogelberg Shopping Centre
Kleinmond Coastal and Mountain Nature Reserve
7-Eleven
PALMIET MOUNTAINS
Kleinmond Primary School
Seemeeu Centre
Beverley Hills
Kleinmond Cemetery
Harbour
Harbour Road Art Gallery
TO BETTY'S BAY

KLERKSDORP KOKSTAD

KNYSNA KOMATIPOORT

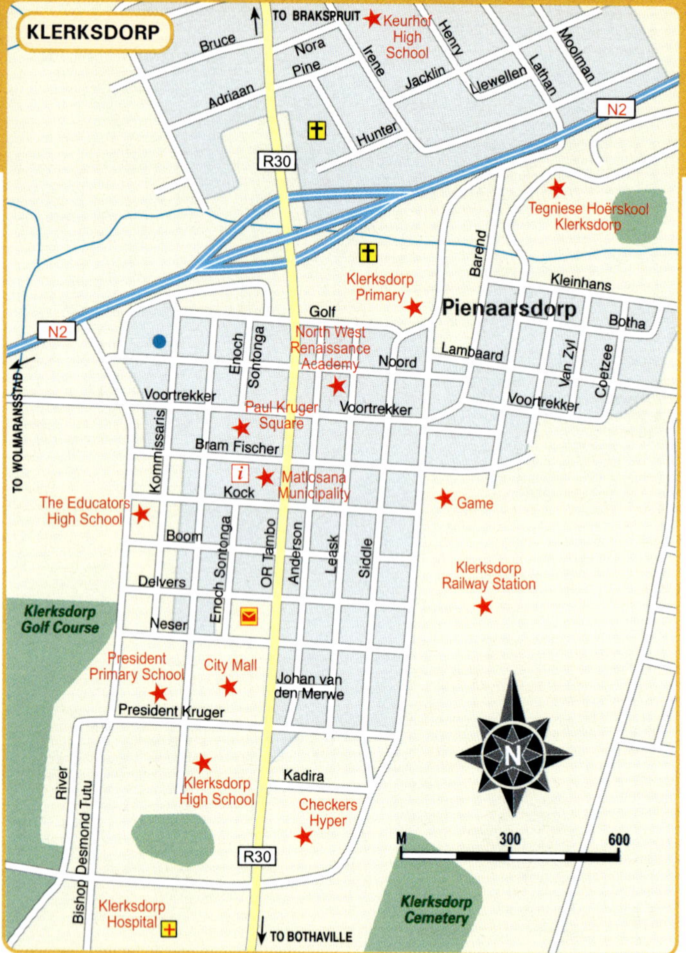

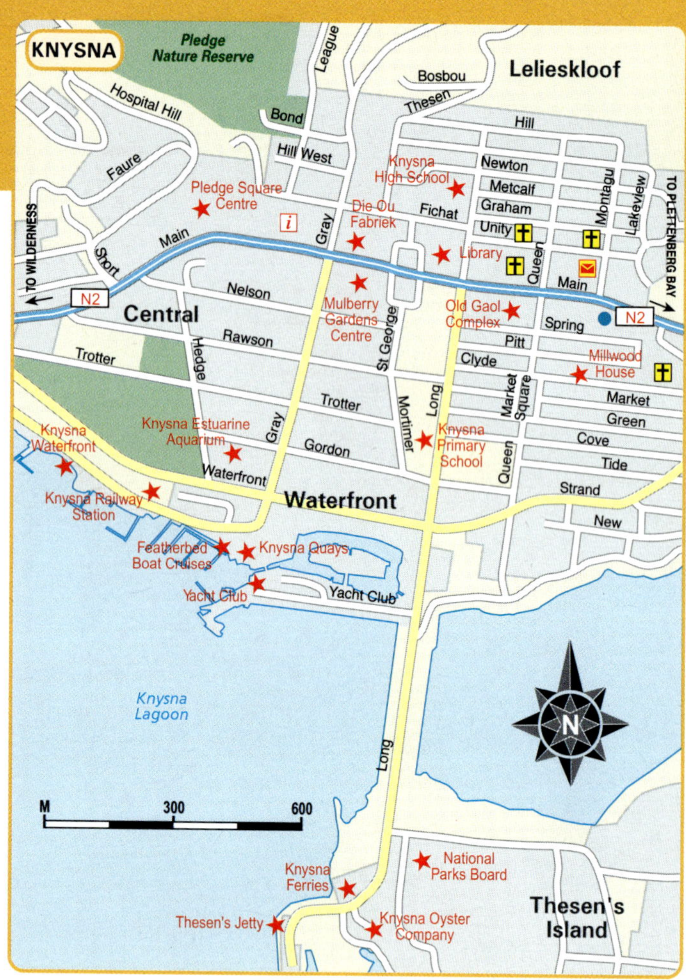

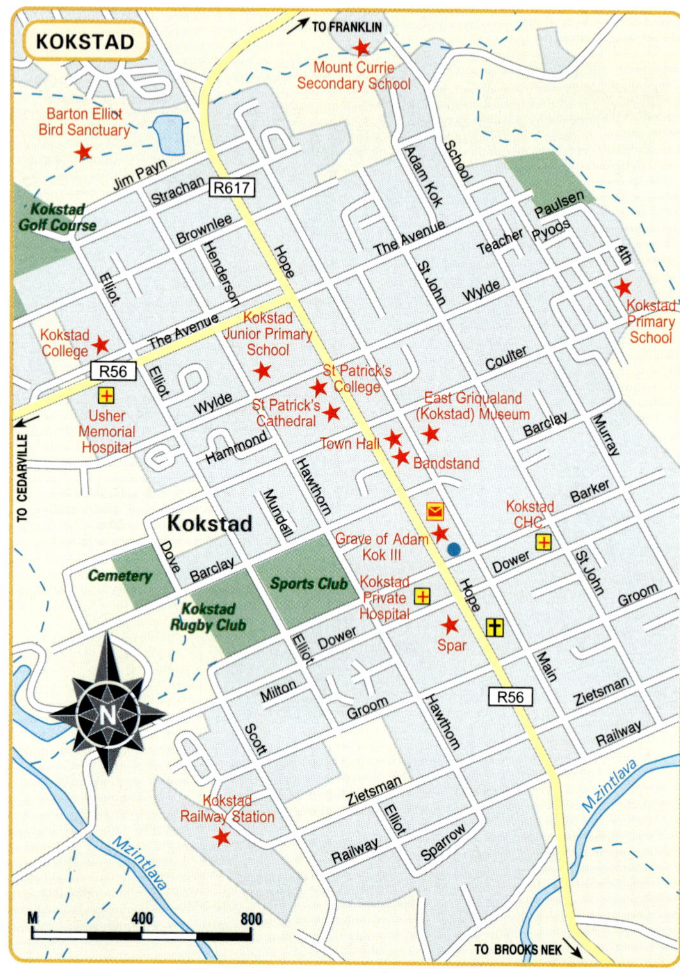

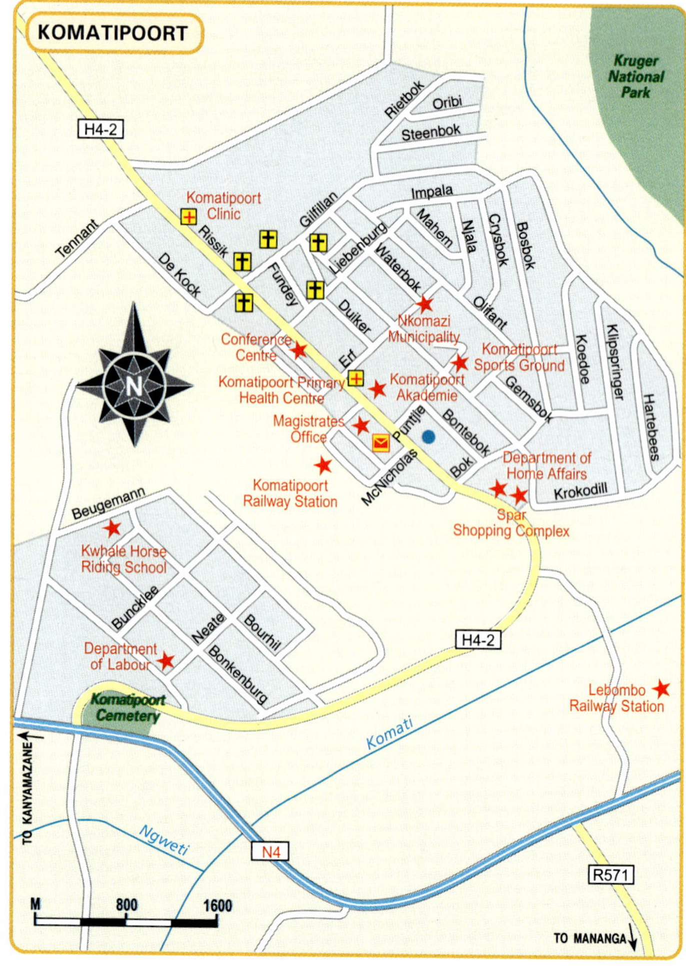

KROONSTAD

Kroonheuwel Primary School
Kroonstad SANDF Base
TO SASOLBURG / JOHANNESBURG
Linky's Lace Mall
Manny's Supermarket
Kroonheuwel
War Cemetery
TO VILJOENSKROON
Kroon Hospital
Pigeon Club
Department of Health
Department of Agriculture
Zenith High School
Spoornet Movement Depot
Kroonstad
Rosebank
TO EDENVILLE
Flavius Mareka FET College
Kroonstad Railway Station
Sentrale Volkskool
Kroonstad Waste Water Treatment Works
Shoprite
SARS
Jukskei Park
JSM Setlolane Secondary School
Calculus College
Moqhaka LM
Border
Kroonstad Country Club
Pick 'n Pay
Library
Swimming Pool
Kroonpark
Alexander Bridge
Kroonstad Academy
Old Town Hall & Leaping Fountain
Gunhill
Goedgedacht
Pick 'n Pay
Wilgenhof
TO STEYNSRUS
TO VENTERSBURG
R78
N1
M 250 500

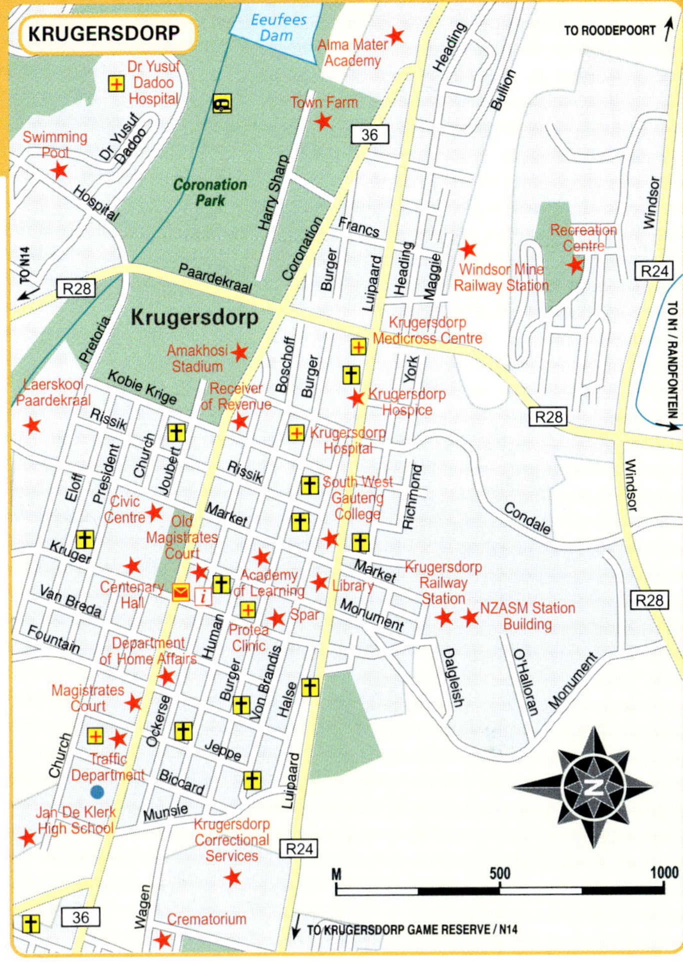

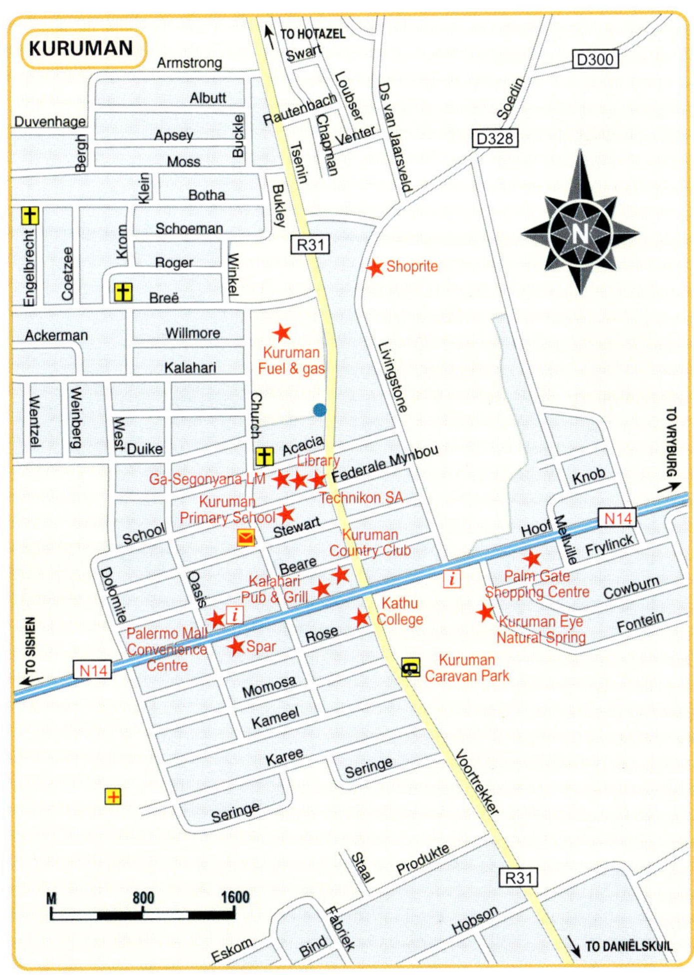

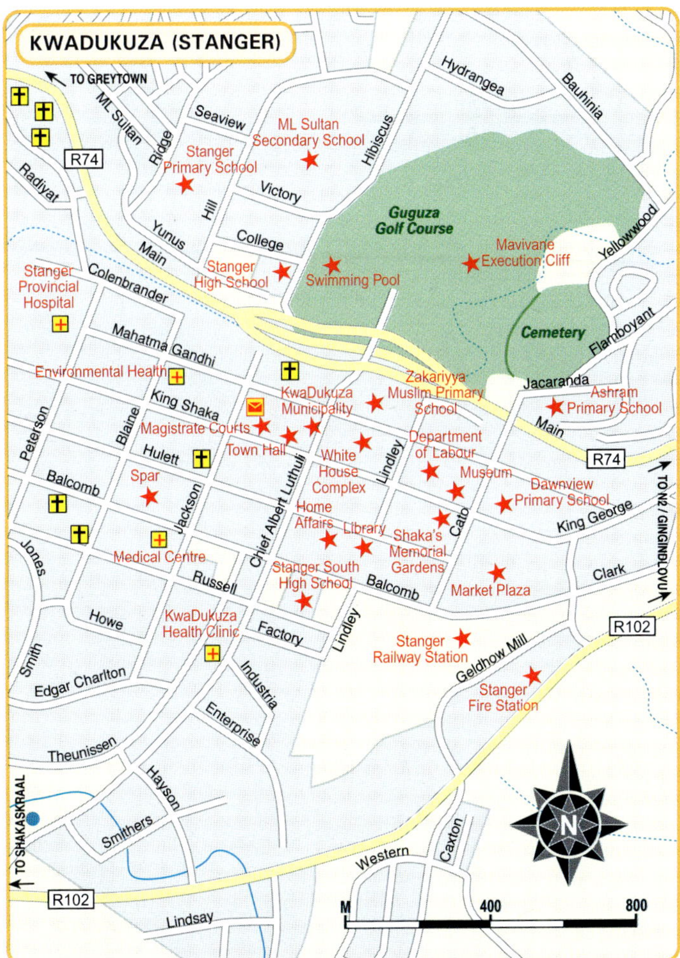

LADISMITH (Western Cape) LADYBRAND
LADYSMITH (KZN) LAMBERTS BAY

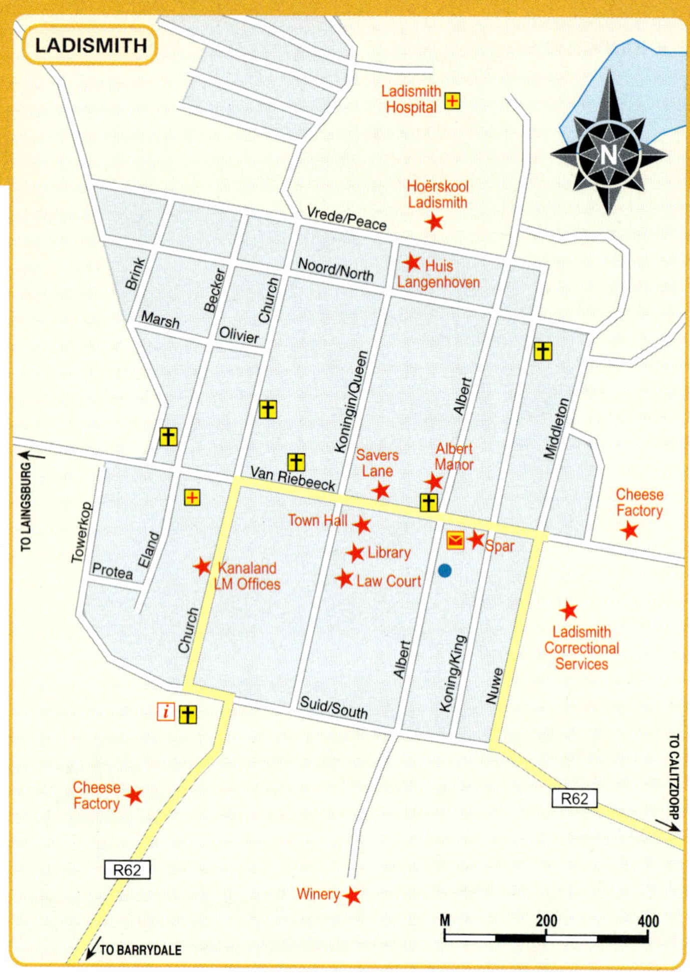

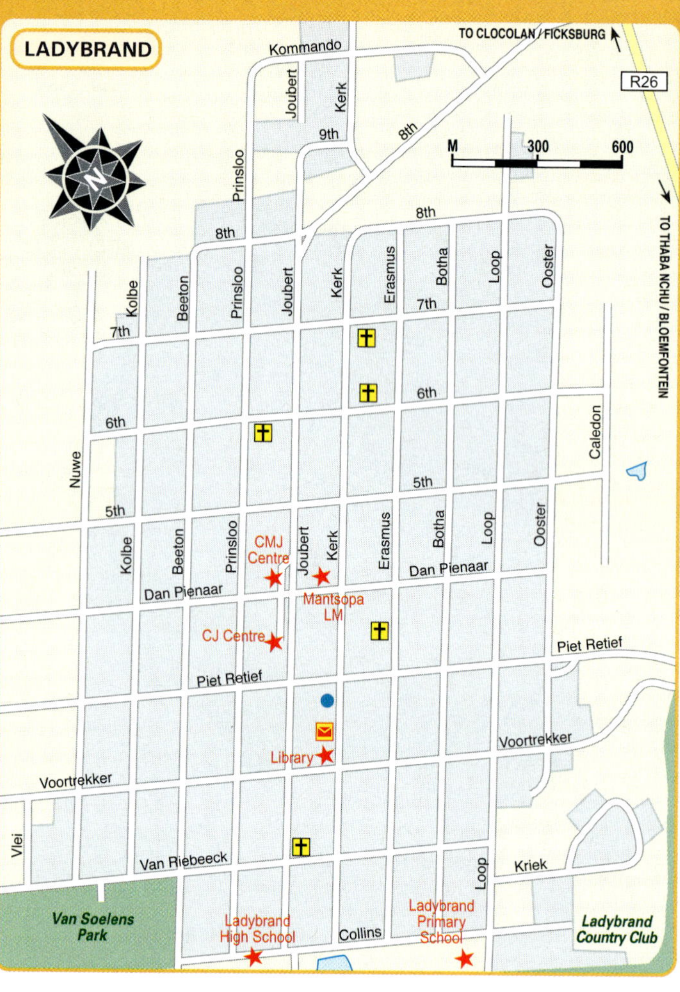

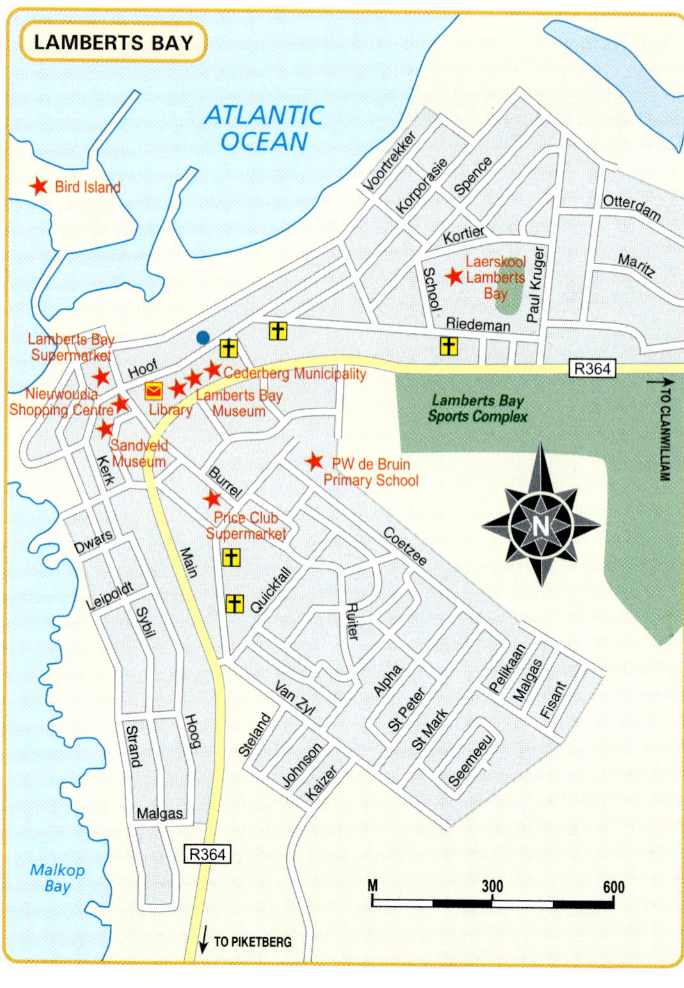

LANGEBAAN LICHTENBURG LEPHALALE (ELLISRAS) eNTOKOZWENI (MACHADODORP)

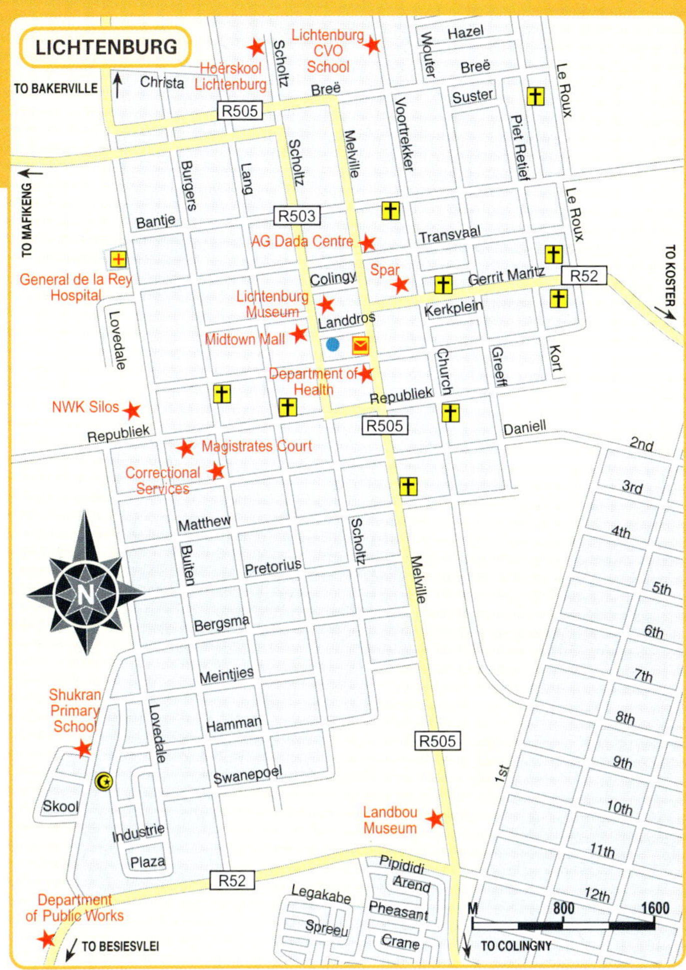

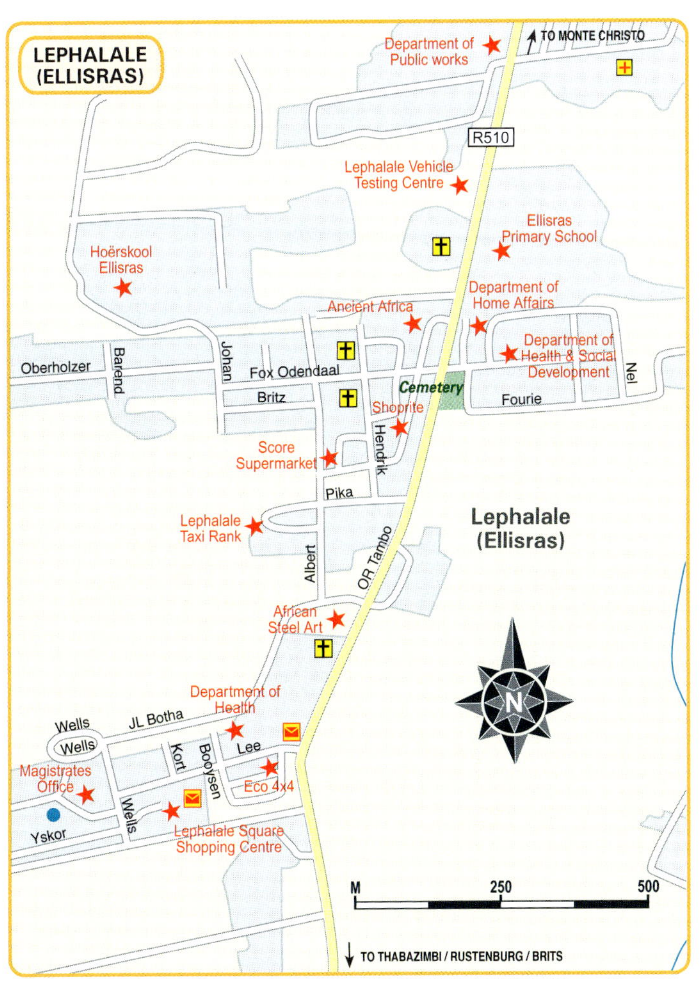

LOUIS TRICHARDT MARGATE

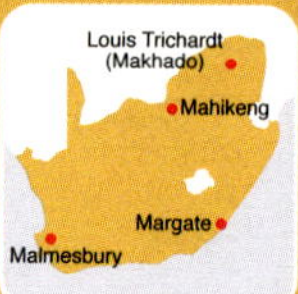

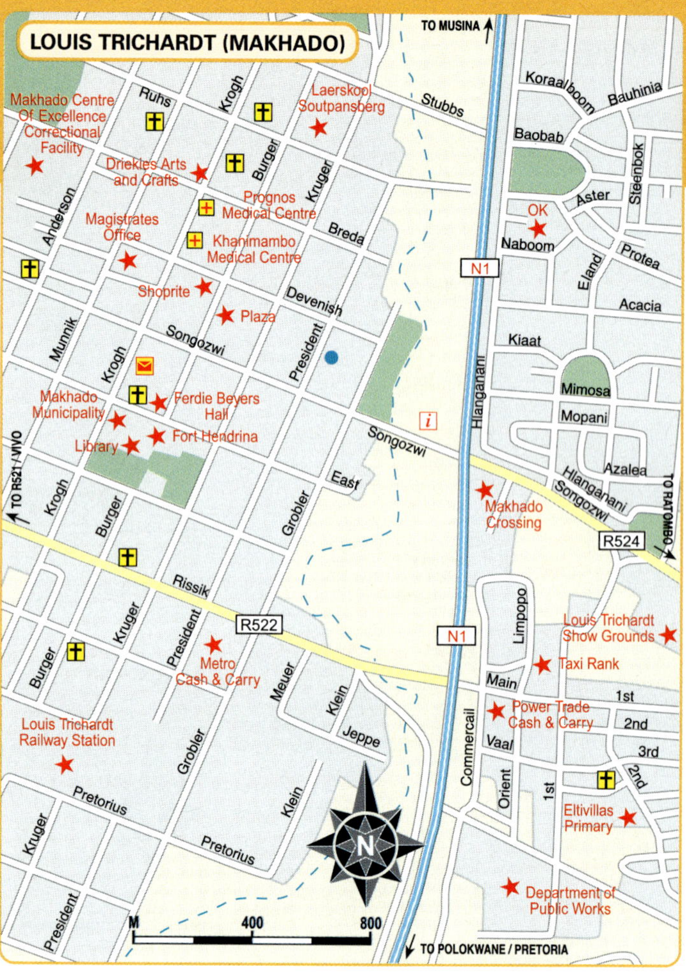

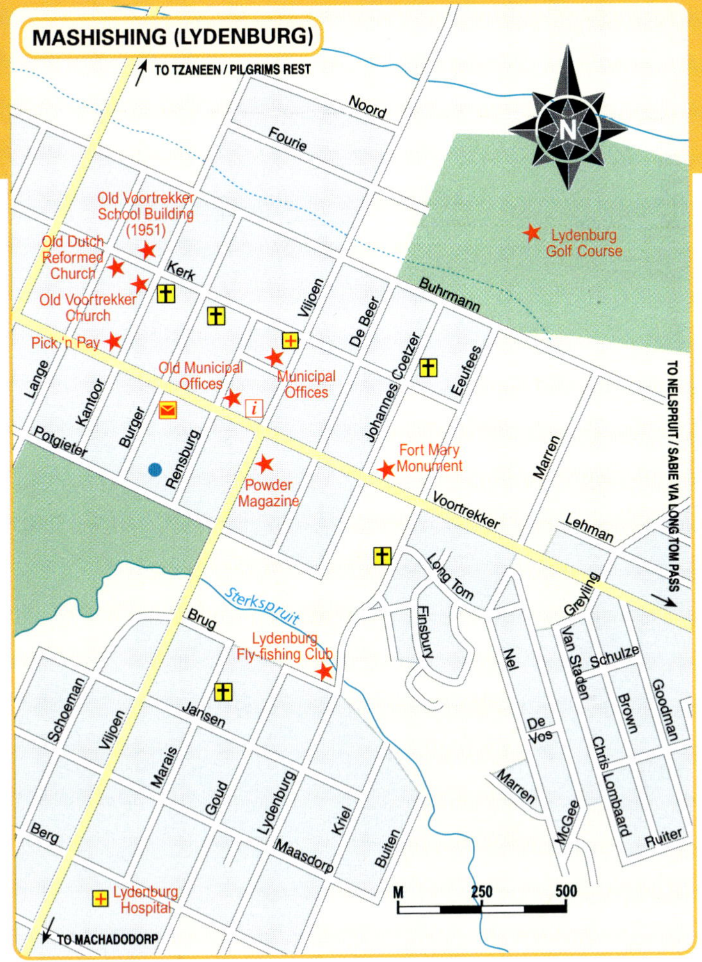
MASHISHING (LYDENBURG)
TO TZANEEN / PILGRIMS REST
Noord
Fourie
Old Voortrekker School Building (1951)
Old Dutch Reformed Church
Old Voortrekker Church
Pick 'n Pay
Kerk
Buhrmann
Lydenburg Golf Course
Viljoen
De Beer
Johannes Coetzer
Eeufees
Old Municipal Offices
Municipal Offices
Lange
Kantoor
Burger
Rensburg
Potgieter
Powder Magazine
Fort Mary Monument
Voortrekker
Marren
Lehman
TO NELSPRUIT / SABIE VIA LONG TOM PASS
Long Tom
Sterkspruit
Brug
Lydenburg Fly-fishing Club
Finsbury
Nel
Greyling
Van Staden
Schulze
Brown
Goodman
De Vos
Chris Lombaard
Schoeman
Viljoen
Jansen
Marais
Goud
Lydenburg
Kriel
Maasdorp
Buiten
Marren
McGee
Ruiter
Berg
Lydenburg Hospital
TO MACHADODORP
M 250 500

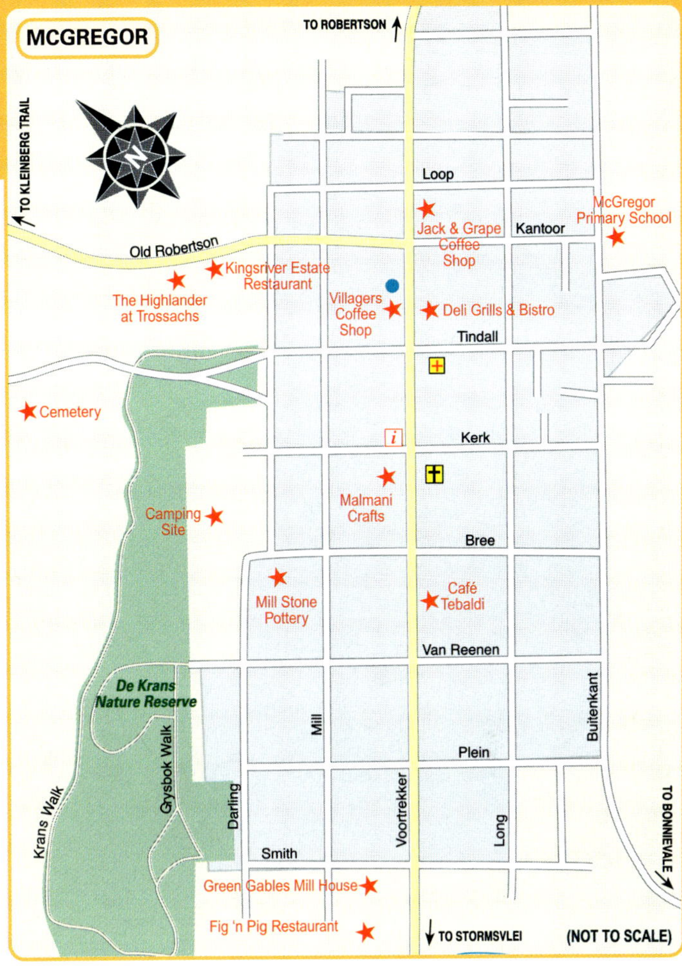
MCGREGOR
TO ROBERTSON
TO KLEINBERG TRAIL
Loop
Jack & Grape Coffee Shop
Kantoor
McGregor Primary School
Old Robertson
Kingsriver Estate Restaurant
The Highlander at Trossachs
Villagers Coffee Shop
Deli Grills & Bistro
Tindall
Cemetery
Kerk
Camping Site
Malmani Crafts
Bree
Mill Stone Pottery
Café Tebaldi
Van Reenen
De Krans Nature Reserve
Mill
Buitenkant
Plein
Krans Walk
Grysbok Walk
Darling
Voortrekker
Long
TO BONNIEVALE
Smith
Green Gables Mill House
Fig 'n Pig Restaurant
TO STORMSVLEI
(NOT TO SCALE)

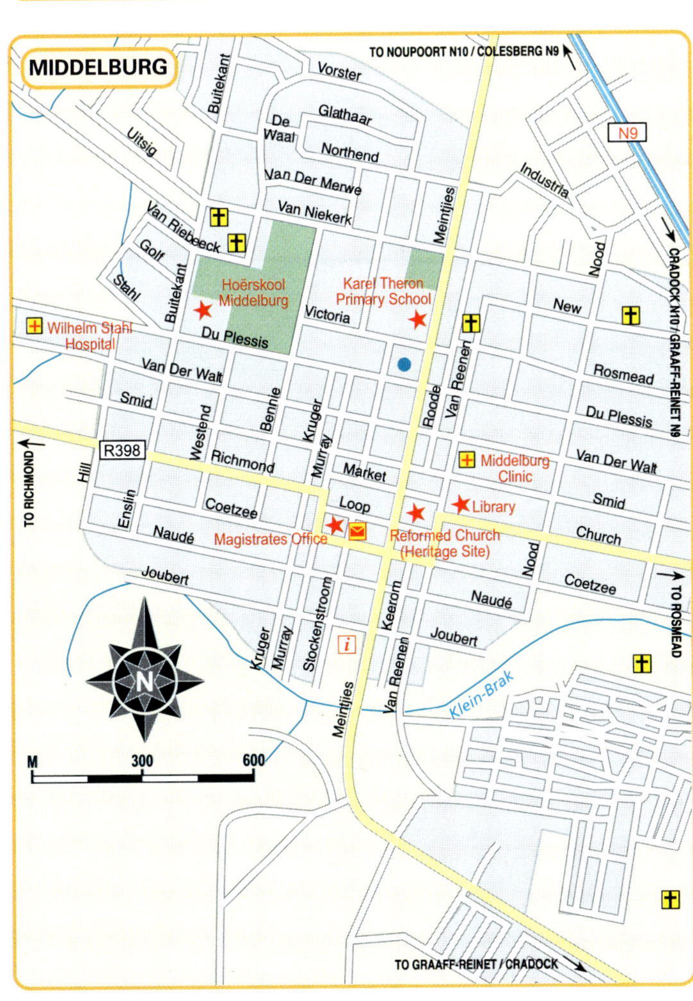
MIDDELBURG
TO NOUPOORT N10 / COLESBERG N9
Buitekant
Vorster
De Waal
Glathaar
Northend
Uitsig
N9
Industria
Van Der Merwe
Van Niekerk
Meintjies
Van Riebeeck
Golf
Stahl
Buitekant
Hoërskool Middelburg
Karel Theron Primary School
Victoria
Nood
New
CRADOCK N10 / GRAAFF-REINET N9
Wilhelm Stahl Hospital
Du Plessis
Van Der Walt
Rosmead
Smid
Westend
Bennie
Kruger
Murray
Roode
Van Reenen
Du Plessis
R398
Richmond
Market
Middelburg Clinic
Van Der Walt
TO RICHMOND
Hill
Enslin
Coetzee
Loop
Library
Smid
Naudé
Magistrates Office
Reformed Church (Heritage Site)
Church
Nood
Coetzee
Joubert
Naudé
TO ROSMEAD
Kruger
Murray
Stockenstroom
Keerom
Joubert
Van Reenen
Meintjies
Klein-Brak
M 300 600
TO GRAAFF-REINET / CRADOCK

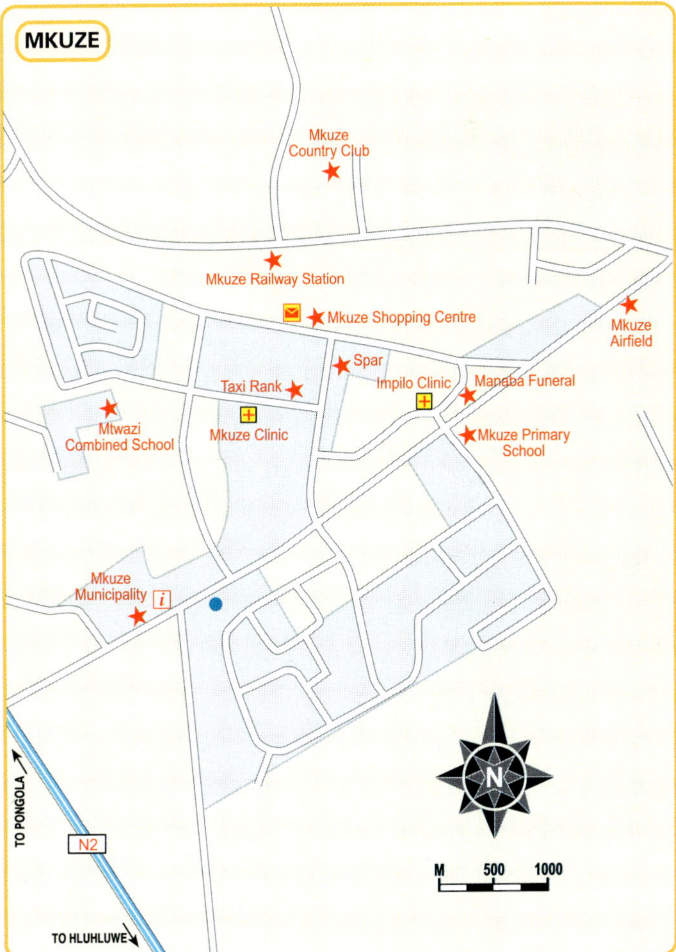
MKUZE
Mkuze Country Club
Mkuze Railway Station
Mkuze Shopping Centre
Mkuze Airfield
Spar
Taxi Rank
Impilo Clinic
Manqba Funeral
Mtwazi Combined School
Mkuze Clinic
Mkuze Primary School
Mkuze Municipality
TO PONGOLA
N2
TO HLUHLUWE
M 500 1000

132 MODIMOLLE (NYLSTROOM) MONTAGU
MOKOPANE MOOI RIVER

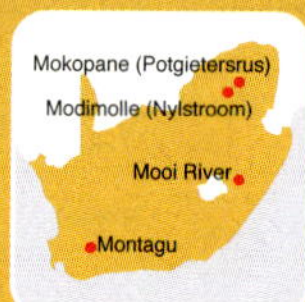

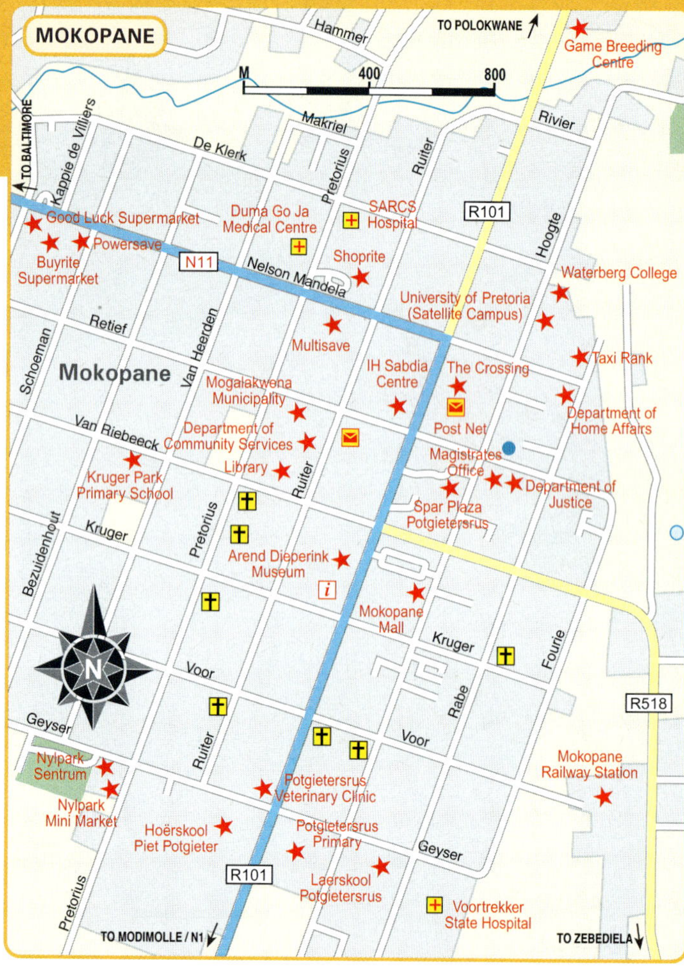

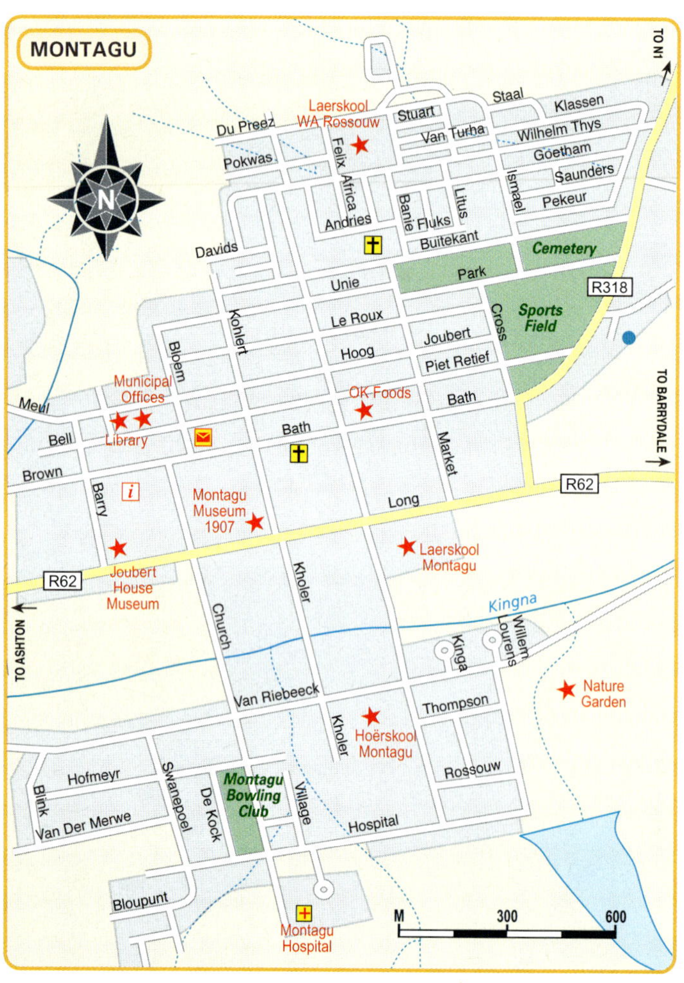

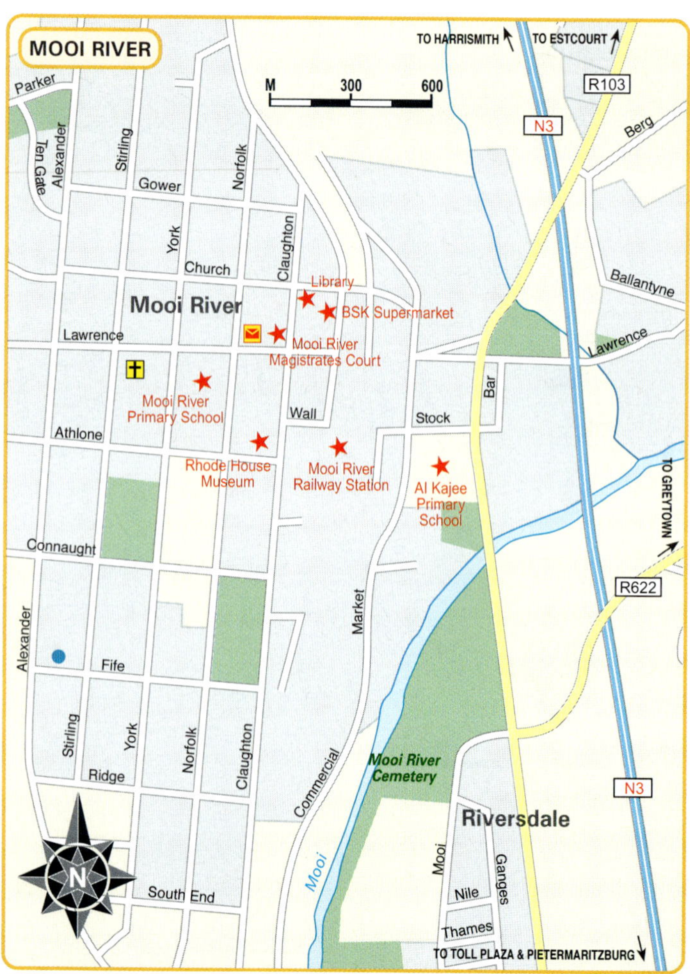

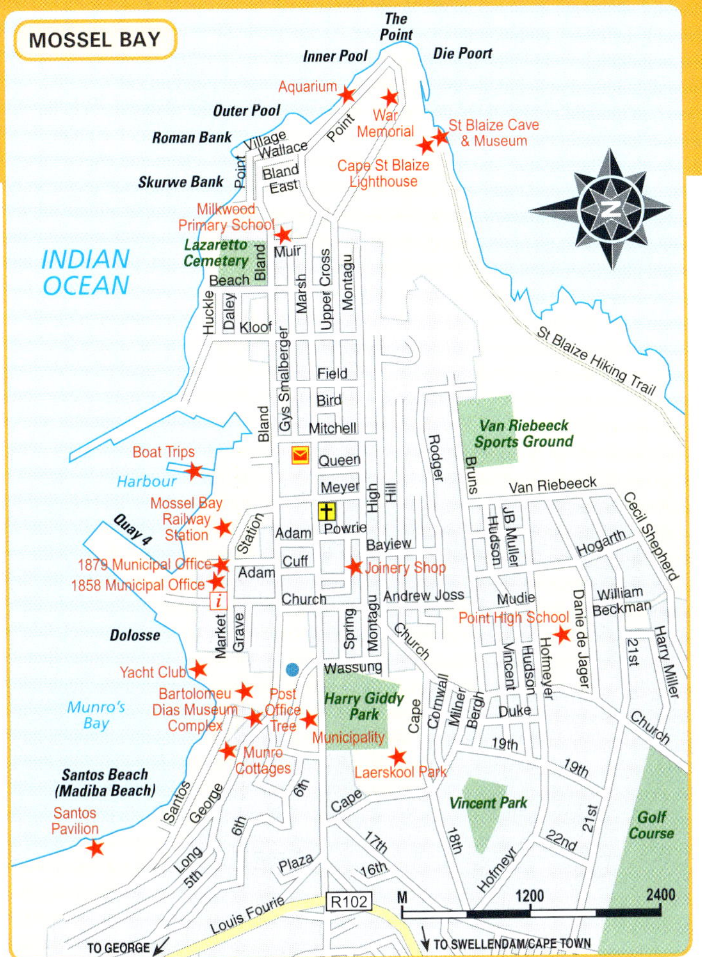
MOSSEL BAY
The Point
Inner Pool
Die Poort
Aquarium
War Memorial
St Blaize Cave & Museum
Outer Pool
Roman Bank
Skurwe Bank
Cape St Blaize Lighthouse
Milkwood Primary School
Lazaretto Cemetery
INDIAN OCEAN
St Blaize Hiking Trail
Boat Trips
Harbour
Mossel Bay Railway Station
Quay 4
Van Riebeeck Sports Ground
1879 Municipal Office
1858 Municipal Office
Joinery Shop
Point High School
Dolosse
Yacht Club
Munro's Bay
Bartolomeu Dias Museum Complex
Post Office Tree
Harry Giddy Park
Municipality
Munro Cottages
Laerskool Park
Santos Beach (Madiba Beach)
Santos Pavilion
Vincent Park
Golf Course
R102
TO GEORGE
TO SWELLENDAM/CAPE TOWN
M 1200 2400

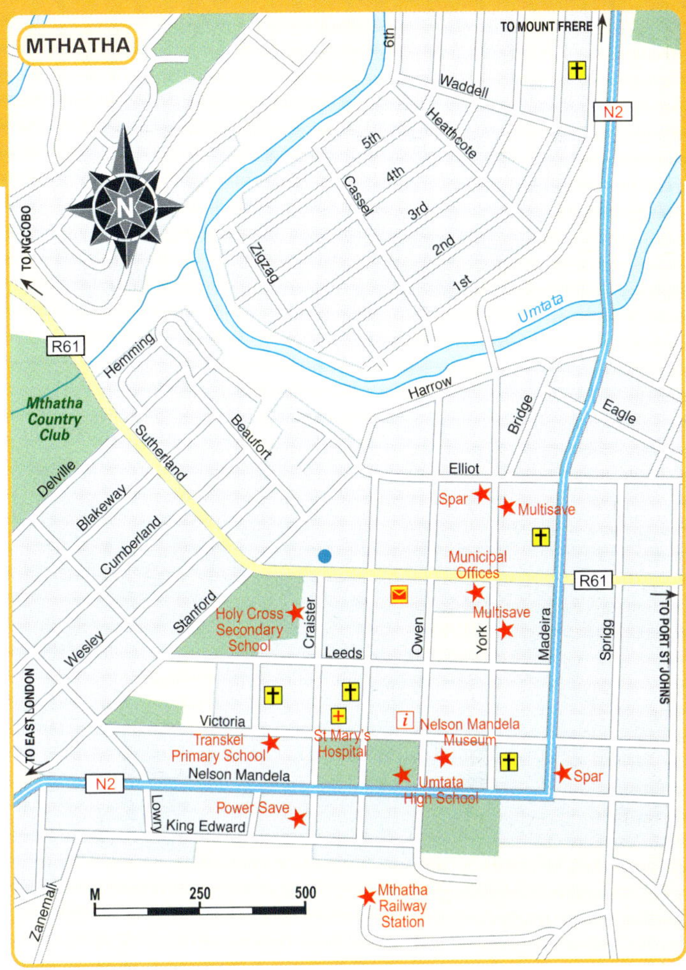
MTHATHA
TO MOUNT FRERE
N2
TO NGCOBO
R61
Umtata
Mthatha Country Club
Spar
Multisave
Municipal Offices
R61
TO PORT ST JOHNS
Holy Cross Secondary School
Multisave
TO EAST LONDON
Transkei Primary School
St Mary's Hospital
Nelson Mandela Museum
Umtata High School
Spar
N2
Power Save
M 250 500
Mthatha Railway Station

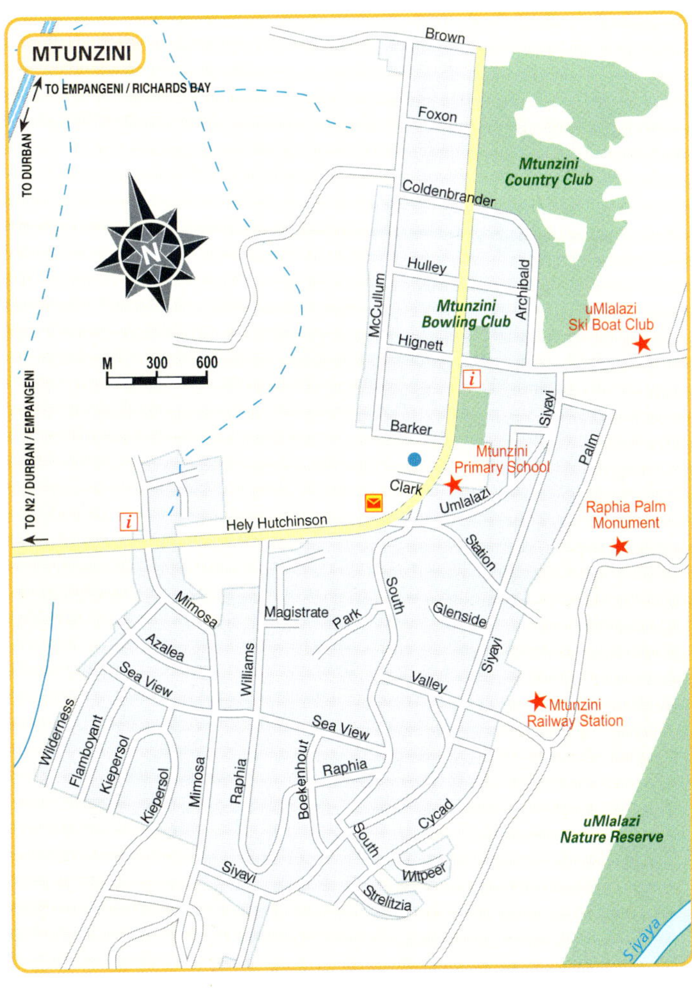
MTUNZINI
TO EMPANGENI / RICHARDS BAY
TO DURBAN
Mtunzini Country Club
Mtunzini Bowling Club
uMlalazi Ski Boat Club
M 300 600
Mtunzini Primary School
TO N2 / DURBAN / EMPANGENI
Raphia Palm Monument
Mtunzini Railway Station
uMlalazi Nature Reserve
Siyaya

MUIZENBERG
Naval Cadet Base
Lakeside Railway Station
Sea Scout Centre
Yacht Club
Park Island
Muizenberg
Muizenberg North
Zandvlei Caravan Park
Muizenberg High School
M4
Zandvlei Sports Complex
Muizenberg 508m
False Bay Railway Station
Muizenberg Primary School
Checkers
R310
TO STELLENBOSCH
Library
West Beach
Natale Labia
Muizenberg Railway Station
Edwardian Beach Houses
M4
TO FISH HOEK
Braeside House
Edwardian Beach Houses
Star of the Sea College
St James Railway Station
False Bay
Historic Houses
St James
M 300 600

MUSINA NEWCASTLE

MBOMBELA (NELSPRUIT) NIGEL

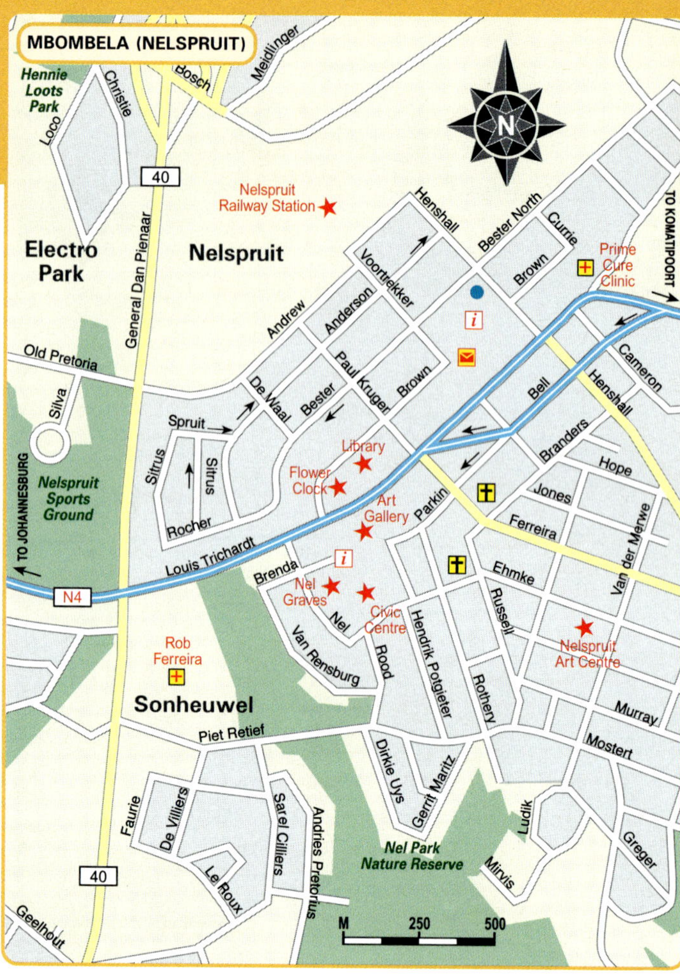

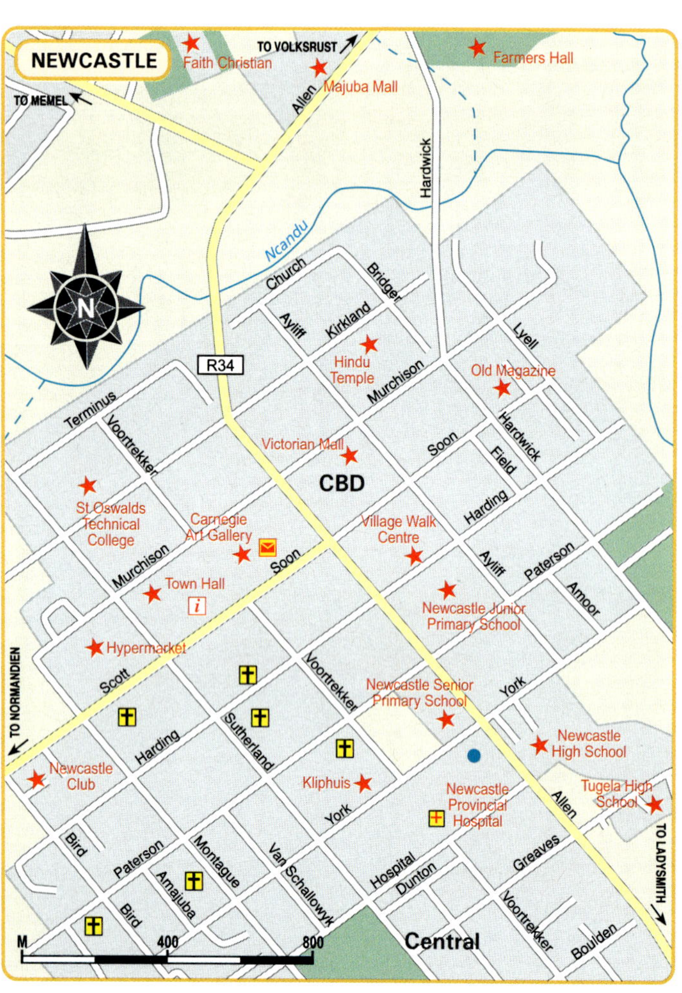

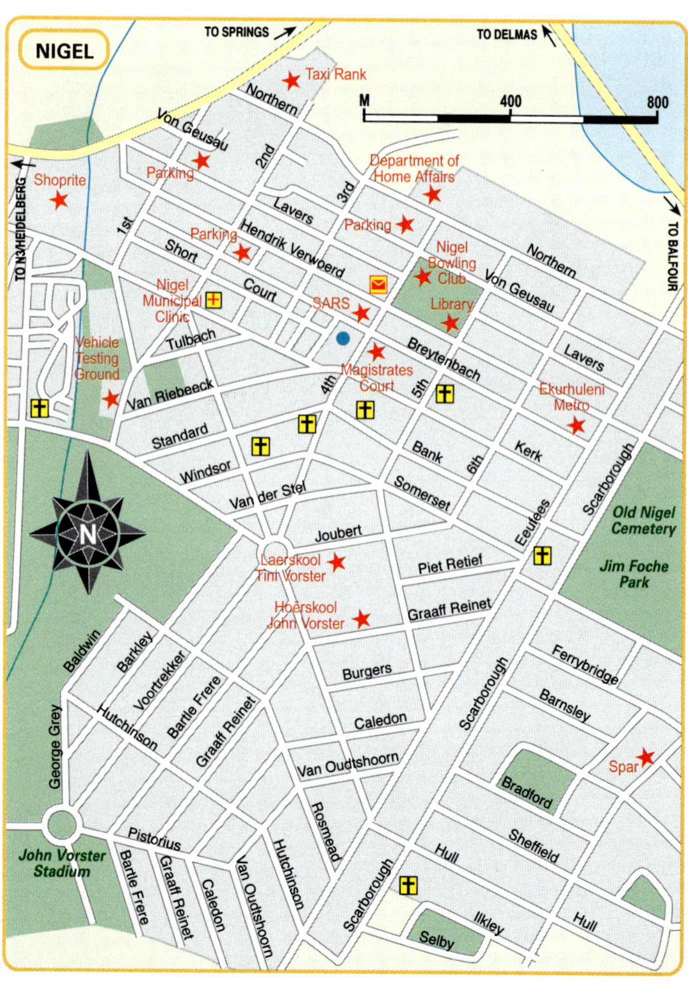

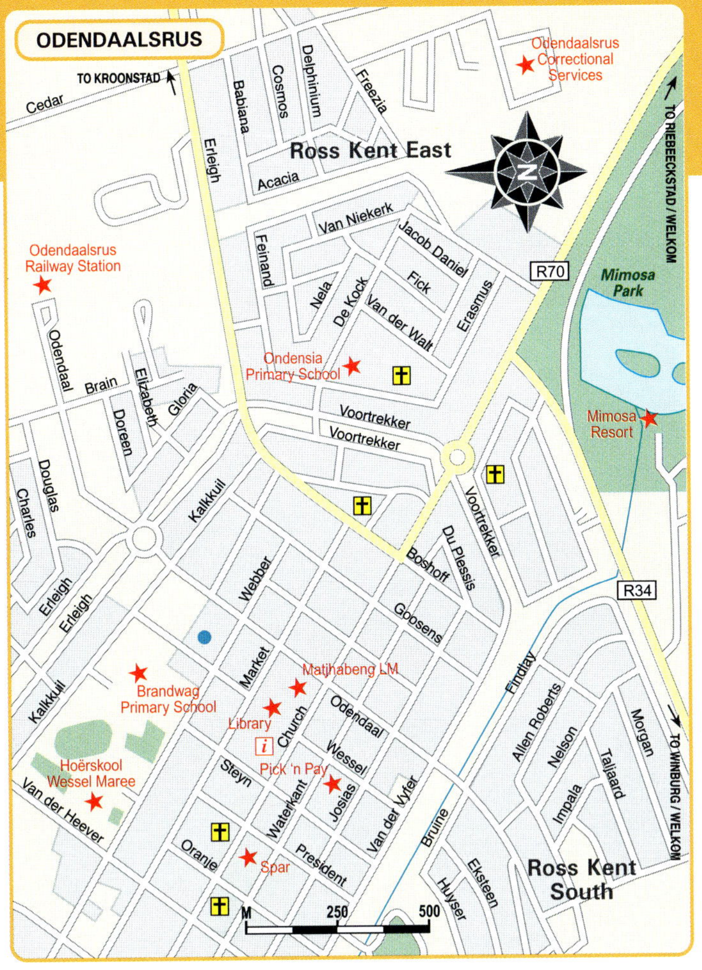

ODENDAALSRUS
TO KROONSTAD
Odendaalsrus Correctional Services
TO RIEBEECKSTAD / WELKOM
Ross Kent East
Odendaalsrus Railway Station
Mimosa Park
Ondensia Primary School
Mimosa Resort
Matjhabeng LM
Brandwag Primary School
Library
Pick 'n Pay
Hoërskool Wessel Maree
Spar
TO WINBURG / WELKOM
Ross Kent South
R70
R34
M 250 500

ORKNEY
Vaal Reefs Bowling Club
Public Swimming Pool
TO POTCHEFSTROOM
Victory Park
Vaal Reefs Cricket Club
TO HARRISBURG / LEEUDORINGSTAD
Macconoche Park
R502
R500
Hoërskool Orkney
Laerskool Orkney
Spar
Ceronio Park
Rotary Park
R30
TO BRAKSPRUIT / VENTERSDORP
M 300 600
Coetzee Park
TO BOTHAVILLE

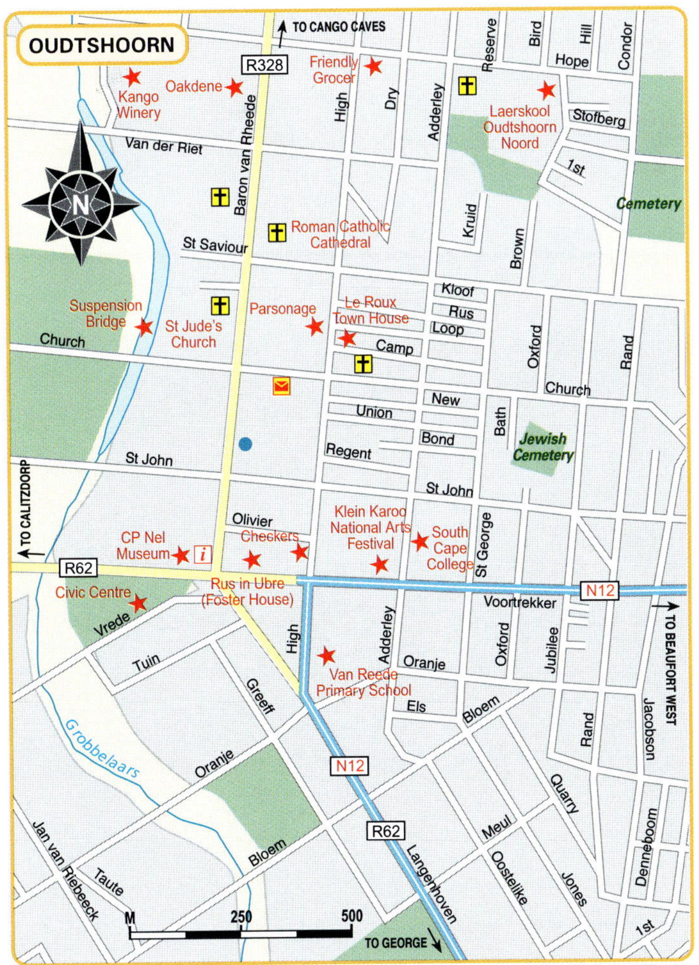

OUDTSHOORN
TO CANGO CAVES
R328
Kango Winery
Oakdene
Friendly Grocer
Laerskool Oudtshoorn Noord
Cemetery
Roman Catholic Cathedral
Suspension Bridge
St Jude's Church
Parsonage
Le Roux Town House
Jewish Cemetery
TO CALITZDORP
CP Nel Museum
Checkers
Klein Karoo National Arts Festival
South Cape College
R62
N12
Civic Centre
Rus in Ubre (Foster House)
Van Reede Primary School
TO BEAUFORT WEST
TO GEORGE
M 250 500

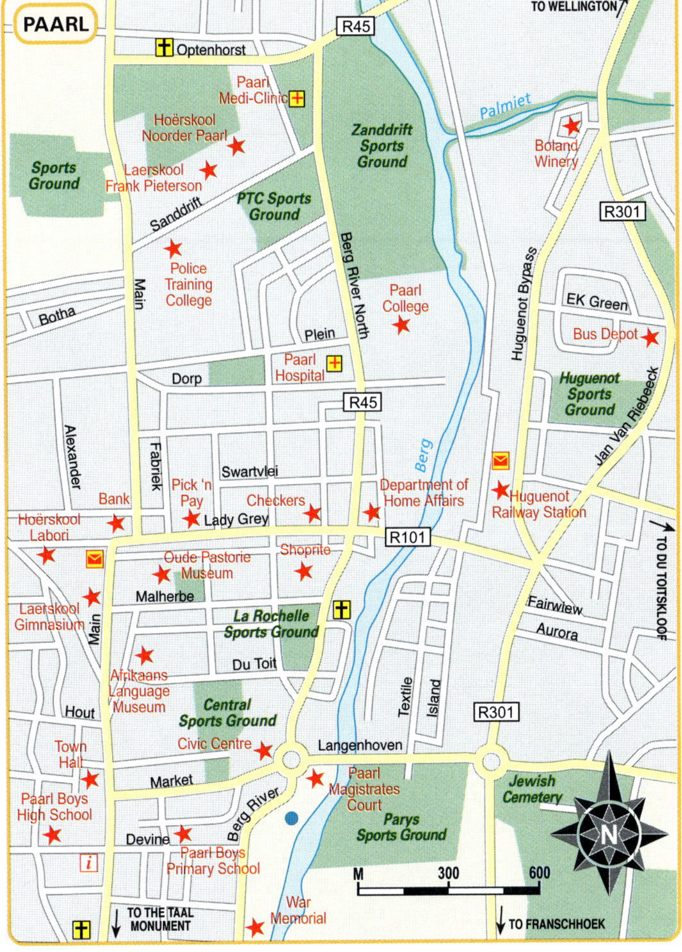

PAARL
TO WELLINGTON
R45
Paarl Medi-Clinic
Zanddrift Sports Ground
Boland Winery
Hoërskool Noorder Paarl
Sports Ground
Laerskool Frank Pieterson
PTC Sports Ground
R301
Police Training College
Paarl College
Bus Depot
Paarl Hospital
Huguenot Sports Ground
Bank
Pick 'n Pay
Checkers
Department of Home Affairs
Huguenot Railway Station
Hoërskool Labori
R101
TO DU TOITSKLOOF
Oude Pastorie Museum
Shoprite
Laerskool Gimnasium
La Rochelle Sports Ground
Afrikaans Language Museum
Central Sports Ground
Civic Centre
Town Hall
Paarl Magistrates Court
Jewish Cemetery
Paarl Boys High School
Parys Sports Ground
Paarl Boys Primary School
War Memorial
TO THE TAAL MONUMENT
TO FRANSCHHOEK
M 300 600

PAULPIETERSBURG eMKHONDO

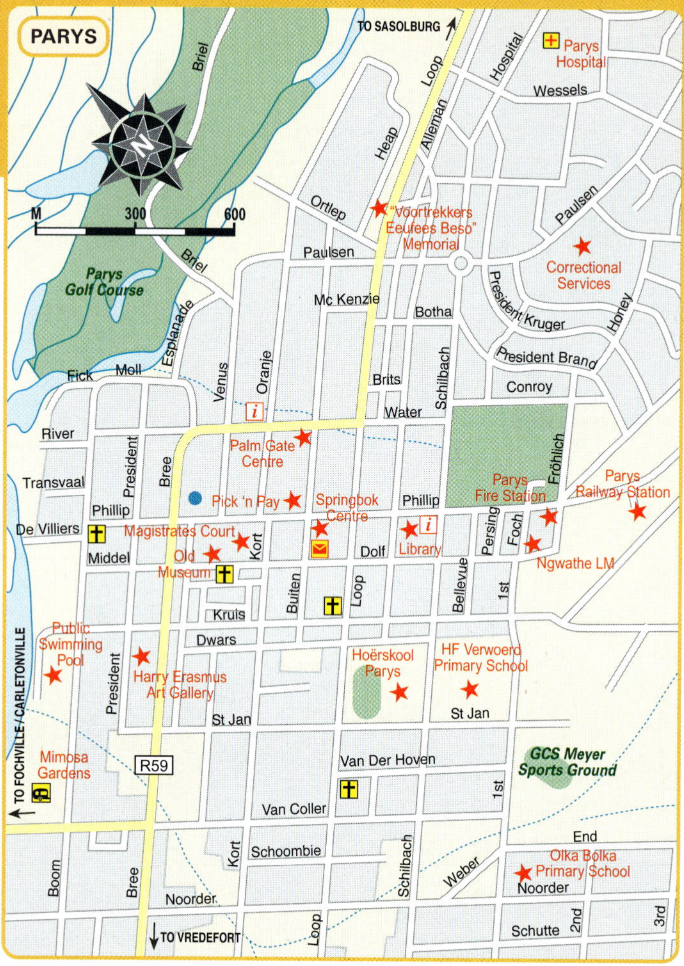

Pilgrims Rest
Pietermaritzburg
Pinetown
Plettenberg Bay

PIETERMARITZBURG
TO MOOI RIVER / ESTCOURT
TO DURBAN
N3
M40
M80
M70
Royal Agricultural Society Showgrounds
Alston Primary School
Open Gate Special School
Pietermaritzburg Primary School
Berg St Primary School
Midlands Medical Centre
Indian Girls High School
Shri Vishnu Primary School
Islamia Primary School
Victoria Railway Station
Gert Maritz Primary School
Voortrekker House
Capital Mall
Park Lane Centre
Supreme Court
Voortrekker Museum
Freedom Square
Cultural Museum
State Archives
City Hall
Natalia (Government Office)
Tatham Art Gallery
St Anne's Hospital
Victorian House
Gandhi Monument
Longmarket Girls' Primary School
Natal Museum
Merchiston Prep. School
St Mary's Anglican Church
Daniel Lindley Bridge
Old Government House
Overpark House
Jubilee Pavilion
McFarlane Bridge
Pietermaritzburg Medi Clinic
Old St Mary's Anglican Church
Macrorie House
Mayor's Garden
Kershaw Park
Victoria Bridge
Woodburn Sports Ground
Scotts Bridge
Garden of Remembrance
Supreme Court
Alexandra Park
Weeping Cross
Clark House & Victoria Hall
Harry Gwala Stadium
Winston Churchill Theatre
M 250 500

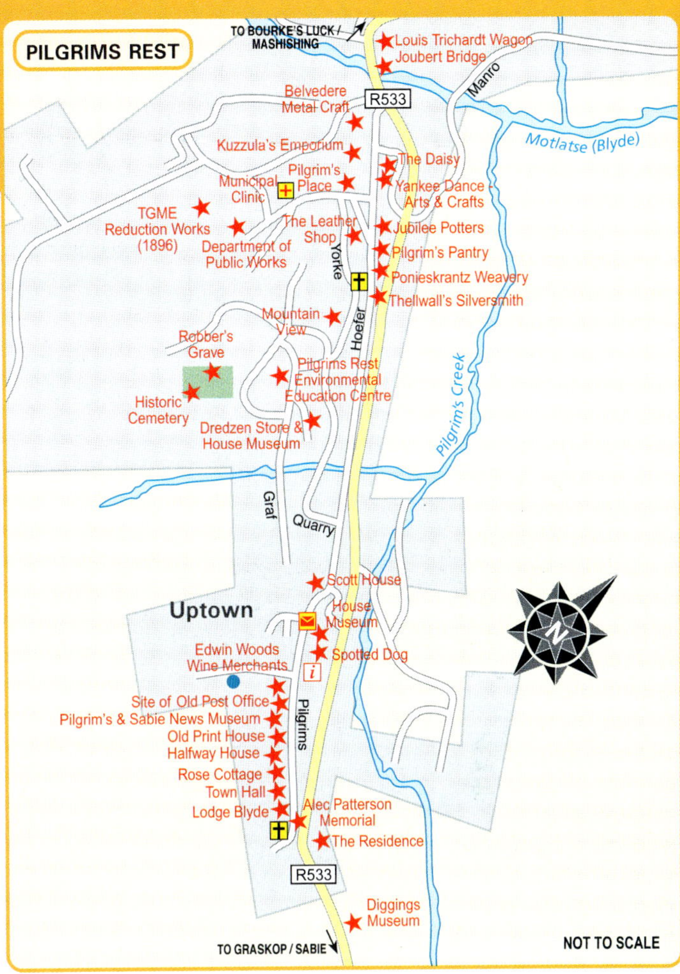
PILGRIMS REST
TO BOURKE'S LUCK / MASHISHING
Louis Trichardt Wagon
Joubert Bridge
Belvedere Metal Craft
R533
Motlatse (Blyde)
Kuzzula's Emporium
The Daisy
Pilgrim's Place
Municipal Clinic
Yankee Dance Arts & Crafts
TGME Reduction Works (1896)
The Leather Shop
Jubilee Potters
Department of Public Works
Pilgrim's Pantry
Ponieskrantz Weavery
Thellwall's Silversmith
Mountain View
Robber's Grave
Pilgrims Rest Environmental Education Centre
Historic Cemetery
Dredzen Store & House Museum
Pilgrim's Creek
Uptown
Scott House
House Museum
Spotted Dog
Edwin Woods Wine Merchants
Site of Old Post Office
Pilgrim's & Sabie News Museum
Old Print House
Halfway House
Rose Cottage
Town Hall
Lodge Blyde
Alec Patterson Memorial
The Residence
Diggings Museum
TO GRASKOP / SABIE
NOT TO SCALE

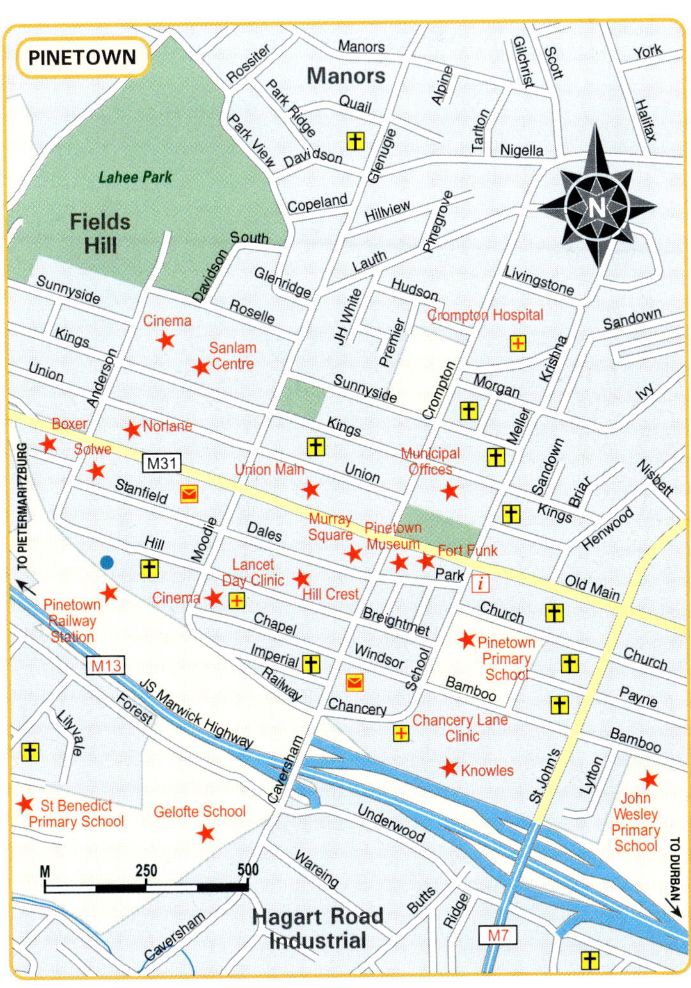
PINETOWN
Manors
Lahee Park
Fields Hill
Crompton Hospital
Cinema
Sanlam Centre
Norlane
M31
Union Main
Municipal Offices
Murray Square
Pinetown Museum
Fort Funk
Lancet Day Clinic
Hill Crest
Cinema
Pinetown Railway Station
Pinetown Primary School
M13
JS Marwick Highway
Chancery Lane Clinic
Knowles
St Benedict Primary School
Gelofte School
John Wesley Primary School
TO PIETERMARITZBURG
TO DURBAN
Hagart Road Industrial
M7
M 250 500

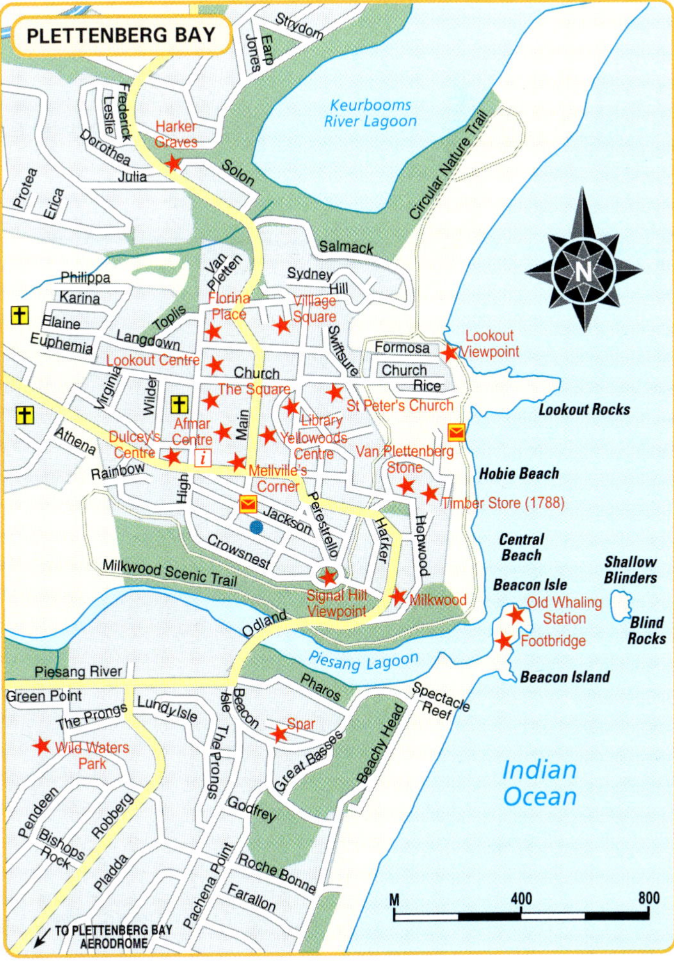
PLETTENBERG BAY
Keurbooms River Lagoon
Harker Graves
Circular Nature Trail
Florina Place
Village Square
Lookout Centre
Lookout Viewpoint
The Square
St Peter's Church
Lookout Rocks
Library
Afrnar Centre
Yellowoods Centre
Dulcey's Centre
Van Plettenberg Stone
Mellville's Corner
Hobie Beach
Timber Store (1788)
Central Beach
Milkwood Scenic Trail
Shallow Blinders
Signal Hill Viewpoint
Milkwood
Beacon Isle
Old Whaling Station
Footbridge
Blind Rocks
Beacon Island
Piesang River
Piesang Lagoon
Spectacle Reef
Wild Waters Park
Spar
Indian Ocean
TO PLETTENBERG BAY AERODROME
M 400 800

POLOKWANE PORT EDWARD

PORT ALFRED PORT ELIZABETH

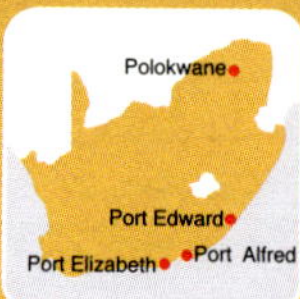

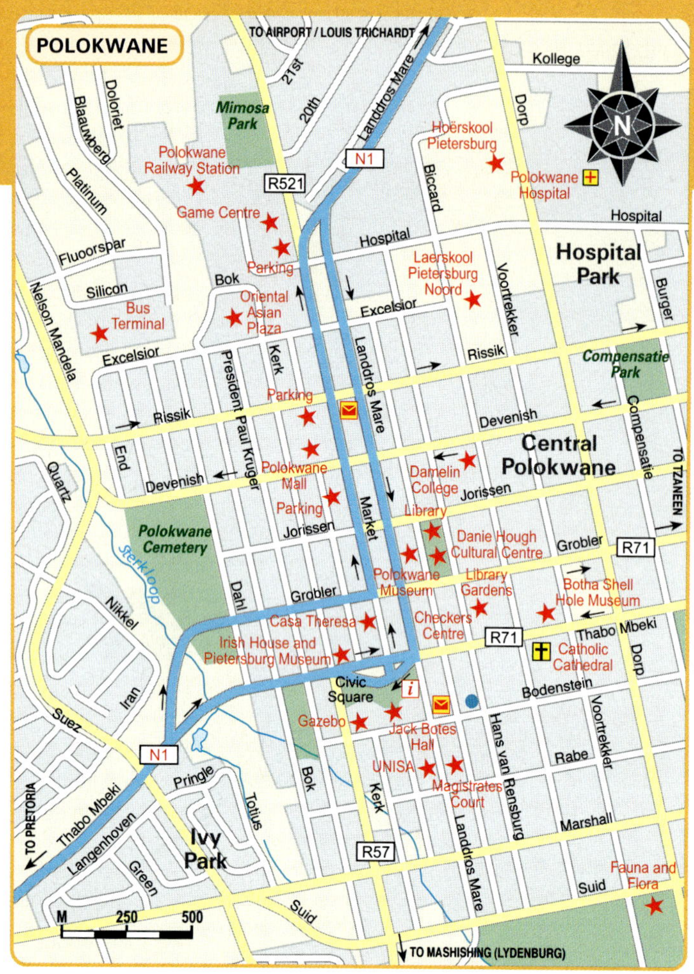

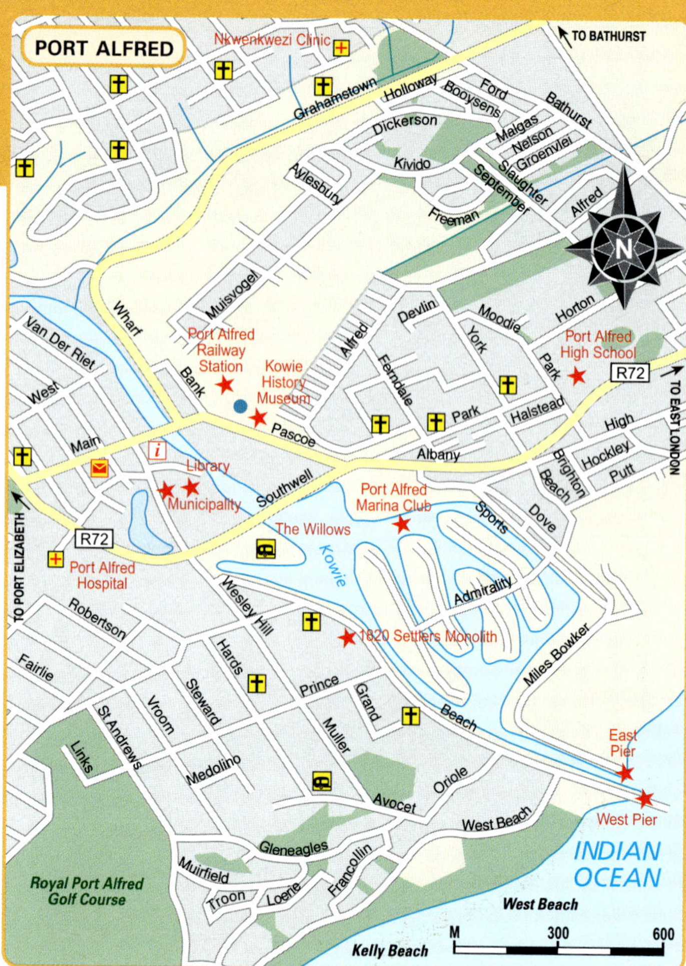

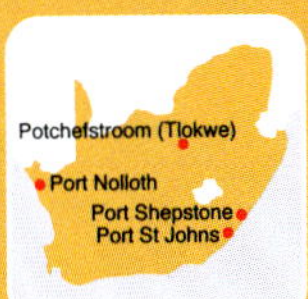

Potchefstroom (Tlokwe)
Port Nolloth
Port Shepstone
Port St Johns

PORT NOLLOTH
TO ALEXANDER BAY
3rd
Bush
Beach
Main
2nd
Soutpan
Noord
Hoërskool Port Nolloth
Port Nolloth Hospital
Magistrates Office
1st
Mark
Sand
Church
Springbok
Agaat
Robyn
Commercial
Alwyn
Bedrock Art Shed
Willem Koegelenberg Park
Port Mark Supermarket
Bay
Gallery Arts & Crafts
Port Nolloth Museum
Richtersveld Municipality
Robson
Rowland
Divers
Alves
Wit
Tieroog
Industria
Spar
Boom
Malherbe
R382
TO STEINKOPF
Emerald
Seagull
McDougall
Carnation
Public Cemetery
Butler
Lantana
Ovenstone
Soccer Field
Diamant
William
Joos
Engelbrecht
Flosse
Duine
Thys Louw
Tinktinkie
Kanarie
Mossel
Rooi
Henry
Burden
Gravenor
Kabeljou
Sardyn
South Point
M 700 1400

PORT SHEPSTONE
TO HIBBERDENE / KINGSBURGH
Memorial
Berea
Robinson
Bisset
Bulwer
Mzimkulu
R102
Dick King Memorial
Ridge
Valley
Andreason
Nicco
Wooley
Muslim Cemetery
Settlers Park
Shepstone Mall
Escombe
Aiken
Riverview
Sandspit Bay
Dennis Shepstone
Library
George
Station
Port Shepstone Lighthouse
McArthur
Hibiscus Civic Centre
Deepvale
Port Shepstone Senior Primary School
Hibiscus Private Hospital
Colley
Port Shepstone Junior Primary School
Oribi Plaza
Port Shepstone Railway Station
Station Bay
Unity
Alamein
George
Bazley
Main
Staunton
Port Shepstone Provincial Hospital
Church
Voortrekker
Victory
Scott
Princess Elizabeth
Port Shepstone High School
Wood
Lucky Dip Bay
Ridge
Tidal Pool
Victory
Mitchell
5th
Port Shepstone Borough Sports Grounds
Fairview
Quarry
Athlone
Swimming Pool
Port Shepstone Museum
Mini Golf, Trampolines, Slide
Kent
Kvalsvig
INDIAN OCEAN
Rathboneville
End
Banana Express Railway Station
Main
Harding
R102
Mbango Bay
Lifeguards
TO N2 / ORIBI GORGE
Sanddune
Boundary
Camp
Marine
North
M 300 600

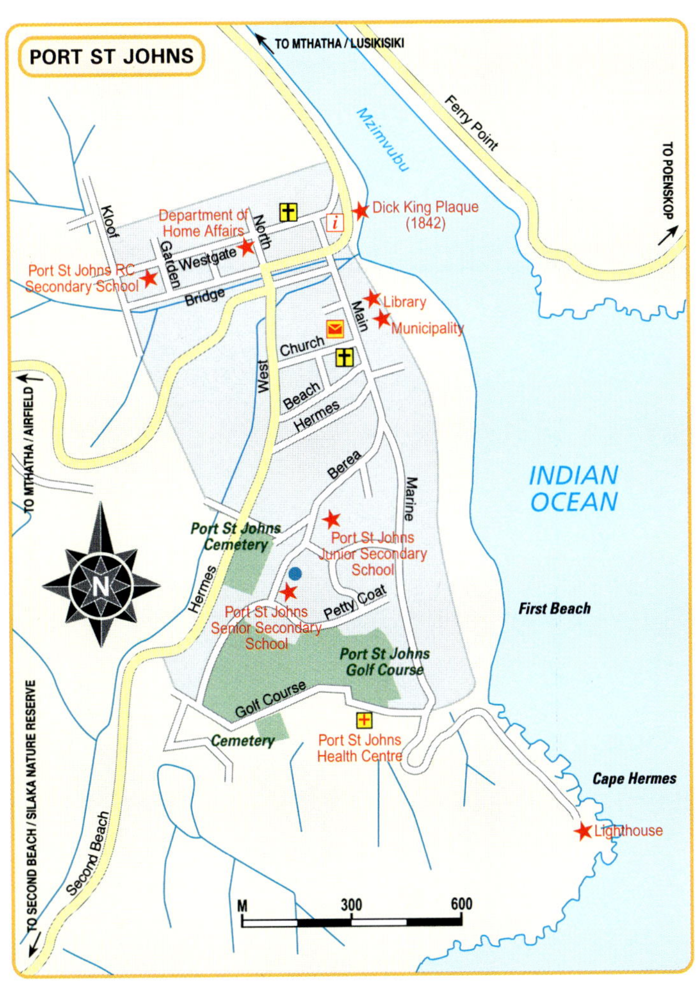

PORT ST JOHNS
TO MTHATHA / LUSIKISIKI
Mzimvubu
Ferry Point
TO POENSKOP
Kloof
Department of Home Affairs
North
Dick King Plaque (1842)
Port St Johns RC Secondary School
Garden
Westgate
Bridge
Library
Main
Municipality
Church
West
Beach
Hermes
TO MTHATHA / AIRFIELD
Berea
Marine
INDIAN OCEAN
Port St Johns Cemetery
Port St Johns Junior Secondary School
Hermes
Port St Johns Senior Secondary School
Petty Coat
First Beach
Port St Johns Golf Course
Golf Course
Cemetery
Port St Johns Health Centre
Cape Hermes
Lighthouse
TO SECOND BEACH / SILAKA NATURE RESERVE
Second Beach
M 300 600

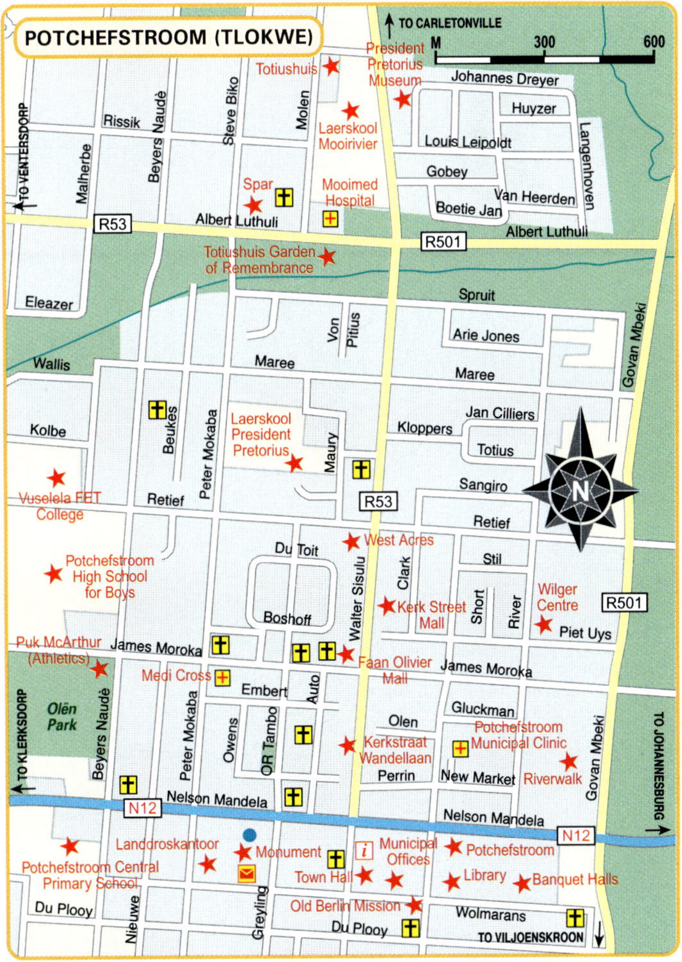

POTCHEFSTROOM (TLOKWE)
TO CARLETONVILLE
President Pretorius Museum
M 300 600
Totiushuis
Johannes Dreyer
Huyzer
TO VENTERSDORP
Rissik
Beyers Naudé
Steve Biko
Molen
Laerskool Mooirivier
Louis Leipoldt
Langenhoven
Malherbe
Gobey
Spar
Mooimed Hospital
Van Heerden
Boetie Jan
R53
Albert Luthuli
R501
Albert Luthuli
Totiushuis Garden of Remembrance
Eleazer
Spruit
Von
Pitius
Arie Jones
Wallis
Maree
Maree
Govan Mbeki
Beukes
Kolbe
Laerskool President Pretorius
Peter Mokaba
Maury
Kloppers
Jan Cilliers
Totius
Vuselela FET College
Retief
R53
Sangiro
Retief
Du Toit
West Acres
Stil
Potchefstroom High School for Boys
Walter Sisulu
Clark
Boshoff
Kerk Street Mall
Short
River
Wilger Centre
R501
Piet Uys
Puk McArthur (Athletics)
James Moroka
Faan Olivier Mall
James Moroka
Medi Cross
Embert
Auto
Olën Park
TO KLERKSDORP
Beyers Naudé
Peter Mokaba
Owens
OR Tambo
Olen
Gluckman
Potchefstroom Municipal Clinic
Kerkstraat Wandellaan
Perrin
New Market
Riverwalk
Govan Mbeki
TO JOHANNESBURG
N12
Nelson Mandela
Nelson Mandela
N12
Landdroskantoor
Monument
Municipal Offices
Potchefstroom
Potchefstroom Central Primary School
Town Hall
Library
Banquet Halls
Du Plooy
Nieuwe
Greyling
Old Berlin Mission
Du Plooy
Wolmarans
TO VILJOENSKROON

PRIESKA RAMSGATE

QUEENSTOWN RANDFONTEIN

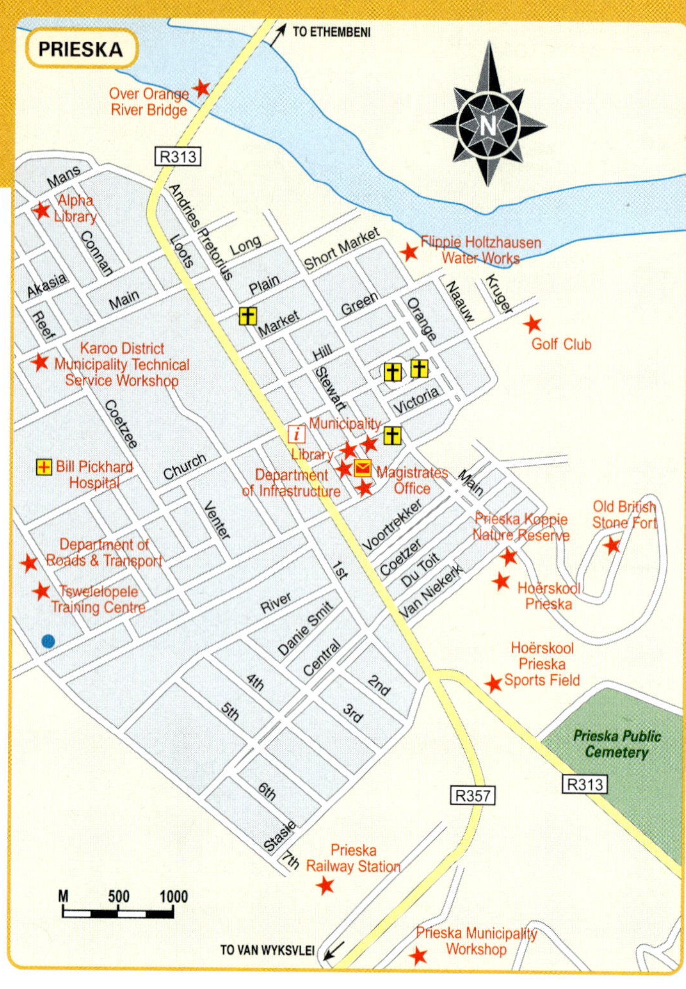

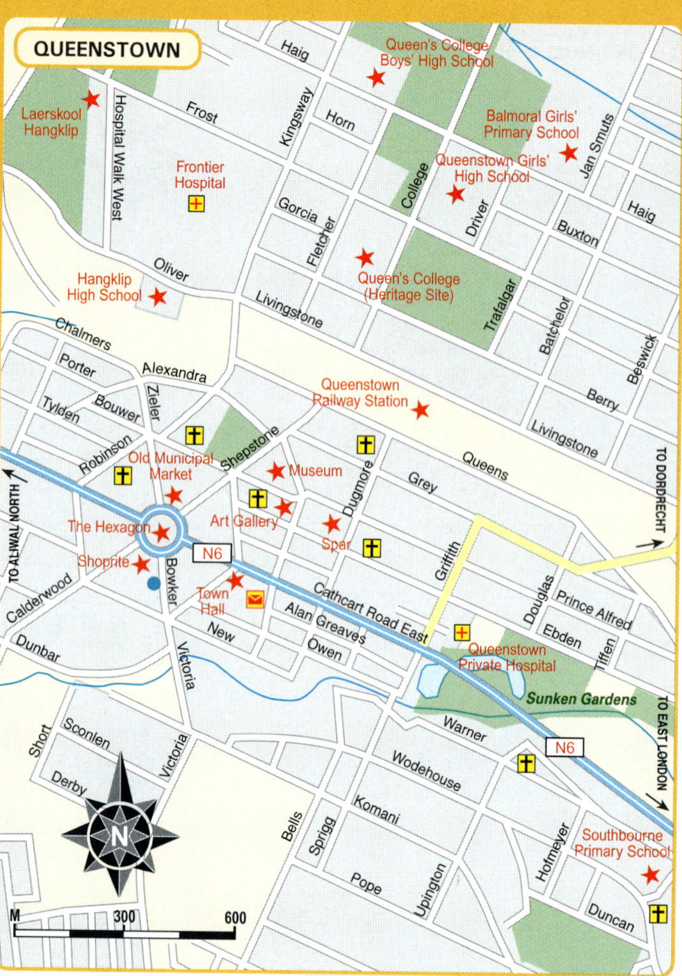

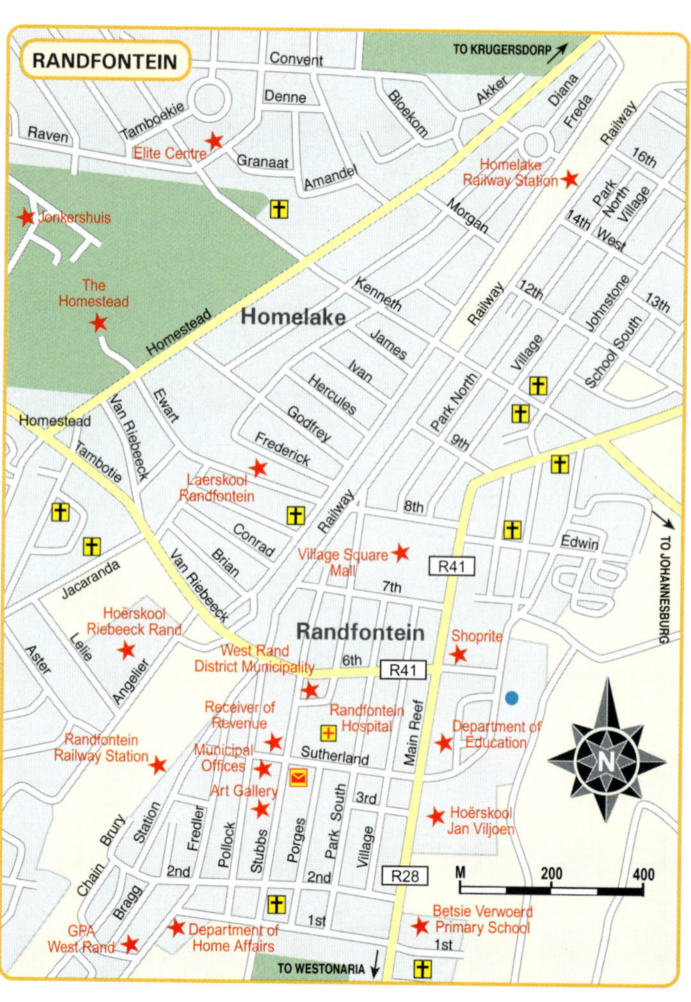

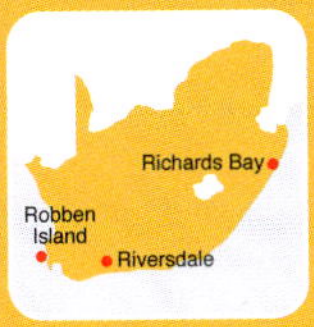

Richards Bay
Robben Island
Riversdale

RICHARDS BAY
TO N2 / EMPANGENI
Lira Link
Krugerrand
The Bay Hospital
Bullion
Boardwalk
Rose Clinic
Shoprite Checkers
Lakeside Mall
Markstrasse
uMhlathuze Municipality
East Central Arterial
White Pear
Alberta
Apiesdoring
Canopy
Albizia
Appelblaar
Ysterhout
Via Richardia
Vaarlands-
Wilg
Tassel Berry
Soap Berry
Sybas
Via Cassiandra
Guldengracht
Pigeon Wood
Sand Olive
Soetdoring-
Sekel
Tambotiehout
Tipuana
Saligna
John Ross College
Wattelgoud
Via Cassiandra
Mango
Avokado
Kroon
Frangipani
Delonix Dune
Cassia
Avokado Kroon
North Central Arterial
Richards Bay Hospice
Rhus Lancea
Koorsboom
Jakaranda
Via Cassiandra
M 250 500
TO N2 / EMPANGENI
R34
John Ross Parkway
TO REPTILE CITY

RIVERSDALE
TO LADISMITH
M 1200 2400
Decora
Ixia
M12
Arendhoogte Bird Sanctuary
Lowrens
Hoërskool Langenhoven
Vet
Freesia
Tritonia
Acacia
Nerina
Badenhorst
Disa
Truter
Pauw
Holtzhausen
Roux
Steyn
Oostehuizen
Bell
Langenhoven
Laerskool Volschenk
Marais
Cronje
Long
Rensburg
De Jager
Mulder
Wilson
Rosenow
Barry
Van Riebeeck
Jager
Albertyn
Olser
Warden
Hudson
Dickson
John
Mitchell
Mitchell
TO HEIDELBERG
N2
Heidelberg
Hessequa Municipality
Main
Friendly Supermarket
Spar
Main
Soloman
Versveld
Reitz
Hospital
Care Cross Clinic
Hofmeyer
Traffic Department
Panorama Primary School
Barry
Riversdale Hospital
Sidney
Becker
Wege
Riversdale Railway Station
Venterrivier
Van Zyl
Volschenk
Theunissen
Varkevisser
Grasskopf
Rose-Innes
Church
Versveld
Oliestager
Cumming
Heese
Petersen
Suikerbos
Maanlig
Varkblom
End
Sonskyn
Aandblom
Panorama
Kloof
Lea
Milner
N2
Bali Shop
Alwyn
Buitekant
Garcia
Uitsig
TO ALBERTINIA

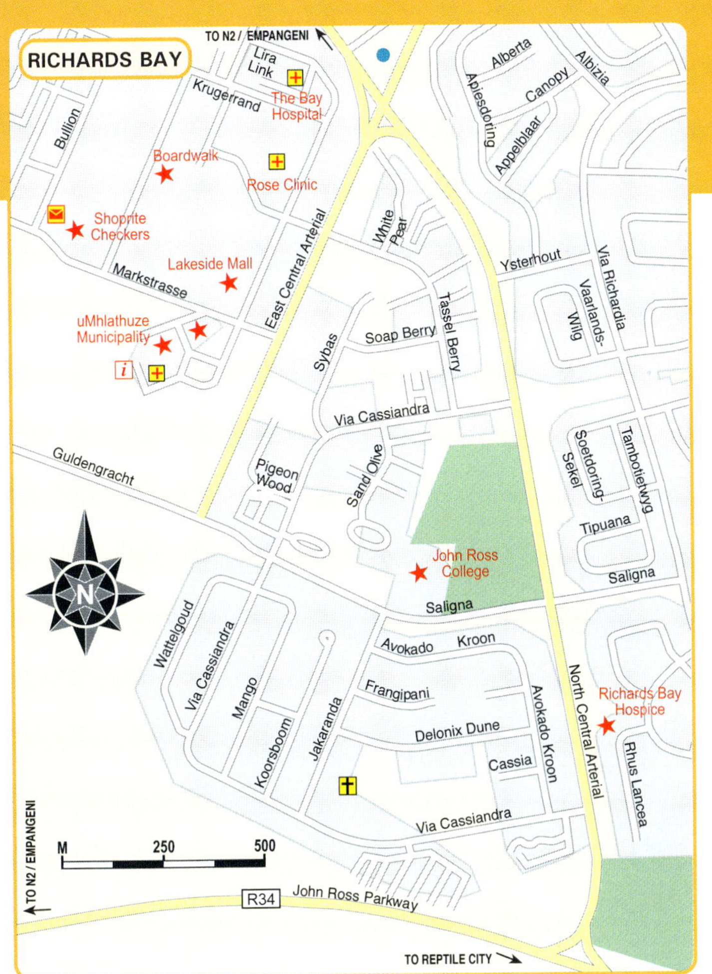

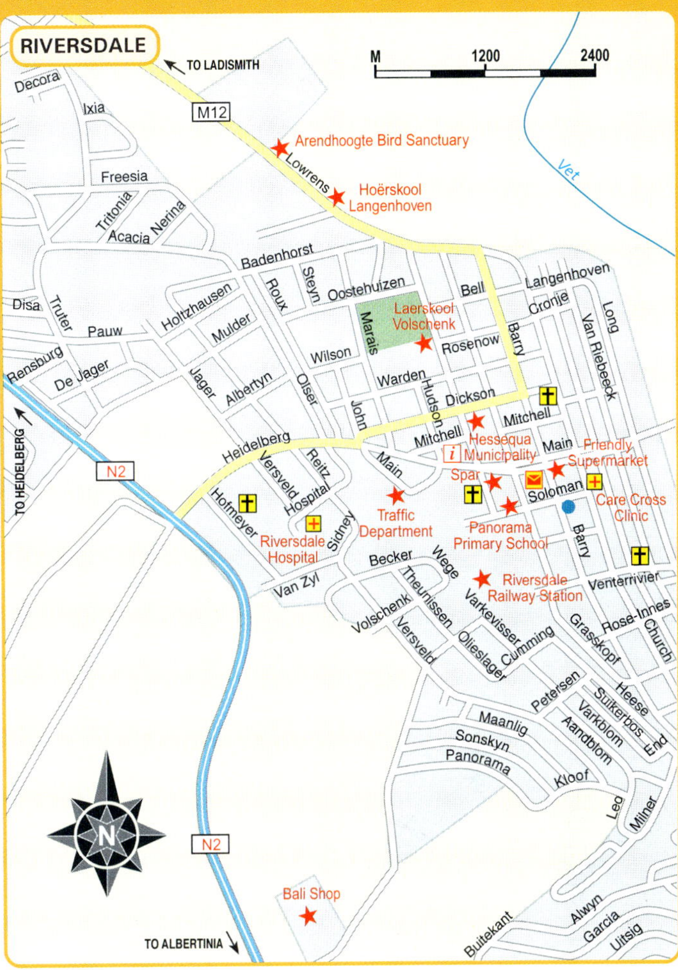

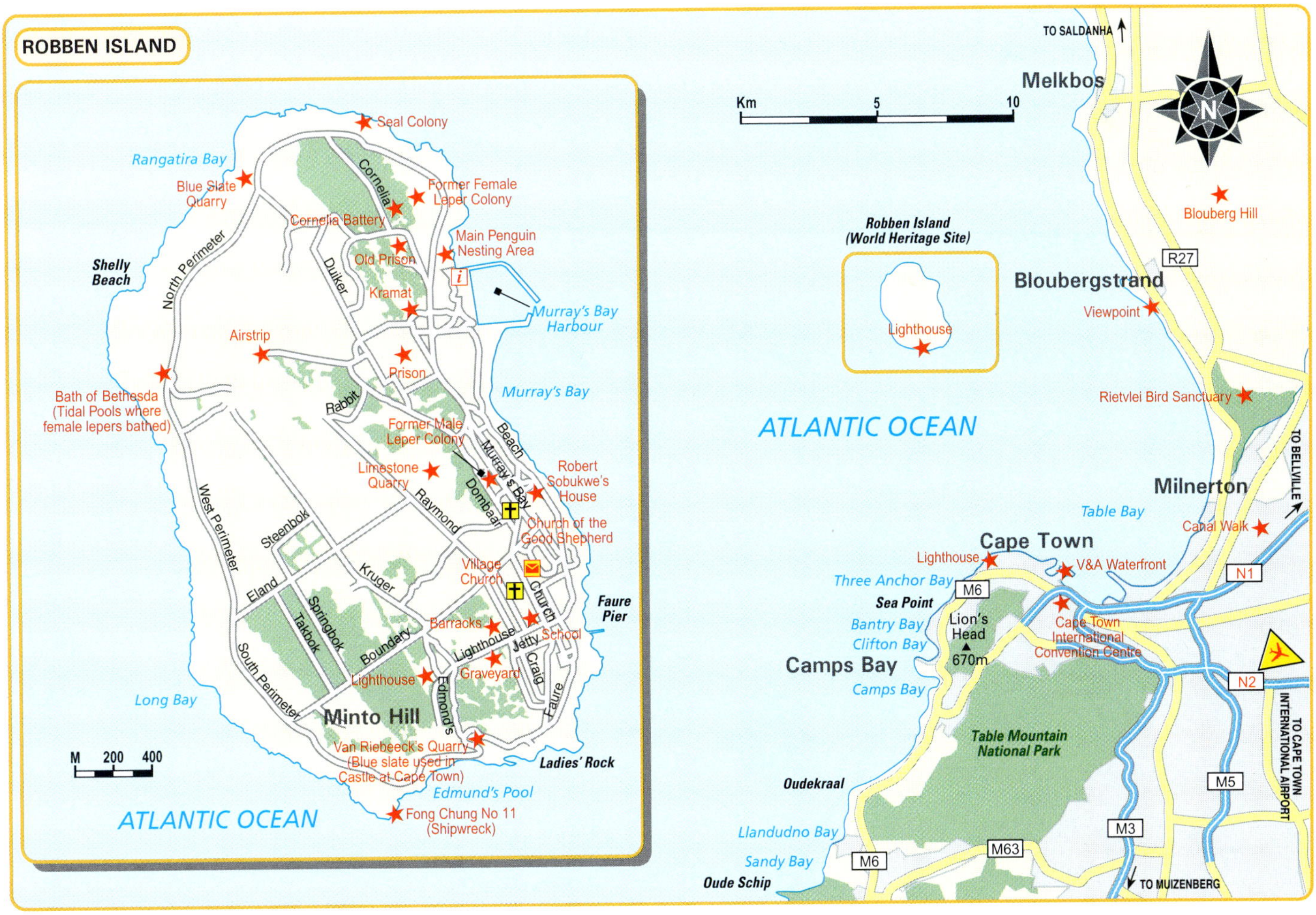

ROBBEN ISLAND
Seal Colony
Rangatira Bay
Blue Slate Quarry
Cornelia
Former Female Leper Colony
Cornelia Battery
Main Penguin Nesting Area
Old Prison
Shelly Beach
North Perimeter
Duiker
Kramat
Murray's Bay Harbour
Airstrip
Prison
Murray's Bay
Bath of Bethesda (Tidal Pools where female lepers bathed)
Rabbit
Former Male Leper Colony
Beach
Limestone Quarry
Murray's Bay
Robert Sobukwe's House
Raymond
Dombaai
West Perimeter
Steenbok
Church of the Good Shepherd
Kruger
Village Church
Church
Faure Pier
Eland
Springbok
Taakbok
Barracks
Lighthouse
Jetty
School
Boundary
Craig
Graveyard
Lighthouse
South Perimeter
Faure
Long Bay
Minto Hill
Edmonds
Van Riebeeck's Quarry (Blue slate used in Castle at Cape Town)
Ladies' Rock
M 200 400
Edmund's Pool
ATLANTIC OCEAN
Fong Chung No 11 (Shipwreck)
TO SALDANHA
Melkbos
Km 5 10
Blouberg Hill
Robben Island (World Heritage Site)
R27
Bloubergstrand
Viewpoint
Lighthouse
Rietvlei Bird Sanctuary
ATLANTIC OCEAN
TO BELLVILLE
Milnerton
Table Bay
Canal Walk
Cape Town
Lighthouse
V&A Waterfront
Three Anchor Bay
M6
N1
Sea Point
Bantry Bay
Lion's Head 670m
Cape Town International Convention Centre
Clifton Bay
Camps Bay
Camps Bay
N2
TO CAPE TOWN INTERNATIONAL AIRPORT
Table Mountain National Park
Oudekraal
M5
Llandudno Bay
M3
Sandy Bay
M6
M63
Oude Schip
TO MUIZENBERG

ROBERTSON RUSTENBURG ROUXVILLE SABIE

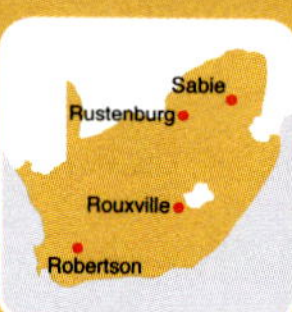

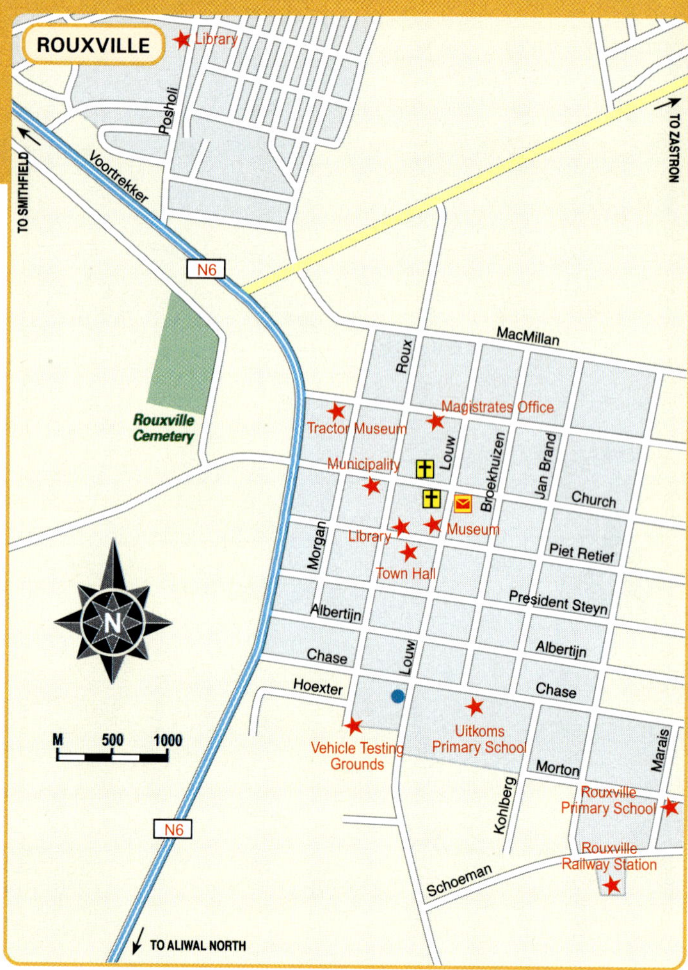

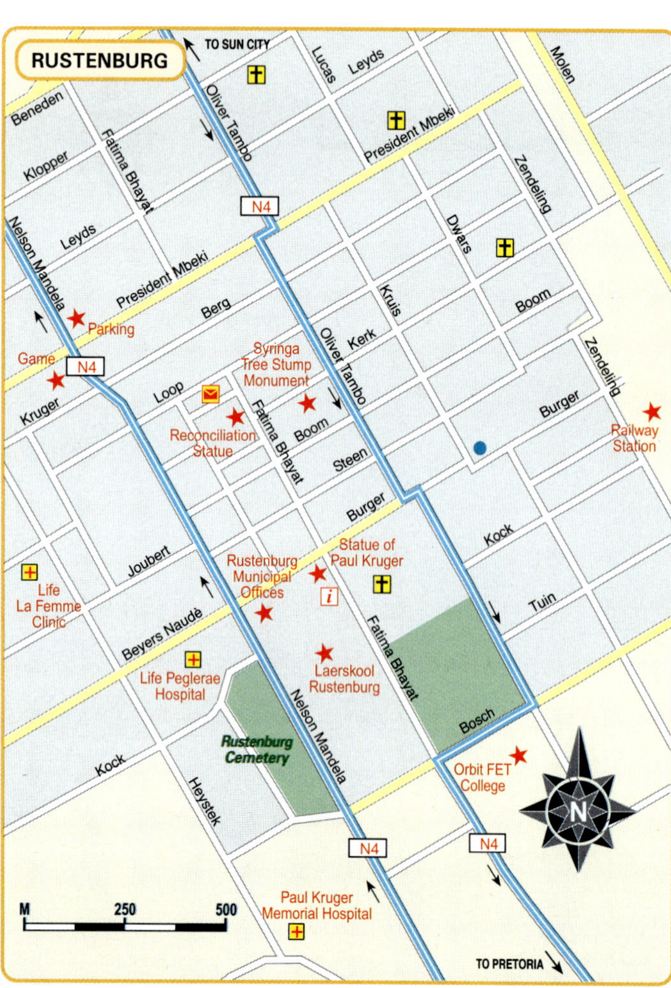

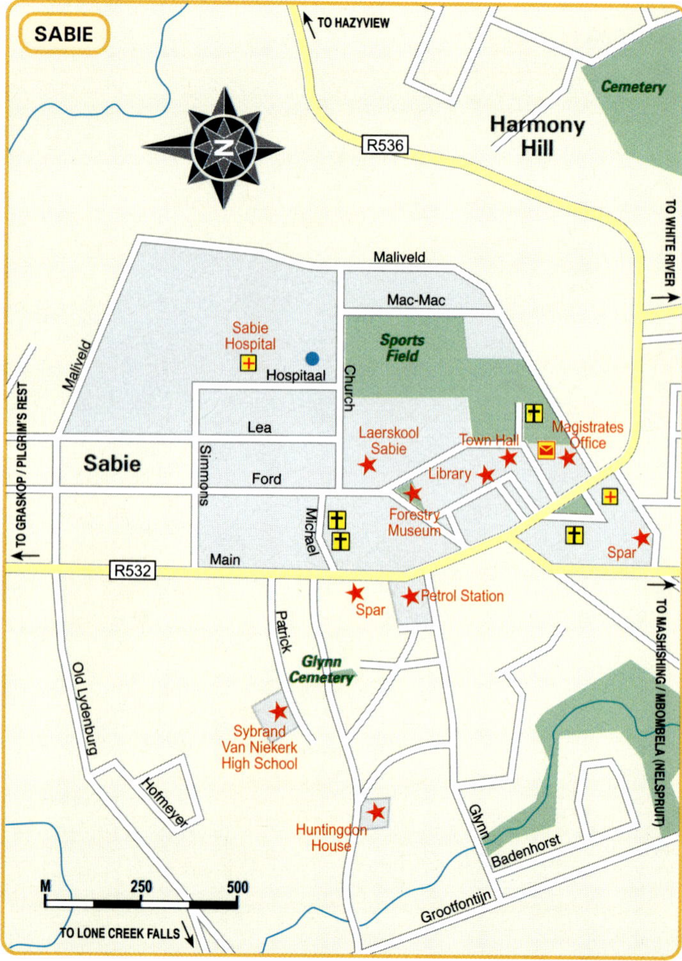

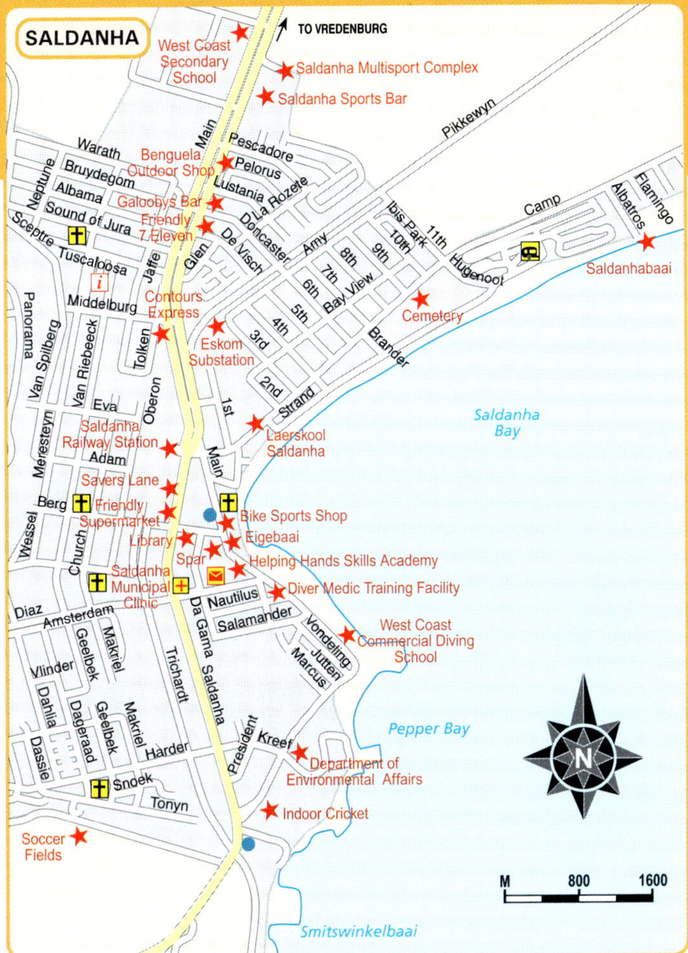
SALDANHA
TO VREDENBURG
West Coast Secondary School
Saldanha Multisport Complex
Saldanha Sports Bar
Pikkewyn
Benguela Outdoor Shop
Galoobys Bar
Friendly 7 Eleven
Contours Express
Eskom Substation
Cemetery
Saldanhabaai
Saldanha Bay
Laerskool Saldanha
Saldanha Railway Station
Savers Lane
Friendly Supermarket
Library
Spar
Bike Sports Shop
Eigebaai
Helping Hands Skills Academy
Diver Medic Training Facility
Saldanha Municipal Clinic
West Coast Commercial Diving School
Pepper Bay
Department of Environmental Affairs
Indoor Cricket
Soccer Fields
Smitswinkelbaai
M 800 1600

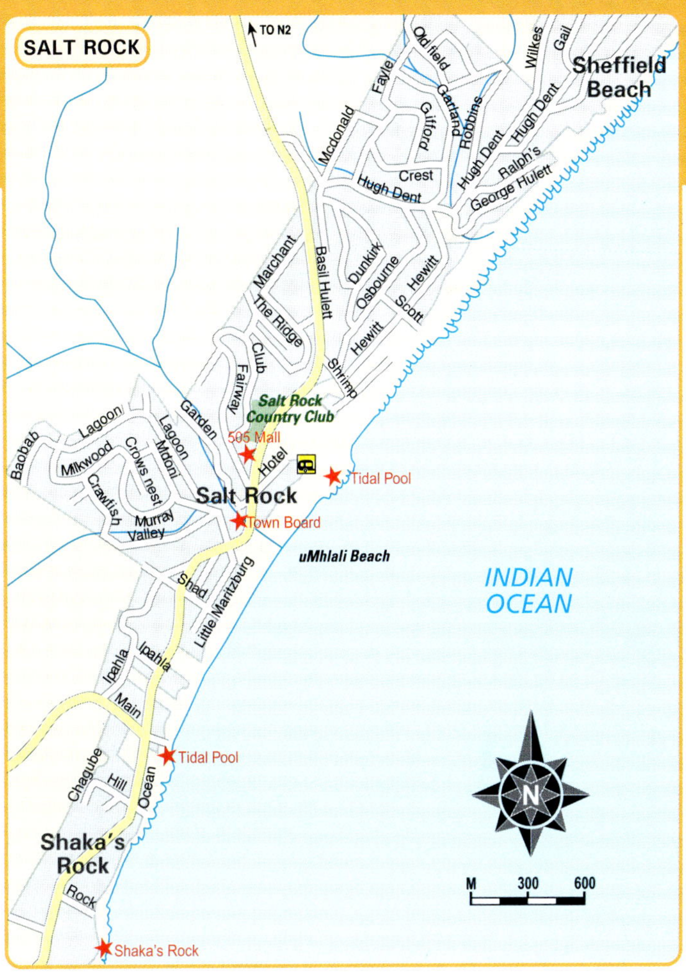
SALT ROCK
TO N2
Sheffield Beach
Salt Rock Country Club
505 Mall
Hotel
Tidal Pool
Salt Rock
Town Board
uMhlali Beach
INDIAN OCEAN
Tidal Pool
Shaka's Rock
Shaka's Rock
M 300 600

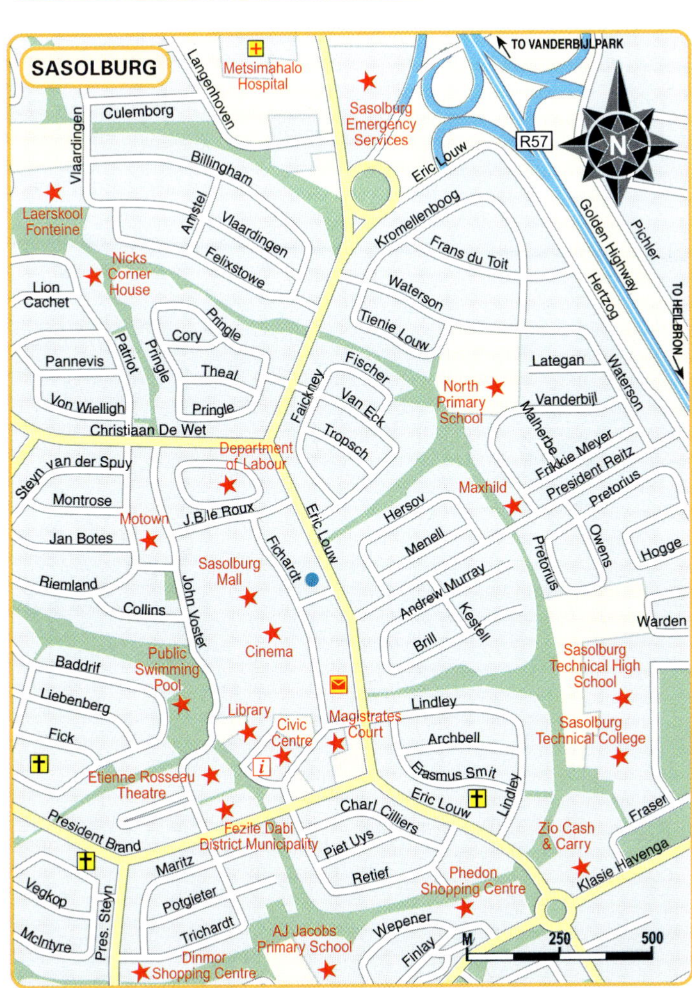
SASOLBURG
TO VANDERBIJLPARK
Metsimaholo Hospital
Sasolburg Emergency Services
R57
Laerskool Fonteine
Nicks Corner House
TO HEILBRON
North Primary School
Department of Labour
Motown
Maxhild
Sasolburg Mall
Cinema
Public Swimming Pool
Library
Civic Centre
Magistrates Court
Sasolburg Technical High School
Sasolburg Technical College
Etienne Rosseau Theatre
Fezile Dabi District Municipality
Zio Cash & Carry
Phedon Shopping Centre
AJ Jacobs Primary School
Dinmor Shopping Centre
M 250 500

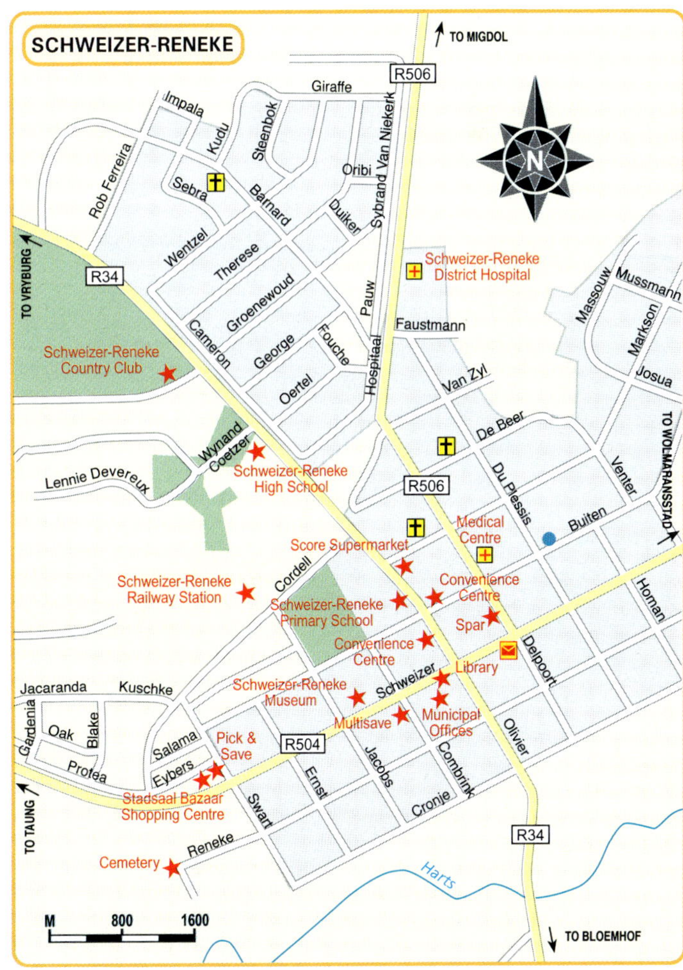
SCHWEIZER-RENEKE
TO MIGDOL
R506
R34
TO VRYBURG
Schweizer-Reneke District Hospital
Schweizer-Reneke Country Club
Schweizer-Reneke High School
R506
TO WOLMARANSSTAD
Medical Centre
Score Supermarket
Convenience Centre
Schweizer-Reneke Railway Station
Schweizer-Reneke Primary School
Spar
Convenience Centre
Library
Schweizer-Reneke Museum
Multisave
Municipal Offices
Pick & Save
R504
Stadsaal Bazaar Shopping Centre
TO TAUNG
Cemetery
R34
Harts
TO BLOEMHOF
M 800 1600

Senekal
Scottburgh
Simon's Town
Sedgefield

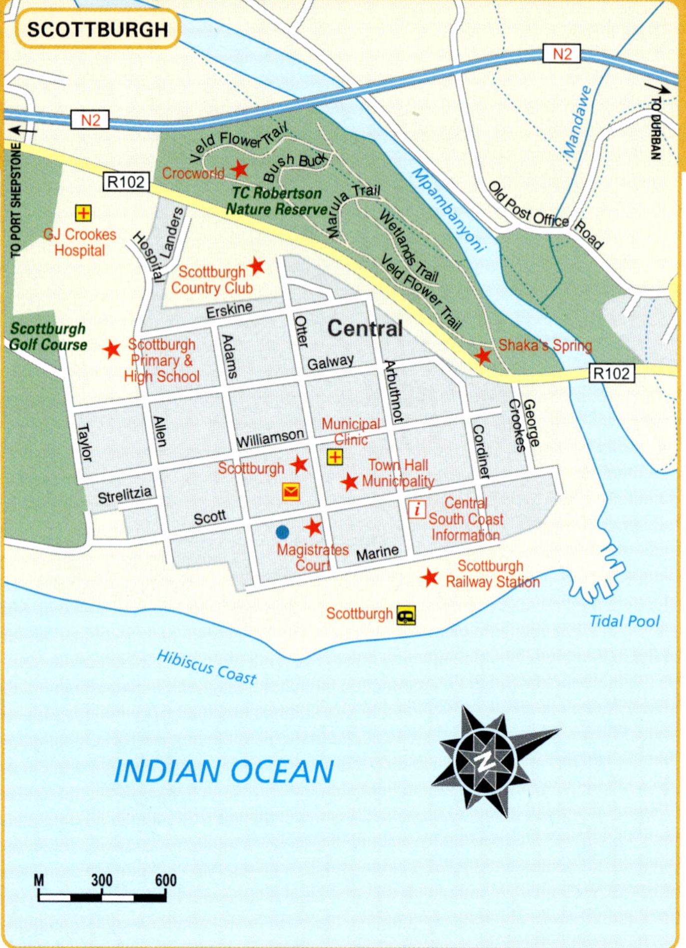
SCOTTBURGH
N2
TO DURBAN
TO PORT SHEPSTONE
R102
Veld Flower Trail
Bush Buck
Crocworld
TC Robertson Nature Reserve
Marula Trail
Wetlands Trail
Veld Flower Trail
Mpambanyoni
Mandawe
Old Post Office Road
GJ Crookes Hospital
Hospital
Landers
Scottburgh Country Club
Erskine
Scottburgh Golf Course
Scottburgh Primary & High School
Adams
Otter
Central
Galway
Arbuthnot
Shaka's Spring
R102
George Crookes
Cordiner
Taylor
Allen
Williamson
Municipal Clinic
Scottburgh
Town Hall Municipality
Strelitzia
Scott
Central South Coast Information
Magistrates Court
Marine
Scottburgh Railway Station
Scottburgh
Tidal Pool
Hibiscus Coast
INDIAN OCEAN
M 300 600

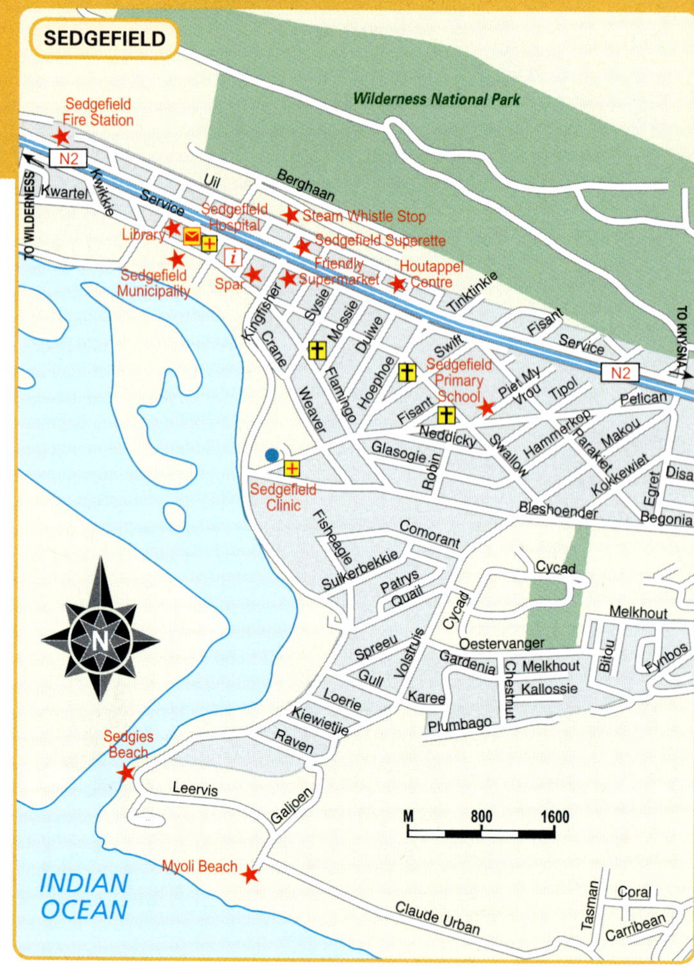
SEDGEFIELD
Sedgefield Fire Station
Wilderness National Park
N2
TO WILDERNESS
Kwartel
Kwikkie
Uil
Berghaan
Service
Sedgefield Hospital
Steam Whistle Stop
Library
Sedgefield Superette
Sedgefield Municipality
Spar
Friendly Supermarket
Houtappel Centre
Tinktinkie
TO KNYSNA
Kingfisher
Crane
Sysie
Mossie
Duiwe
Fisant
Service
Swift
Sedgefield Primary School
N2
Weaver
Flamingo
Hoephoe
Fisant
Piet My Vrou
Tipol
Pelican
Neddicky
Swallow
Hammarkop
Parakiet
Makou
Glasogie
Robin
Kokkewiet
Egret
Disa
Sedgefield Clinic
Bleshoender
Begonia
Fisheagle
Comorant
Suikerbekkie
Patrys
Quail
Cycad
Cycad
Melkhout
Oestervanger
Spreeu
Volstruis
Gardenia
Chestnut
Melkhout
Bitou
Fynbos
Gull
Karee
Kallossie
Loerie
Kiewietjie
Plumbago
Raven
Sedgies Beach
Leervis
Galjoen
M 800 1600
INDIAN OCEAN
Myoli Beach
Claude Urban
Tasman
Coral
Carribean

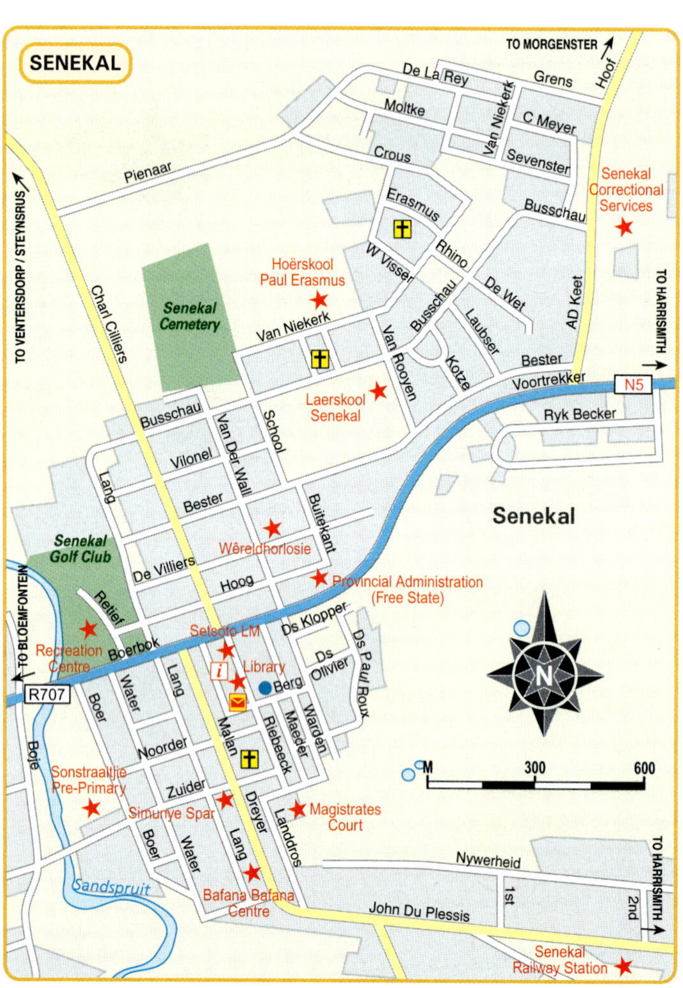
SENEKAL
TO MORGENSTER
De La Rey
Grens
Moltke
Van Niekerk
C Meyer
Hoof
Crous
Sevenster
Pienaar
Senekal Correctional Services
Erasmus
Busschau
TO VENTERSDORP / STEYNSRUS
Rhino
W Visser
De Wet
AD Keet
TO HARRISMITH
Hoërskool Paul Erasmus
Busschau
Senekal Cemetery
Charl Cilliers
Van Niekerk
Van Rooyen
Laubser
Kotze
Bester
Voortrekker
N5
Laerskool Senekal
Ryk Becker
Busschau
Van Der Walt
School
Vilonel
Lang
Bester
Buitekant
Senekal
Senekal Golf Club
Wêreldhorlosie
De Villiers
Hoog
Provincial Administration (Free State)
Reitief
TO BLOEMFONTEIN
Recreation Centre
Boerbok
Setsoto LM
Ds Klopper
Ds Olivier
Ds Paul Roux
Library
R707
Boer
Water
Lang
Berg
Riebeeck
Maeder
Warden
Malan
Noorder
Boje
Sonstraaltjie Pre-Primary
Zuider
Simunye Spar
Dreyer
Magistrates Court
Landdros
Boer
Water
Lang
Nywerheid
Sandspruit
Bafana Bafana Centre
John Du Plessis
1st
2nd
TO HARRISMITH
M 300 600
Senekal Railway Station

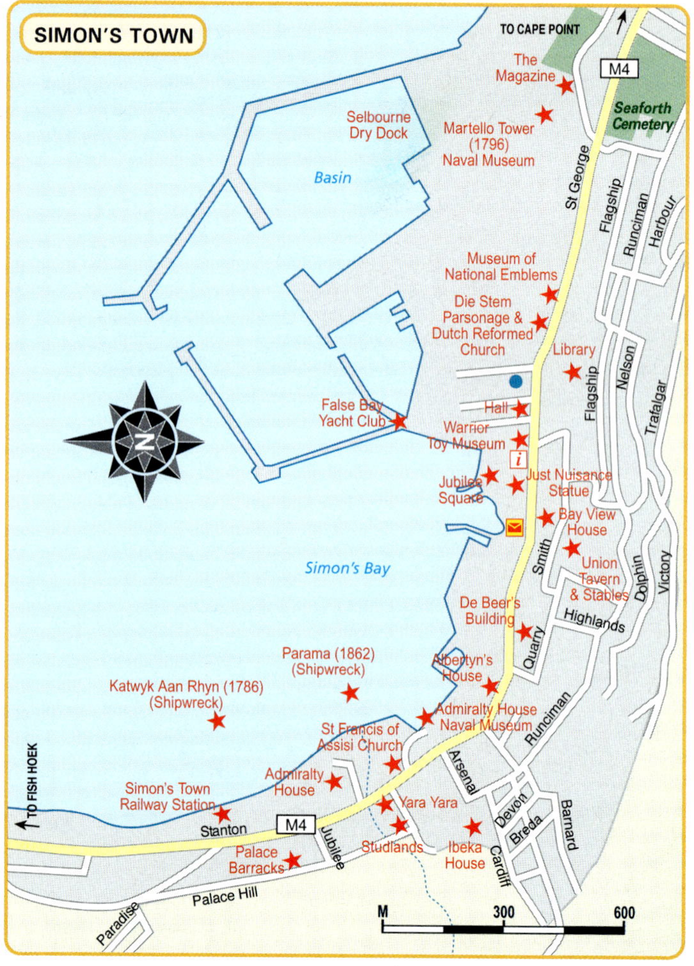
SIMON'S TOWN
TO CAPE POINT
The Magazine
M4
Seaforth Cemetery
Selbourne Dry Dock
Martello Tower (1796) Naval Museum
St George
Flagship
Runciman
Harbour
Basin
Museum of National Emblems
Die Stem Parsonage & Dutch Reformed Church
Library
Nelson
Trafalgar
Flagship
False Bay Yacht Club
Hall
Warrior Toy Museum
Jubilee Square
Just Nuisance Statue
Bay View House
Smith
Union Tavern & Stables
Dolphin
Victory
Simon's Bay
De Beer's Building
Highlands
Quarry
Albertyn's House
Parama (1862) (Shipwreck)
Katwyk Aan Rhyn (1786) (Shipwreck)
Admiralty House Naval Museum
Runciman
St Francis of Assisi Church
Arsenal
TO FISH HOEK
Simon's Town Railway Station
Admiralty House
Yara Yara
Devon
Stanton
M4
Jubilee
Studlands
Ibeka House
Breda
Barnard
Palace Barracks
Cardiff
Palace Hill
Paradise
M 300 600

SISHEN

Sishen Municipality
Sishen Department of Social Development & Population
Sishen Multisport Complex
Library
Sishen Primary School
Dingleton Department of Social Services
Dingleton Supermarket
Sishen Railway Station
M 250 500
TO KATHU / N14

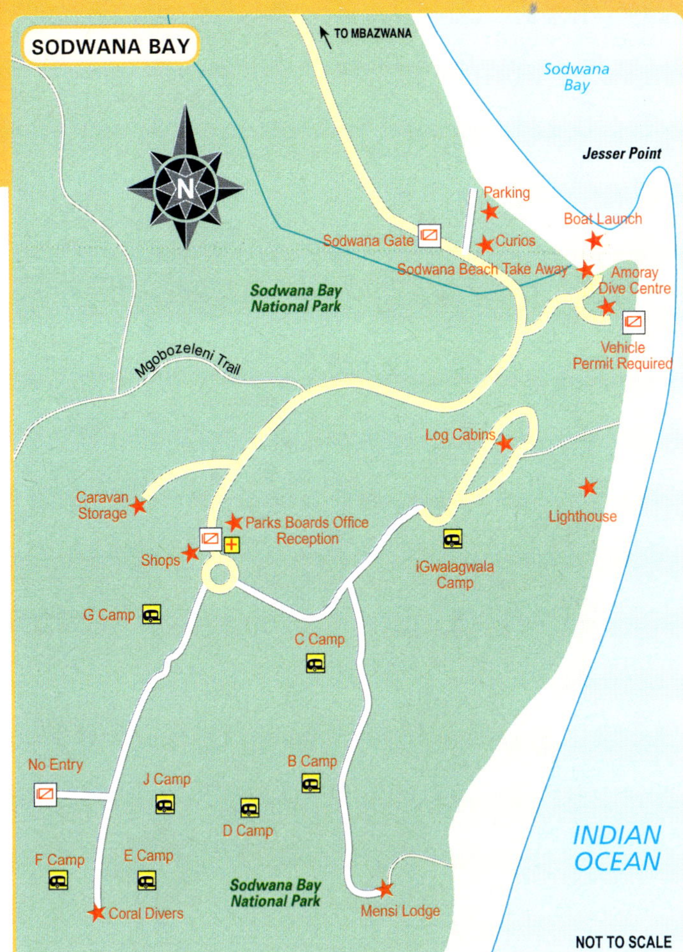

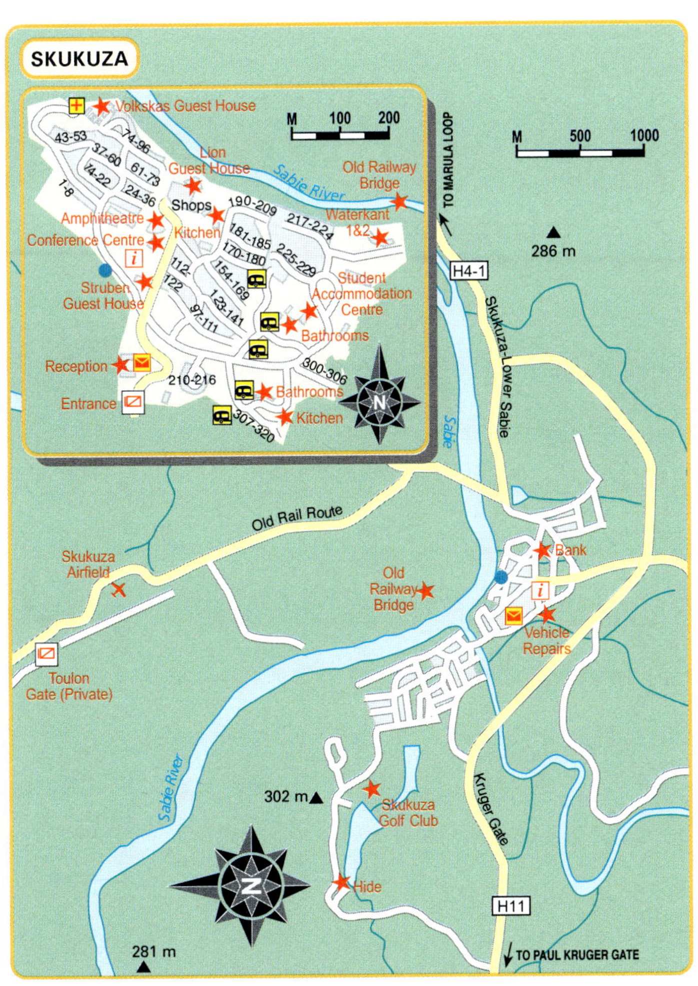

SOMERSET WEST SPRINGBOK SOWETO SPRINGS

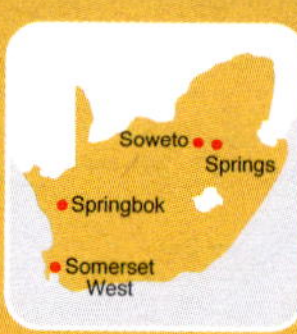

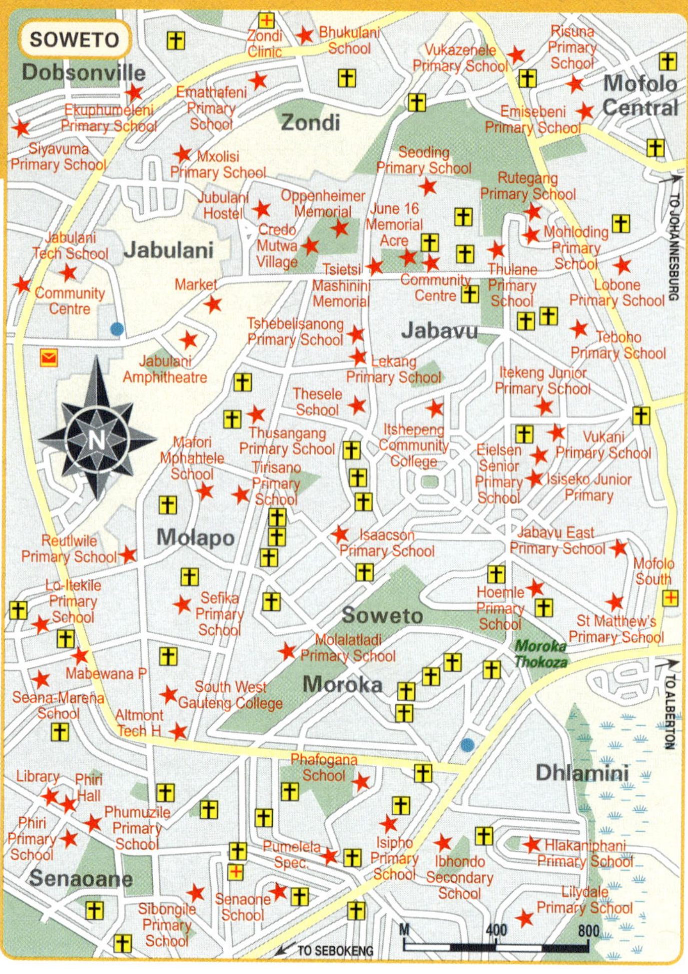

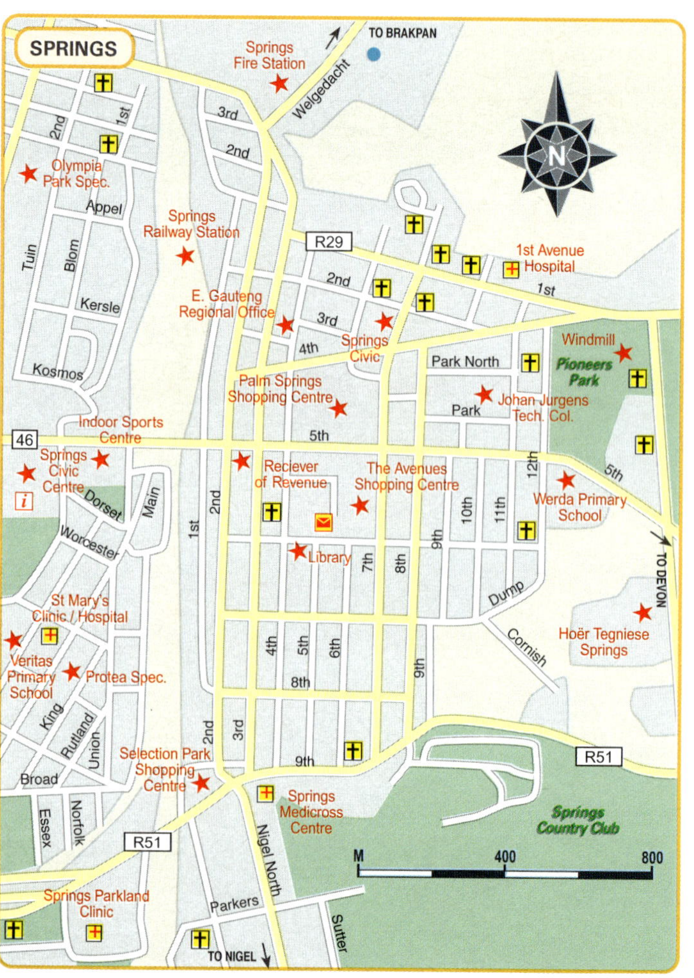

SPRINGBOK

Dr Izak van Niekerk Hospital

King

Breë

Springbok Primary School

Luckhoff

Namaqualand Museum

Library

Kowie Cloete

Monument

Namakwa

Van der Stel

Hospital

Lodge

River

Uitspan

TO N14 / UPINGTON

Koppie

Voortrekker

Shoprite

Keerom

Pieter Malan

Eerstelaan

Showgrounds

Dutch Reformed Church

Tweede-laan

Berg

Multisave

De Waal

Pastorie

Eerstelaan

Welkom

Derdelaan

TO N7 / CAPE TOWN / WINDHOEK

Overberg

M 250 500

Standerton
St Lucia
Stellenbosch
St Francis Bay

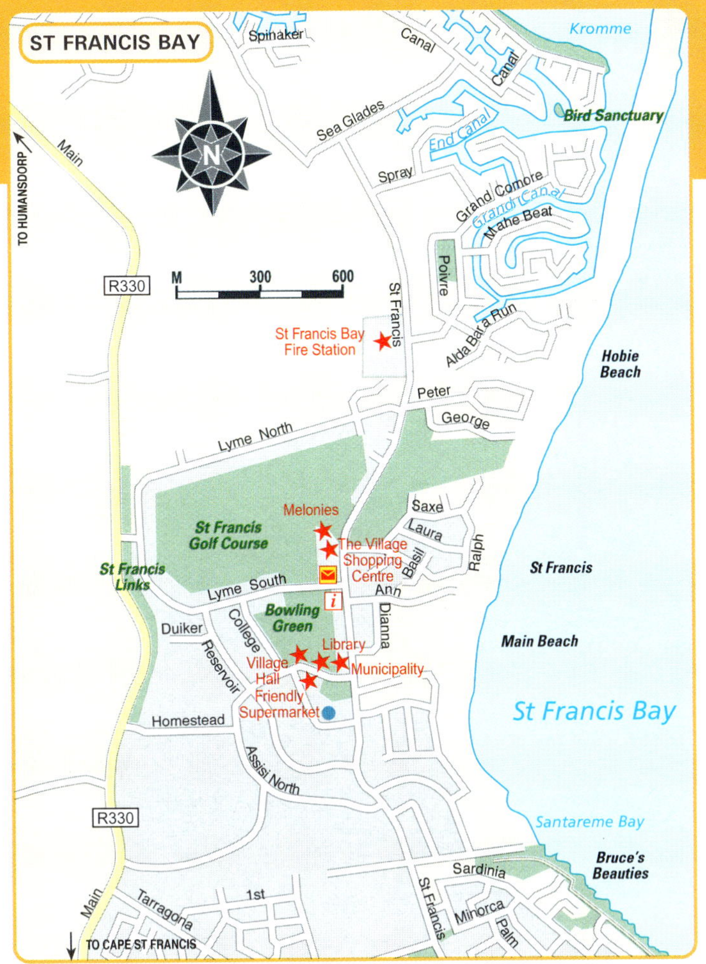
ST FRANCIS BAY
Spinaker
Canal
Kromme
Bird Sanctuary
Sea Glades
End Canal
Spray
Grand Comore
Grand Canal
Mahe Beat
Main
TO HUMANSDORP
R330
M 300 600
Poivre
St Francis
Alda Barra Run
St Francis Bay Fire Station
Hobie Beach
Peter
George
Lyme North
Saxe
Laura
Melonies
St Francis Golf Course
The Village Shopping Centre
Basil
Ralph
St Francis Links
Lyme South
Ann
St Francis
Bowling Green
Duiker
College
Dianna
Main Beach
Library
Village Hall
Municipality
Reservoir
Friendly Supermarket
St Francis Bay
Homestead
Assisi North
R330
Santareme Bay
Bruce's Beauties
Sardinia
Main
Tarragona
1st
St Francis
Minorca
Palm
TO CAPE ST FRANCIS

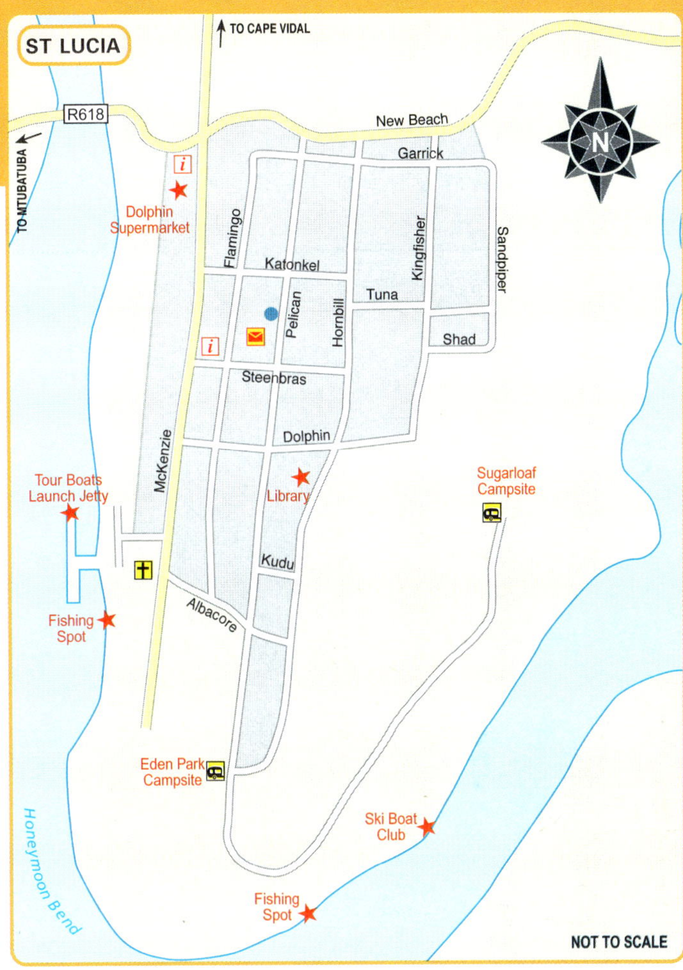
ST LUCIA
TO CAPE VIDAL
R618
TO MTUBATUBA
New Beach
Garrick
Dolphin Supermarket
Flamingo
Kingfisher
Sandpiper
Katonkel
Tuna
Pelican
Hornbill
Shad
Steenbras
Dolphin
McKenzie
Tour Boats Launch Jetty
Library
Sugarloaf Campsite
Kudu
Fishing Spot
Albacore
Eden Park Campsite
Honeymoon Bend
Ski Boat Club
Fishing Spot
NOT TO SCALE

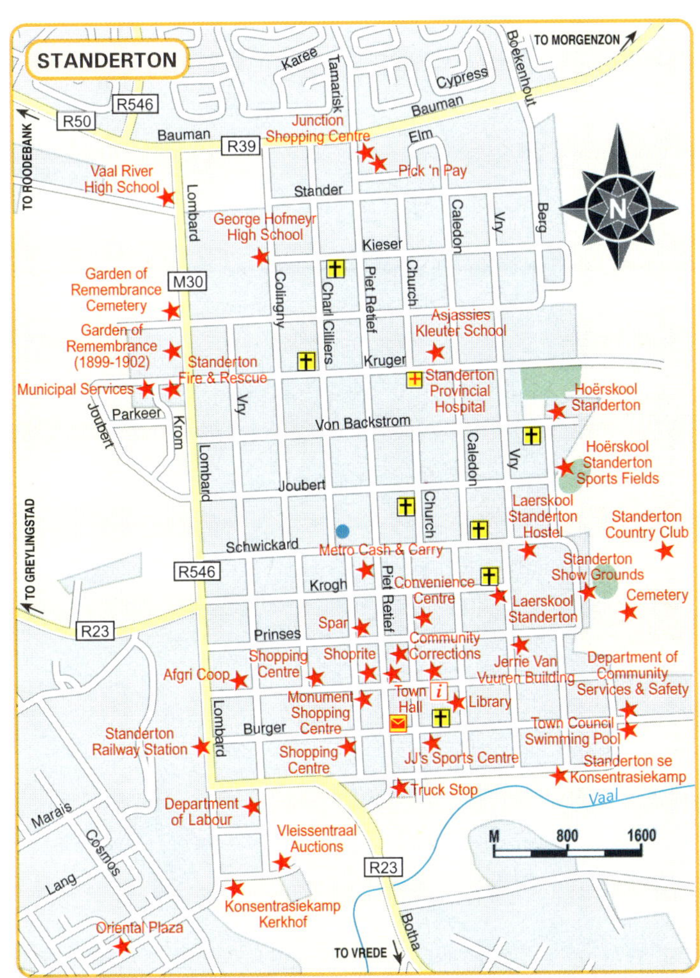
STANDERTON
Karee
Tamarisk
Cypress
Boekenhout
TO MORGENZON
R546
R50
Junction Shopping Centre
Bauman
Bauman
R39
Elm
TO ROODEBANK
Vaal River High School
Pick 'n Pay
Stander
Lombard
Caledon
Vry
Berg
George Hofmeyr High School
Kieser
Garden of Remembrance Cemetery
M30
Collingny
Charl Cilliers
Piet Retief
Church
Garden of Remembrance (1899-1902)
Asjassies Kleuter School
Standerton Fire & Rescue
Kruger
Standerton Provincial Hospital
Municipal Services
Vry
Hoërskool Standerton
Joubert
Parkeer
Krom
Von Backstrom
Caledon
Vry
Hoërskool Standerton Sports Fields
Lombard
Joubert
Church
Laerskool Standerton Hostel
Standerton Country Club
TO GREYLINGSTAD
Schwickard
Metro Cash & Carry
R546
Krogh
Piet Retief
Convenience Centre
Standerton Show Grounds
Laerskool Standerton
Cemetery
R23
Prinses
Spar
Community Corrections
Jerrie Van Vuuren Building
Department of Community Services & Safety
Afgri Coop
Shopping Centre
Shoprite
Monument Shopping Centre
Town Hall
Library
Standerton Railway Station
Lombard
Burger
Town Council Swimming Pool
Shopping Centre
JJ's Sports Centre
Standerton se Konsentrasiekamp
Truck Stop
Vaal
Department of Labour
Marais
Vleissentraal Auctions
M 800 1600
Cosmos
Lang
R23
Konsentrasiekamp Kerkhof
Oriental Plaza
Botha
TO VREDE

STELLENBOSCH
TO N1 / CAPE TOWN / PAARL
R304
R44
Bird
Rand
Conde
Krommerivier
C.S.I.R.
Hammanshand
Stoffel Smit
Adam Tas
Jan Cilliers
Muller
Molteno
Borcherd
Paul Kruger
Ryneveld
Banghoek
TO FRANSCHHOEK
Soeteweide
Stellenbosch Hospital
Dennesig
Andringa
Cederberg Cheese Factory
Merriman
Bosman
Libertas Theatre
Old Court Building
Library
Langenhoven Center
University of Stellenbosch
Victoria College Building
'Neelsie'
Victoria
R44
Van der Stel Sports Club
Bird
Wilgenhof
The Eindler Concert Hall
Hofmeyer
Neethling
Eikestad Mall
Sasol Art Gallery
Du Toit
Murray
Botanical Garden
Stellenbosch Art Gallery
Van Riebeeck
Alexander
The Braak
TO JONKERSHOEK
Toy Museum
Church
Village Museum
Drostdy
Mill
The Avenue
Oom Samie se Winkel
Theological Seminary
Piet Retief
Coetzenburg Sports Ground
Dorp
Vredelust
La Gratitude
Rembrandt van Rijn Art Gallery
Eerste
Suidwal
Danie Craven Stadium
R44
M 300 600
TO STRAND

STILL BAY STUTTERHEIM

STRAND SWELLENDAM

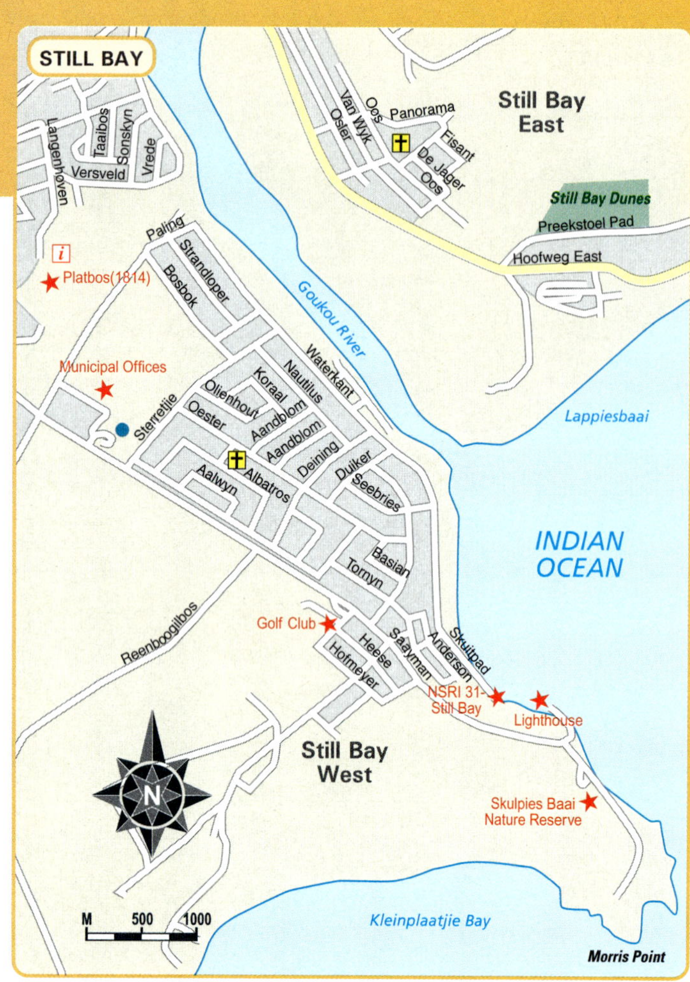

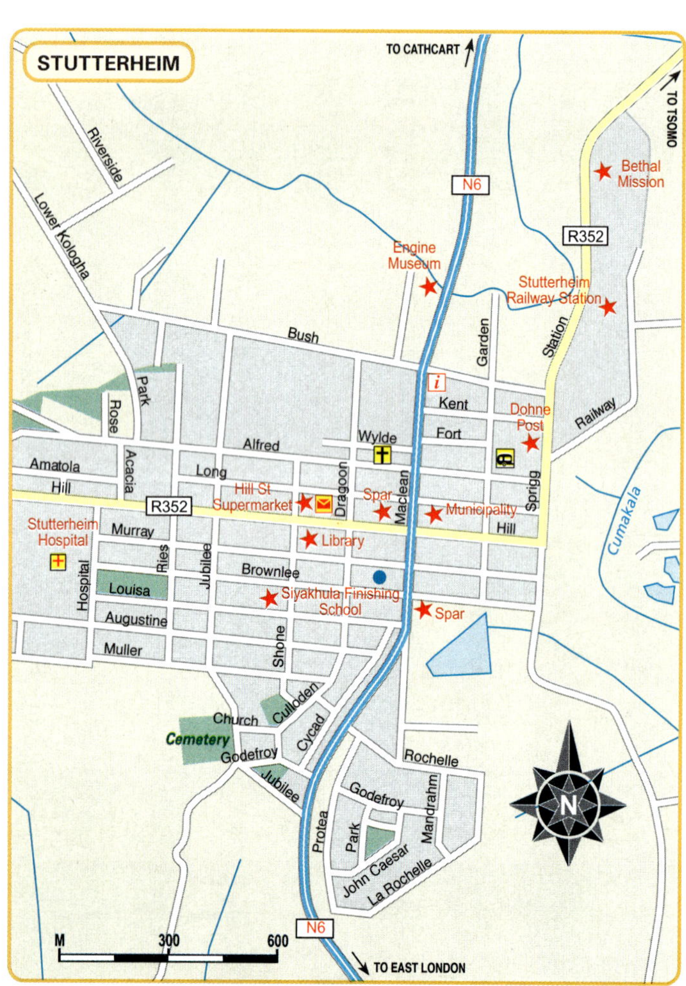

THABAZIMBI TZANEEN

TULBAGH UITENHAGE

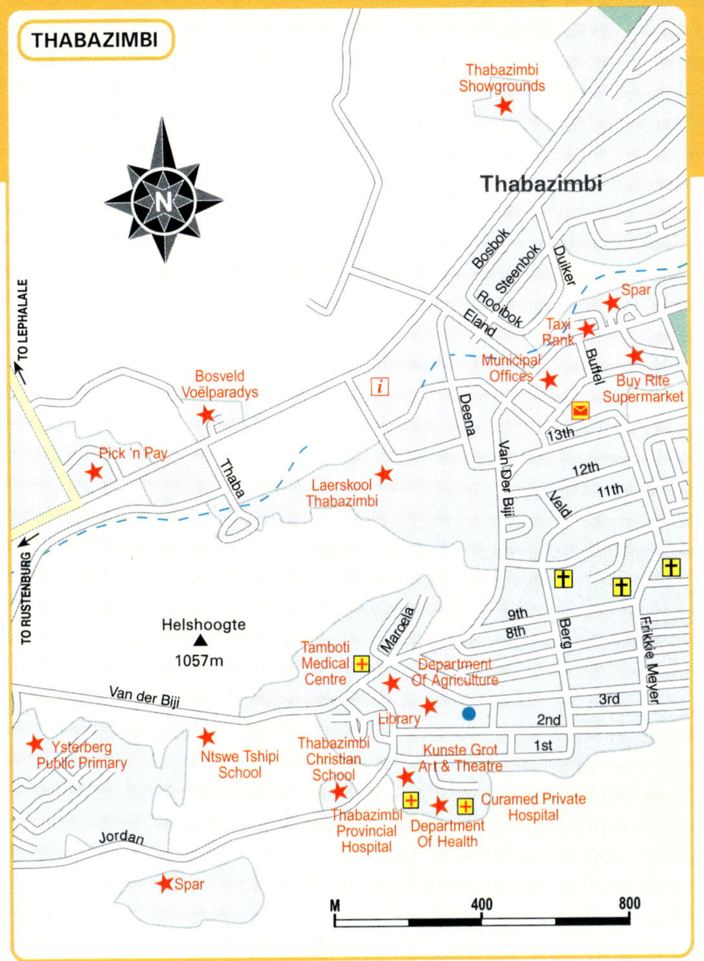

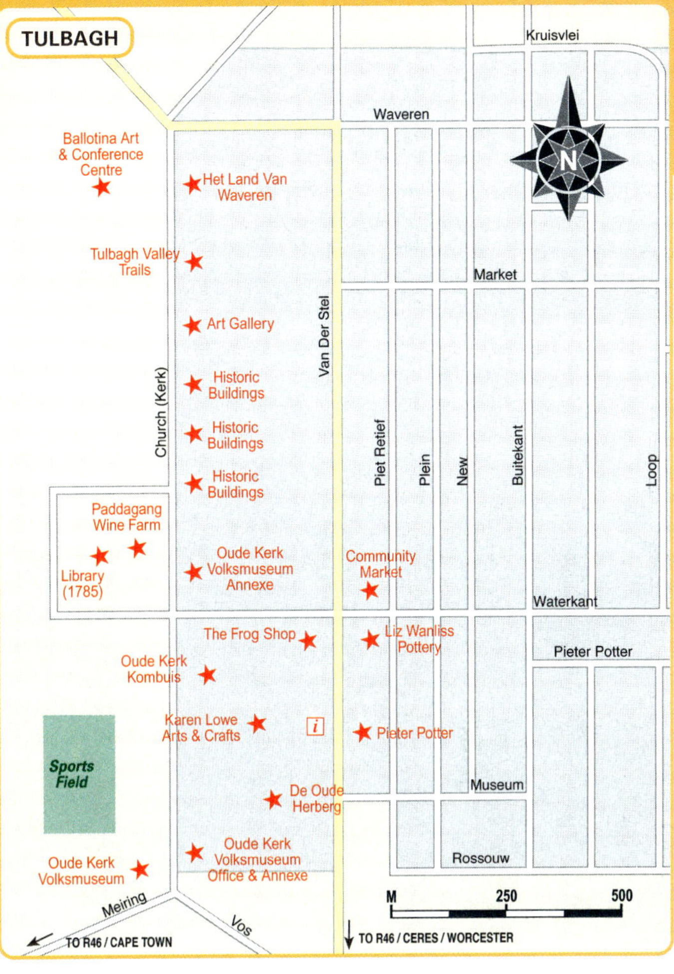

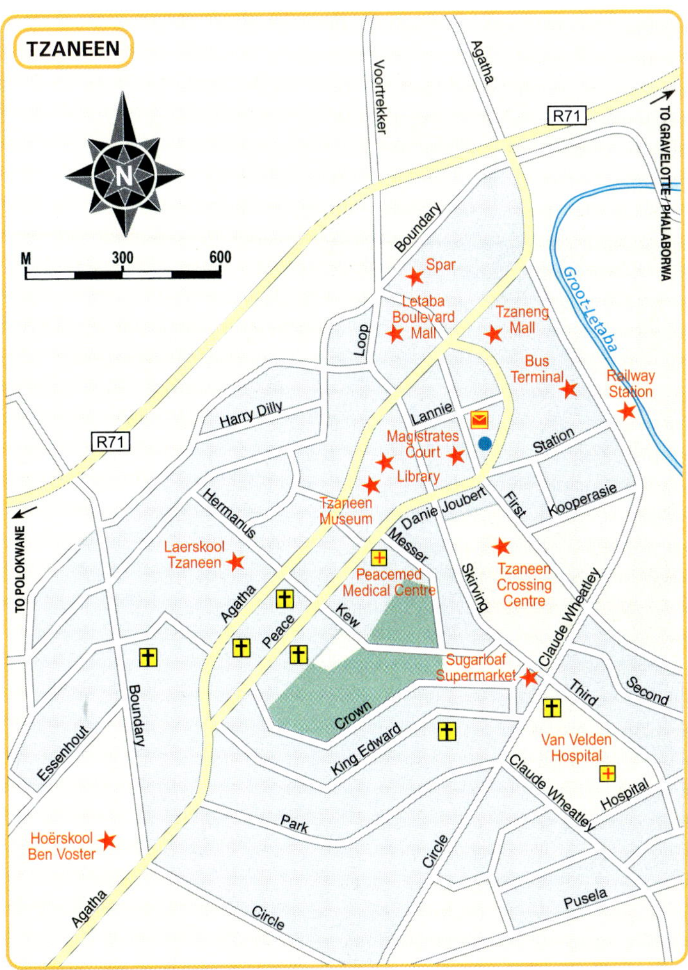

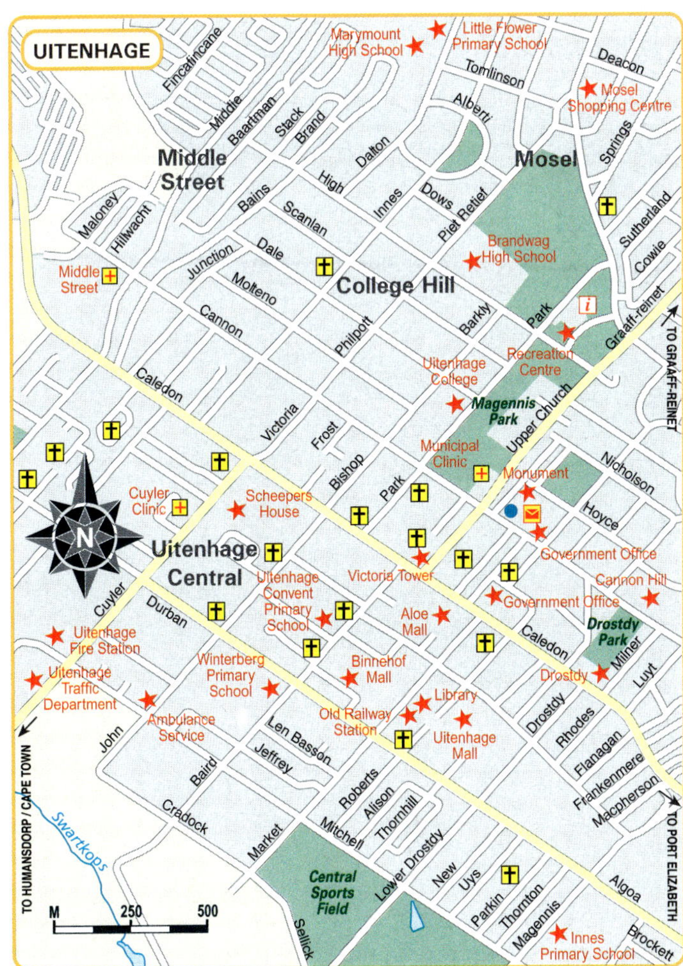

uLUNDI uMKOMAAS

uMHLANGA UNIONDALE

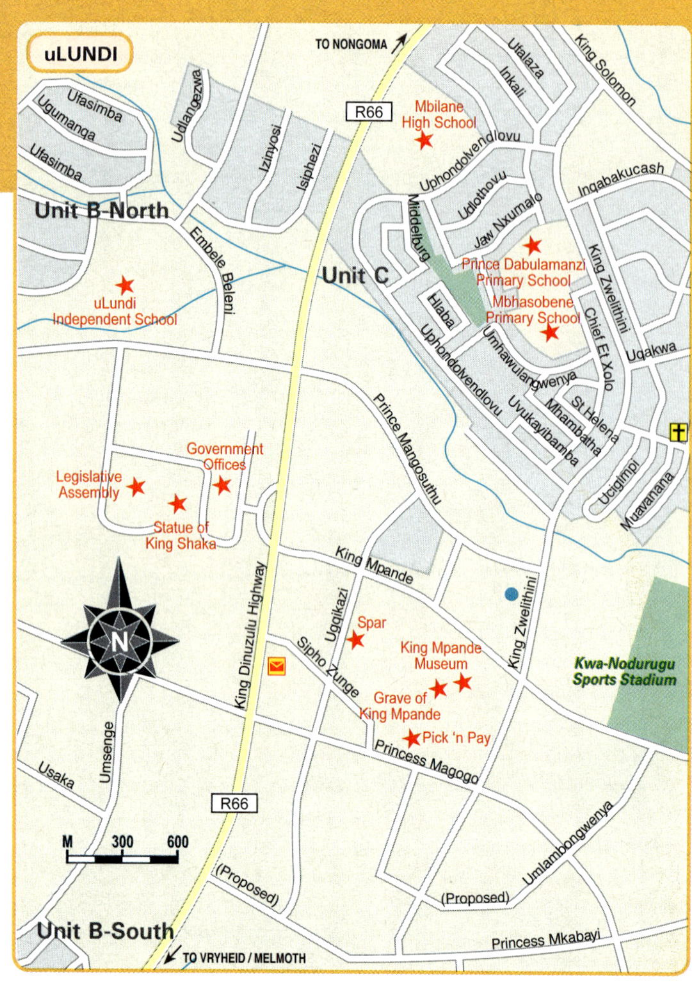

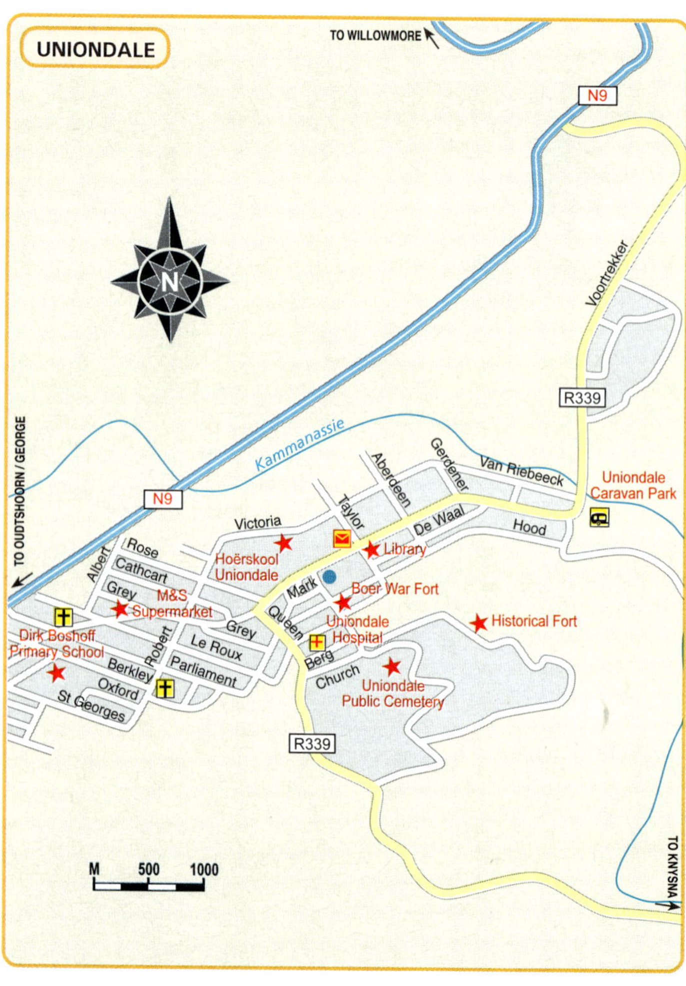

UPINGTON
Upington Railway Station
Danie Kuys Sports Ground
Pioneer Cemetery
Fanie Malan Preparatory School
Vaal University of Technology (Upington Campus)
Pick 'n Pay
Green Kalahari Tourism
Hoërskool Upington
Library
Ancorley Centre
Checkers
Shoprite
Spar
Kalahari Oranje Museum
Orange River
Die Eiland Holiday Resort
TO KARASBURG
TO KURUMAN
TO AUGRABIES FALLS NP / SPRINGBOK
TO LOUISVALE
N10
N14
M 200 400

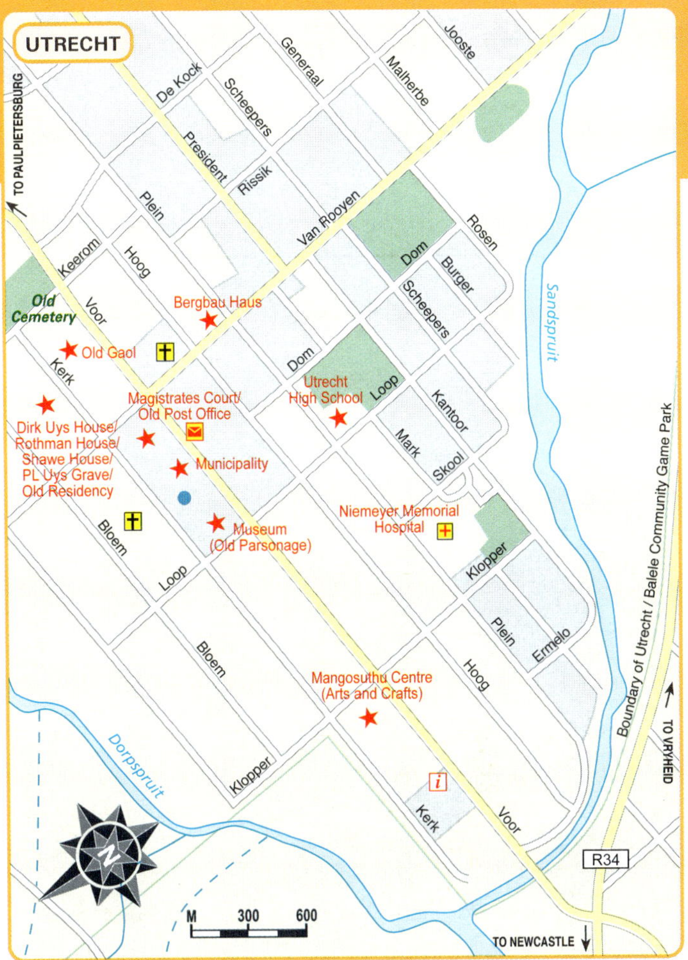
UTRECHT
TO PAULPIETERSBURG
Old Cemetery
Bergbau Haus
Old Gaol
Magistrates Court/ Old Post Office
Utrecht High School
Dirk Uys House/ Rothman House/ Shawe House/ PL Uys Grave/ Old Residency
Municipality
Museum (Old Parsonage)
Niemeyer Memorial Hospital
Mangosuthu Centre (Arts and Crafts)
Sandspruit
Dorpspruit
Boundary of Utrecht / Balele Community Game Park
TO VRYHEID
TO NEWCASTLE
R34
M 300 600

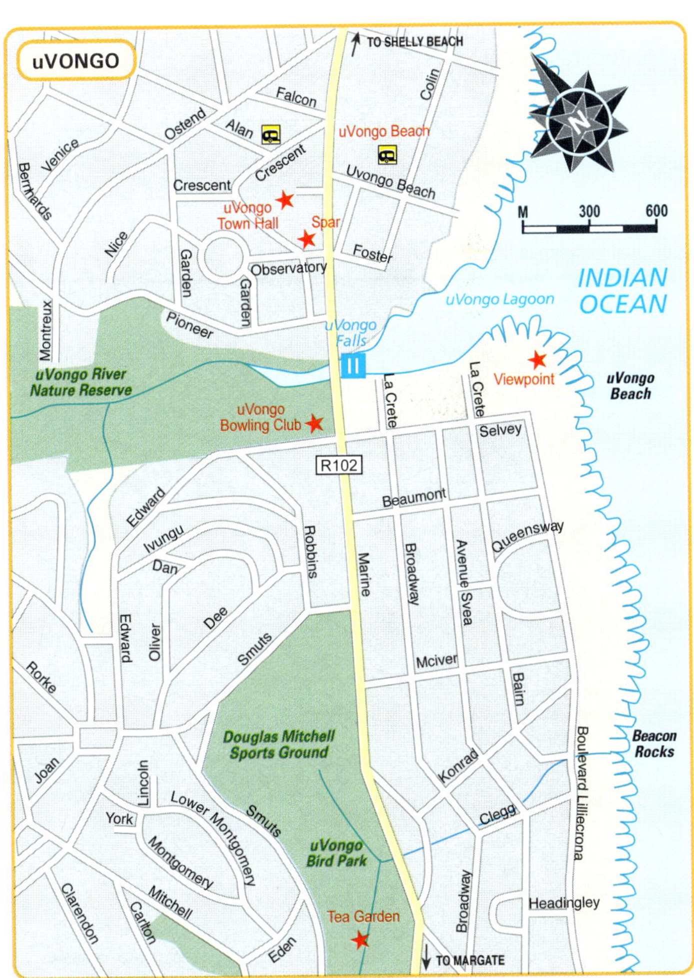
uVONGO
TO SHELLY BEACH
uVongo Beach
uVongo Town Hall
Spar
uVongo Lagoon
INDIAN OCEAN
uVongo Falls
Viewpoint
uVongo Beach
uVongo River Nature Reserve
uVongo Bowling Club
R102
Douglas Mitchell Sports Ground
uVongo Bird Park
Tea Garden
Beacon Rocks
TO MARGATE
M 300 600

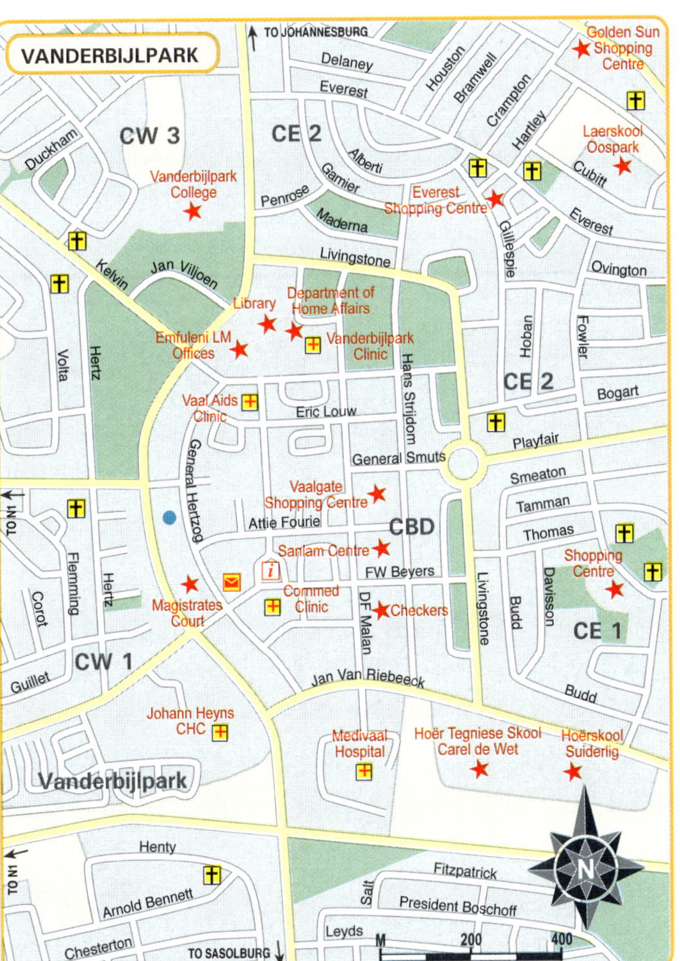
VANDERBIJLPARK
TO JOHANNESBURG
Golden Sun Shopping Centre
CW 3
CE 2
Laerskool Oospark
Vanderbijlpark College
Everest Shopping Centre
Library
Department of Home Affairs
Emfuleni LM Offices
Vanderbijlpark Clinic
Vaal Aids Clinic
CE 2
Vaalgate Shopping Centre
CBD
Sanlam Centre
Magistrates Court
Commed Clinic
Checkers
Shopping Centre
CE 1
CW 1
Johann Heyns CHC
Medivaal Hospital
Hoër Tegniese Skool Carel de Wet
Hoërskool Suiderlig
Vanderbijlpark
TO N1
TO SASOLBURG
M 200 400

VANRHYNSDORP

TO NIEUWOUDTVILLE
R27
Vanrhynsdorp Correctional Services
Vygie
Aalwyn
Botterblom
Skool
Church
Voortrekker
TO VANRHYNSDORP AIRFIELD
Hongerblom
Aandblom
Regional Library
Vanrhynsdorp Municipality and Public Library
Vanrhynsdorp Town Hall
Viooltjie
Hoërskool Vanrhynsdorp
Latsky Radio Museum
Namaqua
Multisave
Paddock
Sanmarislot
Old Gaol Curios
Public Cemetery
Uitsig
De Waal
Van Zyl
Van Rhyn Art Gallery
Lazarus
Riebeek
Grens
Maskam Supermarket
TO NUWERUS
Voortrekker
TO CLANWILLIAM
Mission of the Little Flower
N7
R27
M 150 300
TO VREDENDAL

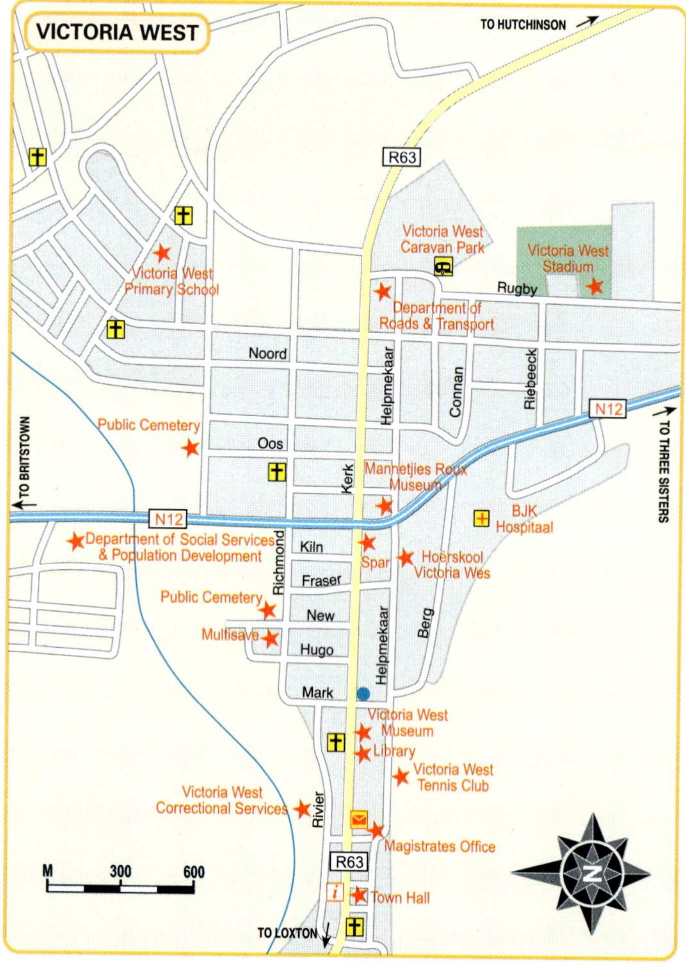

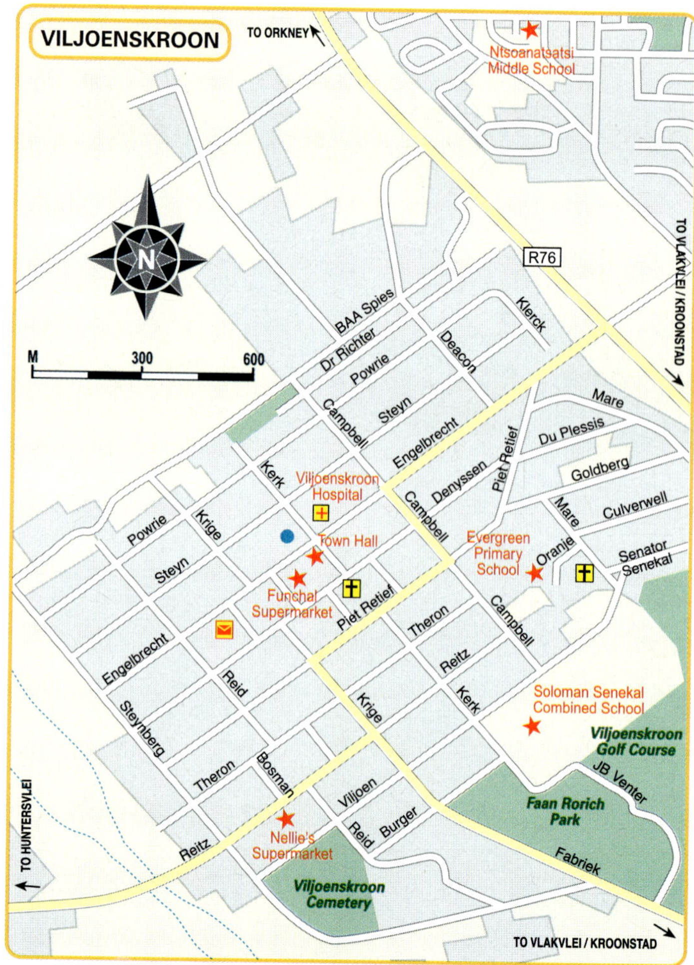

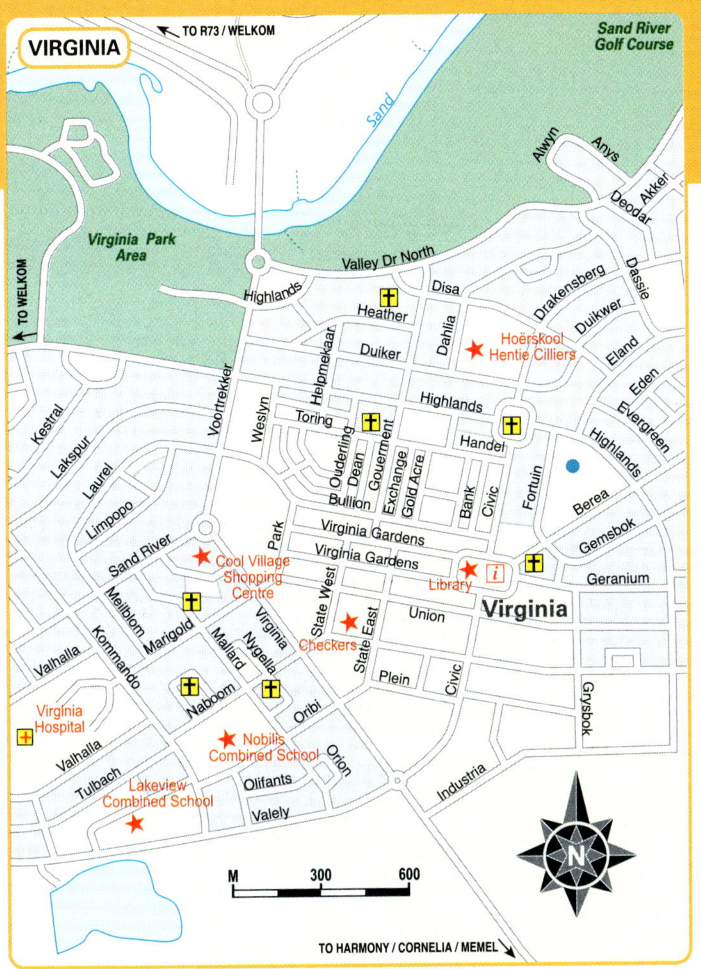
VIRGINIA
TO R73 / WELKOM
Sand River Golf Course
Virginia Park Area
TO WELKOM
Valley Dr North
Highlands
Heather
Disa
Duiker
Dahlia
Hoërskool Hentie Cilliers
Drakensberg
Duikwer
Eland
Eden
Evergreen
Highlands
Toring
Handel
Voortrekker
Weslyn
Helpmekaar
Kestral
Lakspur
Laurel
Limpopo
Sand River
Cool Village Shopping Centre
Virginia Gardens
Library
Virginia
Berea
Gemsbok
Geranium
Union
Plein
Civic
Checkers
State West
State East
Meiblom
Kommando
Marigold
Mallard
Nyegelle
Valhalla
Virginia Hospital
Naboom
Nobilis Combined School
Oribi
Orion
Olifants
Valely
Tulbach
Lakeview Combined School
Industria
Grysbok
TO HARMONY / CORNELIA / MEMEL
M 300 600

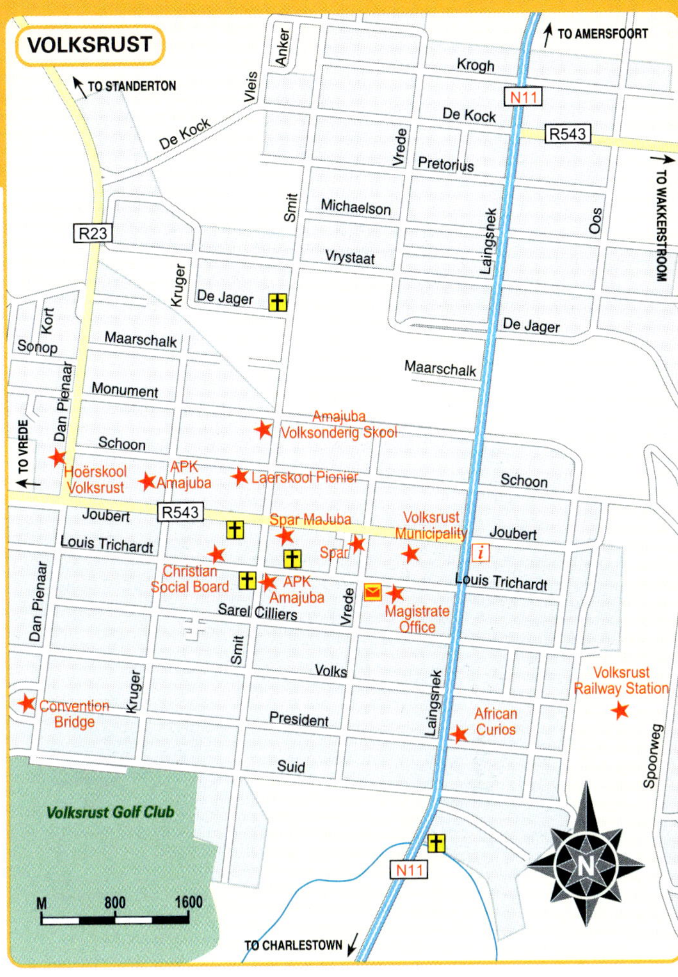
VOLKSRUST
TO STANDERTON
TO AMERSFOORT
TO WAKKERSTROOM
Krogh
De Kock
Pretorius
Michaelson
Vrystaat
De Jager
Maarschalk
Monument
Schoon
Joubert
Louis Trichardt
Amajuba Volksondervig Skool
Hoërskool Volksrust
APK Amajuba
Laerskool Pionier
Spar MaJuba
Spar
Volksrust Municipality
Christian Social Board
APK Amajuba
Sarel Cilliers
Magistrate Office
Volks
President
Suid
Convention Bridge
African Curios
Volksrust Railway Station
Volksrust Golf Club
TO CHARLESTOWN
TO VREDE
N11
R543
R23
M 800 1600

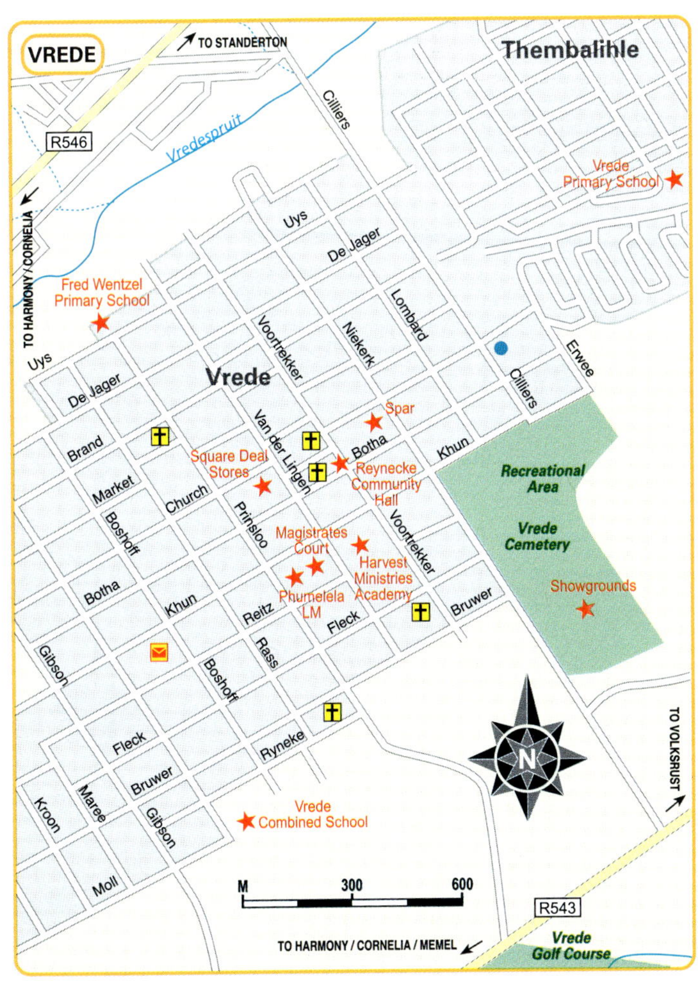
VREDE
TO STANDERTON
Thembalihle
R546
Vredespruit
Vrede Primary School
Fred Wentzel Primary School
TO HARMONY / CORNELIA
Vrede
Spar
Square Deal Stores
Reynecke Community Hall
Magistrates Court
Harvest Ministries Academy
Phumelela LM
Recreational Area
Vrede Cemetery
Showgrounds
Vrede Combined School
TO VOLKSRUST
TO HARMONY / CORNELIA / MEMEL
R543
Vrede Golf Course
M 300 600

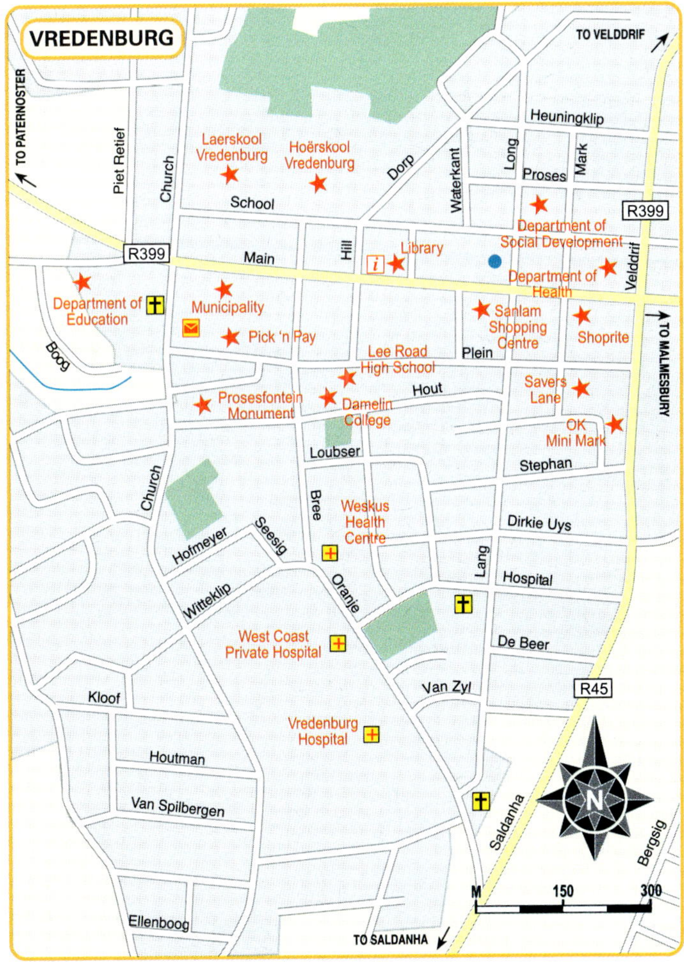
VREDENBURG
TO VELDDRIF
TO PATERNOSTER
Laerskool Vredenburg
Hoërskool Vredenburg
School
Main
R399
Library
Department of Social Development
Department of Health
Department of Education
Municipality
Pick 'n Pay
Sanlam Shopping Centre
Shoprite
Lee Road High School
Prosesfontein Monument
Damelin College
Savers Lane
OK Mini Mark
Weskus Health Centre
West Coast Private Hospital
Vredenburg Hospital
TO MALMESBURY
R45
TO SALDANHA
M 150 300

VRYBURG WELKOM

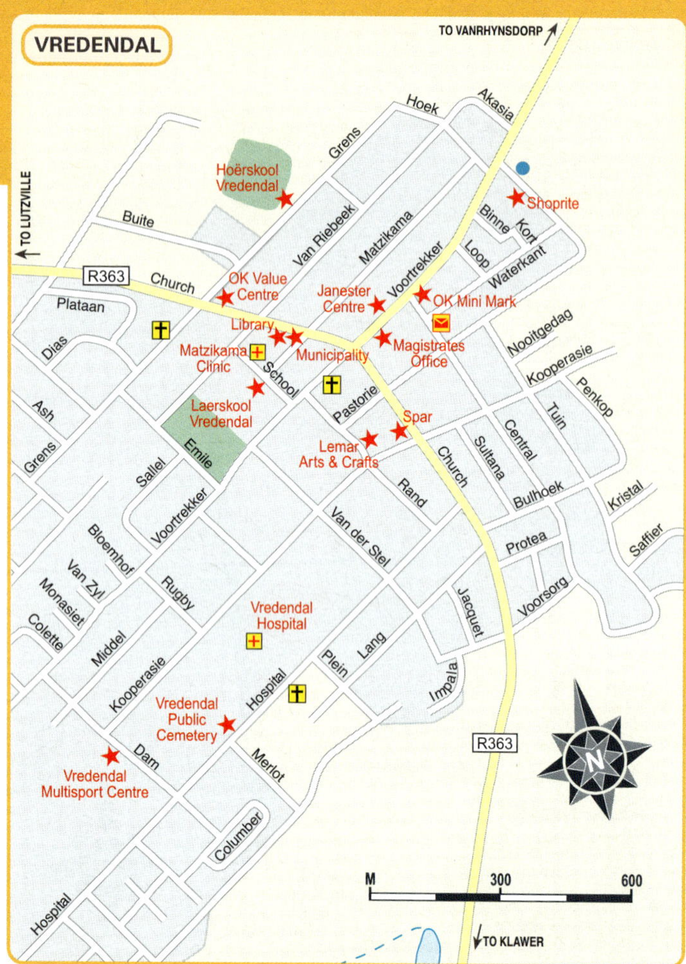

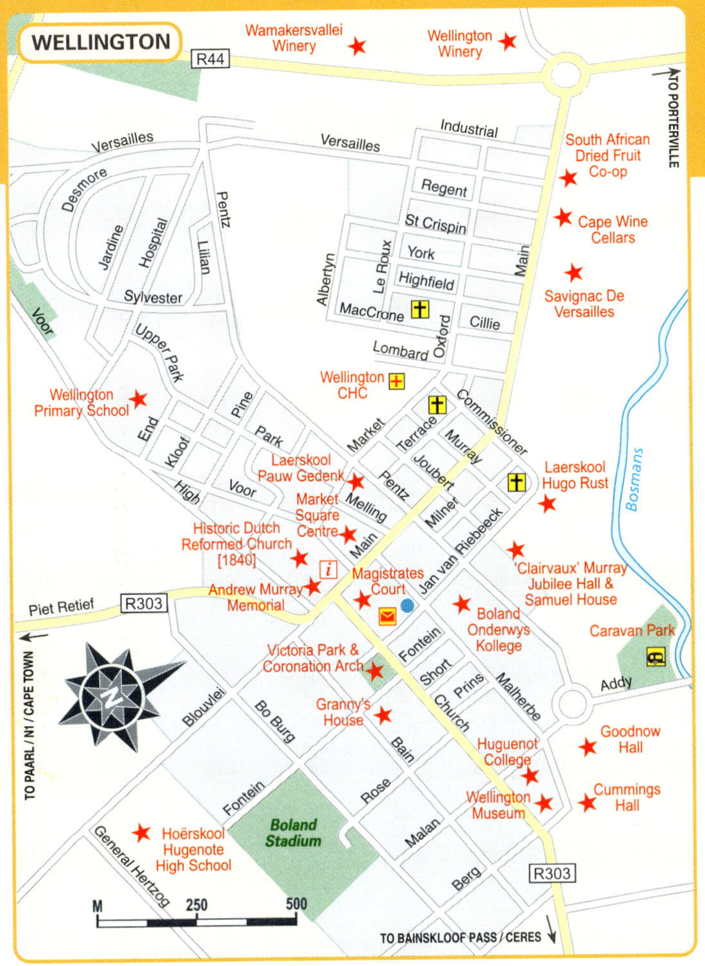
WELLINGTON
Wamakersvallei Winery
Wellington Winery
R44
TO PORTERVILLE
Industrial
Versailles
Versailles
Desmore
Regent
St Crispin
York
Highfield
MacCrone
Cillie
Lombard
Oxford
Albertyn
Le Roux
Main
Pentz
Lilian
Jardine
Hospital
Sylvester
Voor
Upper Park
South African Dried Fruit Co-op
Cape Wine Cellars
Savignac De Versailles
Wellington CHC
Wellington Primary School
End
Kloof
Pine
Park
High
Voor
Laerskool Pauw Gedenk
Market
Terrace
Commissioner
Murray
Joubert
Pentz
Melling
Milner
Market Square Centre
Laerskool Hugo Rust
Bosmans
Historic Dutch Reformed Church [1840]
Main
Jan van Riebeeck
'Clairvaux' Murray Jubilee Hall & Samuel House
Magistrates Court
Andrew Murray Memorial
Piet Retief
R303
Boland Onderwys Kollege
Caravan Park
Fontein
Victoria Park & Coronation Arch
Short
Prins
Malherbe
Addy
TO PAARL / N1 / CAPE TOWN
Blouvlei
Bo Burg
Church
Granny's House
Goodnow Hall
Bain
Huguenot College
Rose
Fontein
Cummings Hall
Wellington Museum
Boland Stadium
Hoërskool Hugenote High School
General Hertzog
Malan
Berg
R303
M 250 500
TO BAINSKLOOF PASS / CERES

WESTONARIA
SPCA (Animal Shelter)
Van Der Bijl
Westonaria Railway Station
Crean
Crean
Doveton
Doveton
Doveton
De Wet
Sampson
TO R28
Briggs
Brits
Malan
Johnstone
Malan
Albrecht
Forbes
Huntley
Bridges
Kemp
Normand
Edwards
Creswell
Codrington
Cross
Edwards
Edwards
McGregor
Briggs
Shopping Centre
Briggs
Briggs
Botha
Hofmeyer
Noel
Allen
Davies
Shopping Centre
Goede Hoop
TO R28
President Kruger
Van Der Stel
Fowler
President Steyn
Diaz
Laerskool Gerrit Maritz
Gilfillan
Botha
Gerrit Maritz
Marble
Da Gama
Brabant
Goud
Haarlem
Westonaria Magistrates Court
Haarlem
Mars
Van Riebeeck
Christian Beyers
Jupiter
Saturnus
Sarel Cilliers
Leo
Westonaria Sports Ground
Mercurius
Westonaria Municipality
Saturnus
Westonaria Primary School
M 250 500
Van Riebeeck
Neptune
Alpha
Centaurus
Galaxia
TO N12 / POTCHEFSTROOM
TO R28

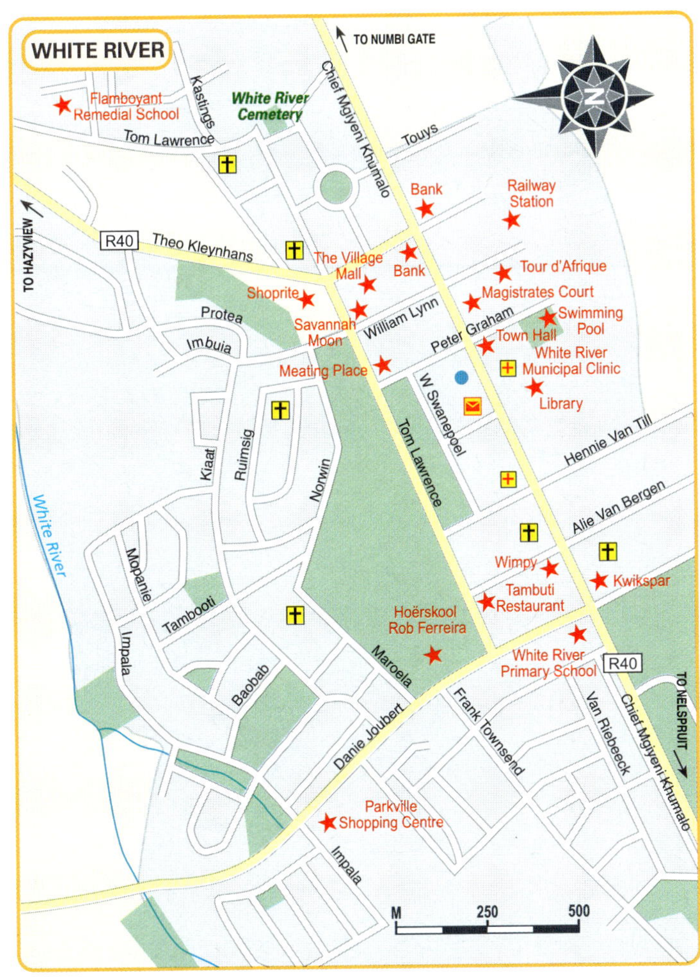
WHITE RIVER
TO NUMBI GATE
Flamboyant Remedial School
Kastings
White River Cemetery
Chief Mgiyeni Khumalo
Touys
Tom Lawrence
Bank
Railway Station
TO HAZYVIEW
R40
Theo Kleynhans
The Village Mall
Bank
Tour d'Afrique
Shoprite
Magistrates Court
Savannah Moon
William Lynn
Peter Graham
Swimming Pool
Protea
Town Hall
Imbuia
White River Municipal Clinic
Meating Place
W Swanepoel
Library
Tom Lawrence
Hennie Van Till
Klaat
Ruimsig
Norwin
Alie Van Bergen
White River
Mopanie
Wimpy
Kwikspar
Tambuti Restaurant
Tambooti
Hoërskool Rob Ferreira
White River Primary School
R40
Impala
Baobab
Maroela
Danie Joubert
Frank Townsend
Van Riebeeck
Chief Mgiyeni Khumalo
TO NELSPRUIT
Parkville Shopping Centre
Impala
M 250 500

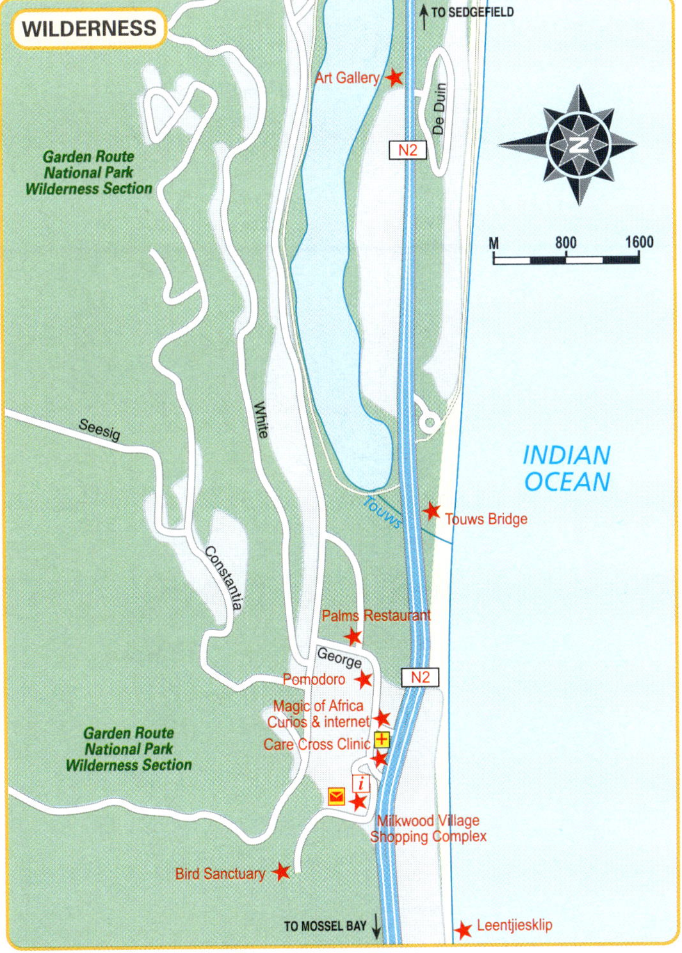
WILDERNESS
TO SEDGEFIELD
Art Gallery
De Duin
N2
Garden Route National Park Wilderness Section
M 800 1600
Seesig
White
INDIAN OCEAN
Touws
Touws Bridge
Constantia
Palms Restaurant
George
Pomodoro
N2
Magic of Africa Curios & internet
Care Cross Clinic
Garden Route National Park Wilderness Section
Milkwood Village Shopping Complex
Bird Sanctuary
TO MOSSEL BAY
Leentjiesklip

WILLISTON eMALAHLENI (WITBANK) WINBURG WITSAND

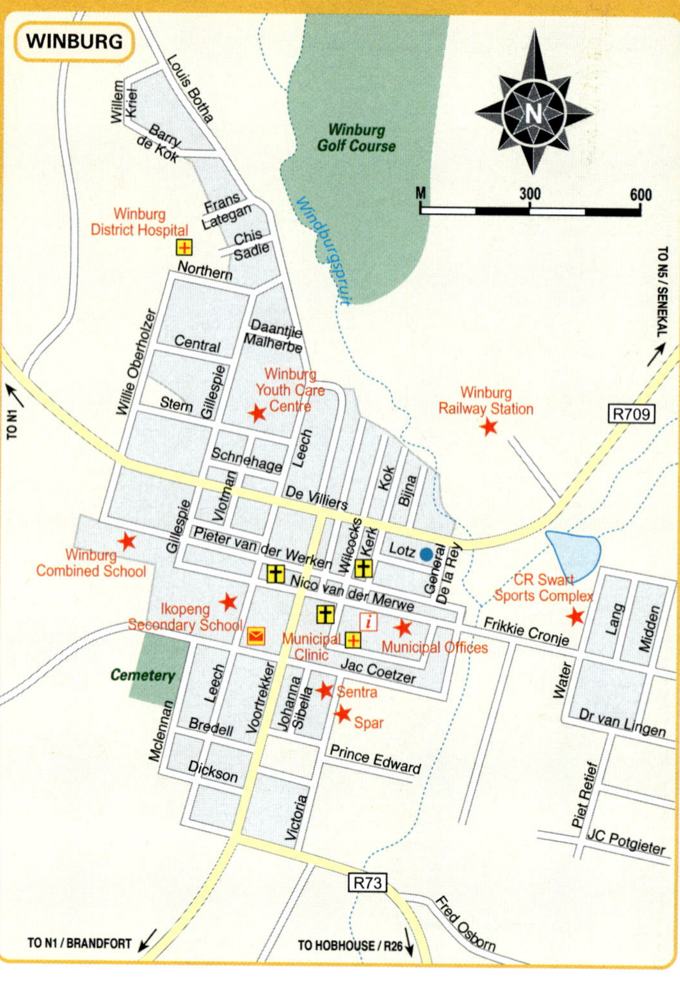

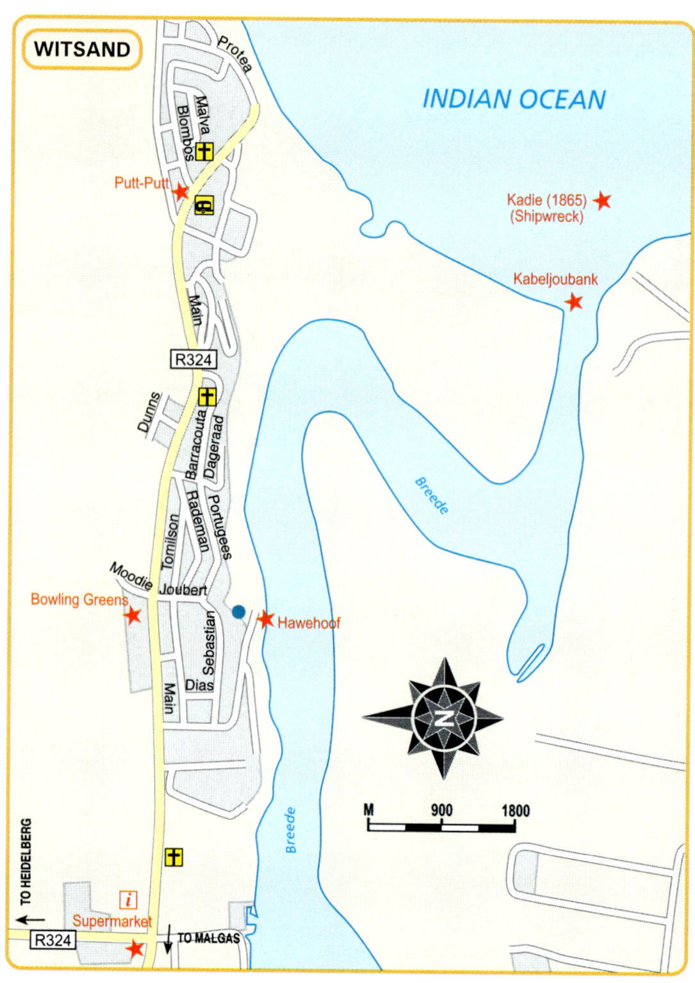

WOLMARANSSTAD WORCESTER ZEERUST

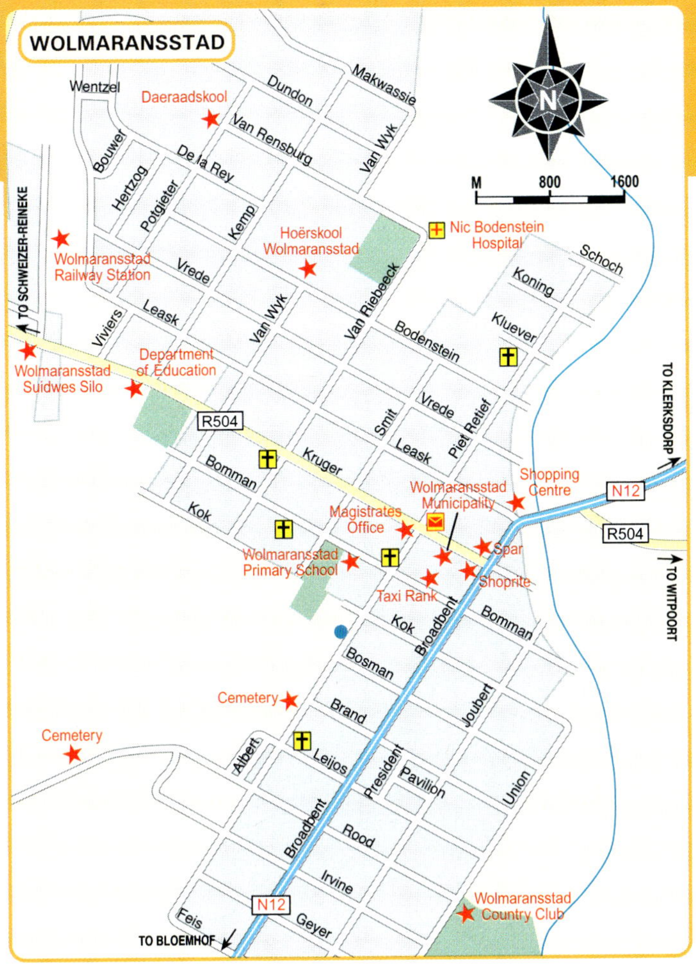

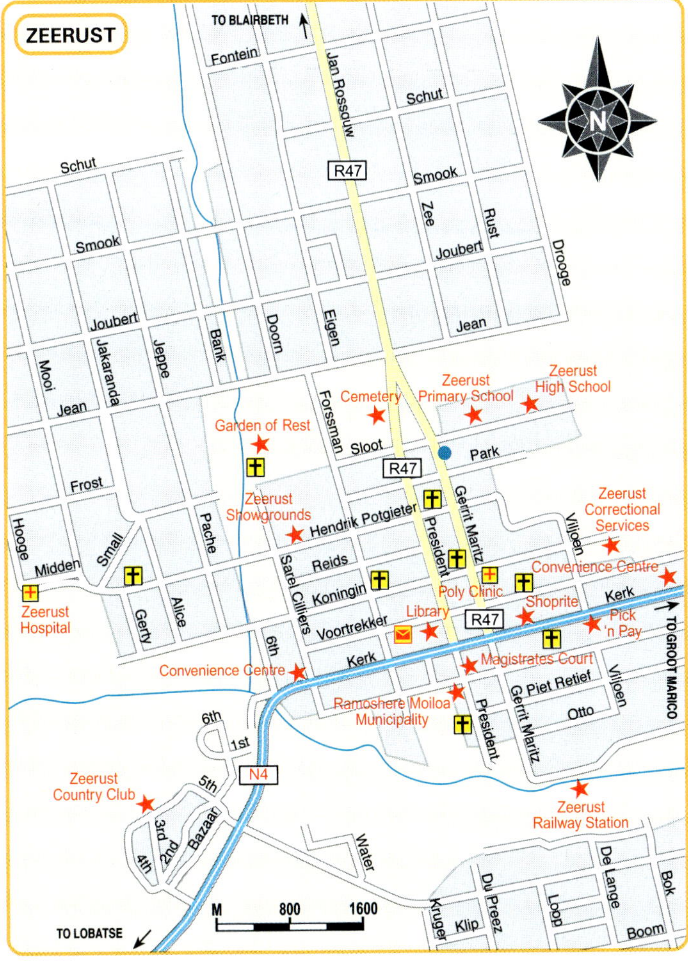

See strip route maps on pages 160 - 167 >>

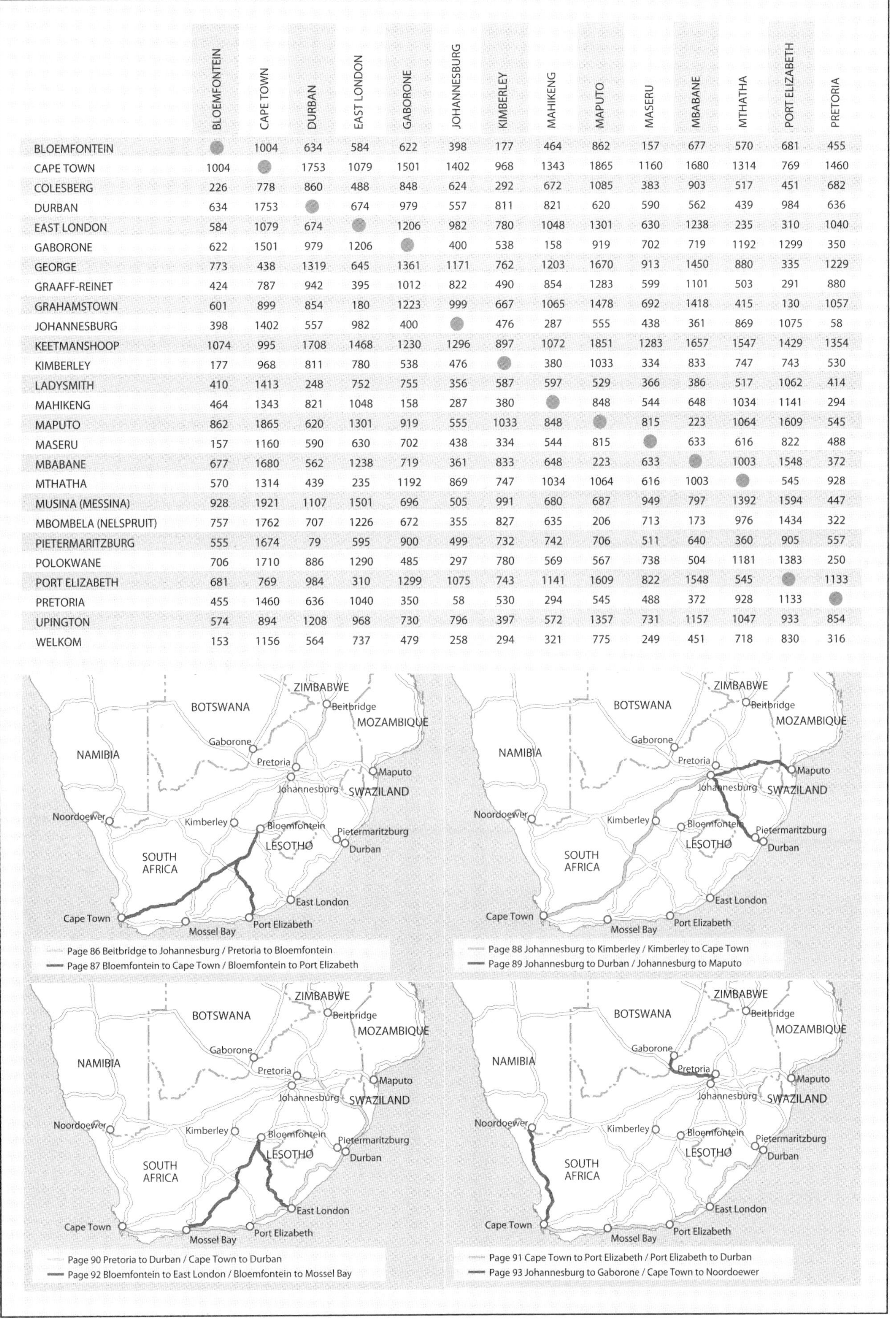

	BLOEMFONTEIN	CAPE TOWN	DURBAN	EAST LONDON	GABORONE	JOHANNESBURG	KIMBERLEY	MAHIKENG	MAPUTO	MASERU	MBABANE	MTHATHA	PORT ELIZABETH	PRETORIA
BLOEMFONTEIN		1004	634	584	622	398	177	464	862	157	677	570	681	455
CAPE TOWN	1004		1753	1079	1501	1402	968	1343	1865	1160	1680	1314	769	1460
COLESBERG	226	778	860	488	848	624	292	672	1085	383	903	517	451	682
DURBAN	634	1753		674	979	557	811	821	620	590	562	439	984	636
EAST LONDON	584	1079	674		1206	982	780	1048	1301	630	1238	235	310	1040
GABORONE	622	1501	979	1206		400	538	158	919	702	719	1192	1299	350
GEORGE	773	438	1319	645	1361	1171	762	1203	1670	913	1450	880	335	1229
GRAAFF-REINET	424	787	942	395	1012	822	490	854	1283	599	1101	503	291	880
GRAHAMSTOWN	601	899	854	180	1223	999	667	1065	1478	692	1418	415	130	1057
JOHANNESBURG	398	1402	557	982	400		476	287	555	438	361	869	1075	58
KEETMANSHOOP	1074	995	1708	1468	1230	1296	897	1072	1851	1283	1657	1547	1429	1354
KIMBERLEY	177	968	811	780	538	476		380	1033	334	833	747	743	530
LADYSMITH	410	1413	248	752	755	356	587	597	529	366	386	517	1062	414
MAHIKENG	464	1343	821	1048	158	287	380		848	544	648	1034	1141	294
MAPUTO	862	1865	620	1301	919	555	1033	848		815	223	1064	1609	545
MASERU	157	1160	590	630	702	438	334	544	815		633	616	822	488
MBABANE	677	1680	562	1238	719	361	833	648	223	633		1003	1548	372
MTHATHA	570	1314	439	235	1192	869	747	1034	1064	616	1003		545	928
MUSINA (MESSINA)	928	1921	1107	1501	696	505	991	680	687	949	797	1392	1594	447
MBOMBELA (NELSPRUIT)	757	1762	707	1226	672	355	827	635	206	713	173	976	1434	322
PIETERMARITZBURG	555	1674	79	595	900	499	732	742	706	511	640	360	905	557
POLOKWANE	706	1710	886	1290	485	297	780	569	567	738	504	1181	1383	250
PORT ELIZABETH	681	769	984	310	1299	1075	743	1141	1609	822	1548	545		1133
PRETORIA	455	1460	636	1040	350	58	530	294	545	488	372	928	1133	
UPINGTON	574	894	1208	968	730	796	397	572	1357	731	1157	1047	933	854
WELKOM	153	1156	564	737	479	258	294	321	775	249	451	718	830	316

Page 86 Beitbridge to Johannesburg / Pretoria to Bloemfontein
Page 87 Bloemfontein to Cape Town / Bloemfontein to Port Elizabeth

Page 88 Johannesburg to Kimberley / Kimberley to Cape Town
Page 89 Johannesburg to Durban / Johannesburg to Maputo

Page 90 Pretoria to Durban / Cape Town to Durban
Page 92 Bloemfontein to East London / Bloemfontein to Mossel Bay

Page 91 Cape Town to Port Elizabeth / Port Elizabeth to Durban
Page 93 Johannesburg to Gaborone / Cape Town to Noordoewer

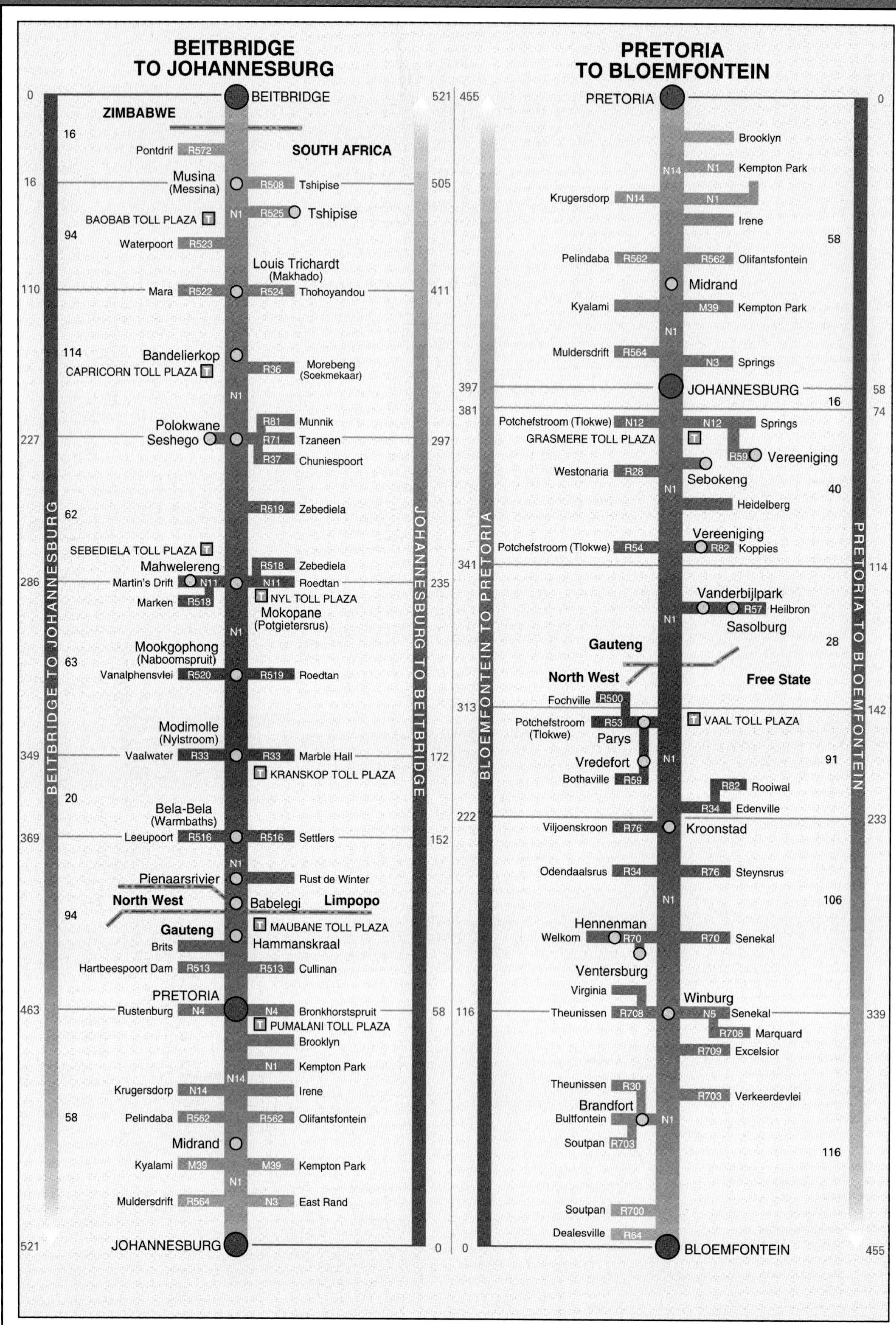
BEITBRIDGE TO JOHANNESBURG
BEITBRIDGE
ZIMBABWE
SOUTH AFRICA
Pontdrif R572
Musina (Messina)
R508 Tshipise
R525 Tshipise
BAOBAB TOLL PLAZA
Waterpoort R523
Louis Trichardt (Makhado)
Mara R522
R524 Thohoyandou
Bandelierkop
CAPRICORN TOLL PLAZA
R36 Morebeng (Soekmekaar)
Polokwane
Seshego
R81 Munnik
R71 Tzaneen
R37 Chuniespoort
R519 Zebediela
SEBEDIELA TOLL PLAZA
Mahwelereng
R518 Zebediela
Martin's Drift N11
N11 Roedtan
Marken R518
NYL TOLL PLAZA
Mokopane (Potgietersrus)
Mookgophong (Naboomspruit)
Vanalphensvlei R520
R519 Roedtan
Modimolle (Nylstroom)
Vaalwater R33
R33 Marble Hall
KRANSKOP TOLL PLAZA
Bela-Bela (Warmbaths)
Leeupoort R516
R516 Settlers
Pienaarsrivier
Rust de Winter
North West
Babelegi
Limpopo
MAUBANE TOLL PLAZA
Gauteng
Brits
Hammanskraal
Hartbeespoort Dam R513
R513 Cullinan
PRETORIA
Rustenburg N4
N4 Bronkhorstspruit
PUMALANI TOLL PLAZA
Brooklyn
N1 Kempton Park
Krugersdorp N14
Irene
Pelindaba R562
R562 Olifantsfontein
Midrand
Kyalami M39
M39 Kempton Park
Muldersdrift R564
N3 East Rand
JOHANNESBURG
BEITBRIDGE TO JOHANNESBURG
JOHANNESBURG TO BEITBRIDGE
0 16 110 227 286 349 369 463 521
16 94 114 62 63 20 94 58
521 505 411 297 235 172 152 58 0
PRETORIA TO BLOEMFONTEIN
PRETORIA
Brooklyn
N14 N1 Kempton Park
Krugersdorp N14
N1
Irene
Pelindaba R562
R562 Olifantsfontein
Midrand
Kyalami
M39 Kempton Park
Muldersdrift R564
N3 Springs
JOHANNESBURG
Potchefstroom (Tlokwe) N12
N12 Springs
GRASMERE TOLL PLAZA
R59 Vereeniging
Westonaria R28
Sebokeng
Heidelberg
Vereeniging
Potchefstroom (Tlokwe) R54
R82 Koppies
Vanderbijlpark
R57 Heilbron
Sasolburg
Gauteng
North West
Free State
Fochville R500
Potchefstroom (Tlokwe) R53
VAAL TOLL PLAZA
Parys
Vredefort
Bothaville R59
R82 Rooiwal
R34 Edenville
Viljoenskroon R76
Kroonstad
Odendaalsrus R34
R76 Steynsrus
Hennenman
Welkom R70
R70 Senekal
Ventersburg
Virginia
Winburg
Theunissen R708
N5 Senekal
R708 Marquard
R709 Excelsior
Theunissen R30
R703 Verkeerdevlei
Brandfort
Bultfontein
Soutpan R703
Soutpan R700
Dealesville R64
BLOEMFONTEIN
BLOEMFONTEIN TO PRETORIA
PRETORIA TO BLOEMFONTEIN
455 397 381 341 313 222 116 0
0 58 74 114 142 233 339 455
58 16 40 28 91 106 116

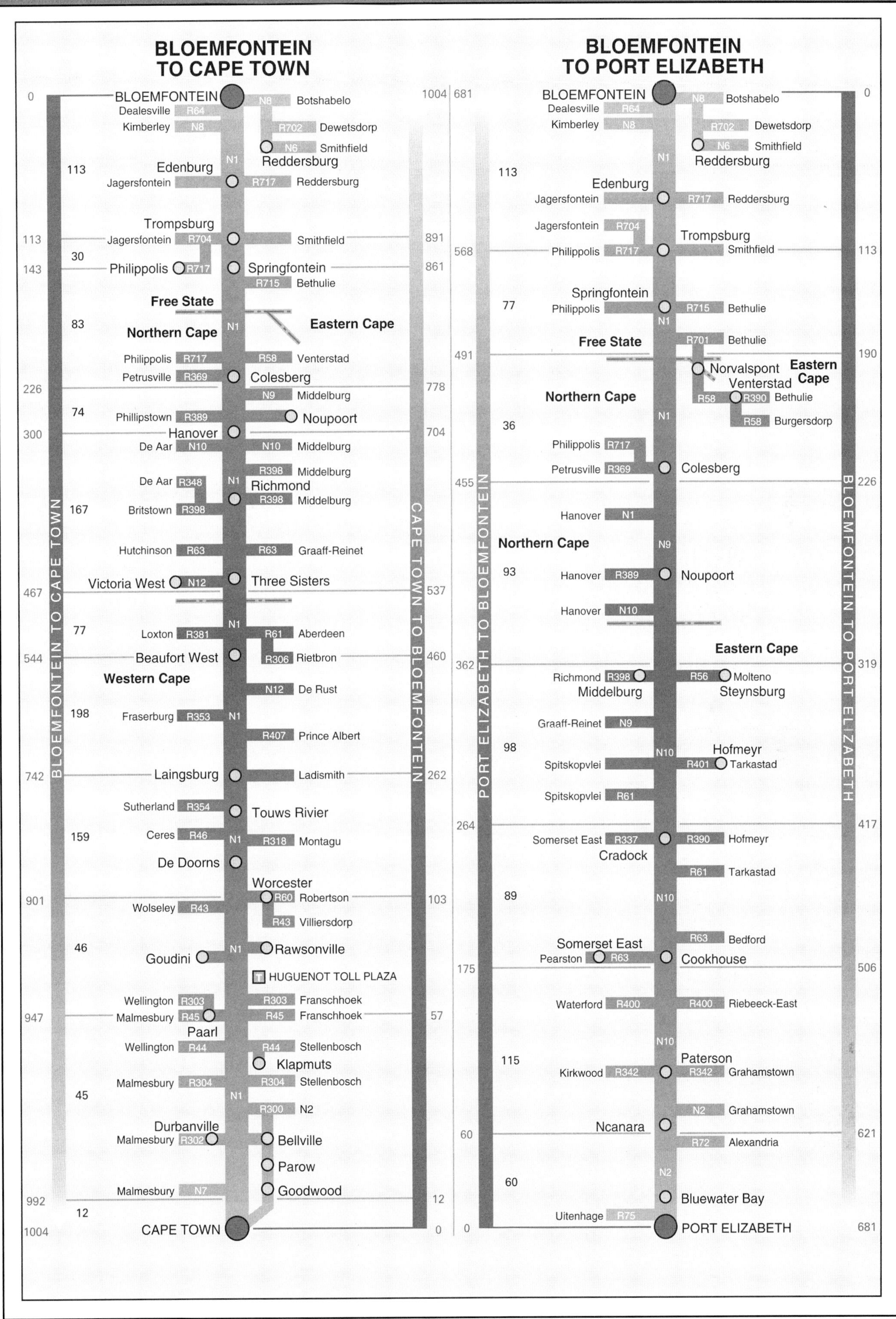
BLOEMFONTEIN TO CAPE TOWN
BLOEMFONTEIN
Dealesville R64
Kimberley N8
N8 Botshabelo
R702 Dewetsdorp
N6 Smithfield
Reddersburg
Edenburg
Jagersfontein
R717 Reddersburg
Trompsburg
Jagersfontein R704
Smithfield
Philippolis R717
Springfontein
R715 Bethulie
Free State
Northern Cape
Eastern Cape
Philippolis R717
R58 Venterstad
Petrusville R369
Colesberg
N9 Middelburg
Phillipstown R389
Noupoort
Hanover
De Aar N10
N10 Middelburg
R398 Middelburg
De Aar R348
Richmond
R398 Middelburg
Britstown R398
Hutchinson R63
R63 Graaff-Reinet
Victoria West N12
Three Sisters
Loxton R381
R61 Aberdeen
Beaufort West
R306 Rietbron
Western Cape
N12 De Rust
Fraserburg R353
R407 Prince Albert
Laingsburg
Ladismith
Sutherland R354
Touws Rivier
Ceres R46
R318 Montagu
De Doorns
Worcester
R60 Robertson
Wolseley R43
R43 Villiersdorp
Rawsonville
Goudini
HUGUENOT TOLL PLAZA
Wellington R303
R303 Franschhoek
Malmesbury R45
R45 Franschhoek
Paarl
Wellington R44
R44 Stellenbosch
Klapmuts
Malmesbury R304
R304 Stellenbosch
R300 N2
Durbanville
Malmesbury R302
Bellville
Parow
Goodwood
Malmesbury N7
CAPE TOWN
BLOEMFONTEIN TO CAPE TOWN
CAPE TOWN TO BLOEMFONTEIN
0 113 143 226 300 467 544 742 901 947 992 1004
113 30 83 74 167 77 198 159 46 45 12
1004 891 861 778 704 537 460 262 103 57 12 0
BLOEMFONTEIN TO PORT ELIZABETH
BLOEMFONTEIN
Dealesville R64
Kimberley N8
N8 Botshabelo
R702 Dewetsdorp
N6 Smithfield
Reddersburg
Edenburg
Jagersfontein
R717 Reddersburg
Jagersfontein R704
Trompsburg
Philippolis R717
Smithfield
Springfontein
Philippolis
R715 Bethulie
R701 Bethulie
Free State
Norvalspont
Venterstad
Eastern Cape
Northern Cape
R58
R390 Bethulie
R58 Burgersdorp
Philippolis R717
Petrusville R369
Colesberg
Hanover N1
Northern Cape
Hanover R389
Noupoort
Hanover N10
Eastern Cape
Richmond R398
Middelburg
R56 Molteno
Steynsburg
Graaff-Reinet N9
Hofmeyr
Spitskopvlei
R401 Tarkastad
Spitskopvlei R61
Somerset East R337
Cradock
R390 Hofmeyr
R61 Tarkastad
R63 Bedford
Somerset East
Pearston R63
Cookhouse
Waterford R400
R400 Riebeeck-East
Paterson
Kirkwood R342
R342 Grahamstown
N2 Grahamstown
Ncanara
R72 Alexandria
Bluewater Bay
Uitenhage R75
PORT ELIZABETH
PORT ELIZABETH TO BLOEMFONTEIN
BLOEMFONTEIN TO PORT ELIZABETH
681 568 491 455 362 264 175 60 0
113 77 36 93 98 89 115 60
0 113 190 226 319 417 506 621 681

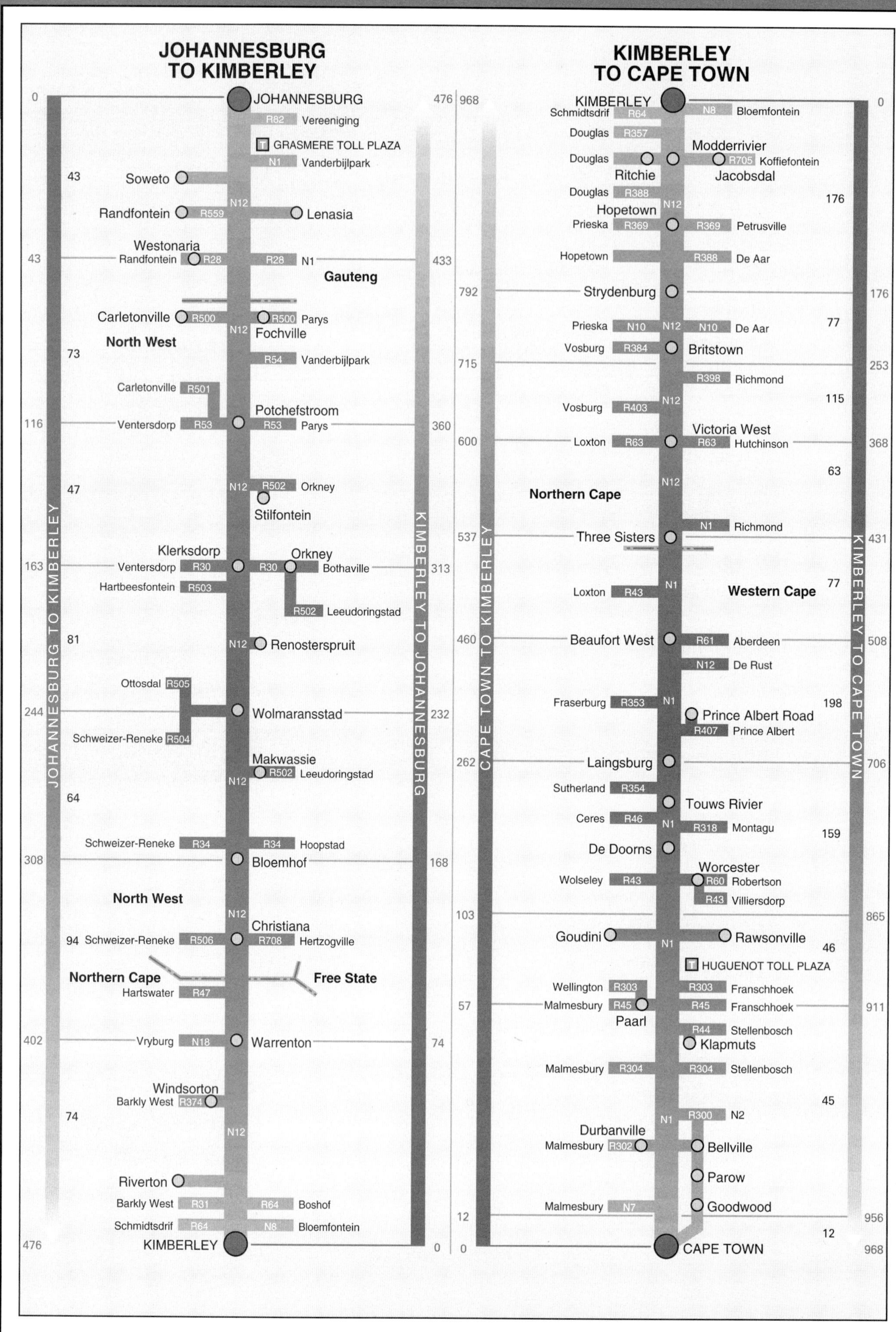
JOHANNESBURG TO KIMBERLEY
JOHANNESBURG
R82 Vereeniging
GRASMERE TOLL PLAZA
N1 Vanderbijlpark
Soweto
Randfontein R559
Lenasia
Westonaria
Randfontein R28
R28 N1
Gauteng
Carletonville R500
R500 Parys
Fochville
North West
R54 Vanderbijlpark
Carletonville R501
Potchefstroom
Ventersdorp R53
R53 Parys
R502 Orkney
Stilfontein
Klerksdorp
Ventersdorp R30
Orkney
R30 Bothaville
Hartbeesfontein R503
R502 Leeudoringstad
Renosterspruit
Ottosdal R505
Wolmaransstad
Schweizer-Reneke R504
Makwassie
R502 Leeudoringstad
Schweizer-Reneke R34
R34 Hoopstad
Bloemhof
North West
Christiana
Schweizer-Reneke R506
R708 Hertzogville
Northern Cape
Free State
Hartswater R47
Vryburg N18
Warrenton
Windsorton
Barkly West R374
Riverton
Barkly West R31
R64 Boshof
Schmidtsdrif R64
N8 Bloemfontein
KIMBERLEY
N12
0 43 73 116 47 163 81 244 64 308 94 402 74 476
476 433 360 313 232 168 74 0
JOHANNESBURG TO KIMBERLEY
KIMBERLEY TO JOHANNESBURG
KIMBERLEY TO CAPE TOWN
KIMBERLEY
Schmidtsdrif R64
N8 Bloemfontein
Douglas R357
Modderrivier
Douglas
R705 Koffiefontein
Ritchie
Jacobsdal
Douglas R388
Hopetown
Prieska R369
R369 Petrusville
Hopetown
R388 De Aar
Strydenburg
Prieska N10
N10 De Aar
Vosburg R384
Britstown
R398 Richmond
Vosburg R403
Victoria West
Loxton R63
R63 Hutchinson
Northern Cape
N1 Richmond
Three Sisters
Loxton R43
Western Cape
Beaufort West
R61 Aberdeen
N12 De Rust
Fraserburg R353
Prince Albert Road
R407 Prince Albert
Laingsburg
Sutherland R354
Touws Rivier
Ceres R46
R318 Montagu
De Doorns
Worcester
Wolseley R43
R60 Robertson
R43 Villiersdorp
Goudini
Rawsonville
HUGUENOT TOLL PLAZA
Wellington R303
R303 Franschhoek
Malmesbury R45
R45 Franschhoek
Paarl
R44 Stellenbosch
Klapmuts
Malmesbury R304
R304 Stellenbosch
R300 N2
Durbanville
Malmesbury R302
Bellville
Parow
Malmesbury N7
Goodwood
CAPE TOWN
N12 N1
968 792 715 600 537 460 262 103 57 12 0
0 176 77 253 115 368 63 431 77 508 198 706 159 865 46 911 45 956 12 968
CAPE TOWN TO KIMBERLEY
KIMBERLEY TO CAPE TOWN

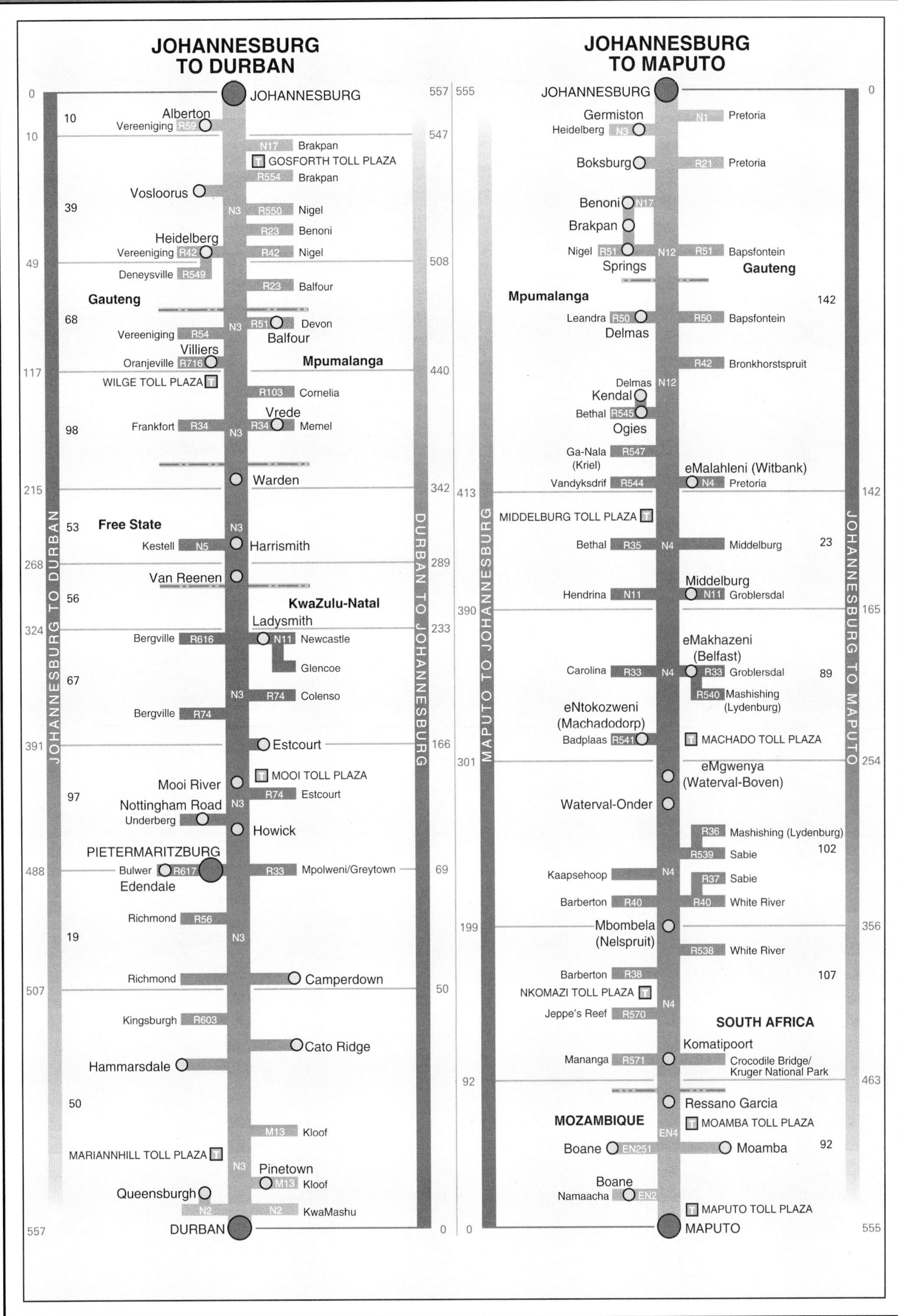
JOHANNESBURG TO DURBAN
JOHANNESBURG
DURBAN
JOHANNESBURG TO DURBAN
DURBAN TO JOHANNESBURG
Alberton
Vereeniging R59
N17 Brakpan
GOSFORTH TOLL PLAZA
R554 Brakpan
Vosloorus
R550 Nigel
R23 Benoni
Heidelberg
Vereeniging R42
R42 Nigel
Deneysville R549
R23 Balfour
Gauteng
Vereeniging R54
R51 Devon
Balfour
Villiers
Oranjeville R716
Mpumalanga
WILGE TOLL PLAZA
R103 Cornelia
Vrede
Frankfort R34
R34 Memel
Warden
Free State
Kestell N5
Harrismith
Van Reenen
KwaZulu-Natal
Ladysmith
Bergville R616
N11 Newcastle
Glencoe
R74 Colenso
Bergville R74
Estcourt
MOOI TOLL PLAZA
Mooi River
R74 Estcourt
Nottingham Road
Underberg
Howick
PIETERMARITZBURG
Bulwer R617
Edendale
R33 Mpolweni/Greytown
Richmond R56
Richmond
Camperdown
Kingsburgh R603
Cato Ridge
Hammarsdale
M13 Kloof
MARIANNHILL TOLL PLAZA
Pinetown
M13 Kloof
Queensburgh
N2 KwaMashu
N3
0 10 49 117 215 268 324 391 488 507 557
10 39 68 98 53 56 67 97 19 50
557 547 508 440 342 289 233 166 69 50 0
JOHANNESBURG TO MAPUTO
JOHANNESBURG
MAPUTO
MAPUTO TO JOHANNESBURG
JOHANNESBURG TO MAPUTO
Germiston
Heidelberg N3
N1 Pretoria
Boksburg
R21 Pretoria
Benoni N17
Brakpan
Nigel R51
N12
R51 Bapsfontein
Springs
Gauteng
Mpumalanga
Leandra R50
R50 Bapsfontein
Delmas
R42 Bronkhorstspruit
Delmas
Kendal
Bethal R545
Ogies
Ga-Nala (Kriel) R547
eMalahleni (Witbank)
Vandyksdrif R544
N4 Pretoria
MIDDELBURG TOLL PLAZA
Bethal R35
N4
Middelburg
Middelburg
Hendrina N11
N11 Groblersdal
eMakhazeni (Belfast)
Carolina R33
R33 Groblersdal
R540 Mashishing (Lydenburg)
eNtokozweni (Machadodorp)
Badplaas R541
MACHADO TOLL PLAZA
eMgwenya (Waterval-Boven)
Waterval-Onder
R36 Mashishing (Lydenburg)
R539 Sabie
Kaapsehoop
R37 Sabie
Barberton R40
R40 White River
Mbombela (Nelspruit)
R538 White River
Barberton R38
NKOMAZI TOLL PLAZA
Jeppe's Reef R570
SOUTH AFRICA
Komatipoort
Mananga R571
Crocodile Bridge/ Kruger National Park
Ressano Garcia
MOZAMBIQUE
MOAMBA TOLL PLAZA
EN4
Boane EN251
Moamba
Boane
Namaacha EN2
MAPUTO TOLL PLAZA
555 413 390 301 199 92 0
0 142 165 254 356 463 555
142 23 89 102 107 92

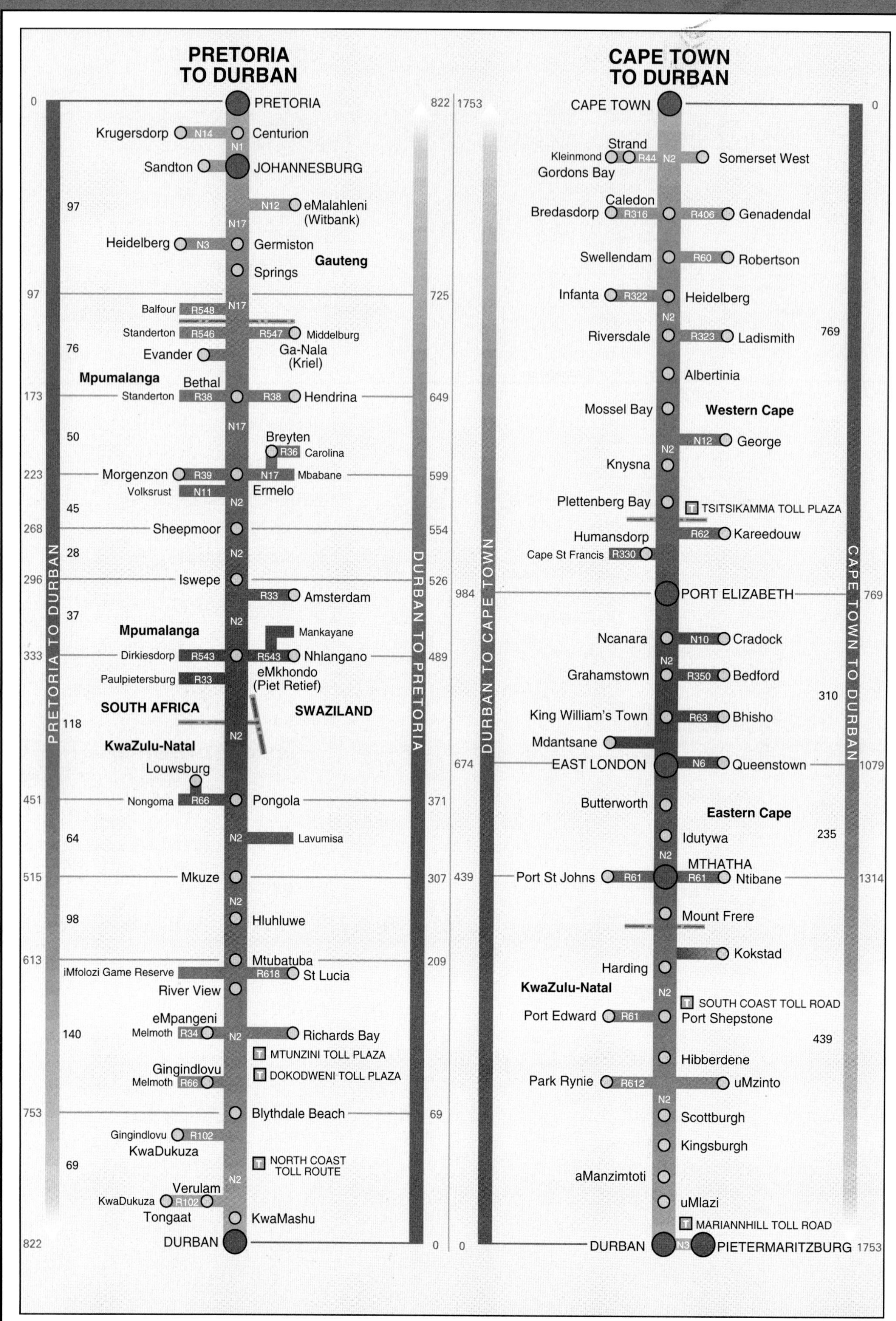
PRETORIA TO DURBAN
PRETORIA
Krugersdorp
N14
Centurion
N1
Sandton
JOHANNESBURG
N12
eMalahleni (Witbank)
N17
Heidelberg
N3
Germiston
Springs
Gauteng
Balfour
R548
Standerton
R546
R547
Middelburg
Evander
Ga-Nala (Kriel)
Mpumalanga
Bethal
Standerton
R38
Hendrina
Breyten
R36
Carolina
Morgenzon
R39
Mbabane
Volksrust
N11
Ermelo
N2
Sheepmoor
Iswepe
R33
Amsterdam
Mpumalanga
Mankayane
Dirkiesdorp
R543
Nhlangano
eMkhondo (Piet Retief)
Paulpietersburg
SOUTH AFRICA
SWAZILAND
KwaZulu-Natal
Louwsburg
Nongoma
R66
Pongola
Lavumisa
Mkuze
Hluhluwe
iMfolozi Game Reserve
Mtubatuba
R618
St Lucia
River View
eMpangeni
Melmoth
R34
Richards Bay
MTUNZINI TOLL PLAZA
Gingindlovu
Melmoth
R66
DOKODWENI TOLL PLAZA
Blythdale Beach
Gingindlovu
R102
KwaDukuza
NORTH COAST TOLL ROUTE
Verulam
KwaDukuza
Tongaat
KwaMashu
DURBAN
PRETORIA TO DURBAN
0 97 173 223 268 296 333 451 515 613 753 822
97 76 50 45 28 37 118 64 98 140 69
DURBAN TO PRETORIA
822 725 649 599 554 526 489 371 307 209 69 0
CAPE TOWN TO DURBAN
CAPE TOWN
Strand
Kleinmond
R44
Somerset West
Gordons Bay
Caledon
Bredasdorp
R316
R406
Genadendal
Swellendam
R60
Robertson
Infanta
R322
Heidelberg
Riversdale
R323
Ladismith
Albertinia
Mossel Bay
Western Cape
N12
George
Knysna
Plettenberg Bay
TSITSIKAMMA TOLL PLAZA
Humansdorp
R62
Kareedouw
Cape St Francis
R330
PORT ELIZABETH
Ncanara
N10
Cradock
Grahamstown
R350
Bedford
King William's Town
R63
Bhisho
Mdantsane
EAST LONDON
N6
Queenstown
Butterworth
Eastern Cape
Idutywa
MTHATHA
Port St Johns
R61
Ntibane
Mount Frere
Kokstad
Harding
KwaZulu-Natal
SOUTH COAST TOLL ROAD
Port Edward
Port Shepstone
Hibberdene
Park Rynie
R612
uMzinto
Scottburgh
Kingsburgh
aManzimtoti
uMlazi
MARIANNHILL TOLL ROAD
DURBAN
N3
PIETERMARITZBURG
DURBAN TO CAPE TOWN
1753 984 674 439 0
CAPE TOWN TO DURBAN
0 769 1079 1314 1753
769 310 235 439

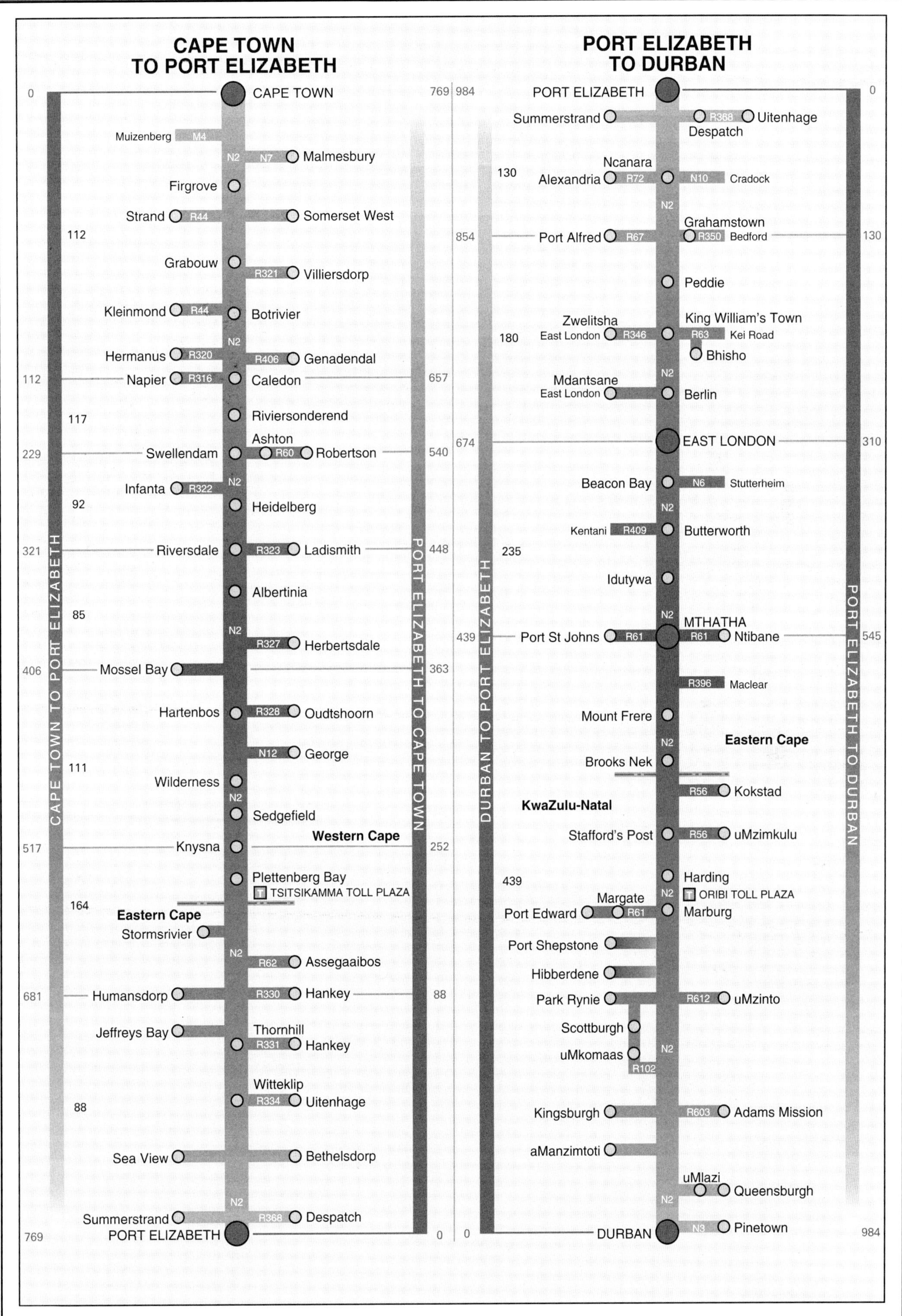
CAPE TOWN TO PORT ELIZABETH
CAPE TOWN
Muizenberg
M4
N2
N7
Malmesbury
Firgrove
Strand
R44
Somerset West
Grabouw
R321
Villiersdorp
Kleinmond
R44
Botrivier
Hermanus
R320
R406
Genadendal
Napier
R316
Caledon
Riviersonderend
Ashton
Swellendam
R60
Robertson
Infanta
R322
Heidelberg
Riversdale
R323
Ladismith
Albertinia
R327
Herbertsdale
Mossel Bay
Hartenbos
R328
Oudtshoorn
N12
George
Wilderness
Sedgefield
Western Cape
Knysna
Plettenberg Bay
TSITSIKAMMA TOLL PLAZA
Eastern Cape
Stormsrivier
R62
Assegaaibos
Humansdorp
R330
Hankey
Jeffreys Bay
Thornhill
R331
Hankey
Witteklip
R334
Uitenhage
Sea View
Bethelsdorp
Summerstrand
R368
Despatch
PORT ELIZABETH
CAPE TOWN TO PORT ELIZABETH
PORT ELIZABETH TO CAPE TOWN
0
112
112
117
229
92
321
85
406
111
517
164
681
88
769
769
657
540
448
363
252
88
0
PORT ELIZABETH TO DURBAN
PORT ELIZABETH
Summerstrand
R368
Uitenhage
Despatch
Ncanara
Alexandria
R72
N10
Cradock
Grahamstown
Port Alfred
R67
R350
Bedford
Peddie
Zwelitsha
East London
R346
King William's Town
R63
Kei Road
Bhisho
Mdantsane
East London
Berlin
EAST LONDON
Beacon Bay
N6
Stutterheim
Kentani
R409
Butterworth
Idutywa
MTHATHA
Port St Johns
R61
R61
Ntibane
R396
Maclear
Mount Frere
Eastern Cape
Brooks Nek
R56
Kokstad
KwaZulu-Natal
Stafford's Post
R56
uMzimkulu
Harding
ORIBI TOLL PLAZA
Margate
Port Edward
R61
Marburg
Port Shepstone
Hibberdene
Park Rynie
R612
uMzinto
Scottburgh
uMkomaas
R102
Kingsburgh
R603
Adams Mission
aManzimtoti
uMlazi
Queensburgh
DURBAN
N3
Pinetown
DURBAN TO PORT ELIZABETH
PORT ELIZABETH TO DURBAN
984
130
854
180
674
235
439
439
0
0
130
310
545
984

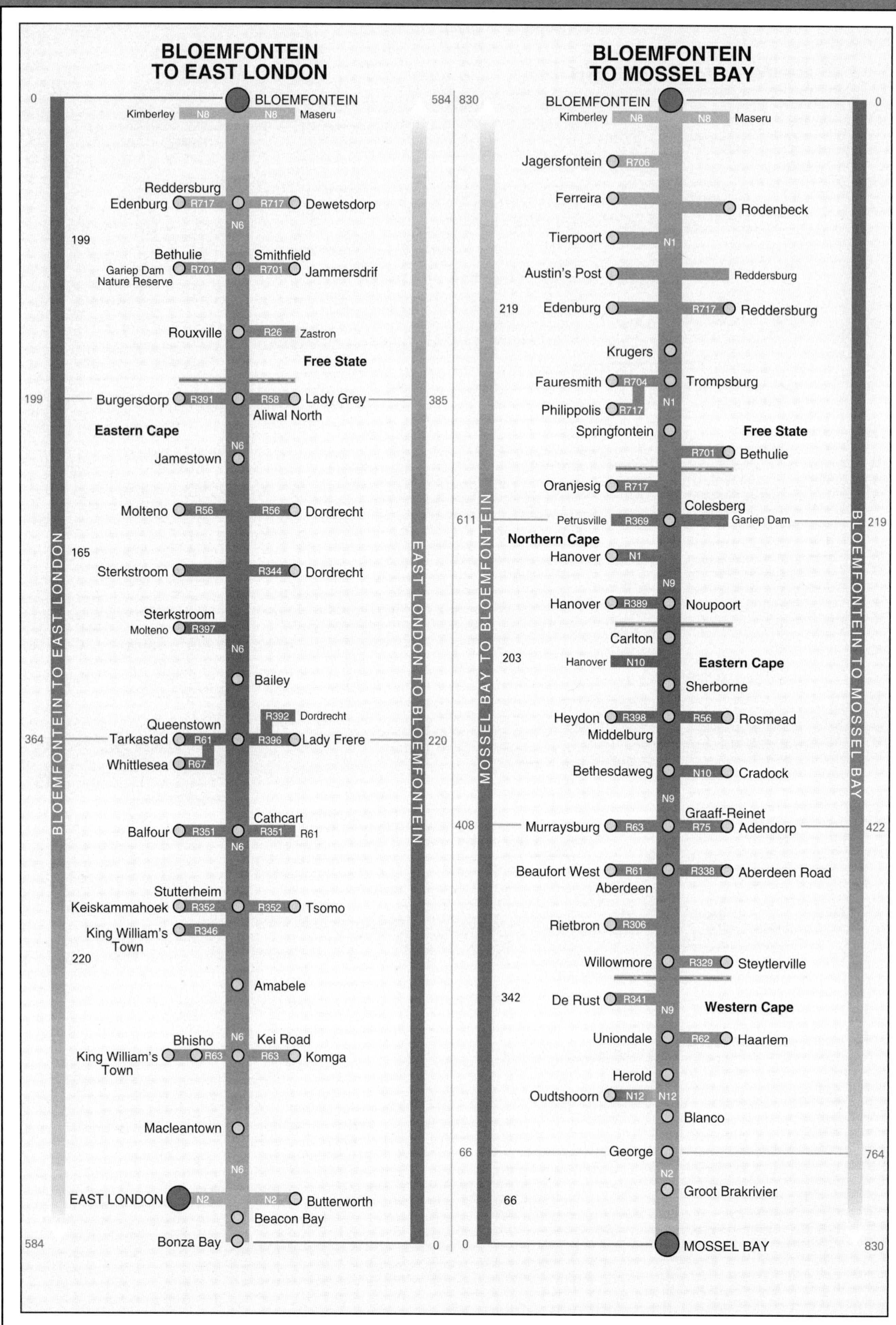
BLOEMFONTEIN TO EAST LONDON
BLOEMFONTEIN
Kimberley
N8
Maseru
Reddersburg
Edenburg
R717
Dewetsdorp
N6
Bethulie
Smithfield
Gariep Dam Nature Reserve
R701
Jammersdrif
Rouxville
R26
Zastron
Free State
Burgersdorp
R391
R58
Lady Grey
Aliwal North
Eastern Cape
Jamestown
Molteno
R56
Dordrecht
Sterkstroom
R344
Dordrecht
Sterkstroom
Molteno
R397
Bailey
R392
Dordrecht
Queenstown
Tarkastad
R61
R396
Lady Frere
Whittlesea
R67
Cathcart
Balfour
R351
R61
Stutterheim
Keiskammahoek
R352
Tsomo
King William's Town
R346
Amabele
Bhisho
Kei Road
King William's Town
R63
Komga
Macleantown
EAST LONDON
N2
Butterworth
Beacon Bay
Bonza Bay
BLOEMFONTEIN TO EAST LONDON
EAST LONDON TO BLOEMFONTEIN
0
199
364
584
199
165
220
584
385
220
0
BLOEMFONTEIN TO MOSSEL BAY
BLOEMFONTEIN
Kimberley
N8
Maseru
Jagersfontein
R706
Ferreira
Rodenbeck
Tierpoort
N1
Austin's Post
Reddersburg
Edenburg
R717
Reddersburg
Krugers
Fauresmith
R704
Trompsburg
Philippolis
R717
Springfontein
Free State
R701
Bethulie
Oranjesig
R717
Colesberg
Petrusville
R369
Gariep Dam
Northern Cape
Hanover
N1
N9
Hanover
R389
Noupoort
Carlton
Hanover
N10
Eastern Cape
Sherborne
Heydon
R398
R56
Rosmead
Middelburg
Bethesdaweg
N10
Cradock
Graaff-Reinet
Murraysburg
R63
R75
Adendorp
Beaufort West
R61
R338
Aberdeen Road
Aberdeen
Rietbron
R306
Willowmore
R329
Steytlerville
De Rust
R341
Western Cape
Uniondale
R62
Haarlem
Herold
Oudtshoorn
N12
Blanco
George
N2
Groot Brakrivier
MOSSEL BAY
MOSSEL BAY TO BLOEMFONTEIN
BLOEMFONTEIN TO MOSSEL BAY
830
219
611
203
408
342
66
66
0
0
219
422
764
830

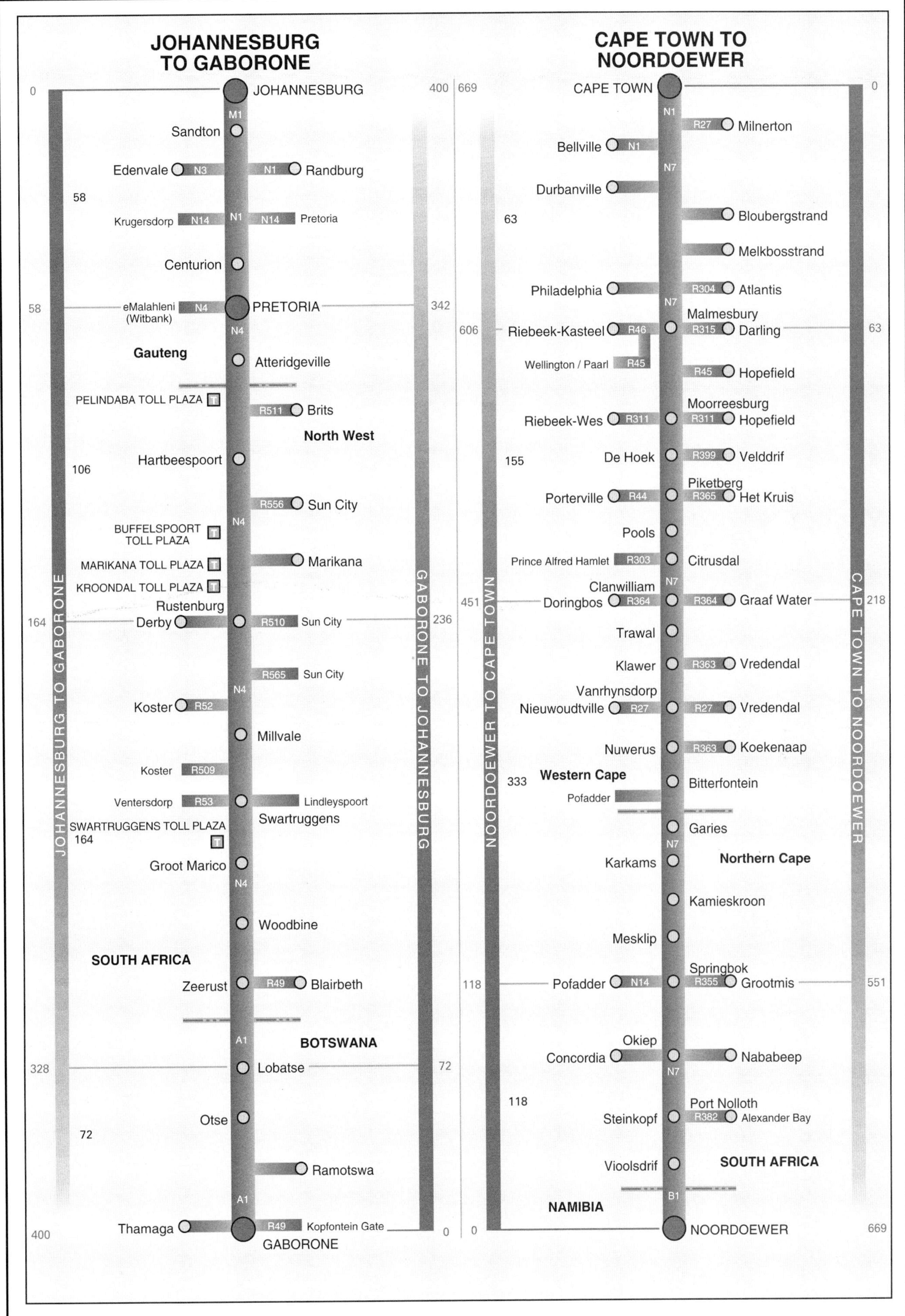
JOHANNESBURG TO GABORONE
JOHANNESBURG
Sandton
Edenvale
Randburg
Krugersdorp
Pretoria
Centurion
eMalahleni (Witbank)
PRETORIA
Gauteng
Atteridgeville
PELINDABA TOLL PLAZA
Brits
North West
Hartbeespoort
Sun City
BUFFELSPOORT TOLL PLAZA
MARIKANA TOLL PLAZA
Marikana
KROONDAL TOLL PLAZA
Rustenburg
Derby
Sun City
Sun City
Koster
Millvale
Koster
Ventersdorp
Lindleyspoort
Swartruggens
SWARTRUGGENS TOLL PLAZA
Groot Marico
Woodbine
SOUTH AFRICA
Zeerust
Blairbeth
BOTSWANA
Lobatse
Otse
Ramotswa
Thamaga
Kopfontein Gate
GABORONE
JOHANNESBURG TO GABORONE
GABORONE TO JOHANNESBURG
CAPE TOWN TO NOORDOEWER
CAPE TOWN
Milnerton
Bellville
Durbanville
Bloubergstrand
Melkbosstrand
Philadelphia
Atlantis
Malmesbury
Riebeek-Kasteel
Darling
Wellington / Paarl
Hopefield
Moorreesburg
Riebeek-Wes
Hopefield
De Hoek
Velddrif
Piketberg
Porterville
Het Kruis
Pools
Prince Alfred Hamlet
Citrusdal
Clanwilliam
Doringbos
Graaf Water
Trawal
Klawer
Vredendal
Vanrhynsdorp
Nieuwoudtville
Vredendal
Nuwerus
Koekenaap
Western Cape
Bitterfontein
Pofadder
Garies
Karkams
Northern Cape
Kamieskroon
Mesklip
Springbok
Pofadder
Grootmis
Okiep
Concordia
Nababeep
Port Nolloth
Steinkopf
Alexander Bay
Vioolsdrif
SOUTH AFRICA
NAMIBIA
NOORDOEWER
NOORDOEWER TO CAPE TOWN
CAPE TOWN TO NOORDOEWER

168 GPS Waypoint map of South Africa

Continues on pages 170 & 171

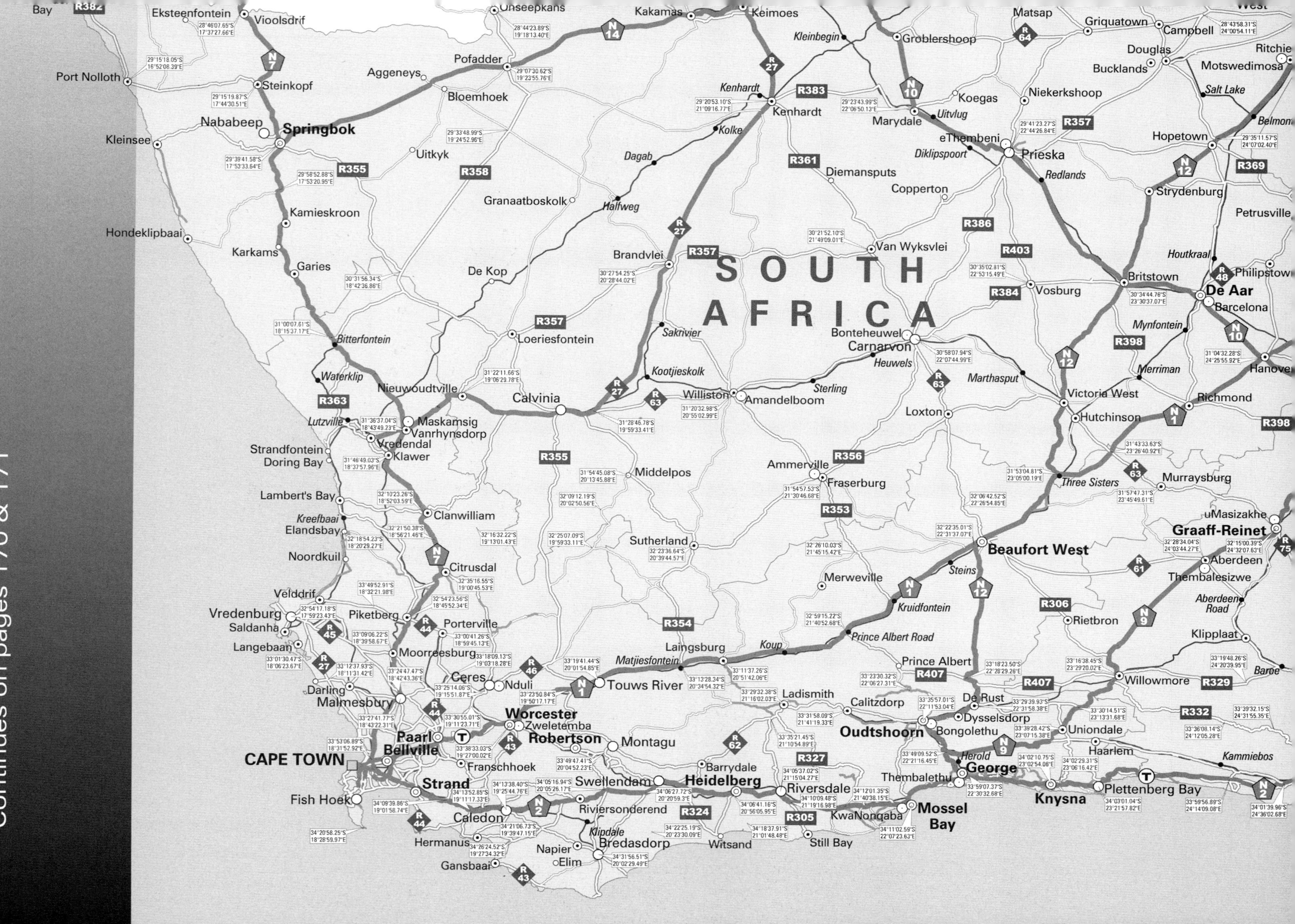

NAMIBIA
BOTSWANA
Karibib
Okahandja
Teufelsbach
Omitara
Omurumendu
Drimiopsis
Buitepos
A2
Tshootsha
Seeis
Witvlei
Gobabis
B6
Babi-Babi
Finkenstein
WINDHOEK
Aris
C28
C20
Dordabis
Doreenville
Nina
Hoaseb
Onderbompa
Nconjane
Tswaane
Takatshwane
Lone Tree
Palamakoloi
Wortel
C14
Rehoboth
Isabis
Kous
C23
Gross Ums
C22
Leonardville
Nauchas
Kobos
Lekkerwater
Derm
Ulhenhorst
C26
Aminuis
Tsetseng
Kang
Klein Aub
Solitaire
B1
Kalkrand
Narib
Lidfontein
C24
Aranos
Hukuntsi
Tshane
Morwamosu
Dutlwe
Gamis
C21
Salzbrunn
Stampriet
Kokong
Sesriem
C14
Hardap
Mariental
Ebeneerde
Akanous
Sekoma
Khakhea
Maltahöhe
C15
C18
Gochas
Gibeon
Witbooisvlei
Werda
Eedsamub
Asab
Brakpan
Twee Rivier
R378
Bray
Terra Firma
Moloporivier
Brukkaros
Vostershoop
Labera
R375
Tses
Helmeringhausen
Shirley
Koës
Tosca
Tshabong
C14
B1
C11
R377
C17
Piet Plessis
Voorspoed
C13
Gariganus
Bethanie
Ganyesa
Tsaukaib
Garub
Aus
B4
Keetmanshoop
C16
R378
Guibes
Goageb
Aroab
Khuis
Aansluit
Feldschuhhorn
Bokspits
Andriesvale
Van Zylsrus
Warmfontein
Cramond
R31
Sonstraal
Hotazel
Vredeshoop
N14
Lykso
Chamieites
Koopan Suid
Lohatlha
R31
Seoding
R27
Obobogorap
Mothibistad
Witpütz
Holoog
Kuruman
Noenieput
R360
Dibeng
R380
Reivilo
Hobas
Grünau
Vrouenspan
Sishen
C13
R31
Ai-Ais
C10
Rosh Pinah
Karasburg
B3
Nakop
N10
Lohatlha
N14
Daniëlskuil
Sendelingsdrif
B1
C10
C10

KIMBERLEY
BLOEMFONTEIN
Jacobsdal
Koffiefontein
Luckhoff
Fauresmith
Dithlake
Vanderkloof
Colesberg
Gariep Dam
Priors
Springfontein
Trompsburg
Edenburg
Reddersburg
Shannon
Smithfield
Bethulie
Noupoort
Middelburg
KwaNonzame
Tafelberg
Conway
Teviot
Steynsburg
Burgersdorp
Aliwal North
Dukathole
Rouxville
Vanstadensrus
Wepener
Botshabelo
Thaba Nchu
Hobhouse
Verkeerdevlei
Brandfort
Clocolan
Ficksburg
Ladybrand
Manyatseng
MASERU
Roma
Peka
Hlotse (Leribe)
Butha-Buthe
Mothae
Lejone
Mokhotlong
Sehlabathebe
Qacha's Nek
Mafeteng
Mohales Hoek
Moyeni (Quthing)
LESOTHO
Zastron
Lady Grey
Barkly East
New England
Jamestown
Dordrecht
Mzanomhle
Nomonde
Molteno
Sterkstroom
Hofmeyr
Tarkastad
Cradock
Lingelihle
Pearston
Somerset East
KwaNojoli
Jansenville
Kirkwood
Addo
Uitenhage
KwaNobuhle
Hankey
Jeffreys Bay
Swartkops
PORT ELIZABETH
Summerstrand
Cookhouse
Bedford
Alicedale
Makanas Kop
Alexandria
GRAHAMSTOWN
Nolukhanyo
Port Alfred
Fort Beaufort
Bofolo
Whittlesea
Sada
Mlungisi
Tylden
Queenstown
Ezibeleni
Lady Frere
Qamata
Cala
Elliot
Ugie
Maclear
Stutterheim
Kubusi
Cathcart
BHISHO
King William's Town
Peddie
Hamburg
Komga
Mdantsane
EAST LONDON
Beacon Bay
Butterworth
Centane
Kei Mouth
Qhorha Mouth
Dutywa
Tsomo
Bityi
MTHATHA
Libode
Port St Johns
Lusikisiki
Flagstaff
Mount Fletcher
Matatiele
Mount Frere
Kokstad
Franklin
Mount Ayliff
Bizana
Harding
Umzimkulu
Donnybrook
Underberg
iXopo
Port Edward
Margate
Port Shepstone
Hibberdene
uMzinto
Scottburgh
aManzimtoti
DURBAN
Queensburgh
Mpumalanga
PIETERMARITZBURG
Edendale
Howick
Nottingham Road
Mooi River
Estcourt
Bergville
Colenso
Weenen
Bruntville
Greytown
Dalton
eNhlalakahle
Verulam
Tongaat
KwaDukuza (Stanger)
Kranskop
eShowe
Gingindlovu
eSikhawini
Felixton
eMpangeni
Richards Bay
N1 N2 N6 N8 N9 N10 R26 R33 R48 R56 R58 R61 R63 R67 R72 R74 R337 R390 R392 R408 R706 R717 A1 A2 A3 A4 A25

ZIMBABWE
MOZAMBIQUE
SWAZILAND
Selebi Phikwe
Serowe
Palapye
Mahalapye
Molepolole
Mochudi
GABORONE
Thamaga
Ramotswa
Kanye
Lobatse
Jwaneng
Musina (Messina)
Beitbridge
Thohoyandou
Louis Trichardt (Makhado)
Giyani
POLOKWANE
Mokopane (Potgietersrus)
Lephalale (Ellisras)
Tzaneen
Phalaborwa
Modimolle (Nylstroom)
Bela-Bela (Warmbaths)
Thabazimbi
Temba
PRETORIA
Brits
Centurion
Tembisa
Sandton
Krugersdorp
JOHANNESBURG
Benoni
Westonaria
Rustenburg
Zeerust
MAHIKENG
Lichtenburg
Vryburg
POTCHEFSTROOM (TLOKWE)
KLERKSDORP
Orkney
Parys
Sebokeng
Vanderbijlpark
Vereeniging
Sasolburg
Heidelberg
Nigel
Middelburg
EMALAHLENI (WITBANK)
MBOMBELA (NELSPRUIT)
Barberton
Komatipoort
White River
Mashishing (Lydenburg)
Sabie
Graskop
Bethal
Secunda
Ermelo
Carolina
Standerton
eMkhondo (Piet Retief)
Volksrust
Newcastle
Dundee
Vryheid
Utrecht
MBABANE
Siteki
MAPUTO
Matola
Manhiça
Marracuene
Xai-Xai
Chokwe
Canicado
Macia
Kroonstad
WELKOM
Virginia
Odendaalsrus
Bethlehem
Harrismith
Frankfort
Heilbron
Christiana
Bloemhof
Schweizer-Reneke
Wolmaransstad
Warrenton
Taung
uLundi

PLACE OF INTEREST	TYPE	GRID	PG
!Khwa ttu Main Gate	Park Entrance	AV 13	26
!Xaus	4x4 Trail	AJ 16	74
16 Mile Beach	Place of Interest	AV 13	26
1820 Settlers Milestone	Historical Site	AU 27	33
1820 Settlers Monument	Historical Site	AV 26	33
1922 Bulhoek Rebellion	Battlefield	AT 26	33
3 Provinsies	4x4 Trail	AL 31	70
4by4	4x4 Trail	AX 17	20
4x4, Mtn Bike, Hiking & Horse-Riding Trails	Hiking	AP 13	49
Aaca Mine	Place of Interest	AN 11	48
Aan-de-Doorns	Wine Farm	AW 15	19
Abrahamsrus	Place of Interest	AK 28	69
Adam Kok Memorial Gate	Park Entrance	AR 31	46
Adam's Mission 1847	Historical Site	AQ 33	47
Addo Eco Trail	4x4 Trail	AW 25	24
Addo Elephant National Park - R342 Entrance	Park Entrance	AW 25	24
Addo Elephant National Park - South Gate	Park Entrance	AW 25	24
Addo Elephant National Park - West Entrance	Park Entrance	AV 24	32
Addo Elephant National Park Gate	Park Entrance	AW 25	24
Adlam's Reef	Dive Site	AM 36	73
African Dawn Wildlife Sanctuary	Place of Interest	AW 24	24
African Hornbill Safaris Game Farm	Nature Reserve	AD 29	86
Agricultural Research Station	Place of Interest	AO 31	58
Agterkliphoogte	Wine Farm	AW 15	19
Air Force Base	Place of Interest	AV 13	26
Al Te Ver Game Farm	Nature Reserve	AD 29	86
Aladdin's-de-Light Studio	Place of Interest	AP 32	59
Alanglade House Museum	Historical Site	AG 33	82
Albasini Ruins	Historical Site	AH 34	83
Algae Reef	Dive Site	AM 36	73
Alkantrant	4x4 Trail	AE 29	86
Alkmaar	4x4 Trail	AH 33	82
Allesverloren	Wine Farm	AV 14	27
Aloe Garden	Place of Interest	AQ 21	41
Aloe Vera Factory	Place of Interest	AX 18	21
Altygedacht	Wine Farm	AW 13	18
Amajuba Mountain 1881	Battlefield	AM 31	70
Amalienstein Mission Station	Place of Interest	AW 18	21
Amanita Game Reserve	Nature Reserve	AF 27	85
Amathunzi Reserve	Nature Reserve	AW 15	19
Amatola Game Reserve	Nature Reserve	AD 31	87
Ambleside Cemetery	Historical Site	AO 31	58
Ambush Rock 1906	Battlefield	AO 33	59
Ana Trees	Nature Reserve	AF 30	87
Ancient Fish Traps (Visvywers)	Place of Interest	AX 18	21
Anderson Museum	Place of Interest	AS 27	44
Andries Pretorius Monument	Historical Site	AU 23	31
Angel Falls	Waterfall	AS 31	46
Anglican Church	Historical Site	AH 25	78
Angling Area	Place of Interest	AP 26	56
Angling Competition	Place of Interest	AP 26	56
Anglo-Boer War Concentration Camp	Historical Site	AP 22	54
Anglo-Boer War Fort	Historical Site	AT 14	27
Anglo-Boer War Monument	Historical Site	AP 23	54
Anglo-Boer War Monument	Historical Site	AR 27	44
Angora Rabbit Farm	Place of Interest	AW 19	21
Annual Crayfish Festival	Place of Interest	AT 13	26
Antipolis 1977	Shipwreck	AW 13	18
Aquarium	Place of Interest	AJ 28	80
Aquila Game Farm	Nature Reserve	AV 15	27
Arabella Country Club	Place of Interest	AX 14	19
Arangieskop Hiking Trail	Hiking	AW 15	19
Arch Rock	Place of Interest	AX 15	19
Archaeological Reserve	Place of Interest	AN 23	54
Ardmore Ceramic Art Studio	Place of Interest	AO 31	58
Aristea 1945	Shipwreck	AQ 11	36
Arniston 1815	Shipwreck	AY 16	20
Arosa 1976	Shipwreck	AQ 11	36
Art & Craft Route	Hiking	AX 15	19
Art & Craft Route	Place of Interest	AV 13	26
Art Gallery	Place of Interest	AP 12	49
Ash Cave	Place of Interest	AP 31	58
Astor	Shipwreck	AX 13	18
Athens 1865	Shipwreck	AW 13	18
Atherstone Nature Reserve	Nature Reserve	AG 26	79
Athina 1967	Shipwreck	AX 21	22
ATKV Holiday Resort	Place of Interest	AX 19	21
Attakwaskloof Monument 1689	Historical Site	AW 19	21
Attaquaskloof	Hiking	AW 19	21
Aufwaerts & Deetlefs	Wine Farm	AW 14	19
Augrabies Falls	Waterfall	AN 16	51
Augrabies National Park Gate	Park Entrance	AO 16	51
Aukoerebis 4x4	4x4 Trail	AN 16	51
Aussenkehr Vineyards	Wine Farm	AN 11	48
Avondale	Wine Farm	AW 14	19
Babalala Picnic Place	Place of Interest	AD 34	89
Baden Powell's Siege Headquarters	Museum	AJ 25	78
Bado Kidogo Bird Farm	Bird Sanctuary	AW 19	21
Bailie's Grave	Historical Site	AU 27	33
Bain Monument	Place of Interest	AW 14	19
Bainbrecht Bridge	Historical Site	AX 15	19
Bakgatla	Park Entrance	AH 27	79
Bakkrans walk	Hiking	AH 33	82
Bakone Maiapa Museum	Historical Site	AF 31	87
Bakoni Malapa Northern Sotho Museum	Historical Site	AF 31	87
Bakubung	Park Entrance	AH 27	79
Balancing Rock	Place of Interest	AX 15	19
Balcony	Dive Site	AX 14	19

PLACE OF INTEREST	TYPE	GRID	PG
Giant's Castle Two Huts Hike	Hiking	AP 31	58
Giant's Cup	Hiking	AP 30	58
Giant's Cup	Hiking	AP 31	58
Gingindlovu	Battlefield	AO 34	60
Giraffe Petroglyph	Historical Site	AB 31	91
Glacial Pavements	Place of Interest	AO 22	54
Glaciated Rocks & Engravings	Place of Interest	AN 23	54
Glaciated Rocks & Engravings	Place of Interest	AO 22	54
Glen Carlou	Wine Farm	AW 14	19
Glen Leary	Historical Site	AH 34	83
Glen Lynden Church 1828	Historical Site	AU 25	32
Glencree Trout Farm	Place of Interest	AQ 30	46
God's Window	Place of Interest	AG 33	82
Godleni Wagpos	Place of Interest	AH 35	83
Goesa Indigenous Forest	Nature Reserve	AW 22	23
Gold Reef City	Place of Interest	AK 28	69
Golf Course	Place of Interest	AE 28	86
Gonjah	4x4 Trail	AW 23	23
Good Hope Cave	Place of Interest	AP 31	58
Goodman Household Aviation Monument	Historical Site	AP 32	59
Gordon Memorial 1879	Historical Site	AN 32	59
Gorge Cave	Place of Interest	AP 31	58
Goudini Spa (Hot Springs)	Place of Interest	AW 14	19
Goudveld Forest Station	Place of Interest	AW 20	22
Goukamma Groenvlei Trail	Hiking	AX 20	22
Gourits River Bridge	Place of Interest	AX 18	21
Gowrie Gate	Park Entrance	AG 34	83
Graceland Casino	Place of Interest	AK 30	70
Graham Beck	Wine Farm	AW 15	19
Graham Beck Reserve	Place of Interest	AW 15	19
Grand West	Place of Interest	AW 13	18
Graskop Gorge	Place of Interest	AG 33	82
Graspan en Enslin Veldslae 1899	Historical Site	AP 23	54
Grassridge Dam Monument	Historical Site	AT 24	32
Grave of Colour Sgt John Pegg	Historical Site	AG 32	82
Grave of Diedrich Coetzee 1820-1891	Historical Site	AH 25	78
Grave of General Joubert	Place of Interest	AL 31	70
Grave of Richard Freyer's Wife	Historical Site	AT 13	26
Grave of Tabu R. Dunn	Historical Site	AO 34	60
Great Kei River Bridge	Place of Interest	AU 28	34
Great Trek 1838	Historical Site	AT 25	32
Great Trek 1838	Historical Site	AU 24	32
Great Trek 1838-1938	Place of Interest	AU 16	28
Greensleeves	Place of Interest	AJ 28	80
Greylands Ostrich Farm	Place of Interest	AW 19	21
Greystone	Historical Site	AO 31	58
Greyton-McGregor Boesmanskloof	Hiking	AW 15	19
Griqua	Historical Site	AX 21	22
Grobler's Bridge 1897	Historical Site	AJ 32	82
Groeneweide Forest Trail	Hiking	AW 20	22
Groenkop	Battlefield	AN 29	57
Groot Constantia 1685	Historical Site	AX 13	18
Groot Kliphuis	Place of Interest	AV 14	27
Groot Suikerboskop Nature Reserve & Dam	Nature Reserve	AH 32	82
Groot Winterhoek Forest Station	Place of Interest	AV 14	27
Grootvaderbosch Nature Reserve	Nature Reserve	AW 17	20
Gruisbank Garden of Remembrance	Historical Site	AO 24	55
Grysbok & Bushbuck Trail	Hiking	AW 17	20
Guided Rooibosch Tours	Place of Interest	AT 14	27
Gunners Memorial 1939-1945	Historical Site	AK 27	68
Gwahumbe Reserve	Nature Reserve	AQ 33	47
Hainshaven Game Farm	Nature Reserve	AF 28	86
Haliartus 1932	Shipwreck	AX 18	21
Hamburg Beach	4x4 Trail	AV 28	34
Hamerkop Hut	Hiking	AX 17	20
Hamilton Russell	Wine Farm	AX 14	19
Hangaboutz Hammocks	Place of Interest	AP 32	59
Hansiesrivier Gold Mine	Historical Site	AX 15	19
Hanzet Distileerders	Wine Farm	AL 27	68
Hard Times Game Farm	Nature Reserve	AE 29	86
Harkerville & Kranshoek Trails	Hiking	AX 21	22
Harmonie Game Farm	Nature Reserve	AD 31	87
Harold Porter Botanical Garden	Nature Reserve	AX 14	19
Harold Trollope Hut	Place of Interest	AH 34	83
Harold Versveld Flower Reserve	Nature Reserve	AV 13	26
Hartebeeshoek Nature Reserve	Nature Reserve	AH 28	80
Hartebeesthoek Satellite Tracking Station	Place of Interest	AJ 28	80
Hartebeesthoek Tracking Station	Place of Interest	AJ 28	80
Havana Hills	Wine Farm	AW 13	18
Hawekwas Connservation Area	Nature Reserve	AW 14	19
Hawkshead Nature Retreat	Place of Interest	AH 32	82
Heavenly Hammocks Arts & Crafts	Place of Interest	AP 32	59
Heerenlogement Cave	Place of Interest	AT 13	26
Heidelberg 4x4 School and Track	4x4 Trail	AK 29	69
Heidelberg Wildflower Garden	Place of Interest	AX 17	20
Heidenhof	Hiking	AX 15	19
Helpmekaar 1900	Battlefield	AN 32	59
Helskloof Gate	Park Entrance	AN 11	48
Hennops Offroad Trail	4x4 Trail	AJ 28	80
Herbert Papenfus KC 1865 - 1937	Historical Site	AG 34	83
Heritage Site	Historical Site	AV 28	34
Herriesklip 1929	Historical Site	AW 20	22
Hester Malan Wild Flower Nature Reserve	Nature Reserve	AP 12	49
Het Huis te Kraaiestein 1698	Shipwreck	AW 13	18
Heuningberg Nature Reserve	Nature Reserve	AX 16	20
Heuningvlei Forest Station	Place of Interest	AT 14	27
Hi-Fly Kites	Place of Interest	AP 32	59
Hibiscus Festival	Place of Interest	AR 32	47
Hide	Bird Sanctuary	AT 23	31

PLACE OF INTEREST	TYPE	GRID	PG
Mitchells Brewery	Place of Interest	AX 21	22
Mkambali Palms	Historical Site	AS 32	47
Mlokolma Royal Graves	Historical Site	AL 34	72
Mlondozi Picnic Spot	Place of Interest	AH 35	83
Mmabatho Airport	Major Airport	AJ 24	78
Mmamagwe Ruins	Historical Site	AC 30	91
Mnweni Cultural Centre	Place of Interest	AO 30	58
Modderrivier 1899	Battlefield	AO 23	54
Modjadji Palms (Cycads)	Nature Reserve	AE 32	88
Moffatt's Mission Church 1833	Historical Site	AL 21	65
Moholoholo Rehabilitation Centre	Place of Interest	AG 33	82
Mokala National Park - Park Gate	Park Entrance	AO 23	54
Mokolodi Nature Reserve	Nature Reserve	AG 25	78
Mokwalo White Lions	Place of Interest	AF 33	88
Monbijou Historical Buildings	Historical Site	AV 14	27
Monkeyland	Place of Interest	AW 21	22
Monkeytown	Place of Interest	AX 14	19
Mons Ruber	Wine Farm	AW 20	22
Monsoon Gallery	Place of Interest	AF 33	88
Monster Rocks	Place of Interest	AP 31	58
Montagu	Wine Farm	AW 16	20
Montagu Mtn Reserve	Nature Reserve	AW 16	20
Montagu Pass & Old Smithy	Place of Interest	AW 20	22
Mont Eco Nature Reserve	Nature Reserve	AW 16	20
Montpellier	Wine Farm	AV 14	27
Montrose Falls	Waterfall	AH 33	82
Monument for Peace & Democracy	Historical Site	AJ 25	78
Mooiplaas	Hiking	AL 27	68
Moolmanshoek	4x4 Trail	AO 28	57
Moonrock	Place of Interest	AN 16	51
Moorddrif Monument 1854	Historical Site	AF 30	87
Moravian Church & Clock	Place of Interest	AX 15	19
Morgan Bay	Lighthouse	AU 29	34
Morgansvlei	Wine Farm	AV 14	27
Morgenhof	Wine Farm	AW 14	19
Morongwa Bush Safaris Reserve	Nature Reserve	AF 27	85
Morula Sun	Place of Interest	AH 29	80
Moshate Ranch Reserve	Nature Reserve	AD 29	86
Moshoeshoe's Mountain Fortress	Historical Site	AP 28	57
Most Southerly Baobab Tree	Place of Interest	AG 34	83
Mostert's Mill	Historical Site	AW 13	18
Moth Memorial	Historical Site	AW 25	24
Mother Goose	Place of Interest	AP 32	59
Motlatse River Canyon Hiking Trail	Hiking	AG 33	82
Motlatse Rivier Canyon	Place of Interest	AG 33	82
Mount Bain	Wine Farm	AW 14	19
Mount Sheba Private Nature Reserve	Place of Interest	AG 33	82
Mountain Lake	Nature Reserve	AQ 30	46
Mountain Oaks	Wine Farm	AW 14	19
Mountain Park Sanctuary	Nature Reserve	AJ 28	80
Mountain Trail	Hiking	AX 15	19
Mountain Zebra National Park - Main Gate	Park Entrance	AT 24	32
Mpande Bay	4x4 Trail	AT 31	35
Mpande's Grave	Historical Site	AN 34	60
Mpenjati NR	Nature Reserve	AR 32	47
Mphafa Hide	Bird Sanctuary	AN 35	60
Mpofu	Hiking	AU 26	33
Mpofu Trail	Hiking	AO 32	59
Mtambalala Forest Station	Place of Interest	AS 31	46
Mtonjaneni Mountain	Historical Site	AN 34	60
Museum	Place of Interest	AO 10	48
Museum	Place of Interest	AV 13	26
Museum & Interpretation Centre	Nature Reserve	AC 31	91
Museum & Succulent Garden	Place of Interest	AW 18	21
Museum of Man	Place of Interest	AG 33	82
Musgrave	Historical Site	AQ 33	47
Mushavi Game Ranch	Nature Reserve	AO 22	54
Mussel Rafts	Place of Interest	AV 12	26
Mvenyane Forest Station	Place of Interest	AR 30	46
Mzama Royal Graves	Historical Site	AL 34	72
Mzamba Cretaceous Deposits	Place of Interest	AS 32	47
Naboom Private Nature Reserve	Nature Reserve	AF 30	87
Nagle Dam Nature Reserve	Nature Reserve	AP 33	59
Nahoon Beach	4x4 Trail	AV 28	34
Namakwa Mariculture Park	Nature Reserve	AO 11	48
Namaqua 1876	Shipwreck	AR 12	37
Namaqualand Mines	Place of Interest	AP 11	48
National Botanical Gardens	Nature Reserve	AP 32	59
National English Literary Museum	Historical Site	AV 26	33
National Exhibition Centre	Place of Interest	AK 28	69
National Railway Museum	Place of Interest	AP 32	59
National Zoo	Place of Interest	AJ 29	80
Natural Rock Bridge	Place of Interest	AG 33	82
Nature Reserve	Nature Reserve	AV 12	26
Nature Trails	Hiking	AX 15	19
Naudé's Nek Monument	Historical Site	AR 29	45
Ndedema Gorge	Place of Interest	AO 31	58
Ndindindi Forest Station	Place of Interest	AR 31	46
Ndongeni's Grave	Historical Site	AR 32	47
Nederburg	Wine Farm	AW 14	19
Neethlingshof	Wine Farm	AW 14	19
Neil Joubert	Wine Farm	AW 14	19
Nel Graves	Historical Site	AH 33	82
Nelson's Bay Cave	Place of Interest	AX 21	22
Nelson's Creek	Wine Farm	AW 14	19
New Agatha Plantation	Historical Site	AF 32	88
Newington Gate	Park Entrance	AG 34	83
Newlands Bhala Bhala Game Lodge	Nature Reserve	AN 23	54
NG Church	Historical Site	AU 20	30

PLACE OF INTEREST	TYPE	GRID	PG
Sudwala Caves	Place of Interest	AH 33	82
Sugarmill Casino	Place of Interest	AP 33	59
Sulphur Springs	Place of Interest	AJ 32	82
Sunday's River Citrus Co.	Historical Site	AV 24	32
Sunken Garden	Place of Interest	AT 27	33
Sunnyside	Battlefield	AO 22	54
Surprise Hill	Place of Interest	AN 31	58
Suspension Bridge	Place of Interest	AG 33	82
Suspension Bridge	Place of Interest	AW 19	21
Suspension Bridge & Hiking Trails	Place of Interest	AW 22	23
Swadini Reptile Park	Nature Reserve	AF 33	88
Swamp Forest	Place of Interest	AN 36	61
Swartberg Trail	4x4 Trail	AV 19	29
Swartland	Wine Farm	AW 14	19
Swartlintjies Mine	Place of Interest	AQ 11	36
Swissland Cheese	Place of Interest	AP 32	59
Swona 1947	Shipwreck	AY 15	19
Taal Monument	Historical Site	AW 14	19
Taalmonument	Place of Interest	AR 26	44
Table Mountain	Place of Interest	AW 13	18
Tafelkop	4x4 Trail	AW 16	20
Takoon 1823	Battlefield	AL 22	66
Tala Private Game Reserve	Nature Reserve	AQ 32	47
Talana 1899	Battlefield	AN 32	59
Talana Museum	Place of Interest	AN 32	59
Talmon Ephriam Lion Cachet 1901	Historical Site	AS 25	43
Tania 1972	Shipwreck	AX 13	18
Tarka Post	Historical Site	AT 26	33
Tea Garden	Place of Interest	AN 31	58
Tearoom and Picnic Spot	Place of Interest	AG 35	83
Tepelkop Hiking Trail	Hiking	AN 29	57
Teresa Mission	Place of Interest	AR 28	45
Tevreden Cheese Farm	Place of Interest	AO 30	58
Thaba Kwena Crocodile Farm	Place of Interest	AG 29	80
Thaba Meetse Game Ranch	Nature Reserve	AF 29	86
Thaba Tholo Eco-park	Nature Reserve	AG 27	79
Thabo's Antiques	Place of Interest	AP 32	59
Thanda Game Reserve	Nature Reserve	AM 35	72
Thandanani Craft Village	Place of Interest	AO 30	58
Thangami Safari	4x4 Trail	AM 34	72
Thatch Roof Church	Place of Interest	AY 16	20
The Big Hole	Historical Site	AO 23	54
The Big Tree	Place of Interest	AC 33	92
The Brightwater Common	Place of Interest	AJ 28	80
The Carousel Entertainment Centre	Place of Interest	AH 29	80
The Cave	Place of Interest	AX 19	21
The Cycads	Historical Site	AP 33	59
The Dunes Trail	4x4 Trail	AT 13	26
The Heads	Place of Interest	AX 21	22
The Hobbit's Hut	Place of Interest	AP 32	59
The Jane Goodall Institute Chimpanzee Eden	Place of Interest	AH 33	82
The Kingdom	Place of Interest	AP 34	60
The Kingfisher	Place of Interest	AH 32	82
The Lavender Co.	Place of Interest	AP 32	59
The Letterklip 1902	Historical Site	AR 12	37
The Lookout	Historical Site	AW 25	24
The Meridian 1821	Shipwreck	AX 14	19
The Observatory	Wine Farm	AW 14	19
The Old Carnegie Museum	Place of Interest	AM 33	71
The Oxwagon 4x4 & Quads Trail	4x4 Trail	AH 31	81
The Pinnacle	Place of Interest	AG 33	82
The Polokwane Museum	Historical Site	AF 31	87
The Rev. George Barre 1857	Historical Site	AU 27	33
The South African Astronomical Observatory	Place of Interest	AU 17	28
The Taung Skull	Historical Site	AM 23	66
The Tengamanzi Trading Post	Historical Site	AH 34	83
The Vale	4x4 Trail	AT 20	30
The Woodturner	Place of Interest	AP 32	59
Theewaterskloof Country Club	Place of Interest	AX 14	19
Thekwane Arts & Crafts	Place of Interest	AF 33	88
Thermopylae 1899	Shipwreck	AW 13	18
Thomas Hart's Grave	Historical Site	AH 34	83
Thomas T Tucker 1942	Shipwreck	AX 13	18
Three Falls Hatchery	Place of Interest	AH 32	82
Thulamela Ruins	Historical Site	AC 34	93
Thunder City	Place of Interest	AW 13	18
Tienie Versveld Flower Reserve & Wetland	Nature Reserve	AV 13	26
Tierhoek Picnic Spot	Place of Interest	AX 16	20
Timavo 1940	Shipwreck	AM 36	73
Timbavati Gate	Park Entrance	AF 34	89
Timbila Game Reserve	Nature Reserve	AV 22	31
Tlholego Eco Village	Place of Interest	AJ 27	79
Toll House	Historical Site	AW 18	21
Tonteldoos Mampoer Distillery	Place of Interest	AH 32	82
Touch the Sky Trail	4x4 Trail	AS 26	44
Touchstone Game Ranch	Nature Reserve	AE 29	86
Tourism Centre	Place of Interest	AP 32	59
Touwsberg Private Nature Reserve	Nature Reserve	AW 17	20
Touwsrivier Nature Reserve	Nature Reserve	AV 16	28
Tower College & Memorial Tower	Historical Site	AQ 33	47
Towersig	Hiking	AW 18	21
Township Tours	Place of Interest	AP 11	48
Tractor Trips	Place of Interest	AW 15	19
Transport Museum	Historical Site	AK 29	69
Trawal	Wine Farm	AT 13	26
Treverton College	Place of Interest	AO 32	59
Triangular Trail	Hiking	AW 16	20
Tribal Office	Place of Interest	AT 30	35
Trichardt Memorial	Historical Site	AG 35	83

PLACE OF INTEREST	TYPE	GRID	PG
Triple Jump Falls	Waterfall	AX 14	19
Trooper Knight 1906	Historical Site	AP 33	59
Trout Hatchery	Place of Interest	AH 32	82
Trout Hideaway	Place of Interest	AG 33	82
Tsaba-Tsaba Nature Reserve	Nature Reserve	AY 16	20
Tshugulu Gate	Park Entrance	AC 30	91
Tsitsikamma Trail	Hiking	AW 22	23
Tsoelike Falls	Waterfall	AQ 30	46
Tswaing Meteorite Crater and Museum	Place of Interest	AH 29	80
Tswana Game Farm	Nature Reserve	AF 28	86
Tugela 1838	Battlefield	AO 34	60
Tugela Gorge	Waterfall	AO 32	59
Tugela Gorge Walk	Hiking	AO 30	58
Tuinskloof	4x4 Trail	AW 23	23
Tula Tula Game Reserve	Nature Reserve	AO 22	54
Tulbagh (Porterville)	Wine Farm	AV 14	27
Tunnel	Place of Interest	AJ 28	80
Twee Jonge Gezellen	Wine Farm	AV 14	27
Two-Mile Reef	Dive Site	AM 36	73
Tyityaba Game Reserve	Nature Reserve	AU 29	34
Tzaarsbank Picnic Area	Place of Interest	AV 12	26
Ubejane Trail	4x4 Trail	AT 24	32
Ubizane Wildlife Reserve	Nature Reserve	AN 35	60
Ugab Guided Tour	Hiking	AT 19	29
Uitvlucht	Place of Interest	AH 32	82
Uitvlucht Ponds	Place of Interest	AH 32	82
Ultimatum Tree	Historical Site	AP 34	60
uLundi 1879	Historical Site	AN 34	60
uLundi Fort	Historical Site	AN 34	60
Umgungundhlovu 1838	Battlefield	AN 34	60
uMhlanga Lagoon Nature Reserve	Place of Interest	AP 33	59
Umtiza NR	Nature Reserve	AV 28	34
Umtombe Picnic Site	Place of Interest	AO 32	59
Umtunzini Picnic Site	Place of Interest	AO 32	59
uNkonka Trail	Hiking	AR 32	47
Upington International Airport	Major Airport	AN 18	52
Upper iNjasuthi Cave	Place of Interest	AO 31	58
uShaka Marine World	Place of Interest	AQ 33	47
uVongo Beach	4x4 Trail	AR 32	47
V & A Waterfront	Place of Interest	AW 13	18
Vaal Race Course	Place of Interest	AK 28	69
Vaalkrans 1900	Battlefield	AO 31	58
Vaalkrans Hut	Hiking	AX 17	20
Valley of 1000 Hills	Place of Interest	AP 33	59
Valley of Ancient Voices	Place of Interest	AV 26	33
Valley of Desolation	Historical Site	AU 23	31
Valley of Ferns	Place of Interest	AW 21	22
Valley of the Rainbow	Place of Interest	AH 32	82

PLACE OF INTEREST	TYPE	GRID	PG
Van Loveren	Wine Farm	AW 16	20
Van Riebeeck's Hedge	Place of Interest	AW 13	18
Van Stadens	Hiking	AW 24	24
Van Stadens Wild Flower Reserve	Nature Reserve	AW 24	24
Van Zylshof	Wine Farm	AW 16	20
Vanrhijn & Latsky Radio Museum	Place of Interest	AS 14	38
Vasco da Gama Nautical Museum	Place of Interest	AU 12	26
Vechtkop	Battlefield	AM 28	69
Vegloer	Battlefield	AO 31	58
'Veldskoen' Shoe Factory	Place of Interest	AU 14	27
Verdun Ruins	Historical Site	AD 31	87
Vergelegen	Wine Farm	AX 14	19
Verlorenkloof	4x4 Trail	AU 16	28
Verwoerd Tunnels	Historical Site	AD 32	88
Victorian Architecture	Place of Interest	AS 13	37
Victorian, Edwardian & Georgian Buildings	Historical Site	AW 14	19
Viewpoint	Place of Interest	AH 34	83
Viewpoint	Place of Interest	AJ 33	82
Viewpoint	Place of Interest	AA 35	93
Viewpoint	Place of Interest	AK 36	73
Villa Spa	4x4 Trail	AQ 33	47
Village & Craft Market	Place of Interest	AM 35	72
Villiera	Wine Farm	AW 14	19
Villiersdorp Nature Rerserve	Nature Reserve	AW 14	19
Virginia Aerodrome	Major Airport	AP 33	59
Visitor's Centre	Place of Interest	AO 30	58
Vlcermuisklip 1661	Historical Site	AS 13	37
Vlei Trails	Hiking	AX 16	20
VOC Beacon	Historical Site	AV 13	26
Volkspele Monument	Historical Site	AN 24	55
Vollgraaf Monument 1838-1938	Historical Site	AO 19	52
Von Regen Wines	Wine Farm	AO 17	51
Voortrekker Fort	Historical Site	AG 33	82
Voortrekker Gedenkplaat	Historical Site	AW 19	21
Voortrekker Graves	Historical Site	AG 33	82
Voortrekker Memorial	Historical Site	AO 31	58
Voortrekker Memorial	Historical Site	AV 19	29
Voortrekker Monument	Historical Site	AJ 29	80
Voortrekker Monument	Historical Site	AN 27	56
Voortrekkergedenksaal 1828-1874	Historical Site	AU 26	33
Vrede en Lust	Wine Farm	AW 14	19
Vredefort Dome (WHS)	Place of Interest	AL 27	68
Vredendal	Wine Farm	AT 13	26
Vredesboom	Place of Interest	AJ 28	80
Vukuzenzele	Place of Interest	AP 32	59
Vulamehlo Curio Stall	Place of Interest	AN 35	60
Vulture Hide	Bird Sanctuary	AO 31	58
Vulture Hide	Bird Sanctuary	AP 31	58
Vulture Restaurant	Historical Site	AJ 25	78
Vulture Restaurant & Feeding Scheme	Bird Sanctuary	AN 30	58

H

198 INDEX Place Names

Main map pages 18 - 93

Main map pages 18 - 93

N

Main map pages 18 - 93

Main map pages 18 - 93

S

Main map pages 18 - 93

U

V

OTHER MapStudio atlas products

www.mapstudio.co.za

OTHER ATLASES AVAILABLE FROM MAP STUDIO

AFRICA ROAD ATLAS
ISBN 9781868098019
Overview maps include parks throughout Africa, towns within African countries and adventure activities available in various African countries. Key plan to 62 street maps (e.g. Accra, Algiers, Beira, Durban, Gaborone, Harare, Johannesburg). Coverage includes all African countries and the Indian Ocean Islands at scales of 1 : 1 500 000 and 1 : 3 000 000.

AFRICAN CITIES & TOWNS ROAD ATLAS
ISBN 9781770260719
Comprehensive atlas featuring all the capital cities of Africa. Additional tourist and business centres also included. The atlas includes country locators, hotels, accommodation, places of interest, detailed index of street names, important buildings, police stations, post offices, hospitals, route markers and road classifications. Coverage: Abidjan, Abuja, Accra, Addis Ababa, Algiers Alexandria, Antenanarivo, Asmara, Bamako, Bangui, Banjul, Beira, Bissau, Blantyre, Brazzavlile, Bujumbura, Cairo, Cape Town, Conakry, Dakar, Dar Es Salaam & Zanzibar, Djibouti,Dodoma, Durban, Freetown, Gaborone, Harare, Johannesburg & surrounds inset, Kampala, Khartoum, Kigali, Kinshasa, Lagos, Libreville, Lilongwe, Lome, Luanda, Lusaka, Maputo, Malabo, Maseru, Mbabane, Mogadishu, Mombasa, Monrovia, N'Djamena, Nairobi, Niamey, Nouakchott, Ouagadougou, Port Elizabeth, Port Louis, Porto-Novo, Pretoria, Rabat, Tangier, Tripoli, Tunis, Victoria, Victoria Falls & Livingstone, Walvis Bay, Windhoek, Yamoussoukro and Yaounde.

CAPE TOWN TO PORT ELIZABETH ROAD ATLAS
ISBN 9781770262195
The Cape Town to Port Elizabeth Road Atlas covers the main coastal route of the Western Cape and Garden Route between Cape Town and East London. The atlas provides tourist friendly information, tourism contact details and resources. Included are 1:750 000 scaled maps of the region, a detailed index and street plans of Cape Town, Knysna, Port Elizabeth (including Summerstrand), East London, Mossel Bay, Stellenbosch, Franschhoek, Worcester, Struis Bay, Hermanus, Swellendam, Montagu, Cape Infanta, Hartenbos, Oudtshoorn, George, Wilderness, Sedgefield, St Francis Bay, Jeffrey's Bay, Kenton on Sea, Grahamstown, Port Alfred, Beacon Bay and Kei Mouth.

SOUTH AFRICA GLOVEBOX ROAD ATLAS
ISBN 9781770261051
This revised and updated compact atlas includes detailed and continuous map section, highlights seven major tourist areas and features eleven street maps. The maps show freeways, national roads, route numbers, nature reserves and parks, places of interest, tourist information, index to place names and GPS co-ordinates. Coverage includes a detailed map of South Africa at a scale of 1 : 1 500 000. The seven major tourist areas of the Cape Peninsula, South Western Cape and Overberg region, Garden Route, Gauteng, Kruger National Park, Drakensberg and Kwazulu-Natal coast. The eleven street maps are of Pietermaritzburg, Durban, Nelspruit, Polokwane, Pretoria, Johannesburg, Bloemfontein, Kimberley, East London, Port Elizabeth and Cape Town.

SOUTH AFRICA POCKET ROAD ATLAS
ISBN 9781770261068
This updated edition 36 page atlas includes new place names, a main map section, national parks and game reserves, places of interest and historic sites, road distances, freeways, major routes and secondary roads (tarred and untarred), route numbers, mountain passes, airports and airfields, toll roads, border posts, mountain ranges, rivers, lakes, waterfalls and dams. The maps show international and provincial boundaries, selected accommodation, battlefields, town plans, post offices, hospitals and clinics, police stations, schools, tourist offices, parks, recreation areas, distance chart, place names index. Coverage includes the whole of South Africa as detailed road maps at a scale of 1 : 2 000 000. Featuring nine detailed street maps of Bloemfontein, Cape Town, Durban, East London, Johannesburg, Nelspruit, Pietermaritzburg, Port Elizabeth and Pretoria.

SOUTH AFRICA ROAD ATLAS, 23RD EDITION
ISBN 9781770261549
This new edition South Africa Road Atlas is completely revised and updated to suit your needs. It now includes all satellite towns and provides GPS co-ordinates for major road junctions. It provides 34 pages of detailed topography in a continuous map section at a scale of 1:1 250 000. The atlas contains 16 detailed tourist area maps which cover the Cape Peninsula, South Western Cape, Overberg, Garden Route, Eastern Cape, Kwa-Zulu Natal coastline, Drakensburg, midlands meander, Kwa-Zulu Natal battlefields, St Lucia (isimangaliso), uMfolozi Hluhluwe region, Gauteng region, Magaliesburg, Sun City and Pilanesberg and Kruger National Park. The atlas provides 46 detailed street maps covering Cape Town, Stellenbosch, Langebaan, Simonstown, Worcester, Swellendam, Oudtshoorn, George, Mossel Bay, Knysna, Plettenberg Bay, Upington, Port Elizabeth, Grahamstown, Port Alfred, East London, Bhisho, Mthatha, Durban, Margate, Richards Bay, Ladysmith Ulundi, Kimberly, Bloemfontein, Welkom, Kroonstad, Klerksdorp, Potchefstroom, Johannesburg 'ring road' regional, Johannesburg central, Rosebank and Sandton (JHB), Midrand, Pretoria, Hartbeespoort Mafikeng, Rustenberg, Polokwane, Witbank (Emalahleni), Nelspruit white river and Phalaborwa. Includes three detailed airport map layouts for O.R. Tambo, King Shaka and Cape Town International airports. Includes 16 accurate and easy-to-use strip routes across South Africa.

SOUTHERN & EAST AFRICA ROAD ATLAS
ISBN 9781868098439
Maps of Southern Africa, physical and political, climate and vegetation. Information about each country with statistics, flags and interesting facts. Key plans, 107 pages of maps of Southern and East Africa, 11 pages covering 6 major tourist areas, 18 pages covering the main cities and towns, distance chart and index to place names. Countries covered are Angola, Botswana, Democratic Republic of the Congo, Kenya, Malawi, Mozambique, Namibia, South Africa, Tanzania, Zambia, Zimbabwe, Lesotho, Swaziland, Uganda, Burundi, Rwanda.

WESTERN CAPE ROAD ATLAS
ISBN 9781868099054
Detailed map of the Western Cape, coverage of main towns, detailed touring maps, tourist site map, top tips and tourism resources, historic sites and activity coverage, places of interest, route numbers, nature reserves and parks, index to place names. Coverage includes Cape Town and the Winelands region, the Breede River Valley, Overberg, the Garden Route and Route 62, the Klein Karoo.

EASTERN CAPE ROAD ATLAS
ISBN 9781770261891
This updated edition tourist atlas of the Eastern Cape Province now includes GPS co-ordinates. Includes coverage of main towns, tourist site maps, top tourist sites per region and tourism resources, parks and reserves. Regions covered include Tsitsikamma, the Sunshine Coast, Karoo heartland, Amatola Mountains, the route along the N6, the Wild Coast, Sundays River Valley and settler country. The atlas contains town plans of St Francis Bay area, Alexandria, Beacon Bay, East London, Gonubie, Grahamstown, Humansdorp, Jeffrey's Bay, Kenton-on-Sea, Peddie, Port Elizabeth, Port Alfred, Summerstrand and Uitenhage.

KWAZULU-NATAL ROAD ATLAS
ISBN 9781770261709
This revised and updated edition includes GPS co-ordinates and the new Durban street names. This tourist atlas provides detailed coverage of the entire KwaZulu-Natal province with main towns and tourist sites. It gives top travel tips and information on tourism resources. Coverage of the north coast includes Umhlanga, Ballito, Shaka's Rock, Salt Rock, Gingindlovu, Mtunzini and inland to Eshowe. The coverage of Zululand and surrounds includes Empangeni, Richards Bay, Ulundi, Melmoth, Zululand's Wildlife, St Lucia Wetland Reserve, Zululand parks and reserves, St Lucia, Sodwana, Kosi Bay and continues into Mozambique. The south coast coverage includes Amanzimtoti, Kingsburgh, Scottburgh, Hibberdene and Port Shepstone, Oribi Gorge, Margate, Uvongo, Uvongo River nature reserve, Ramsgate, Port Edward, Kokstad, Mount Currie nature reserve and Route 617. Coverage from Kloof to Mooi River features Valley of 1000 Hills, Pietermaritzburg, Howick and Midmar region, Howick, Albert Falls, Midlands Meander, Mooi River, Bushmans River region, Estcourt, Weenen nature reserve, Winterton, Bergville and Spioenkop Dam.

MOZAMBIQUE ROAD ATLAS
I SBN 9781770260306
Includes key route map and distance chart. Information about Mozambique's' main sites and parks, historical information, activities, getting around on the roads, what to pack, eating and sleeping. Includes GPS co-ordinates for major road junctions, detailed 1 : 1 430 000 scale road atlas section, map covering the entire country, complete map index. Detailed street maps including smaller towns and villages. Information on shopping, hot spots with contact details, detailed tourism contacts and resources, tourist regions. Coverage includes a road atlas section at a 1 : 1 430 000 scale, Maputo and Maputaland region, Punto de Ouro, Maputo Bay and the Southern region, Maputo Elephant Reserve, Bilene, Xai-Xai, Chockwe and surrounds, Xai-Xai and Praia do Xai-Xai, Great Limpopo Transfrontier Reserve, Zinave National Park, Banhine National Park, Inhambane and surrounds, Vilankulo, Tofo, Bazaruto Archipelago, Beira Corridor, Gorongosa National Park, Tete, Zambezi and Zambezi Delta, Quelimane and Surrounds, Gili Reserve and surrounds, Nampula and Cuamba surrounds, Mozambique Island, Pemba street plan map, IBO street plan map, Mocimboa De Praia, Quirimba Archipelago and Region, Niassa Reserve, Lichinga Area, Lake Niassa (Lake Malawi).

MPUMALANGA & KRUGER NATIONAL PARK ROAD ATLAS
ISBN 9781868098989
Perfect for the first time visitor, colour photographs, detailed continuous map section, street maps, tourist areas, indexed place names, contact information, small towns, accommodation, nature reserves, national parks, route planner, shopping, hot spots, history, activities.

NAMIBIA ROAD ATLAS
ISBN 9781770261693
This updated edition features a continuous detailed map section that includes GPS co-ordinates for major road junctions. Perfect for the first time visitor, colour photographs, tourist areas, sites, place names index, contact information, small towns, reserves, national parks, route planner, shopping, hot spots, historic sites, activities, detailed atlas section. Coverage includes detailed map section covering the whole of Namibia. Street maps of Windhoek, Swakopmund, Walvis Bay, Luderitz, Sesfontein, Opuwo, Oshakati, Rundu, Katima Mulilo, Tsumeb, Grootfontein, Otavi, Otjiwarongo, Outjo, Omaruru, Gobabis, Okahandja, Rehoboth, Mariental and Keetmanshoop.

ACTIVITY ATLAS SOUTHERN AFRICA
ISBN 9781770260023
This atlas includes introductory maps, a brief history, people and culture, natural wonders, animals and plants and adventure regions. All countries are listed with adventures by region and include contact details, popular routes, suggested sites and activities route maps, regional maps, site maps, city and town maps, national parks and reserves, information on people and places, showing a distance chart and detailed resource section. Coverage includes South Africa, Lesotho, Swaziland, Namibia, Botswana, Zimbabwe, Mozambique, Zambia, Tanzania, Kenya, Uganda, Rwanda, Burundi, Madagascar, the Indian Ocean Islands and Malawi.

CAPE TOWN & PENINSULA VISITOR'S GUIDE
ISBN 9781770260009
Detailed visitors guide and touring map to the Cape Peninsula, detailed routeplanner, points of interest and activity areas plus a check list for major sites. Coverage includes Cape Town CBD, Victoria and Alfred Waterfront, Robben Island, Oudekraal, Hout Bay, Constantia tourist region, Kirstenbosch, Simon's Town, Boulders Penguin Colony, Table Mountain National Park, greater Cape Town, the West Coast, Winelands and Hoerikwaggo Trail.

DRIVE SOUTHERN AFRICA
ISBN 9781770260085
This pictorial journey of Southern Africa divides the region into seven major driving routes. Each driving route opens with pictorial spread containing a strip map showing distances and places along the route. Beautiful images show the reader the visual journey they are about to drive. The route is then split into smaller more detailed routes covering areas of interest along the route. Sites of special interest are highlighted in more detail with images or maps. 60 top sites along each route are covered as a double page, with more detailed mapping and images. The town plans section has 96 city and town maps, covering all the capital cities and important towns along the chosen route. This comprehensive road atlas has 64 pages of seamless mapping covering the entire Southern African region at a scale of 1.5 million. The resource section has 11 pages of contact details and listings of tour operators and tourist authorities. Coverage includes South Africa, Swaziland, Lesotho, Namibia, Botswana, Zimbabwe and Mozambique.

GARDEN ROUTE & ROUTE 62 VISITOR'S GUIDE
ISBN 9781770261860
This new edition includes GPS co-ordinates along with a route planner that details points of interest and activity areas, major sites and how to reach them, detailed resource section, extra detail on sites to visit along the way, cross-referenced to other applicable products focusing on major sites within towns on the way. The new main map section provides coverage of Montagu, Robertson, Ladismith and Barrydale, the start of Route 62, Mossel Bay, Oudtshoorn and George, Knysna Feature, Plettenberg Bay, Jeffery's Bay and national parks of the Garden Route.

NATIONAL PARKS & RESERVES OF SOUTH AFRICA
ISBN 9781868098422 (ENGLISH)
ISBN 9781868098736 (AFRIKAANS)
The Atlas covers all national parks and reserves within South Africa. Detailed coverage includes over 300 parks and reserves. Contains useful information, detailed site and location maps, includes over 150 photographs.

OUR TOP 4X4 TRIPS
ISBN 9781770260177
This product features the Cederberg and Biedouw Valley, Gannaga Ouberg and Tankwa Karoo National Park, Swartberg, Die Hel and Meiringspoort passes, Baviaanskloof, Mountain Zebra National Park and Camdeboo, Lesotho-Drakensberg region, iSimangaliso Wetland Park, Sodwana and Hluhluwe-iMfolozi National Park, Kgalagadi Transfrontier Park, Northern Namibia and Southern Namibia.
Each route has been driven and verified by the author. They include turn-by-turn descriptions of the routes along with the best and worst experiences of each trip. Includes detailed information on accommodation listings, top sites, gear guide on what to pack, geological information, interesting facts on regions visited and full color photographs throughout the book. Contains checklists of fauna, flora and lists likely to see birds and animals. The maps include detailed information on the routes, street plans of towns near the main routes, GPS points throughout the route areas, a road atlas section of Southern Africa and the distances travelled.

THE ULTIMATE AFRICA ATLAS
ISBN 9781868099245
The Ultimate Africa Atlas covers 57 countries of the continent, it includes traveling tips, information on the cultures within the countries and the environment across all featured places. This colour coded atlas features activities, places of interest, entertainment, climatology, awareness of risk factors, important facilities and it gives a guide on the ideal wardrobe to pack for each and every country featured.

TOP 12 HIKING TRAILS OF THE WESTERN CAPE
ISBN 9781770260313
Features the top 12 hiking routes of the Western Cape region. The trails covered include the Cederberg Heritage Route, the West Coast Crayfish Trail, Whale Trail (De Hoop Nature Reserve), Boland Hiking Trail, Hoerikwaggo Tented Classic (Table Mountain), Swellendam Hiking Trail, Postberg Wild Flower Trail, Oystercatcher Trail (Mossel Bay), Otter and Tsitsikamma Trails. Each chapter contains a detailed contour map of the trail. Information includes location map, detailed legend, trail route walked and alternative routes, peak heights and names, difficulty rating, distances in kilometres, GPS points for overnight stops and camps. The author provides an overview of each route and its history along with a day-by-day description of the route walked and a summary. The book includes mountain bike routes in the vicinity detailing the trail name, distance, time taken to ride and a brief description of the ride.

4X4 ROUTES THROUGH SOUTHERN AFRICA
ISBN 9781770262904 (ENGLISH)
ISBN 9781770262928 (AFRIKAANS)
'4x4 Routes through Southern Africa' takes a detailed look at 20 great 4x4 routes across Southern Africa from the popular Cederberg and Richtersveld regions of South Africa to the Namib Desert in Namibia and East to Lesotho and Mozambique, even as far afield as Tanzania. Each of the 20 routes are described in vast detail with contributions from reputable 4x4 operators, giving the book a unique perspective with descriptions as seen through the eyes of local experts. Each chapter contains a detailed day-by-day description of a 4x4 route together with maps, colour images and GPS waypoints for use in conjunction with any GPS navigation system. The book is also jam-packed with information about the local fauna & flora and includes interesting facts about each of the regions travelled as well as tourist information and accommodation listings to help plan an overnight stay. For the serious adventurer – each chapter indicates specific vehicle requirements, a kit checklist, road conditions & warnings, multi-day trails with expert advice, special vehicle driving skills required, self-sufficiency ratings and detailed distance charts for each route. '4x4 Routes through Southern Africa' includes a FREE bonus CD with downloadable GPS tracks of all the routes, a digital packing list and PDF format maps.

BIKE - Tar & Gravel Adventures in South Africa
ISBN 9781770262942

TOP MTB TRAILS - Western, Eastern and Northern Cape
ISBN 9781770262775

TO REVIEW ANY OF OUR PRODUCTS CONTACT
SANDY CHRISTIE
0860 10 50 50
sandyc@mapstudio.co.za

CUSTOMISED MAPPING

MapStudio now offer a full custom mapping service which is available to all customers. Whether you're looking for a map which pinpoints your sales regions or a map of The World with your company branding, we can do it all. Simply call our dedicated custom mapping sales agent to discuss your requirements. Once we have established your needs, we'll then send you a quote and have our team of cartographers create a map just for you!

Now you can customise your own map online with the simple click of a button. Visit www.mapstudio.co.za and access the 'Business' tab to enter our custom mapping portal. For orders and enquiries, kindly contact Charles at 0860 10 50 50 or charlesc@mapstudio.co.za